WHAT THE BIBLE SAYS ABOUT... THE TEN COMMANDMENTS

WHAT THE BIBLE SAYS ABOUT... THE TEN COMMANDMENTS

LEADERSHIP
MINISTRIES
WORLDWIDE

P.O. Box 21310, Chattanooga, Tennessee

What The Bible Says About The Ten Commandments is written for God's people to use both in their personal lives and in their teaching. Leadership Ministries Worldwide wants God's people to use What The Bible Says About The Ten Commandments. The purpose of the copyright is to prevent the reproduction, misuse, and abuse of the material.

May our Lord bless us all as we live, preach, teach, and write for Him, fulfilling His great commission to live righteous and godly lives and to make disciples of all nations.

Please address all requests for information or permission to:
Leadership Ministries Worldwide
PO Box 21310
Chattanooga TN 37424-0310
Ph.# (423) 855-2181   FAX (423) 855-8616   E-Mail outlinebible@compuserve.com
http://www.outlinebible.org

Library of Congress Catalog Card Number: 97-077562
International Standard Book Number: 1-57407-068-1

PRINTED IN THE U.S.A.

PUBLISHED BY LEADERSHIP MINISTRIES WORLDWIDE

Dedicated

To all the men and women of the world
who preach and teach the Gospel of our
Lord Jesus Christ.

And to the mercy and Grace of God.

———◆◆◆———

Demonstrated to us through Christ

*"In whom we have redemption through His
blood, the forgiveness of sins, according to the
riches of His grace."* (Eph. 1:7)

Out of the mercy and grace of God, His Word has flowed. Let
every person know that God will have mercy upon him, forgiving and using him to fulfill His glorious plan of salvation.

*"For God so loved the world, that he gave
his only begotten Son, that whosoever believeth
in him should not perish, but have everlasting
life. For God sent not his Son into the world to
condemn the world; but that the world through
him might be saved."* (Jn. 3:16-17)

*"For this is good and acceptable in the
sight of God our Saviour; who will have all
men to be saved, and to come unto the knowledge of the truth."* (I Tim. 2:3-4)

———◆◆◆———

This book is written and prepared for God's people to use in
their preparation for preaching and teaching.

Published by

LEADERSHIP
MINISTRIES
WORLDWIDE

LEADERSHIP MINISTRIES WORLDWIDE

OUR FIVEFOLD MISSION & PURPOSE:

- To share the Word of God with the world.
- To help the believer, both minister and layman alike, in his understanding, preaching, and teaching of God's Word.
- To do everything we possibly can to lead men, women, boys, and girls to give their hearts and lives to Jesus Christ and to secure the eternal life which He offers.
- To do all we can to minister to the needy of the world.
- To give Jesus Christ His proper place, the place which the Word gives Him. Therefore — No work of Leadership Ministries Worldwide will ever be personalized.

This material, like similar works, has come from imperfect man and is thus susceptible to human error. We are nevertheless grateful to God for both calling us and empowering us through His Holy Spirit to undertake this task. Because of His goodness and grace, *The Preacher's Outline & Sermon Bible®* - New Testament is complete in 14 volumes as well as the single volume of **The Minister's Handbook**.

God has given the strength and stamina to bring us this far. Our confidence is that, as we keep our eyes on Him and grounded in the undeniable truths of the Word, we will continue working through the Old Testament Volumes and introduce a new series known as *The Teacher's Outline & Study Bible.* Future materials will include CD-ROM, The Believer's *Outline* Bible, and similar *Outline* and **Handbook** materials.

To everyone, everywhere who preaches and teaches the Word, we offer this material firstly to Him in whose name we labor and serve, and for whose glory it has been produced.

Our daily prayer is that each volume will lead thousands, millions, yes even billions, into a better understanding of the Holy Scriptures and a fuller knowledge of Jesus Christ the incarnate Word, of whom the Scriptures so faithfully testify.

As you have purchased this volume, you will be pleased to know that a portion of the price you paid goes to underwrite providing similar volumes at affordable prices in other languages (Russian, Korean, Spanish and others yet to come) to a preacher, pastor, church leader, or Bible student somewhere around the world, who will present God's message with clarity, authority, and understanding beyond their own.
Amen.

- *Equipping God's Servants Worldwide with OUTLINE Bible Materials* -
— LMW is a 501(c)3 nonprofit, international nondenominational mission agency —   8/97

**LEADERSHIP
MINISTRIES
WORLDWIDE**

P.O. Box 21310, 515 Airport Road, Suite 107
Chattanooga, TN 37424-0310
(423) 855-2181 FAX (423) 855-87616
E-Mail - outlinebible@compuserve.com
www.outlinebible.org [Free download samples]

Materials Published & Distributed by LEADERSHIP MINISTRIES WORLDWIDE:

- *THE PREACHER'S OUTLINE & SERMON BIBLE®*— DELUXE EDITION
  - Volume 1 .... St. Matthew I (chapters 1-15)   3-Ring, looseleaf binder
  - Volume 2 .... St. Matthew II (chapters 16-28)
  - Volume 3 .... St. Mark
  - Volume 4 .... St. Luke
  - Volume 5 .... St. John
  - Volume 6 .... Acts
  - Volume 7 .... Romans
  - Volume 8 .... 1, 2 Corinthians (1 volume)
  - Volume 9 .... Galatians, Ephesians, Philippians, Colossians (1 volume)
  - Volume 10 .... 1,2 Thessalonians, 1,2 Timothy, Titus, Philemon (1 volume)
  - Volume 11 .... Hebrews-James (1 volume)
  - Volume 12 .... 1,2 Peter, 1,2,3 John, Jude (1 volume)
  - Volume 13 .... Revelation
  - Volume 14 .... Master Outline & Subject Index
  - FULL SET — 14 Volumes

- *THE PREACHER'S OUTLINE & SERMON BIBLE®* — OLD TESTAMENT
  - Volume 1 .... Genesis I (chapters 1-11)
  - Volume 2 .... Genesis II (chapters 12-50)
  - Volume 3 .... Exodus I (chapters 1-18)
  - Volume 4 .... Exodus II (chapters 19-40)   New volumes release periodically

- *THE PREACHER'S OUTLINE & SERMON BIBLE®* — SOFTBOUND EDITION
  Identical content as Deluxe above. Lightweight, compact, and affordable for overseas & traveling.

- The Minister's Personal Handbook - What the Bible Says...to the Minister
  12 Chapters — 127 Subjects — 400 Verses *OUTLINED* — Standard, Deluxe, 3-ring
  * More than 400 verses from OT and NT dealing with God's minister and servant; all assembled in
  the unique *Outline* style. Features God's Word for His chosen and called servants who minister the Word.

- Translations of N.T. Volumes and Minister's Handbook: Limited Quantities
  Russian — Spanish — Korean • *Future:* Portuguese, Hindi, Chinese + others
  — *Contact us for Specific Language and Prices* —

- *THE TEACHER'S OUTLINE & STUDY BIBLE*™ • New Testament Books •
  Average 17 lessons/book & 205 pages • Verse-by-Verse Study •• Also: Student Journal Guides

- CD-ROM New Testament - (Windows/STEP) - WORD*Search* 4™

All these great Volumes & Materials are also available at affordable prices in
quantity orders, particularly for overseas ministry, by contacting:

LEADERSHIP MINISTRIES WORLDWIDE   *Your OUTLINE Bookseller*
PO Box 21310
Chattanooga, TN 37424-0310
(423) 855-2181 (8:30 - 5:00 ET) • FAX (423) 855-8616 (24 hrs)
E•Mail - outlinebible@compuserve.com.
      ⇥ FREE Download Sample Pages — www.outlinebible.org

• *Equipping God's Servants Worldwide with OUTLINE Bible Materials* •
— LMW is a 501(c)3 nonprofit, international nondenominational mission agency — 8/97

The Ten
Commandments...

CONTENTS
CHAPTER BY CHAPTER

Part Two: The Laws Governing Man's Duty to Others

159

CONTENTS
POINT BY POINT

Part One: The Laws Governing Man's Duty to God

Part Two: The Laws Governing Man's Duty to Others

The Purposes for the Law: Why God Gave the Ten Commandments to the World, Ex.20:18-26

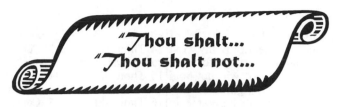

INTRODUCTION

THE TEN COMMANDMENTS—
NECESSARY LAWS TO GOVERN
MAN AND SOCIETY
Exodus 20:1-26

The most important document ever written is *the Ten Commandments*. The influence of the Ten Commandments upon nations and societies could never be measured; indeed the importance of the Ten Commandments can never be overstressed. For this reason, the Ten Commandments need to be looked at as a whole before they are studied in detail. This book outlines and discusses each commandment separately for those who wish to study, preach, or teach a series on the Ten Commandments. For those who wish to preach or teach just two or perhaps three messages on the Ten Commandments, the following overall outline is given as an aid.

	A. The Ten Commandments (Part 1): The Laws Governing Man's Duty to God, Ex.20:1-11	thing that is in heaven above, or that is in the earth beneath, or that is in the water under the earth:	a. The commandment forbids the making of any idols: Things in heaven, earth, or water
1. The basis of the 10 com.		5 Thou shalt not bow down thyself	b. The reasons
a. God's existence: "And God"	And God spake all these words, saying,	to them, nor serve them: for I the	
b. God's Word: "God spoke," (v.1)	2 I am the LORD thy God, which	LORD thy God am a jealous God,	1) God is a jealous God
c. God's name: The LORD	have brought thee	visiting the iniquity	2) The influence & result of idolatry
d. God's relationship with man: "Your God"	out of the land of Egypt, out of	of the fathers upon the children unto	are passed down from fathers to
e. God's salvation, deliverance, & redemption	the house of bondage.	the third and fourth generation of them	children
2. Com. 1 concerns *God's being*: **Have no other gods** *whatsoever*	3 Thou shalt have no other gods before me.	that hate me; 6 And showing	3) The influence of loving & obeying God lasts for a
3. Com. 2 concerns *God's* *worship*: **Do not make, worship, or serve any other god** *whatsoever*	4 Thou shalt not make unto thee any graven image, or any likeness of any	mercy unto thousands of them that love me, and keep my commandments. 7 Thou shalt not	thousand generations **4. Com. 3 concerns** *God's*

1

name: Do not misuse the LORD's name
a. He is the LORD your God
b. He will hold you accountable

5. Com. 4 concerns *God's day*: Keep the Sabbath day holy
a. The commandment:
   1) Work for six days
   2) Rest & worship on the seventh day
b. The reasons:
   1) Because the 7th day is the LORD's: No work whatsoever is to be done on the Sabbath, not by anyone
   2) Because the LORD created the universe in six days, & then rested on the seventh day
   3) Because the LORD blessed the seventh day & made it holy

1. Com. 5 concerns *man's parents*: Honor your father & mother
a. Helps a person to live longer
b. Helps a person to inherit the promised land
2. Com. 6 concerns

take the name of the LORD thy God in vain; for the LORD will not hold him guiltless that taketh his name in vain.
8 Remember the sabbath day, to keep it holy.
9 Six days shalt thou labour, and do all thy work:
10 But the seventh day is the sabbath of the LORD thy God: in it thou shalt not do any work, thou, nor thy son, nor thy daughter, thy manservant, nor thy maidservant, nor thy cattle, nor thy stranger that is within thy gates:
11 For in six days the LORD made heaven and earth, the sea, and all that in them is, and rested the seventh day: wherefore the LORD blessed the sabbath day, and hallowed it.

B. The Ten Commandments (Part 2): The Law Governing Man's Duty to Others, Ex.20:12-17

12 Honour thy father and thy mother: that thy days may be long upon the land which the LORD thy God giveth thee.
13 Thou shalt not

kill.
14 Thou shalt not commit adultery.
15 Thou shalt not steal.
16 Thou shalt not bear false witness against thy neighbour.
17 Thou shalt not covet thy neighbour's house, thou shalt not covet thy neighbour's wife, nor his manservant, nor his maidservant, nor his ox, nor his ass, nor any thing that is thy neighbour's.

C. The Purposes for the Ten Commandments: Why God Gave the Ten Commandments to the World, Ex.20:18-26

18 And all the people saw the thunderings, and the lightnings, and the noise of the trumpet, and the mountain smoking: and when the people saw it, they removed, and stood afar off.
19 And they said unto Moses, Speak thou with us, and we will hear: but let not God speak with us, lest we die.
20 And Moses said unto the people, Fear not: for God is come to prove you, and that his fear may be before

man's life
3. Com. 7 concerns *man's family*: Forbids adultery
4. Com. 8 concerns *man's property*
5. Com. 9 concerns *man's word*: Forbids lying or speaking falsely against anyone
6. Com. 10 concerns *man's desires & security*: Forbids coveting anything that belongs to your neighbor—his house, wife, servant, workers, animals, or anything else

1. To reveal the glorious majesty & holiness of God: Showing that a great barrier—a great gulf—exists between man and God

2. To reveal man's need for a mediator, for a person who can approach God on behalf of man

3. To test man
a. To see if man will walk in the fear & reverence of God
b. To see if man will truly obey God & not sin

	your faces, that ye sin not.	shalt sacrifice thereon thy burnt	ship was to be of earth: A non-
c. To see if man will trust the mediator appointed by God	21 And the people stood afar off, and Moses drew near unto the thick darkness where God was.	offerings, and thy peace offerings, thy sheep, and thine oxen: in all places where I record my name I will	showy, non-costly material provided (created) by God alone
4. To teach that God alone is the LORD: He alone has truly revealed Himself, has spoken to man from heaven	22 And the LORD said unto Moses, Thus thou shalt say unto the children of Israel, Ye have seen that I have talked with you from heaven.	come unto thee, and I will bless thee. 25 And if thou wilt make me an altar of stone, thou shalt not build it of hewn stone:	2) The altar of worship was to be made of natural, undressed stones: A material provided by God, not defiled & polluted by man
5. To teach how God alone is to be approached & worshipped a. No idolatry: No gods whatsoever are to be made or worshipped b. No pageantry: 1) The altar of wor-	23 Ye shall not make with me gods of silver, neither shall ye make unto you gods of gold. 24 An altar of earth thou shalt make unto me, and	for if thou lift up thy tool upon it, thou hast polluted it. 26 Neither shalt thou go up by steps unto mine altar, that thy nakedness be not discovered thereon.	c. No unrefined behavior: The altar was not to have steps that would expose a person's nakedness (symbolized self-righteousness, man ascending up to God)

1. The Ten Commandments have influenced the world and the civil laws of nations more than any other document ever devised. Any nation that is being formed or has been newly formed—who will use the Ten Commandments as the basis for its laws—will grow into one of the most blessed societies upon earth: a just, orderly, compassionate, and law-abiding society, a society that is strong, strong in growth and development. Maxie Dunnam says this:

> "I doubt if any document has influenced Western culture to the degree that the Ten Commandments have. In Western civilization, they have a position of inescapable significance....The civil law of many lands has rootage in this covenant law of God given at Sinai."[1]

2. The Ten Commandments spell out the duty of God's people: *obedience*. God has always demanded only one thing of believers: *obedience*. Both Old and New Testament believers are given the same charge: obey God. Norman L. Geisler says this:

> "Duty follows deliverance. Complete redemption involved more than getting Israel out of Egypt. It also involved getting 'Egypt' (i.e., the world) out of them. Not unlike believers of today, the Israelites often

[1] Maxie Dunnam. *Mastering The Old Testament, Volume 2: Exodus.* (Dallas, TX: Word Publishing, 1987), p.247.

lusted for the things of Egypt (16:3) instead of fulfilling their duty. Their duty was to follow God's law in order to receive God's blessing."[2]

3. The Ten Commandments have been given as a condition for receiving the blessings of God (Ex.19:5-6). The Israelites had to obey God in order to receive the blessings and promises of God. What was to be Israel's response in the coming centuries? Failure. The rest of the Old Testament is primarily...

- a record of Israel's gross disobedience to God.
- a record of the prophets' denunciation of Israel's sin.
- a record of the warning of coming judgment upon all the disobedient of this earth, upon both the Jew and the Gentile.
- a record of a people failing to become what God wanted them to become.
- a record of a people failing to do what God wanted them to do.

(The idea for the above statements has been gleaned from F.B. Huey, Jr., Exodus.[3])

4. The Ten Commandments are called by several names throughout the Bible.
  a. In the Old Testament the Ten Commandments are referred to as...
   - The *Ten Commandments* or *Ten Words* (the literal translation of the Hebrew) or the *Decalogue* (the literal Greek term for the Ten Commandments).

     "And he was there with the LORD forty days and forty nights; he did neither eat bread, nor drink water. And he wrote upon the tables the words of the covenant, the ten commandments" (Ex.34:28).
     "And he declared unto you his covenant, which he commanded you to perform, even ten commandments [ten words, decalogue]; and he wrote them upon two tables of stone" (Dt.4:13).
     "And he wrote on the tables, according to the first writing, the ten commandments, which the LORD spake unto you in the mount out of the midst of the fire in the day of the assembly: and the LORD gave them unto me" (Dt.10:4).

   - The *Words of the covenant*.

     "And he was there with the LORD forty days and forty nights; he did neither eat bread, nor drink water. And he wrote upon the tables the words of the covenant, the ten commandments" (Ex.34:28).

   - The *Words spoken by the LORD* (Jehovah, Yahweh)

     "And God spake all these words, saying..." (Ex.20:1).

---

[2]   Norman L. Geisler. *A Popular Survey of the Old Testament*. (Grand Rapids, MI: Baker Book House, 1977), p.58.

[3]   F.B. Huey, Jr. *A Study Guide Commentary, Exodus*. (Grand Rapids, MI: Zondervan Publishing House, 1977), p.81.

"And the LORD said unto Moses, Write thou these words: for after the tenor of these words I have made a covenant with thee and with Israel" (Ex.34:27).

"These words the LORD spake unto all your assembly in the mount out of the midst of the fire, of the cloud, and of the thick darkness, with a great voice: and he added no more. And he wrote them in two tables of stone, and delivered them unto me" (Dt.5:22).

"And I will write on the tables the words that were in the first tables which thou brakest, and thou shalt put them in the ark" (Dt.10:2)

- The *testimony of God*

   "As the LORD commanded Moses, so Aaron laid it up before the Testimony, to be kept" (Ex.16:34).

   "And thou shalt put into the ark the testimony which I shall give thee" (Ex.25:16).

- The *two tablets of stone*

   "And the LORD said unto Moses, Come up to me into the mount, and be there: and I will give thee tables of stone, and a law, and commandments which I have written; that thou mayest teach them" (Ex.24:12).

   "And he gave unto Moses, when he had made an end of communing with him upon mount Sinai, two tables of testimony, tables of stone, written with the finger of God" (Ex.31:18).

   "And Moses turned, and went down from the mount, and the two tables of the testimony were in his hand: the tables were written on both their sides; on the one side and on the other were they written. And the tables were the work of God, and the writing was the writing of God, graven upon the tables" (Ex.32:15-16).

   "And the LORD delivered unto me two tables of stone written with the finger of God; and on them was written according to all the words, which the LORD spake with you in the mount out of the midst of the fire in the day of the assembly" (Dt.9:10).

   "And I took the two tables, and cast them out of my two hands, and brake them before your eyes" (Dt.9:17).

b. In the New Testament the Ten Commandments are simply referred to as *commandments*:

   "And he said unto him, Why callest thou me good? [there is] none good but one, [that is], God: but if thou wilt enter into life, keep the commandments. He saith unto him, Which? Jesus said, Thou shalt do no murder, Thou shalt not commit adultery, Thou shalt not steal,

> **Thou shalt not bear false witness, Honour thy father and [thy] mother: and, Thou shalt love thy neighbour as thyself" (Mt.19:17-19).**
>
> **"Honour thy father and mother; (which is the first commandment with promise;)" (Eph.6:2).**

5. The Bible does not number the Ten Commandments; consequently, they are numbered differently by different commentators.
   ⇒ The verses concerning God and idols, verses 3-6, are combined as one commandment by some commentators (primarily Lutherans and Roman Catholics). When these are combined, the commandment concerning coveting (v.17) is usually split into two commandments. The first sentence of verse 17 is counted as the ninth commandment, and the rest of the verse is counted as the tenth commandment. The ninth and tenth commandments would then look like this:

   9. *Thou shalt not covet thy neighbour's house.*
   10. *Thou shalt not covet thy neighbour's wife, nor his manservant, nor his maidservant, nor his ox, nor his ass, nor any thing that is thy neighbour's.*

6. The Ten Commandments are repeated in the New Testament.
   1. *Commandment 1 concerning God's being: have no other gods whatsoever (Acts 14:15; 1 Cor.10:14; 1 Jn.5:21).*
   2. *Commandment 2 concerning God's worship: do not make, worship, nor serve any other god whatsoever (Acts 17:29; Ro.1:22-23; 1 Jn.5:21; 1 Cor. 10:7, 14).*
   3. *Commandment 3 concerning God's name: do not misuse the LORD's name (Jas.5:12; Mt.5:33-37; 6:5-9).*
   4. *Commandment 4 concerning God's day: keep the Sabbath day holy. This is not directly repeated anywhere in the New Testament, but Christ faithfully observed the Sabbath and New Testament believers faithfully kept the LORD's Day (Mk.1:21; 6:2; Lk.4:16; Acts 17:2; 18:4; Heb.10:25).*
   5. *Commandment 5 concerning man's parents: honor your father and mother (Mt.19:18-19; Eph.6:1-4).*
   6. *Commandment 6 concerning man's life: prohibits murder (1 Jn.3:15; Mt.5:21-22; 19:18-19).*
   7. *Commandment 7 concerning man's family: forbids adultery (Mt.5:27-28; 19:18-19; 1 Cor.5:1-13; 6:9-20; Heb.13:4).*
   8. *Commandment 8 concerning man's property: prohibits stealing (Mt.19:18-19; Eph.4:28; 2 Th.3:10-12; Jas.5:1-4).*
   9. *Commandment 9 concerning man's word: forbids lying or speaking falsely against anyone (Mt.19:18-19; Col.3:9; Eph.4:25).*
   10. *Commandment 10 concerning man's security: forbids coveting anything that belongs to your neighbor—his house, wife, servant, workers, animals, or anything else (Mt.19:18-19; Eph.5:3; Lk.12:15-21).*

7. The New Testament gives several summaries of the commandments.

> **"He saith unto him, Which? Jesus said, Thou shalt do no murder, Thou shalt not commit adultery, Thou shalt not steal, Thou shalt not bear false witness, Honour thy father and [thy] mother: and, Thou shalt love thy neighbour as thyself" (Mt.19:18-19; cp. Mk.10:18-19; Lk.18:18-19).**
>
> **"Owe no man any thing, but to love one another: for he that loveth another hath fulfilled the law. For this, Thou shalt not commit adultery, Thou shalt not kill, Thou shalt not steal, Thou shalt not bear false witness, Thou shalt not covet; and if there be any other commandment, it is briefly comprehended in this saying, namely, Thou shalt love thy neighbour as thyself. Love worketh no ill to his neighbour: therefore love is the fulfilling of the law" (Ro.13:8-10).**

8. It is important to note the form of the Ten Commandments, just how they are written. Note these facts:
   a. The Ten Commandments are stated as *moral absolutes*. They absolutely must be kept. There is no equivocation and no condition attached to the commandments—no *ifs*, *ands*, or *buts*. The commandments are to be kept.
   b. The Ten Commandments are written in the second person singular, "*you*." This means that the Ten Commandments apply to you, the individual, as well as to you, a community or society of people.
   c. The commandments fall into a natural division:
      ⇒ The first four commandments concern *man's relationship to God*.
      ⇒ The next six commandments concern *man's relationship to others*.

9. Eight of the Ten Commandments are stated negatively, and two commandments are stated positively. Note that the eight negative commandments imply the positive and the two positive commandments imply the negative. The commandments even arouse the mind to immediately think of the opposite statement. This was obviously the very reason God stated the commandments so simply. A double focus or imprint is made upon the mind, both a negative and positive emphasis when the commandments are read.
   a. "You shall have no other gods before me" (Ex.20:3) implies that "you shall believe and follow the only living and true God, the LORD Himself."
   b. "You shall not make for yourself [worship] any graven image [idol]" (Ex.20:4-6) implies that "you shall worship only the LORD, Him and Him alone."
   c. "You shall not take the name of the LORD your God in vain" (Ex.20:7) implies that "you shall always honor the name of the LORD your God."
   d. "Remember the Sabbath day to keep it holy" (Ex.20:8-11) implies that "you shall not neglect nor abuse the Sabbath day."

e. "Honor you father and your mother" (Ex.20:12) implies that "you shall not mistreat your father and mother."

f. "You shall not kill" (Ex.20:13) implies that "you shall respect and reverence life."

g. "You shall not commit adultery" (Ex.20:14) implies that "you shall be sexually moral and faithful."

h. "You shall not steal" (Ex.20:15) implies that "you shall be honest."

i. "You shall not bear false witness" (Ex.20:16) implies that "you shall tell the truth."

j. "You shall not covet (Ex.20:17) implies that "you shall be content with what you have."

10. Both the Old Testament and the New Testament tell us why God gave the Ten Commandments. There were at least nine purposes.

a. The Ten Commandments were given to mark believers, to mark them as the true followers of God, as being God's holy and treasured people.

> "Now therefore, if ye will obey my voice indeed, and keep my covenant, then ye shall be a peculiar treasure unto me above all people: for all the earth is mine: And ye shall be unto me a kingdom of priests, and an holy nation. These are the words which thou shalt speak unto the children of Israel" (Ex.19:5-6).
>
> "He showeth his word unto Jacob, his statutes and his judgments unto Israel. He hath not dealt so with any nation: and as for his judgments, they have not known them. Praise ye the LORD" (Ps.147:19-20).
>
> "My brethren, my kinsmen according to the flesh: Who are Israelites; to whom pertaineth the adoption, and the glory, and the covenants, and the giving of the law, and the service of God, and the promises; Whose are the fathers, and of whom as concerning the flesh Christ came, who is over all, God blessed for ever. Amen" (Ro.9:3^b-5).

b. The Ten Commandments were given to mark believers as the priests, the true witnesses and servants of God upon earth.

> "Now therefore, if ye will obey my voice indeed, and keep my covenant, then ye shall be a peculiar treasure unto me above all people: for all the earth is mine: And ye shall be unto me a kingdom of priests, and an holy nation. These are the words which thou shalt speak unto the children of Israel" (Ex.19:5-6).
>
> "But ye shall be named the Priests of the LORD: men shall call you the Ministers of our God: ye shall eat the riches of the Gentiles, and in their glory shall ye boast yourselves" (Is.61:6).
>
> "Ye also [all believers], as lively stones, are built up a spiritual house, an holy priesthood, to offer up spiritual sacrifices, acceptable to God by Jesus Christ" (1 Pt.2:5).

c. The Ten Commandments were given to show man that he is sinful, that he is far short of God's glory, that he is not perfect.

> "Moreover the law entered, that the offence might abound. But where sin abounded, grace did much more abound" (Ro.5:20).
>
> "What shall we say then? Is the law sin? God forbid. Nay, I had not known sin, but by the law: for I had not known lust, except the law had said, Thou shalt not covet" (Ro.7:7).
>
> "Wherefore then serveth the law? It was added because of transgressions, till the seed should come to whom the promise was made; and it was ordained by angels in the hand of a mediator" (Gal.3:19).
>
> "Knowing this, that the law is not made for a righteous man, but for the lawless and disobedient, for the ungodly and for sinners, for unholy and profane, for murderers of fathers and murderers of mothers, for manslayers, for whoremongers, for them that defile themselves with mankind, for menstealers, for liars, for perjured persons, and if there be any other thing that is contrary to sound doctrine" (1 Tim.1:9-10).
>
> "For the law having a shadow of good things to come, and not the very image of the things, can never with those sacrifices which they offered year by year continually make the comers thereunto perfect" (Heb.10:1).
>
> "As it is written, There is none righteous, no, not one....Now we know that what things soever the law saith, it saith to them who are under the law: that every mouth may be stopped, and all the world may become guilty before God. Therefore by the deeds of the law there shall no flesh be justified in his sight: for by the law is the knowledge of sin" (Ro.3:10, 19-20).

d. The Ten Commandments were given to show man that he can never be justified by the law, never be perfected by the law, never keep the law perfectly. In fact, he comes ever so short of keeping the law, ever so short of perfection.

> "Therefore by the deeds of the law there shall no flesh be justified in his sight: for by the law is the knowledge of sin" (Ro.3:20).
>
> "For the law having a shadow of good things to come, and not the very image of the things, can never with those sacrifices which they offered year by year continually make the comers thereunto perfect" (Heb.10:1).
>
> "For all have sinned, and come short of the glory of God" (Ro.3:23).

e. The Ten Commandments were given to show man that he needs a Savior, a Savior who can deliver him from the curse and penalty of the law.

"For as many as are of the works of the law are under the curse: for it is written, Cursed is every one that continueth not in all things which are written in the book of the law to do them. But that no man is justified by the law in the sight of God, it is evident: for, The just shall live by faith. And the law is not of faith: but, The man that doeth them shall live in them. Christ hath redeemed us from the curse of the law, being made a curse for us: for it is written, Cursed is every one that hangeth on a tree" (Gal.3:10-13).

"But when the fulness of the time was come, God sent forth his Son, made of a woman, made under the law, To redeem them that were under the law, that we might receive the adoption of sons. And because ye are sons, God hath sent forth the Spirit of his Son into your hearts, crying, Abba, Father" (Gal.4:4-6; cp. Gal.1:4).

"Therefore by the deeds of the law there shall no flesh be justified in his sight: for by the law is the knowledge of sin. But now the righteousness of God without the law is manifested, being witnessed by the law and the prophets; Even the righteousness of God which is by faith of Jesus Christ unto all and upon all them that believe: for there is no difference" (Ro.3:20-22).

"For all have sinned, and come short of the glory of God; Being justified freely by his grace through the redemption that is in Christ Jesus" (Ro.3:23-24).

"There is therefore now no condemnation to them which are in Christ Jesus, who walk not after the flesh, but after the Spirit. For the law of the Spirit of life in Christ Jesus hath made me free from the law of sin and death. For what the law could not do, in that it was weak through the flesh, God sending his own Son in the likeness of sinful flesh, and for sin, condemned sin in the flesh: That the righteousness of the law might be fulfilled in us, who walk not after the flesh, but after the Spirit" (Ro.8:1-4).

"Knowing that a man is not justified by the works of the law, but by the faith of Jesus Christ, even we have believed in Jesus Christ, that we might be justified by the faith of Christ, and not by the works of the law: for by the works of the law shall no flesh be justified" (Gal.2:16).

"For the law made nothing perfect, but the bringing in of a better hope [in Christ] did; by the which we draw nigh unto God" (Heb.7:19).

f. The Ten Commandments were given to show man that he needs a mediator to approach God. God appointed Moses to be the mediator between Himself and Israel, but Moses was only a type of the promised *Mediator and Prophet*, the Lord Jesus Christ...
    * who was to be *raised up* by God Himself
    * who was to be the very *Prophet* of God Himself
    * who was to be the *Savior and Messiah* of the world
    * who was to be the *High Priest* of God Himself

"The LORD thy God will raise up unto thee a Prophet from the midst of thee, of thy brethren, like unto me; unto him ye shall hearken; According to all that thou desiredst of the LORD thy God in Horeb in the day of the assembly, saying, Let me not hear again the voice of the LORD my God, neither let me see this great fire any more, that I die not. And the LORD said unto me, They have well spoken that which they have spoken. I will raise them up a Prophet from among their brethren, like unto thee, and will put my words in his mouth; and he shall speak unto them all that I shall command him. And it shall come to pass, that whosoever will not hearken unto my words which he shall speak in my name, I will require it of him" (Dt.18:15-19).

"Then those men, when they had seen the miracle that Jesus did, said, This is of a truth that prophet that should come into the world" (Jn.6:14).

"Repent ye therefore, and be converted, that your sins may be blotted out, when the times of refreshing shall come from the presence of the Lord; And he shall send Jesus Christ, which before was preached unto you: Whom the heaven must receive until the times of restitution of all things, which God hath spoken by the mouth of all his holy prophets since the world began. For Moses truly said unto the fathers, A prophet shall the Lord your God raise up unto you of your brethren, like unto me; him shall ye hear in all things whatsoever he shall say unto you" (Acts 3:19-22).

"Wherefore he is able also to save them to the uttermost that come unto God by him, seeing he ever liveth to make intercession for them. For such an high priest became us, who is holy, harmless, undefiled, separate from sinners, and made higher than the heavens" (Heb.7:25-26).

g. The Ten Commandments were given to be a guide (a schoolmaster or guardian), a guide who would lead people to Christ.

"Wherefore the Ten Commandments were our schoolmaster to bring us unto Christ, that we might be justified by faith" (Gal.3:24).

h. The Ten Commandments were given to arouse people to seek both life and the promised land.

"Now therefore hearken, O Israel, unto the statutes and unto the judgments, which I teach you, for to do them, that ye <u>may live, and go in and possess the land</u> which the LORD God of your fathers giveth you. Ye shall not add unto the word which I command you, neither shall ye diminish ought from it, that ye may keep the commandments of the LORD your God which I command you" (Dt.4:1-2).

> "Ye shall observe to do therefore as the LORD your God hath commanded you: ye shall not turn aside to the right hand or to the left. Ye shall walk in all the ways which the LORD your God hath commanded you, <u>that ye may live</u>, and that it may be well with you, and that ye may prolong your days in the land which ye shall possess" (Dt.5:32-33).

i. The Ten Commandments were given to show man how to live a peaceful and productive life upon earth, how to be at peace with God and man and to live a life that overflows with the blessings of God. Note the commandments, how each...
   - leads either to peace with God or peace with man
   - leads to a productive and fruitful life upon earth
     Commandment 1: *Never believe in false gods.*
     Commandment 2: *Never make nor worship false gods.*
     Commandment 3: *Never misuse God's name; never use vulgarity.*
     Commandment 4: *Keep the Sabbath day holy.*
     Commandment 5: *Honor your father and mother.*
     Commandment 6: *Never kill.*
     Commandment 7: *Never commit adultery or immorality.*
     Commandment 8: *Never steal.*
     Commandment 9: *Never lie or speak falsely against anyone.*
     Commandment 10: *Never covet anything that belongs to a neighbor—his house, wife, servant, workers, animals, or anything else.*

11. Scripture tells us several things that the Ten Commandments cannot and do not do.
   a. The law cannot save a person because no person can keep the law perfectly.

   > "But that no man is justified by the law in the sight of God, it is evident: for, The just shall live by faith" (Gal.3:11).
   > "Therefore by the deeds of the law there shall no flesh be justified in his sight: for by the law is the knowledge of sin" (Ro.3:20).

   b. The law cannot make a person perfect.

   > "For the law made nothing perfect, but the bringing in of a better hope did; by the which we draw nigh unto God" (Heb.7:19, cp. Heb.7:11-18).

   c. The law cannot justify a person from sin.

   > "Be it known unto you therefore, men and brethren, that through this man is preached unto you the forgiveness of sins: And by him all that believe are justified from all things, from which ye could not be justified by the law of Moses" (Acts 13:38-39).

"Now we know that what things soever the law saith, it saith to them who are under the law: that every mouth may be stopped, and all the world may become guilty before God. Therefore by the deeds of the law there shall no flesh be justified in his sight: for by the law is the knowledge of sin. But now the righteousness of God without the law is manifested, being witnessed by the law and the prophets; Even the righteousness of God which is by faith of Jesus Christ unto all and upon all them that believe: for there is no difference: For all have sinned, and come short of the glory of God; Being justified freely by his grace through the redemption that is in Christ Jesus: Whom God hath set forth to be a propitiation through faith in his blood, to declare his righteousness for the remission of sins that are past, through the forbearance of God; To declare, I say, at this time his righteousness: that he might be just, and the justifier of him which believeth in Jesus. Where is boasting then? It is excluded. By what law? of works? Nay: but by the law of faith. Therefore we conclude that a man is justified by faith without the deeds of the law" (Ro.3:19-28).

d. The law cannot make us righteous, cannot impute righteousness to man.

"Therefore by the deeds of the law there shall no flesh be justified in his sight: for by the law is the knowledge of sin. But now the righteousness of God without the law is manifested, being witnessed by the law and the prophets; Even the righteousness of God which is by faith of Jesus Christ unto all and upon all them that believe: for there is no difference" (Ro.3:20-22).

"For he hath made him to be sin for us, who knew no sin; that we might be made the righteousness of God in him" (2 Cor.5:21).

"I do not frustrate the grace of God: for if righteousness come by the law, then Christ is dead in vain" (Gal.2:21).

"Who his own self bare our sins in his own body on the tree, that we, being dead to sins, should live unto righteousness: by whose stripes ye were healed" (1 Pt.2:24).

e. The law cannot give life to man.

"Is the law then against the promises of God? God forbid: for if there had been a law given which could have given life, verily righteousness should have been by the law" (Gal.3:21).

12. Jesus Christ taught that the Ten Commandments are timeless and universal laws: they are given to all people of all nations for all time. Everyone is to keep the Ten Commandments. The Ten Commandments are to underlie all civil laws of a nation.

What about Christian believers: Are we required to keep the Ten Commandments? Are we not saved by grace and not by law? Yes, we are saved by grace, but the Ten Commandments are still binding upon us. Jesus Christ made this clear time and again.

a. Jesus Christ declared that He came to fulfill the law not destroy (abolish) it.

> "Think not that I am come to destroy the law, or the prophets: I am not come to destroy, but to fulfil" (Mt.5:17).

What does this mean? It means that Jesus Christ embraced the law, kept and fulfilled it. As such, He embodies the law and so much more. Therefore, the person who follows Jesus Christ embraces and keeps the Ten Commandments. For example, the person who follows Jesus Christ does not steal, kill, commit adultery, nor break any of the other commandments.

The person who follows Jesus Christ focuses upon Jesus Christ not upon the law. He looks to Christ, focuses upon Him, seeking to live a righteous and godly life just as Christ lived a righteous and godly life. By so doing, the believer keeps the law and fulfills it. In fact, when the believer follows Jesus Christ, he keeps the Ten Commandments and a whole lot more.

b. Jesus Christ condensed the law into one simple statement:

> "Therefore all things whatsoever ye would that men should do to you, do ye even so to them: for this is the law and the prophets" (Mt.7:12).

c. Jesus Christ said that love is the basis of the law, that the law can be summarized in two commandments:

> "Then one of them, which was a lawyer, asked him a question, tempting him, and saying, Master, which is the great commandment in the law? Jesus said unto him, Thou shalt love the Lord thy God with all thy heart, and with all thy soul, and with all thy mind. This is the first and great commandment. And the second [is] like unto it, Thou shalt love thy neighbour as thyself. On these two commandments hang all the law and the prophets" (Mt.22:35-40).

> "And thou shalt love the LORD thy God with all thine heart, and with all thy soul, and with all thy might" (Dt.6:5).

> "Thou shalt not avenge, nor bear any grudge against the children of thy people, but thou shalt love thy neighbour as thyself: I am the LORD" (Lev.19:18).

d. Jesus Christ enlarged upon the commandment to love our neighbors: He declared that His followers must love one another just as He loved them. How did Christ love us? Sacrificially, even to the point of dying for us.

"A new commandment I give unto you, That ye love one another; as I have loved you, that ye also love one another. By this shall all [men] know that ye are my disciples, if ye have love one to another" (Jn.13:34-35).

"This is my commandment, That ye love one another, as I have loved you. Greater love hath no man than this, that a man lay down his life for his friends" (Jn.15:12-13).

"These things I command you, that ye love one another" (Jn.15:17).

"And walk in love, as Christ also hath loved us, and hath given himself for us an offering and a sacrifice to God for a sweetsmelling savour" (Eph.5:2).

"Hereby perceive we the love of God, because he laid down his life for us: and we ought to lay down our lives for the brethren. But whoso hath this world's good, and seeth his brother have need, and shutteth up his bowels of compassion from him, how dwelleth the love of God in him? My little children, let us not love in word, neither in tongue; but in deed and in truth" (1 Jn.3:16-18).

The International Standard Bible Encyclopaedia says this:

> "'Thou shalt love' is the first word and the last in the teaching of Our Lord. His teaching is positive rather than negative, and so simple that a child can understand it. For the Christian, the Decalogue [the Ten Commandments] is no longer the highest summary of human duty. He must ever read it with sincere respect as one of the great monuments of the love of God in the moral and religious education of mankind; but it has given place to the higher teaching of the Son of God."[4]

e. Jesus Christ declared that a person proves his love by obeying the commandments:

"He that hath my commandments, and keepeth them, he it is that loveth me: and he that loveth me shall be loved of my Father, and I will love him, and will manifest myself to him" (Jn.14:21).

"Jesus answered and said unto him, If a man love me, he will keep my words: and my Father will love him, and we will come unto him, and make our abode with him" (Jn.14:23).

"For this is the love of God, that we keep his commandments: and his commandments are not grievous" (1 Jn.5:3).

"Here is the patience of the saints: here are they that keep the commandments of God, and the faith of Jesus" (Rev.14:12).

---

[4] *The International Standard Bible Encyclopaedia*, Vol.V. (Grand Rapids, MI: Eerdmans Publishing Co., 1939), p.2946-2947.

13. The relationship of Jesus Christ to the law is of critical importance.

   a. Jesus Christ obeyed the Ten Commandments; He never transgressed the Ten Commandments, not even once. He was without sin.

> "For it became him, for whom are all things, and by whom are all things, in bringing many sons unto glory, to make the captain of their salvation perfect through sufferings" (Heb.2:10).
>
> "For we have not an high priest which cannot be touched with the feeling of our infirmities; but was in all points tempted like as we are, yet without sin" (Heb.4:15).
>
> "And being made perfect, he became the author of eternal salvation unto all them that obey him" (Heb.5:9).
>
> "For such an high priest became us, who is holy, harmless, undefiled, separate from sinners, and made higher than the heavens" (Heb.7:26).
>
> "For the law maketh men high priests which have infirmity; but the word of the oath, which was since the law, maketh the Son, who is consecrated for evermore" (Heb.7:28).
>
> "Which of you convinceth me of sin? And if I say the truth, why do ye not believe me?" (Jn.8:46).
>
> "For he hath made him to be sin for us, who knew no sin; that we might be made the righteousness of God in him" (2 Cor.5:21).
>
> "But with the precious blood of Christ, as of a lamb without blemish and without spot" (1 Pt.1:19).
>
> "Who did no sin, neither was guile found in his mouth" (1 Pt.2:22).

   b. Jesus Christ declared that He came to fulfill the Ten Commandments not to destroy them.

> "Think not that I am come to destroy the law, or the prophets: I am not come to destroy, but to fulfil" (Mt.5:17).

Christ said He was neither contradicting nor destroying the law nor was He standing against it. He was fulfilling and completing the law, embracing, keeping, and obeying the commandments with all His heart and life. There are several ways in which Jesus Christ fulfilled the law.

⇒ Before Christ, the law described how God wanted man to live. The law was the ideal, the words that told man what he was to do. But Christ fulfilled and completed the law; that is, God gave man more than just mere words to describe how He wants man to live. He gave man the Life, the Person who perfectly pictures and demonstrates the law before the world's very eyes. Jesus Christ is the Picture, the Living Example, the Pattern, the Demonstration of life as it is to be lived. He is the Perfect Picture of *God's Will and Word*, the Ideal Man, the Representative Man, the Pattern for all men.

> **"And the Word was made flesh, and dwelt among us, (and we beheld his glory, the glory as of the only begotten of the Father,) full of grace and truth" (Jn.1:14).**

⇒ Before Christ, the law was only words and rules. It could only inject the idea of behavior into the mind of a person. It had no spirit, no life, no power to enable a person to do the law, not perfectly. But Christ fulfilled and completed the law. He was *Spirit and Life*, so He was able to put spirit and life to the words and rules of the law. He was able to live the life described by the words and rules. As such, He was able to inject both the idea and the power to behave into a person's mind and life. It is now His life that sets the standard and the rule for the believer; it is His Spirit and life that give the believer power to obey.

> **"There is therefore now no condemnation to them which are in Christ Jesus, who walk not after the flesh, but after the Spirit. For the law of the Spirit of life in Christ Jesus hath made me free from the law of sin and death. For what the law could not do, in that it was weak through the flesh, God sending his own Son in the likeness of sinful flesh, and for sin, condemned sin in the flesh: that the righteousness of the law might be fulfilled in us, who walk not after the flesh, but after the Spirit" (Ro.8:1-4).**

⇒ Before Christ, the law stated only the rule and the principle of behavior. It did not explain the rule nor the spirit behind the rule. Neither did the law give the full meaning of the rule. The law always had to have an interpreter. But Christ fulfilled and completed the law. He explained the rule and the spirit behind the rule. He interpreted the law. He gave the law its real and full meaning.

> **"But before faith came, we were kept under the law, shut up unto the faith which should afterwards be revealed. Wherefore the law was our schoolmaster to bring us unto Christ, that we might be justified by faith" (Gal.3:23-24).**

⇒ Before Christ, the law demanded perfect righteousness; it demanded a perfect life. But man failed at certain points. Man just could not obey the law perfectly; he fell short of perfect righteousness. But Christ fulfilled and completed the law. He kept the law in *every de-*

tail. He secured the *perfect righteousness* demanded by the law. He fulfilled all the requirements, all the types, and all the ceremonies of the law—perfectly. As such, He became the Perfect Man, the Ideal Man, the Representative Man for all men. As the Ideal Man, He simply embraced all men; He embodied the righteousness that man must now have.

> **"For he hath made him to be sin for us, who knew no sin; that we might be made the righteousness of God in him" (2 Cor.5:21).**

⇒ Before Christ, the law demanded punishment for disobedience. If a man broke the law, he was to be punished. But Christ fulfilled and completed the law. In fact, He went to the furthest point possible in fulfilling the law. He paid the maximum price and showed the ultimate love. He bore the punishment of the law for every man's disobedience; He took the punishment of the law upon Himself. As the Ideal Man, He not only embodies the righteousness that must cover all men, He also frees all men from the penalty of the law. And He makes them sons of God. (Cp. Ro.8:15-17; Gal.3:13-14; 4:1-7.)

> **"For God sent not his Son into the world to condemn the world; but that the world through him might be saved" (Jn.3:17).**
>
> **"Who his own self bare our sins in his own body on the tree, that we, being dead to sins, should live unto righteousness: by whose stripes ye were healed" (1 Pt.2:24).**

14. Jesus Christ expects us—all believers—to obey the Ten Commandments. He even expects believers to go beyond the Ten Commandments and do far more than just the rules laid down by the commandments. Note what He had to say about each of the commandments.

   a. **Commandment 1**: Jesus Christ declared that there is *only One LORD GOD* of the universe, and that we are to love Him with all our hearts, souls, and minds.

> **"Then one of them, which was a lawyer, asked him a question, tempting him, and saying, Master, which is the great commandment in the law? Jesus said unto him, Thou shalt love the LORD thy God with all thy heart, and with all thy soul, and with all thy mind. This is the first and great commandment. And the second [is] like unto it, Thou shalt love thy neighbour as thyself. On these two commandments hang all the law and the prophets" (Mt.22:35-40).**

b. **Commandment 2**: Jesus Christ declared that *God is Spirit* and that He must be worshipped in spirit and in truth. Consequently, all the images of gods, whether created by the hands of people or simply existing in the imaginations of people, are merely dead, helpless and false gods.

> "God [is] a Spirit: and they that worship him must worship [him] in spirit and in truth" (Jn.4:24).

c. **Commandment 3**: Jesus Christ declared that man is not to swear.

> "But I say unto you, Swear not at all; neither by heaven; for it is God's throne: Nor by the earth; for it is his footstool: neither by Jerusalem; for it is the city of the great King. Neither shalt thou swear by thy head, because thou canst not make one hair white or black. But let your communication be, Yea, yea; Nay, nay: for whatsoever is more than these cometh of evil" (Mt.5:34-37).

d. **Commandment 4**: Jesus Christ faithfully worshipped on the Sabbath, and He declared that we are to worship the Lord our God and Him alone.

> "Then saith Jesus unto him, Get thee hence, Satan: for it is written, Thou shalt worship the Lord thy God, and him only shalt thou serve" (Mt.4:10).
> "And he came to Nazareth, where he had been brought up: and, as his custom was, he went into the synagogue on the sabbath day, and stood up for to read" (Lk.4:16).

e. **Commandment 5**: Jesus Christ declared that man is always to honor father and mother even above vows and offerings and that man is never to curse father and mother.

> "For God commanded, saying, Honour thy father and mother: and, He that curseth father or mother, let him die the death. But ye say, Whosoever shall say to [his] father or [his] mother, [It is] a gift, by whatsoever thou mightest be profited by me; And honour not his father or his mother, [he shall be free]. Thus have ye made the commandment of God of none effect by your tradition" (Mt.15:4-6).

Jesus Christ also declared that the fifth commandment governing the honor of parents must be obeyed. He insisted that a person had to honor his father and mother in order to inherit eternal life.

> "And when he was gone forth into the way, there came one running, and kneeled to him, and asked him, Good Master, what shall I do that I may inherit eternal life? And Jesus said unto him, Why callest thou me good? [there is] none good but one, [that is], God. Thou

knowest the commandments, Do not commit adultery, Do not kill, Do
not steal, Do not bear false witness, Defraud not, Honour thy father
and mother" (Mk.10:17-19).

f. **Commandment 6**: Jesus Christ declared that the law governing murder
goes much deeper than the act itself: it covers the deep-seated feelings of
unjustified anger.

> "Ye have heard that it was said by them of old time, Thou shalt
> not kill; and whosoever shall kill shall be in danger of the judgment:
> But I say unto you, That whosoever is angry with his brother without
> a cause shall be in danger of the judgment: and whosoever shall say
> to his brother, Raca, shall be in danger of the council: but whosoever
> shall say, Thou fool, shall be in danger of hell fire" (Mt.5:21-22).

Jesus Christ also declared that the sixth commandment governing
murder must be obeyed: "Do not kill."

> "Thou knowest the commandments, Do not commit adultery, Do
> not kill, Do not steal, Do not bear false witness, Defraud not, Honour
> thy father and mother" (Mk.10:19).

g. **Commandment 7**: Jesus Christ declared that the law governing adultery
goes much deeper than the act itself: it covers the feelings of lust within
the human heart.

> "Ye have heard that it was said by them of old time, Thou shalt
> not commit adultery: But I say unto you, That whosoever looketh on
> a woman to lust after her hath committed adultery with her already
> in his heart. And if thy right eye offend thee, pluck it out, and cast [it]
> from thee: for it is profitable for thee that one of thy members should
> perish, and not [that] thy whole body should be cast into hell. And if
> thy right hand offend thee, cut it off, and cast [it] from thee: for it is
> profitable for thee that one of thy members should perish, and not
> [that] thy whole body should be cast into hell. It hath been said, Who-
> soever shall put away his wife, let him give her a writing of divorce-
> ment: But I say unto you, That whosoever shall put away his wife,
> saving for the cause of fornication, causeth her to commit adultery:
> and whosoever shall marry her that is divorced committeth adultery"
> (Mt.5:27-32).

Jesus Christ also declared that the seventh commandment must be
obeyed: "Do not commit adultery."

"Thou knowest the commandments, Do not commit adultery, Do not kill, Do not steal, Do not bear false witness, Defraud not, Honour thy father and mother" (Mk.10:19).

h. **Commandment 8**: Jesus Christ declared that the eighth commandment governing stealing must be obeyed: "Do not defraud."

"Thou knowest the commandments, Do not commit adultery, Do not kill, Do not steal, Do not bear false witness, Defraud not, Honour thy father and mother" (Mk.10:19).

i. **Commandment 9**: Jesus Christ not only upheld the ninth commandment against bearing false witness, He enlarged it to include...
- evil thoughts
- blasphemy
- idle words

"Wherefore I say unto you, All manner of sin and blasphemy shall be forgiven unto men: but the blasphemy [against] the [Holy] Ghost shall not be forgiven unto men" (Mt.12:31).
"But I say unto you, That every idle word that men shall speak, they shall give account thereof in the day of judgment" (Mt.12:36).
"For out of the heart proceed evil thoughts, murders, adulteries, fornications, thefts, false witness, blasphemies" (Mt.15:19).
"Thou knowest the commandments, Do not commit adultery, Do not kill, Do not steal, Do not bear false witness, Defraud not, Honour thy father and mother" (Mk.10:19).

j. **Commandment 10**: Jesus Christ warned people against covetousness.

"And he said unto them, Take heed, and beware of covetousness: for a man's life consisteth not in the abundance of the things which he possesseth" (Lk.12:15; cp. v.16-21).

15. The Ten Commandments are meant for all people of all generations. They are not just religious records or archives limited to a particular sect of people. God's law has been placed in the heart, in the very conscience of every man, woman, and child—no matter what a person may claim. God has stamped a sense of morality deep into man's innermost being. God's Word declares this fact:

"([People] show the work of the law written in their hearts, their conscience also bearing witness, and their thoughts the mean while accusing or else excusing one another)" (Ro.2:15).

How the Ten Commandments are Outlined and Discussed

The Ten Commandments are being outlined as the Scripture dictates. But remember, several of the Ten Commandments are forcefully stated in one brief sentence. Because our purpose is to give an overall discussion of the Ten Commandments, not to limit our discussion just to the brief statement of Scripture, additional outline points have been adopted and discussed for each of the commandments. This is being done to help us in studying and understanding the commandments.

The message of the Ten Commandments is desperately needed by our society, a society and world that is rapidly becoming lawless, immoral, perverted, and desensitized, losing all sense of conscience, all sense of right and wrong. Our purpose is to cover the full teaching of Scripture about each of the commandments. This is done with the conviction and hope that this study will be of far greater value to God's dear people as they study, preach, and teach His Holy Commandments. Some or all of the following outline points are discussed for each of the Ten Commandments.

I. Who is to obey this commandment?

II. How long was this commandment to be in force?

III. What is forbidden by this commandment? or What is the charge of this commandment?

IV. What are the Biblical consequences of breaking this commandment?

V. What are the Biblical benefits of keeping this commandment?

VI. What is the teaching of Jesus Christ concerning this commandment?

VII. What is the decision demanded or required by this commandment?

The Ten Commandments

And God spake all these words, saying, I am the LORD thy God...

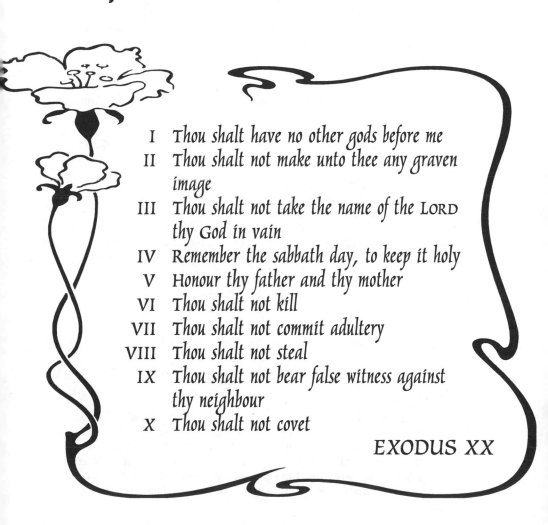

I   Thou shalt have no other gods before me

II   Thou shalt not make unto thee any graven image

III   Thou shalt not take the name of the LORD thy God in vain

IV   Remember the sabbath day, to keep it holy

V   Honour thy father and thy mother

VI   Thou shalt not kill

VII   Thou shalt not commit adultery

VIII   Thou shalt not steal

IX   Thou shalt not bear false witness against thy neighbour

X   Thou shalt not covet

EXODUS XX

THE TEN COMMANDMENTS

You hold in your hands the most important document in all of history, a document that was given to the world by God Himself. Down through history, the Ten Commandments have influenced people and societies more than any other single document. The importance of the Ten Commandments can never be overstated. The Ten Commandments are...

- The pattern for a righteous society, for establishing fair and just laws within society.

  > "Keep therefore and do them; for this is your wisdom and your understanding in the sight of the nations, which shall hear all these statutes, and say, Surely this great nation is a wise and understanding people" (Dt.4:6).
  > "Righteousness exalteth a nation: but sin is a reproach to any people" (Pr.14:34).
  > "Wherefore the law is holy [set apart, consecrated by God as His very special laws], and the commandment holy, and just, and good [for society]" (Ro.7:12).

- The basic laws that will govern lawlessness, that will bring about a safe, orderly, peaceful, and just society.

  > "Knowing this, that the law is not made for a righteous man, but for the lawless and disobedient, for the ungodly and for sinners, for unholy and profane, for murderers of fathers and murderers of mothers, for manslayers, for whoremongers, for them that defile themselves with mankind, for menstealers, for liars, for perjured persons, and if there be any other thing that is contrary to sound doctrine" (1 Tim.1:9-10).

- The means that God uses to bring us to Christ.

  > "Wherefore the law was our schoolmaster to bring us unto Christ, that we might be justified by faith" (Gal.3:24).

- The main laws that are to be taught and learned by every citizen, family, and child.

  > "And thou shalt love the LORD thy God with all thine heart, and with all thy soul, and with all thy might. And these words, which I command thee this day, shall be in thine heart: And thou shalt teach them diligently unto thy children, and shalt talk of them when thou sittest in thine house, and when thou walkest by the way, and when thou liest down, and when thou risest up" (Dt.6:5-7).

(The idea for the above chart was stirred by the *Ten Commandments* poster produced by the American Rights Coalition, Chattanooga, TN.)

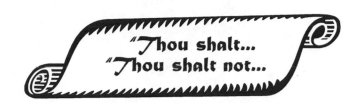

"Thou shalt...
"Thou shalt not...

The Great Basis of The Ten Commandments: The Person and Work of God Himself Exodus 20:1-2

Contents

The Great Basis of the Ten Commandments: The Person and Work of God Himself
Exodus 20:1-2

THE GREAT BASIS OF THE TEN COMMANDMENTS	
1. God's existence: "And God" 2. God's Word: "God spoke" 3. God's name: The LORD 4. God's relationship with man: "Your God" 5. God's salvation, deliverance, & redemption: "Brought you out"	And God spake all these words, saying, 2 I am the LORD thy God, which have brought thee out of the land of Egypt, out of the house of bondage.

What is the basis of morality? Who can be absolutely sure what is right or wrong? The world offers various opinions. But a question needs to be asked, and the question must be answered objectively and most of all honestly: Is it left up to man to formulate his own values, his own system of morality and ethics? Is there no being higher than man, no being who can give more sure and permanent guidance than the frail human mind? Generation after generation of men have spoken in uncertain voices, voices which believe and proclaim that anything goes, ideas that encourage...

- taking what a person wants
- doing what a person wants
- saying what a person wants
- believing what a person wants

The result has been tragic: man is losing control of society and the world. Sin and evil are sweeping the world, running rampant, out of control, the sin and evil of...

- lawlessness
- alcohol
- murder
- abuse
- drugs
- violence
- immorality

At times, the problems of sin and evil seem insurmountable. Humanly there seems to be no answer to the problems of society; the situation appears almost hopeless. But note: there is good news. The solution for a world that has gone berserk does not lie with man. Thousands of years ago, God gave man a plan for order within society, a plan for morality and ethics that was to guide man down through the centuries, a plan that will work today as much as it would have worked in ancient history. What is that plan? The *Ten Commandments*. The Ten Commandments will work within any generation—if man will just institute and enforce them. God's *Ten Commandments* can bring order to the world—the most beneficial system of morality and ethics possible to man, a morality and ethics that will bring peace and abundance to man. How can we say this? Because the Ten Commandments were given by God Himself. The Ten Commandments are not based upon...

- the prejudices and morality of men
- the latest popularity polls
- the worldly desires of people
- the purposes of government

The basis of the Ten Commandments has been set in stone, in the Rock of Ages, in the One who is the Alpha and Omega, the Beginning and the End, the First and the Last. The basis of the Ten Commandments is God Himself. Therefore, the Ten Commandments work. They work because God knows man, knows exactly what man needs to live a fulfilled and orderly life. The Ten Commandments are based upon God Himself, upon His person and work, upon His knowledge of what man needs, upon His understanding and wisdom. This is the important focus of our study: *The Great Basis of the Ten Commandments: The Person and Work of God Himself,* Ex.20:1-2.

I. God's existence: "And God" (v.1).

II. God's Word: "God spoke" (v.1).

III. God's Name: "the LORD [Yahweh]" (v.2).

IV. God's relationship with man: "Your God" (v.2).

V. God's salvation, deliverance, and redemption: "Brought you out" (v.2).

I. The First Basis of the Ten Commandments Is God's Existence, His Eternal Existence (20:1).

God exists. Moreover, God planned and created the world, and He gave His commandments to the people He had created. Note the words "And God." The existence of God is declared. His existence is not argued or debated. There is no attempt to prove God's existence. Scripture assumes that everyone is *thoughtful and honest, thoughtful and honest* enough to know and acknowledge that God exists. Therefore, Scripture declares without any hesitation or explanation, "And God"; that is, God exists. Consequently, because God exists, He is bound to show man how to live; He is bound to give His commandments to the people He created. This is what the Ten Commandments are: they are the commandments of God Himself, the commandments that tell us how to live. The Ten Commandments are to be the *basic laws* of society, the *basic laws* that govern human relationships and the relationship between God and man. And they are to *govern* man down through history, *govern* every generation and every society of man.

God Himself is the Person who worked out and spoke forth the Ten Commandments. God Himself is the source of the Ten Commandments. God Himself—His existence, His eternal existence—is the basis of the Ten Commandments. The Ten Commandments exist because God Himself exists, and He wants us to know how to live.

<u>Thought.</u>

What does it mean for God to be the basis, the source, the One who has given us the Ten Commandments? It means that the Ten Commandments are true; the Ten Commandments should be the basic laws that govern our lives and our society. The Ten Commandments...

- are the basic laws that show us how to live
- are the basic laws that can help us live a fruitful and productive life
- are the basic laws that can help us live together in love, joy, and peace

> "In the beginning God created the heaven and the earth" (Gen.1:1).
> "Hear, O Israel: The LORD our God is one LORD: And thou shalt love the LORD thy God with all thine heart, and with all thy soul, and with all thy might. And these words, which I command thee this day, shall be in thine heart: And thou shalt teach them diligently unto thy children, and shalt talk of them when thou sittest in thine house, and when thou walkest by the way, and when thou liest down, and when thou risest up" (Dt.6:4-7).
> "And he said, LORD God of Israel, there is no God like thee, in heaven above, or on earth beneath, who keepest covenant and mercy with thy servants that walk before thee with all their heart" (1 Ki.8:23).
> "But seek ye first the kingdom of God, and his righteousness; and all these things shall be added unto you" (Mt.6:33).
> "Thou wilt keep him in perfect peace, whose mind is stayed on thee: because he trusteth in thee" (Is.26:3).

II. The Second Basis of the Ten Commandments Is God's Word, the Fact that God Speaks to Man, That God Communicates with Man (20:1).

What a glorious truth this is: God speaks to us. Despite our rejection of Him—our denial, cursing, and rebellion—God cares for us. Therefore, He has communicated with us, telling us how to live. Note how this verse reads:

> "And God spake all these words, saying,"

Men try to make false gods speak and sometimes even claim that they do speak, but they are mistaken. They are deceived and are making deceptive claims. False gods cannot speak. Scripture declares:

> "They [idols] *are* upright as the palm tree, <u>but speak not</u>: they must needs be borne, because they cannot go. Be not afraid of them; for they cannot do evil, neither also *is it* in them to do good" (Jer.10:5).
>
> "That which may be known of God is manifest in them; for God hath showed it unto them. For the invisible things of him from the creation of the world are clearly seen, being understood by the things that are made, even his eternal power and Godhead; so that they are without excuse: Because that, when they knew God, they glorified him not as God, neither were thankful; but became vain in their imaginations, and their foolish heart was darkened" (Ro.1:19-21).

The LORD God, the only true and living God, has chosen to speak to us. Moreover, He has chosen to speak in a way that can be clearly understood. How has God chosen to speak?

⇒ Through His written Word, the Holy Scripture.

⇒ Through the Living Word, the Lord Jesus Christ, the Son of God Himself.

The present passage of Scripture covers how God has given us part of the written Word, in particular the Ten Commandments. God Himself spoke and gave the law to man. God did not leave man in the dark, wondering how he is to live. Man does not have to stumble around in the dark groping and grasping after the truth, wondering how to bring peace and reconciliation to the world, wondering how to please God and become acceptable to Him. God has spoken to man and declared His Word to man; but more than just speaking, God has seen to it that His law is written down for man. God has spoken and given His law in the most permanent way possible: in *written form*. God has communicated the Holy Law of God in written form so that man will always have access to the Ten Commandments, will always know how to relate and live in peace and reconciliation.

Thought.

God has spoken to us, telling us how to live. Note what Scripture declares:
a) God has given us the written Word of God.

> "For whatsoever things were written aforetime were written for our learning, that we through patience and comfort of the scriptures might have hope" (Ro.15:4).
>
> "Now all these things happened unto them for examples: and they are written for our admonition, upon whom the ends of the world are come" (1 Cor.10:11).

"All scripture is given by inspiration of God, and is profitable for doctrine, for reproof, for correction, for instruction in righteousness" (2 Tim.3:16).

"For the prophecy came not in old time by the will of man: but holy men of God spake as they were moved by the Holy Ghost" (2 Pt.1:21).

b) God has given us the *living Word of God*, the Lord Jesus Christ Himself. God did not just give us the written Word of God, but He sent His own Son to demonstrate and show us how to live out His Word.

"In the beginning was the Word, and the Word was with God, and the Word was God. The same was in the beginning with God. All things were made by him; and without him was not any thing made that was made. In him was life; and the life was the light of men. And the light shineth in darkness; and the darkness comprehended it not" (Jn.1:1-5).

"And the Word was made flesh, and dwelt among us, (and we beheld his glory, the glory as of the only begotten of the Father,) full of grace and truth" (Jn.1:14).

"God, who at sundry times and in divers manners spake in time past unto the fathers by the prophets, Hath in these last days spoken unto us by his Son, whom he hath appointed heir of all things, by whom also he made the worlds" (Heb.1:1-2).

"That which was from the beginning, which we have heard, which we have seen with our eyes, which we have looked upon, and our hands have handled, of the Word of life; (For the life was manifested, and we have seen it, and bear witness, and show unto you that eternal life, which was with the Father, and was manifested unto us;) That which we have seen and heard declare we unto you, that ye also may have fellowship with us: and truly our fellowship is with the Father, and with his Son Jesus Christ" (1 Jn.1:1-3).

"And this is his commandment, That we should believe on the name of his Son Jesus Christ, and love one another, as he gave us commandment" (1 Jn.3:23).

III. The Third Basis of the Ten Commandments Is God's Name (20:2).

Note that the name of God is the LORD (Jehovah - Yahweh).

- The name of God means that He is the great I AM: "I AM THAT I AM" (Ex.3:14-15). God is the Essence, Force, and Energy of Being, the Self-existent One.

- The name of God means that He is the God of salvation, deliverance, and redemption.

- The name of God means that He is the God of revelation.

God's very name means that He is the Source of all being; that He created man; that He loves man; that He saves, delivers, and redeems man; that He reveals and unveils the truth to man; that He reveals the truth of God and of the world to man. This is what the Ten Commandments (the law of God) are: the revelation of a loving God seeking to help man, showing man how to live. The very name of God tells us this. God's name is the basis, the very reason, the Ten Commandments are given to us. The name of God tells us that the LORD Himself loves us: He saves, delivers, and redeems us. He reveals the truth to us, showing us how to live and relate to Him, how to relate to one another. This He has done in the Ten Commandments. Simply stated, the LORD God loves us and wants us to know how to live; therefore, He gave us the Ten Commandments.

> "And God said unto Moses, I AM THAT I AM: and he said, Thus shalt thou say unto the children of Israel, I AM hath sent me unto you. And God said moreover unto Moses, Thus shalt thou say unto the children of Israel, The LORD God of your fathers, the God of Abraham, the God of Isaac, and the God of Jacob, hath sent me unto you: this is my name for ever, and this is my memorial unto all generations" (Ex.3:14-15).
>
> "Hear, O Israel: The LORD our God is one LORD: And thou shalt love the LORD thy God with all thine heart, and with all thy soul, and with all thy might. And these words, which I command thee this day, shall be in thine heart: And thou shalt teach them diligently unto thy children, and shalt talk of them when thou sittest in thine house, and when thou walkest by the way, and when thou liest down, and when thou risest up" (Dt.6:4-7).
>
> "For the LORD is our judge, the LORD is our lawgiver, the LORD is our king; he will save us" (Is.33:22).
>
> "Hearken unto me, my people; and give ear unto me, O my nation: for a law shall proceed from me, and I will make my judgment to rest for a light of the people. My righteousness is near; my salvation is gone forth, and mine arms shall judge the people; the isles shall wait upon me, and on mine arm shall they trust" (Is.51:4-5).

IV. The Fourth Basis of the Ten Commandments Is God's Relationship with Man (20:2).

Note that God is said to be the LORD *your* God. God is not far off in outer space someplace, unreachable, unapproachable. God is near, near enough for us to speak to Him. In fact, God wants us to speak with Him; God wants to develop a relationship with us, a personal, loving relationship. This is the reason God gave us the Ten Commandments. He is the great Creator and Father of mankind. Therefore, He gave us the commandments to nourish the relationship between Him and the people He created. He gave us the Ten Commandments to guide us into a closer relationship with Him.

"Now therefore, if ye will obey my voice indeed, and keep my covenant, then ye shall be a peculiar treasure unto me above all people: for all the earth is mine: And ye shall be unto me a kingdom of priests, and an holy nation. These are the words which thou shalt speak unto the children of Israel" (Ex.19:5-6).

"O that there were such an heart in them, that they would fear me, and keep all my commandments always, that it might be well with them, and with their children for ever!" (Dt.5:29).

"He that hath my commandments, and keepeth them, he it is that loveth me: and he that loveth me shall be loved of my Father, and I will love him, and will manifest myself to him" (Jn.14:21).

"Jesus answered and said unto him, If a man love me, he will keep my words: and my Father will love him, and we will come unto him, and make our abode with him" (Jn.14:23).

"Wherefore come out from among them, and be ye separate, saith the LORD, and touch not the unclean thing [keep God's commandments]; and I will receive you, And will be a Father unto you, and ye shall be my sons and daughters, saith the LORD Almighty" (2 Cor.6:17-18).

V. The Fifth Basis of the Ten Commandments Is God's Salvation, Deliverance, and Redemption (20:2).

Note that God Himself rescued Israel from the evil place of bondage, the land of Egypt (a symbol of the world). God gave us the Ten Commandments to save us from the evil and lawlessness of this world, evil and lawlessness such as...

- covetousness
- greed
- lying
- stealing

- adultery
- murder
- abuse
- cursing God

- false worship
- unbelief, denial of God
- violating the Sabbath, the day of rest & worship

Thought.

Evil and lawlessness have always swept the world in places where the Ten Commandments were not present and followed. The commandments help us only if we keep them. This is the reason God demands one thing above all else: *obedience*. God is our Savior and Deliverer. He wants us out of harm's way, living like we should, living in peace and reconciliation, both with Him and with one another. Therefore, He gave us the Ten Commandments. God's salvation, deliverance, and redemption are the bases of the Ten Commandments.

"O that there were such an heart in them, that they would fear me, and keep all my commandments always, that it might be well with them, and with their children for ever!" (Dt.5:29).

"But the salvation of the righteous is of the LORD: he is their strength in the time of trouble" (Ps.37:39).

"Behold, God is my salvation; I will trust, and not be afraid: for the LORD JEHOVAH is my strength and my song; he also is become my salvation" (Is.12:2).

"And it shall be said in that day, Lo, this is our God; we have waited for him, and he will save us: this is the LORD; we have waited for him, we will be glad and rejoice in his salvation" (Is.25:9).

"The LORD thy God in the midst of thee is mighty; he will save, he will rejoice over thee with joy; he will rest in his love, he will joy over thee with singing" (Zeph.3:17).

"This book of the law shall not depart out of thy mouth; but thou shalt meditate therein day and night, that thou mayest observe to do according to all that is written therein: for then thou shalt make thy way prosperous, and then thou shalt have good success" (Josh.1:8).

"For the grace of God that bringeth salvation hath appeared to all men, Teaching us that, denying ungodliness and worldly lusts, we should live soberly, righteously, and godly, in this present world; Looking for that blessed hope, and the glorious appearing of the great God and our Saviour Jesus Christ" (Tit.2:11-13).

Part One: The Laws Governing Man's Duty to God

Commandment One Concerns God's Being— Never Believe in Other Gods Exodus 20:3

Contents

Commandment One Concerns God's Being—Never Believe in Other Gods
Exodus 20:3

COMMANDMENT 1: Have no other gods *whatsoever*	3 Thou shalt have no other gods before me.

God is; God exists. There is a Creator of the universe: the one true and living God. He is the LORD GOD Himself (Jehovah, Yahweh). He created everything that exists, including man; therefore, God cares for man. He cares about man's welfare, what happens to man as he walks throughout life day by day. But God cares about something else as well: God cares about what man thinks of Him. What people think about God determines their eternal fate. God wants, even longs, for us all to live with Him eternally. This is the reason God gave us this first commandment:

"Thou shalt have no other gods before me" (Ex.20:3).

But the great tragedy is this: not all of us will live with God eternally. Why? Because many do not live with God now.

1. There are some who deny God: they just do not believe that God is, that God exists.

⇒ Some persons are secularists, people who believe that this physical world is all that exists.

⇒ Still others are evolutionists, people who believe that man has evolved to be the ultimate being of this earth, evolved to be the god of this earth.

⇒ Other persons are humanists, people who believe that man—his knowledge, his science, his technology—determines the destiny of man and of all else in this world.

Now if a person denies God, he naturally does not live with God, not now nor will he in the future. He has cut himself off from God. This commandment is directed to the atheists, secularists, humanists, and evolutionists.

"Thou shalt have no other gods before me"—not this secular world and universe and certainly not man himself who is ever so frail. Man's life is as a vapor that appears for just a brief time and then vanishes ever so quickly.

2. There are some people who question God's existence: God may exist, but He may not exist. There may be a God behind the universe, but there may not be. They just do not know, not for sure. How could they ever know? They are skeptical toward God. They are agnostics.

If a person questions God's existence, he naturally does not live with God, not now nor will he in the future. This commandment is directed to the agnostic:

"Thou shalt have no other gods before me"—not man's questioning and reasoning ability, not his science, technology, or exploratory abilities.

3. There are other people who believe in many gods, believe that the destiny of man and his world are in the hands of many powers and authorities throughout the universe (polytheism). This commandment is directed to all who believe in many gods. There is only one true and living God.

"Thou shalt have no other gods before me" (Ex.20:3).

4. There are many, many people who believe in one god and only in one god. But that god is not the true and living God, *not the God and Father of the Lord Jesus Christ*. Many people, especially within industrialized nations, say that the god worshiped by the Moslems, Buddhists, Christians, and others is the same god, that we all just call god by different names. But this is not true, not according to Scripture, not according to the *Father of our Lord Jesus Christ*.

The *Father of our Lord Jesus Christ* claims to be the only living and true God. He declares that this is the very reason He sent His Son, Jesus Christ, into the world: to reveal Himself—to reveal the truth to us—that there is only one true and living God. And this is the key belief: the god most people believe in is not the God and Father of our Lord Jesus Christ. He and He alone is the true and living God. He and He alone is the One who sent Jesus Christ to reveal the truth of Himself and the world to us.

This commandment is directed to those who believe in only one god, but who believe that he is the god of all people and religions of the earth.

"Thou shalt have no other gods before me" (Ex.20:3).

As stated above, God loves all people and longs for all to live with Him eternally. But so many of us are mistaken about God; so many of us deny, question, and have wrong images of God; so many of us tragically reject the Father of our Lord Jesus Christ. And all who reject the Father of our Lord Jesus Christ reject the only living and true God. And if we reject Him, we doom ourselves to be separated forever from God. This is the reason God gives us the first great commandment: to warn us, to warn us that there is only one true and living God.

"Thou shalt have no other gods before me" (Ex.20:3).

This is the first of the Ten Commandments: *Commandment One Concerns God's Being—Never Believe in Other Gods*, Ex.20:3.

I.   Who is to obey this commandment (v.3)?
II. How long was this commandment to be in force (v.3)?
III. What is forbidden by this commandment (v.3)?
IV. What are the Biblical consequences of breaking this commandment?
V.   What are the Biblical benefits of keeping this commandment?
VI. What is the teaching of Jesus Christ concerning this commandment?
VII. What is the decision required by this commandment (v.3)?

I. Who Is to Obey This Commandment?

The first commandment is personal. Note the word "you." The commandment is addressed to each person, each individual. Keep in mind that God is the Sovereign LORD and Majesty of the universe, the only living and true God. His commandments are, therefore, bound to be addressed to every person throughout the universe. No person—believer or unbeliever—would ever be exempt from the commandments given by the Sovereign LORD and God of the universe. Every person is required to obey God's commandments.

You yourself are personally responsible; *you yourself* are held accountable to obey this commandment.

> "Now therefore, if ye will obey my voice indeed, and keep my covenant, then ye shall be a peculiar treasure unto me above all people: for all the earth is mine: And ye shall be unto me a kingdom of priests, and an holy nation" (Ex.19:5-6).
> "This day the LORD thy God hath commanded thee to do these statutes and judgments: thou shalt therefore keep and do them with all thine heart, and with all thy soul" (Dt.26:16).
> "This book of the law shall not depart out of thy mouth; but thou shalt meditate therein day and night, that thou mayest observe to do according to all that is written therein: for then thou shalt make thy way prosperous, and then shalt have good success" (Josh.1:8).
> "Not every one that saith unto me, Lord, Lord, shall enter into the kingdom of heaven; but he that doeth the will of my Father which is in heaven" (Mt.7:21).

II. How Long Was This Commandment to Be in Force?

Was this commandment given by God to Israel alone, or was it given through Israel to the whole world? At least three facts show us that this commandment is to be obeyed by all people of all generations, to be obeyed as long as the universe stands.

First, God is the LORD (Jehovah, Yahweh), the Sovereign Majesty of the universe, the only living and true God (cp. v.2). There is no other God, not a living God, not a true God. You can search throughout the whole world—travel throughout the entire universe—and you will never find another true and living God. There is only one Creator and Sustainer of the universe: the LORD God Himself (cp. v.1-2). He is; He exists. The LORD God always has existed, is now existing, and always will exist. Therefore, as long as God exists and as long as the universe stands—as long as there are generations of people—God will command and demand: "You shall have no other gods before me" (v.3).

Second, Jesus Christ Himself told us that the Ten Commandments are meant for all generations of people.

> **"Think not that I am come to destroy the law, or the prophets: I am not come to destroy, but to fulfil" (Mt.5:17).**

Jesus Christ declared that He *fulfilled* the law: He completed and perfected the law. He never failed to keep the law, not even in one minute point. Therefore, He fulfilled the demands of the law perfectly. The point is this: by fulfilling the law, Jesus Christ embraces and upholds the law. He embodies, encompasses, integrates, and contains the law within His very being. The law of God is part of the very being of Jesus Christ, of God Himself.

Thought.

When a person looks at Jesus Christ, he sees the law of God in all its perfection. True, he sees more, much more. The person sees within Jesus Christ the very embodiment and perfection of love, mercy, compassion, joy, peace, longsuffering, gentleness, goodness, faithfulness, meekness, control, power, and justice. The person sees all that God Himself is. But in addition to all this, when the person sees Jesus Christ, he sees the law of God embodied within the very being of Jesus Christ. Therefore, when a person gives his life to follow Jesus Christ, that person follows the law of God and all else that Christ is.

Now, how long was this commandment to be in force? How many generations are to obey this commandment? As long as God loves the world and as long as Jesus Christ is the Savior of the world, people are to obey this commandment. All generations of people are to follow Christ and obey Him. They are to obey all that Christ is, which includes the Ten Commandments—the Ten Commandments plus so much more.

> **"O that there were such an heart in them, that they would fear me, and keep all my commandments always, that it might be well with them, and with their children for ever!" (Dt.5:29).**
> **"Hear, O Israel: The LORD our God is one LORD: And thou shalt love the LORD thy God with all thine heart, and with all thy soul, and with all thy might. And these words, which I command thee this day, shall be in thine heart: And thou shalt teach them diligently unto thy**

children, and shalt talk of them when thou sittest in thine house, and when thou walkest by the way, and when thou liest down, and when thou risest up" (Dt.6:4-7).

"Be ye therefore very courageous to keep and to do all that is written in the book of the law of Moses, that ye turn not aside therefrom to the right hand or to the left" (Josh.23:6).

"For verily I say unto you, Till heaven and earth pass, one jot or one tittle shall in no wise pass from the law, till all be fulfilled" (Mt.5:18).

"Heaven and earth shall pass away: but my words shall not pass away" (Lk.21:33).

III. What Is Forbidden by This First Commandment?

How is this commandment broken, violated? This commandment concerns God's being. God is declaring that He alone is the *Supreme Being*, the absolute authority of the universe. There is no other *supreme being*, no other god who created and who rules and reigns over the universe. He alone is the LORD, the only living and true God, the only living and true Creator.

Note that God makes three stringent demands, three clear requirements in this commandment.
1. Man is to have no other gods, none whatsoever (v.3).
   a. Man is not to set himself up as a god. Man is not to believe that he himself nor any other being or energy in the universe is the ultimate source of the universe.
      ⇒ Man is not to deny God, declaring there is no God (atheism).
      ⇒ Man is not to question God, saying God may exist but He also may not exist (agnosticism).
      ⇒ Man is not to declare that man himself is the supreme being, the ultimate authority of his world (humanism).
      ⇒ Man is not to look to science and technology as the ultimate power in life (secularism).
      ⇒ Man is not to hold that his own knowledge and reasoning ability are the ultimate control of the universe.
      ⇒ Man is not to believe that the spirit of man (the combined spirit of all men) is the ultimate energy of the universe.
      ⇒ Man is not to proclaim some impersonal mass, energy, or gas in the universe as *the force* behind all things.
   b. Man is not to believe that other beings, animals, or material things are God. Man is not to look in the sky above nor in the earth below nor in the sea and its depths and declare that something therein is God.

⇒ Man is not to look at the sky and declare the heavenly bodies and beings to be the supreme force of the universe: not the sun, moon, stars, angels, principalities, powers nor any other creature of any world or any dimension of being.

⇒ Man is not to look at the earth nor at some material substance of the earth and declare it to be God.

⇒ Man is not to look upon animals as some god, no matter what the animal is.

⇒ Man is not to consider the physical mass nor energy or gases that comprise the basic substance of things as a god: not the atoms, protons, neutrons nor whatever the most minute building-block of existence may be.

c. Man is not to believe in many gods (polytheism). There is only one living and true God, only one true Creator, only one LORD and Majesty of the universe (monotheism). Therefore, man is to have no other gods whatsoever. All other so-called gods are nothing more than...

• things created by the imaginations and thoughts of people

• things called gods by people

• things that are lifeless and powerless

• things that are only images made out of metal, wood, stone, chemicals, or dirt

2. God also makes a second demand of man: "You shall have no other gods <u>before me</u>" (v.3). The words "before me" (alpamaya) mean literally *before my face, against my face, in hostility toward me, in my presence, in my sight.* It means that man...

• is to set no god *before* the LORD God

• is to set no god *beside* the LORD God

• is to set no god *in the presence* of the LORD God

• is to set no god *in the face* of the LORD God

The great nineteenth century commentator George Bush makes several excellent statements that tell us exactly what the first commandment means:

⇒ "[Creating idols] may be done mentally as well as manually. There may be idolatry without idols.

⇒ "[This commandment] forbids the making of any other objects [as gods] whether persons or things, real or imaginary."

⇒ "[Our] supreme regard, reverence, esteem, affection, and obedience [is due] God alone.

⇒ "God is the fountain of happiness, and no intelligent being can be happy but through him... [consequently] whoever seeks for supreme happiness in the creature instead of the Creator is guilty of a violation of this command."[1]

If we set up anything that is a rival interest in our hearts and minds, anything that absorbs the love and service which belong only to the true God, then that thing becomes another god. Whatever the heart clings to, that becomes our god. Consequently...

- the proud man who idolizes himself makes himself a god
- the ambitious man who pays homage to popular applause makes his ambition and the praise of men his god
- the covetous person who craves money and things makes a god out of money and things
- the greedy person who hoards possessions makes possessions his god
- the immoral person who craves sex makes sex his god
- the glutton who craves food makes eating his god
- the doting lover—whether husband, wife, mother or father—who sets his supreme affection on the person loved instead of upon God makes that person his god [2]

3. God also makes a third demand of us: man is to know and acknowledge the only true and living God—the LORD God Himself.
  a. God declares that people who think there is no God are wrong (atheists). I AM the LORD God, the true and living God. *Atheists* may deny God, and *agnostics* may question if God really exists, but God is forceful in His declaration.
  ⇒ "I AM—I AM the LORD Your God" (v.2).

  "The fool hath said in his heart, There is no God" (Ps.14:1).

  b. No other object and no other being are ever to be set up as a so-called god. Taking ideas or objects or beings and calling them God is forbidden, absolutely forbidden.
  ⇒ The LORD Himself (Jehovah, Yahweh) emphatically declares:

  "I am the LORD: that is my name: and my glory will I not give to another, neither my praise to graven images" (Is.42:8).

---

[1] George Bush. *Exodus*. (Minneapolis, MN: Klock & Klock Christian Publishers, Inc., 1981), p.260.
[2] The idea for this paragraph was also taken from George Bush, *Exodus*, p.260.

⇒ The great apostle Paul declared:

"For though there be [many] that are called gods, whether in heaven or in earth, (as there be gods many, and lords many,) But to us there is but one God, the Father, of whom are all things" (1 Cor.8:5-6).

We make a god out of anything that we esteem or love, fear or serve more than God. Again, whatever the heart clings to, that is a person's god. It may be oneself. Frankly, many people focus upon pleasing and satisfying themselves. They live by their own values and are concerned primarily with their own feelings, comfort, desires, and pleasures. They simply live like they want, doing their own thing. They have exalted themselves to be their own gods. Other people make gods out of...

- heavenly bodies
- animals
- property
- fame, recognition
- family
- pleasure

- sports
- images
- position, career
- recreation
- sex
- cars, trucks

- force, energy
- money
- science
- power
- food
- the latest style of clothing

A god can be anything or any person. Man's first allegiance, first loyalty, first devotion is to be to the LORD God. The LORD God is to be first in a man's life; He is to be enthroned in the heart of man. Man is to know and acknowledge that there is one God and one God alone. The first commandment of the LORD is to be obeyed:

"You shall have no other gods before me" (v.3).

Thought 1.
Note several points:
a) The so-called gods of heaven and earth are nothing more than the creation of man's imagination and hands.

"To whom then will ye liken God? or what likeness will ye compare unto him? The workman melteth a graven image, and the goldsmith spreadeth it over with gold, and casteth silver chains. He that is so impoverished that he hath no oblation [offering] chooseth a tree that will not rot; he seeketh unto him a cunning workman to prepare a graven image, that shall not be moved. Have ye not known? have ye not heard? hath it not been told you from the beginning? have ye not understood from the foundations of the earth? It is he that sitteth upon the circle of the earth, and the inhabitants thereof are as grasshoppers; that stretcheth out the heavens as a curtain, and spreadeth them out as a tent to dwell in....Lift up your eyes on high, and behold who hath created these things, that bringeth out their host by number: he calleth

them all by names by the greatness of his might, for that he is strong in power; not one faileth" (Is.40:18-22, 26; cp. Ps.115:4-8; Jer.10:2-5).

"Assemble yourselves and come; draw near together, ye that are escaped of the nations: they have no knowledge that set up the wood of their graven image, and pray unto a god that cannot save" (Is.45:20).

"For as I [Paul the apostle] passed by, and beheld your devotions, I found an altar with this inscription, TO THE UNKNOWN GOD. Whom therefore ye ignorantly worship, him declare I unto you. God that made the world and all things therein, seeing that he is LORD of heaven and earth, dwelleth not in temples made with hands; Neither is worshipped with men's hands, as though he needed any thing, seeing he giveth to all life, and breath, and all things; And hath made of one blood all nations of men for to dwell on all the face of the earth, and hath determined the times before appointed, and the bounds of their habitation; That they should seek the LORD, if haply they might feel after him, and find him, though he be not far from every one of us: For in him we live, and move, and have our being; as certain also of your own poets have said, For we are also his offspring. Forasmuch then as we are the offspring of God, we ought not to think that the Godhead is like unto gold, or silver, or stone, graven by art and man's device. And the times of this ignorance God winked at; but now commandeth all men every where to repent: Because he hath appointed a day, in the which he will judge the world in righteousness by that man whom he hath ordained; whereof he hath given assurance unto all men, in that he hath raised him from the dead" (Acts 17:23-31).

"Professing themselves to be wise, they became fools, And changed the glory of the uncorruptible God into an image made like to corruptible man, and to birds, and fourfooted beasts, and creeping things" (Ro.1:22-23).

b) There is only one true and living God, the LORD Himself (Jehovah, Yahweh).

"For thus saith the LORD that created the heavens; God himself that formed the earth and made it; he hath established it, he created it not in vain, he formed it to be inhabited: I am the LORD; and there is none else" (Is.45:18; cp. Dt.4:35; 6:4-5; 2 Sam. 7:22; 1 Chron.17:20; Ps.83:18; Ps.86:10; Is.43:10-11; Is.44:6).

"Look unto me, and be ye saved, all the ends of the earth: for I am God, and there is none else" (Is.45:22).

"And Jesus answered him, The first of all the commandments [is], Hear, O Israel; The LORD our God is one LORD: And thou shalt love the LORD thy God with all thy heart, and with all thy soul, and with all thy mind, and with all thy strength: this [is] the first commandment" (Mk.12:29-30; cp. 1 Cor.8:4-6; Eph.4:6).

"And the scribe said unto him, Well, Master, thou hast said the truth: for there is one God; and there is none other but he" (Mk.12:32).

> "For there is one God, and one mediator between God and men, the man Christ Jesus" (1 Tim.2:5).

c) There is only one sovereign Creator who meets the needs of man.

> "By the word of the LORD were the heavens made; and all the host of them by the breath of his mouth....The LORD looketh from heaven; he beholdeth all the sons of men....Behold, the eye of the LORD is upon them that fear him, upon them that hope in his mercy; To deliver their soul from death, and to keep them alive in famine. Our soul waiteth for the LORD: he is our help and our shield" (Ps.33:6, 13, 18-20).

> "Of old hast thou laid the foundation of the earth: and the heavens are the work of thy hands. They shall perish, but thou shalt endure: yea, all of them shall wax old like a garment; as a vesture shalt thou change them, and they shall be changed: But thou art the same, and thy years shall have no end. The children of thy servants shall continue, and their seed shall be established before thee" (Ps.102:25-28).

> "Fear thou not; for I am with thee: be not dismayed; for I am thy God: I will strengthen thee; yea, I will help thee; yea, I will uphold thee with the right hand of my righteousness" (Is.41:10).

> "And even to your old age I am he; and even to hoar [gray] hairs will I carry you: I have made, and I will bear; even I will carry, and will deliver you....Remember the former things of old: for I am God, and there is none else; I am God, and there is none like me, Declaring the end from the beginning, and from ancient times the things that are not yet done, saying, My counsel shall stand, and I will do all my pleasure" (Is.46:4, 9-10).

Thought 2.

The very first commandment says, "You shall have no other gods *before me*" (v.3). Note the words *"before me."* This suggests at least two facts:
a) If we set some so-called god *"before God,"* He knows it. We cannot hide the fact from Him.
b) If we set a god *"before Him,"* His anger is aroused.

> "If we have forgotten the name of our God, or stretched out our hands to a strange god; Shall not God search this out? for he knoweth the secrets of the heart" (Ps.44:20-21).

> "I am the LORD: that is my name: and my glory will I not give to another, neither my praise to graven images" (Is.42:8).

> "For the wrath of God is revealed from heaven against all ungodliness and unrighteousness of men, <u>who hold the truth in unrighteousness</u>" (Ro.1:18).

IV. What Are the Consequences of Breaking This Commandment?

The first commandment does not cover the consequences. The reason is seen in the first two verses of Exodus, chapter twenty (20:1-2). The motivation for keeping the Ten Commandments is not to be fear, fear of the judgment of God. The reason for keeping the commandments is to be the love of God, the glorious salvation and deliverance He has provided. Note what God says:

> "I am the LORD thy God, which have brought thee out of the land of Egypt, out of the house of bondage" (v.2).

The Israelites were to keep the Ten Commandments because God had delivered them out of Egypt, out of slavery and bondage. Remember, Egypt is a picture of the world, and Israel's slavery to Egypt is a picture of man's enslavement to the world, to its bondages of sin and death. But God loves us; therefore, He has provided salvation for us in Christ Jesus our Lord. It is this—the love of God—that is to compel us to keep His commandments. But having said this, there are other reasons covered throughout Scripture for obeying the commandments. Scripture declares that there are severe consequences for violating or breaking the Ten Commandments. Our purpose in discussing the Ten Commandments is to give an overall discussion. For this reason, we are including the consequences for breaking each of the commandments. In relation to the first commandment, Scripture declares the following consequences.

1. There are the consequences upon God.

   a. The person who does not follow God cuts the heart of God: causes pain and hurt for Him.

      > "And the LORD said unto Samuel, Hearken unto the voice of the people in all that they say unto thee: for they have not rejected thee, but they have rejected me, that I should not reign over them" (1 Sam.8:7).
      > "But my people would not hearken to my voice; and Israel would none of me" (Ps. 81:11).
      > "The LORD is not slack concerning his promise, as some men count slackness; but is longsuffering to us, not willing that any should perish, but that all should come to repentance" (2 Pt.3:9).

   b. The person who does not follow God causes the name of God to be blasphemed.

      > "Thou that makest thy boast of the law, through breaking the law dishonourest thou God? For the name of God is blasphemed among the Gentiles [the unsaved] through you, as it is written" (Ro.2:23-24).

   c. The person who does not follow God lives a life that is detestable to God.

      > "They profess that they know God; but in works they deny him, being abominable [detestable], and disobedient, and unto every good work reprobate [worthless, NASB]" (Tit.1:16).

2. There are the consequences upon oneself, one's day-to-day life.

   a. The person who does not follow God follows after dumb, lifeless idols, man-made gods that can never help him.

"Shall a man make gods unto himself, and they are no gods?" (Jer.16:20).

"Ye know that ye were Gentiles, carried away unto these dumb idols, even as ye were led" (1 Cor.12:2).

b. The person who does not follow God exchanges a life of glory for a life that does not profit, a life that is worthless.

"Hath a nation changed their gods, which are yet no gods? but my people have changed their glory for that which doth not profit" (Jer.2:11).

c. The person who does not follow God experiences a life of emptiness and trouble, missing out on the spiritual rest and peace of God.

"Let us labour therefore to enter into that rest, lest any man fall after the same example of unbelief" (Heb.4:11).

"For all this they sinned still, and believed not for his wondrous works. Therefore their days did he consume in vanity [emptiness], and their years in trouble" (Ps.78:32-33).

d. The person who does not follow God lives a life of hopelessness.

"That at that time ye were without Christ, being aliens from the commonwealth of Israel, and strangers from the covenants of promise, having no hope, and without God in the world" (Eph.2:12).

e. The person who does not follow God lives a life that is enslaved to sin.

"Howbeit then, when ye knew not God, ye did service unto them which by nature are no gods. But now, after that ye have known God, or rather are known of God, how turn ye again to the weak and beggarly elements, whereunto ye desire again to be in bondage?" (Gal.4:8-9).

f. The person who does not follow God lives a hypocritical life, a life that denies the truth.

"Having a form of godliness, but denying the power thereof: from such turn away" (2 Tim.3:5).

"For the wrath of God is revealed from heaven against all ungodliness and unrighteousness of men, who hold the truth in unrighteousness; Because that which may be known of God is manifest in them; for God hath showed it unto them. For the invisible things of him from the creation of the world are clearly seen, being understood by the things that are made, even his eternal power and Godhead; so that they are without excuse: Because that, when they knew God, they glorified him not as God, neither were thankful; but became vain in their imaginations, and their foolish heart was darkened. Professing themselves to be wise, they became fools, And changed the glory of the uncorruptible God into an image made like to corruptible man, and to birds, and fourfooted beasts, and creeping things" (Ro.1:18-23).

g. The person who does not follow God defiles his mind and conscience.

"Unto the pure all things are pure: but unto them that are defiled and unbelieving is nothing pure; but even their mind and conscience is defiled" (Tit.1:15).

h. The person who does not follow God experiences the most illogical life that can be lived: the life of a fool.

"The fool hath said in his heart, There is no God. They are corrupt, they have done abominable works, there is none that doeth good" (Ps.14:1).

i. The person who does not follow God has no root and falls away when temptation comes.

"Those by the way side are they that hear; then cometh the devil, and taketh away the word out of their hearts, lest they should believe and be saved. They on the rock are they, which, when they hear, receive the word with joy; and these have no root, which for a while believe, and in time of temptation fall away" (Lk.8:12-13).

j. The person who does not follow God is blinded in his mind, unable to see the saving light of the gospel of Christ.

"In whom the god of this world hath blinded the minds of them which believe not, lest the light of the glorious gospel of Christ, who is the image of God, should shine unto them" (2 Cor.4:4).

k. The person who does not follow God lives a life of ungodly lusts, a life that mocks God and His Son, the Lord Jesus Christ.

"Then certain philosophers of the Epicureans, and of the Stoicks, encountered him. And some said, What will this babbler say? other some, He seemeth to be a setter forth of strange gods: because he preached unto them Jesus, and the resurrection" (Acts 17:18).
"Knowing this first, that there shall come in the last days scoffers, walking after their own lusts, And saying, Where is the promise of his coming? for since the fathers fell asleep, all things continue as they were from the beginning of the creation. For this they willingly are ignorant of, that by the word of God the heavens were of old, and the earth standing out of the water and in the water" (2 Pt.3:3-5).

"But, beloved, remember ye the words which were spoken before of the apostles of our LORD Jesus Christ; How that they told you there should be mockers in the last time, who should walk after their own ungodly lusts" (Jude 1:17-18; cp. Ps.73:11-12).

3. There are the consequences of judgment.

   a. The person who does not follow God does not inherit the kingdom of God.

"Know ye not that the unrighteous shall not inherit the kingdom of God? Be not deceived: neither fornicators, nor idolaters, nor adulterers, nor effeminate, nor abusers of themselves with mankind, Nor thieves, nor covetous, nor drunkards, nor revilers, nor extortioners, shall inherit the kingdom of God" (1 Cor.6:9-10).

   b. The person who does not follow God displeases God, arousing His anger and wrath.

"He that believeth on the Son hath everlasting life: and he that believeth not the Son shall not see life; but the wrath of God abideth on him" (Jn.3:36).
"I said therefore unto you, that ye shall die in your sins: for if ye believe not that I am he, ye shall die in your sins" (Jn.8:24).
"That they all might be damned who believed not the truth, but had pleasure in unrighteousness" (2 Th.2:12).
"I will therefore put you in remembrance, though ye once knew this, how that the LORD, having saved the people out of the land of Egypt, afterward destroyed them that believed not" (Jude 1:5).

   c. The person who does not follow God is broken off, separated, cut loose, turned away from by God.

"Well; because of unbelief they were broken off, and thou standest by faith. Be not highminded, but fear" (Ro.11:20).
"And the word of the LORD came unto me, saying, Son of man, these men have set up their idols in their heart, and put the stumblingblock of their iniquity before their face: should I be inquired of at all by them? Therefore speak unto them, and say unto them, Thus saith the Lord GOD; Every man of the house of Israel that setteth up his idols in his heart, and putteth the stumblingblock of his iniquity before his face, and cometh to the prophet; I the LORD will answer him that cometh according to the multitude of his idols; That I may take the house of Israel in their own heart, because they are all estranged [separated] from me through their idols" (Ezk.14:2-5).

   d. The person who does not follow God experiences the judicial judgment of God: God gives him over to his sin, to reap what he sows.

> "And even as they did not like to retain God in their knowledge, God gave them over to a reprobate [depraved] mind, to do those things which are not convenient" (Ro.1:28).

e. The person who does not follow God shall not enter heaven, no matter what he professes to have done in the name of God.

> "Not every one that saith unto me, LORD, LORD, shall enter into the kingdom of heaven; but he that doeth the will of my Father which is in heaven. Many will say to me in that day, LORD, LORD, have we not prophesied in thy name? and in thy name have cast out devils? and in thy name done many wonderful works? And then will I profess unto them, I never knew you: depart from me, ye that work iniquity" (Mt.7:21-23).

f. The person who does not follow God shall face the fierce judgment of God and perish.

> "He that rejecteth me, and receiveth not my words, hath one that judgeth him: the word that I have spoken, the same shall judge him in the last day" (Jn.12:48).
> "But the heavens and the earth, which are now, by the same word are kept in store, reserved unto fire against the day of judgment and perdition of ungodly men" (2 Pt.3:7).
> "And Enoch also, the seventh from Adam, prophesied of these, saying, Behold, the LORD cometh with ten thousands of his saints, To execute judgment upon all, and to convince all that are ungodly among them of all their ungodly deeds which they have ungodly committed, and of all their hard speeches which ungodly sinners have spoken against him" (Jude 1:14-15; cp. Ps.1:4-6; Jer.5:7-9).

g. The person who does not follow God shall face the terrible experience of dying in his sins and going to hell.

> "I said therefore unto you, that ye shall die in your sins: for if ye believe not that I am he, ye shall die in your sins" (Jn.8:24).
> "But the fearful, and unbelieving, and the abominable, and murderers, and whoremongers, and sorcerers, and idolaters, and all liars, shall have their part in the lake which burneth with fire and brimstone: which is the second death" (Rev.21:8).

h. The person who does not follow God is deluded and damned.

> "And for this cause God shall send them strong delusion, that they should believe a lie: That they all might be damned who believed not the truth, but had pleasure in unrighteousness" (2 Th.2:11-12).

i. The person who does not follow God causes God to hide His face from him.

> "And he said, I will hide my face from them, I will see what their end shall be: for they are a very froward generation, children in whom is no faith" (Dt.32:20).

j. The person who does not follow God brings judgment upon his children.

> "Ahaziah the son of Ahab began to reign over Israel in Samaria the seventeenth year of Jehoshaphat king of Judah, and reigned two years over Israel. And he did evil in the sight of the LORD, and walked in the way of his father, and in the way of his mother, and in the way of Jeroboam the son of Nebat, who made Israel to sin: For he served Baal, and worshipped him, and provoked to anger the LORD God of Israel, according to all that his father had done" (1 Ki.22:51-53).
>
> "He [Ahaziah] also walked in the ways of the house of Ahab: for his mother was his counsellor to do wickedly. Wherefore he did evil in the sight of the LORD like the house of Ahab: for they were his counsellers after the death of his father to his destruction" (2 Chron.22:3-4).
>
> "But I said unto their children in the wilderness, Walk ye not in the statutes of your fathers, neither observe their judgments, nor defile yourselves with their idols: I am the LORD your God; walk in my statutes, and keep my judgments, and do them; And hallow my sabbaths; and they shall be a sign between me and you, that ye may know that I am the LORD your God. Notwithstanding the children rebelled against me: they walked not in my statutes, neither kept my judgments to do them, which if a man do, he shall even live in them; they polluted my sabbaths: then I said, I would pour out my fury upon them, to accomplish my anger against them in the wilderness" (Ezk.20:18-21).

V. What Are the Benefits of Keeping This Commandment?

The LORD (Jehovah, Yahweh) is the only living and true God. Consequently, He is bound to pour out the richest blessings imaginable upon the person who keeps this commandment, upon the person who truly believes and follows Him.

1. The person who believes God—genuinely believes God—will be saved, never condemned, through God's Son, the LORD Jesus Christ.

> "For God so loved the world, that he gave his only begotten Son, that whosoever believeth in him should not perish, but have everlasting life. For God sent not his Son into the world to condemn the world; but that the world through him might be saved. He that believeth on him is not condemned: but he that believeth not is condemned already, be-

cause he hath not believed in the name of the only begotten Son of God" (Jn.3:16-18).

"For the wages of sin is death; but the gift of God is eternal life through Jesus Christ our Lord" (Ro.6:23).

"That if thou shalt confess with thy mouth the Lord Jesus, and shalt believe in thine heart that God hath raised him from the dead, thou shalt be saved. For with the heart man believeth unto righteousness; and with the mouth confession is made unto salvation" (Ro.10:9-10).

"For by grace are ye saved through faith; and that not of yourselves: it is the gift of God: Not of works, lest any man should boast. For we are his [God's] workmanship, created in Christ Jesus unto good works, which God hath before ordained that we should walk in them" (Eph.2:8-10).

2. The person who believes God will be redeemed, never condemned.

"The LORD redeemeth the soul of his servants: and none of them that trust in him shall be desolate [condemned]" (Ps.34:22).

3. The person who believes God will escape the wrath of God and live forever, live eternally with God and with His Son, the Lord Jesus Christ.

"He that believeth on the Son hath everlasting life: and he that believeth not the Son shall not see life; but the wrath of God abideth on him" (Jn.3:36).

"Verily, verily, I say unto you, He that heareth my word, and believeth on him that sent me, hath everlasting life, and shall not come into condemnation; but is passed from death unto life" (Jn.5:24).

"Jesus said unto her, I am the resurrection, and the life: he that believeth in me, though he were dead, yet shall he live" (Jn.11:25).

"Let not your heart be troubled: ye believe in God, believe also in me. In my Father's house are many mansions: if [it were] not [so], I would have told you. I go to prepare a place for you" (Jn.14:1-2).

"That if thou shalt confess with thy mouth the LORD Jesus, and shalt believe in thine heart that God hath raised him from the dead, thou shalt be saved" (Ro.10:9).

4. The person who believes God will be justified: God will count his faith for righteousness.

"Therefore it [the promise of righteousness, of eternal life] is of faith, that it might be by grace; to the end the promise might be sure to all the seed; not to that only which is of the law, but to that also which is of the faith of Abraham; who is the father of us all, (As it is written, I have made thee a father of many nations,) before him whom he believed, even God, who quickeneth the dead, and calleth those things which be not as though they were" (Ro.4:16-17).

> "Now it was not written for his sake alone, that it [righteousness] was imputed to him; But for us also, to whom it shall be imputed, if we believe on him that raised up Jesus our LORD from the dead; Who was delivered for our offences, and was raised again for our justification" (Ro.4:23-25).

5. The person who believes God—genuinely believes—will be a member of God's family, His treasured possession, and receive unbelievable reward.

> "Now therefore, if ye will obey my voice indeed, and keep my covenant, then ye shall be a peculiar treasure unto me above all people: for all the earth is mine" (Ex.19:5).
>
> "This day the LORD thy God hath commanded thee to do these statutes and judgments: thou shalt therefore keep and do them with all thine heart, and with all thy soul. Thou hast avouched the LORD this day to be thy God, and to walk in his ways, and to keep his statutes, and his commandments, and his judgments, and to hearken unto his voice: And the LORD hath avouched thee this day to be his peculiar people, as he hath promised thee, and that thou shouldest keep all his commandments; And to make thee high above all nations which he hath made, in praise, and in name, and in honour; and that thou mayest be an holy people unto the LORD thy God, as he hath spoken" (Dt.26:16-19).
>
> "Therefore, my beloved brethren, be ye stedfast, unmoveable, always abounding in the work of the LORD, forasmuch as ye know that your labour is not in vain in the LORD" (1 Cor.15:58).
>
> "And I saw a new heaven and a new earth: for the first heaven and the first earth were passed away; and there was no more sea....And God shall wipe away all tears from their eyes; and there shall be no more death, neither sorrow, nor crying, neither shall there be any more pain: for the former things are passed away" (Rev.21:1, 4).
>
> "And, behold, I come quickly; and my reward is with me, to give every man according as his work shall be" (Rev.22:12).

6. The person who believes God will come to know God personally, in an intimate way.

> "Ye are my witnesses, saith the LORD, and my servant whom I have chosen: that ye may know and believe me, and understand that I am he: before me there was no God formed, neither shall there be after me" (Is.43:10).
>
> "That I may know him [Jesus Christ], and the power of his resurrection, and the fellowship of his sufferings, being made conformable unto his death" (Ph.3:10; cp. Dt.4:35; Jn.7:16-17).

7. The person who believes God will live in perfect peace, assurance, and confidence as he walks throughout life, as he trusts God and keeps his mind upon Him.

"Thou wilt keep him in perfect peace, whose mind is stayed on thee: because he trusteth in thee" (Is.26:3).

"Therefore being justified by faith, we have peace with God through our Lord Jesus Christ" (Ro.5:1).

"Finally, brethren, whatsoever things are true, whatsoever things are honest, whatsoever things are just, whatsoever things are pure, whatsoever things are lovely, whatsoever things are of good report; if there be any virtue, and if there be any praise, think on these things. Those things, which ye have both learned, and received, and heard, and seen in me [Paul], do: and the God of peace shall be with you" (Ph.4:8-9).

8. The person who believes God will be given the strength of God day by day, even the everlasting strength of God Himself.

"Trust ye in the LORD for ever: for in the LORD Jehovah is everlasting strength" (Is.26:4).

9. The person who believes God will be secure through the trials and temptations of life, safe from all the enemies of life.

"The fear of man bringeth a snare: but whoso putteth his trust in the LORD shall be safe" (Pr.29:25).

"Who shall separate us from the love of Christ? shall tribulation, or distress, or persecution, or famine, or nakedness, or peril, or sword? Nay, in all these things we are more than conquerors through him that loved us. For I am persuaded, that neither death, nor life, nor angels, nor principalities, nor powers, nor things present, nor things to come....Nor height, nor depth, nor any other creature, shall be able to separate us from the love of God, which is in Christ Jesus our LORD" (Ro.8:35, 37-39).

10. The person who believes God will be looked after and taken care of by God.

"Commit thy way unto the LORD; trust also in him; and he shall bring it to pass" (Ps.37:5).

"Casting all your care upon him; for he careth for you" (1 Pt.5:7).

"But seek ye first the kingdom of God, and his righteousness; and all these things shall be added unto you" (Mt.6:33).

11. The person who believes God will be guided and directed by God.

"Trust in the LORD with all thine heart; and lean not unto thine own understanding. In all thy ways acknowledge him, and he shall direct thy paths" (Pr.3:5-6).

12. The person who believes God will experience the love and power of God: all things will work out for good.

"And we know that all things work together for good to them that love God, to them who are the called according to his purpose" (Ro.8:28).

13. The person who believes God overcomes the world.

> "For whatsoever is born of God overcometh the world: and this is the victory that overcometh the world, even our faith. Who is he that overcometh the world, but he that believeth that Jesus is the Son of God?" (1 Jn.5:4-5).

14. The person who believes God overcomes the temptations of the devil.

> "Above all, taking the shield of faith [in God], wherewith ye shall be able to quench all the fiery darts of the wicked" (Eph.6:16).

15. The person who believes God is given the righteousness and justification of God.

> "But now the righteousness of God without the law is manifested, being witnessed by the law and the prophets; Even the righteousness of God which is by faith of Jesus Christ unto all and upon all them that believe: for there is no difference: For all have sinned, and come short of the glory of God; Being justified freely by his grace through the redemption that is in Christ Jesus" (Ro.3:21-24).
>
> "And be found in him, not having mine own righteousness, which is of the law, but that which is through the faith of Christ, the righteousness which is of God by faith" (Ph.3:9; cp. 2 Cor.5:21; Jer.9:24).

16. The person who believes God receives what he asks in prayer.

> "And all things, whatsoever ye shall ask in prayer, believing, ye shall receive" (Mt.21:22).

17. The person who believes God will be greatly rewarded by God.

> "But without faith it is impossible to please him: for he that cometh to God must believe that he is, and that he is a rewarder of them that diligently seek him"(Heb.11:6).

18. The person who believes God will experience the glorious goodness and blessings of God.

> "Oh how great is thy goodness, which thou hast laid up for them that fear thee; which thou hast wrought for them that trust in thee before the sons of men!" (Ps.31:19).

VI.   What Is the Teaching of Jesus Christ Concerning This Commandment?

1. Jesus Christ declared that there is *only one true and living God, One Sovereign LORD and Majesty* of the universe, and that we are to love Him with all our hearts, souls, and minds.

"Then one of them, which was a lawyer, asked him a question, tempting him, and saying, Master, which is the great commandment in the law? Jesus said unto him, Thou shalt love the Lord thy God with all thy heart, and with all thy soul, and with all thy mind. This is the first and great commandment. And the second is like unto it, Thou shalt love thy neighbour as thyself. On these two commandments hang all the law and the prophets" (Mt.22:35-40).

Thought.

We are to know and acknowledge the only true and living God, Him and Him alone. We must not believe nor follow any other gods, none whatsoever. We are...

- to set no other god *before* the LORD God
- to set no other god *beside* the LORD God
- to set no other god "in the presence" of the LORD God
- to set no other god in the face of the LORD God

"Ye are my witnesses, saith the LORD, and my servant whom I have chosen: that ye may know and believe me, and understand that I am he: before me there was no God formed, neither shall there be after me" (Is.43:10).

"Thus saith the LORD the King of Israel, and his redeemer the LORD of hosts; I am the first, and I am the last; and beside me there is no God" (Is.44:6).

"Fear ye not, neither be afraid: have not I told thee from that time, and have declared it? ye are even my witnesses. Is there a God beside me? yea, there is no God; I know not any" (Is.44:8).

"I am the LORD, and there is none else, there is no God beside me: I girded thee, though thou hast not known me" (Is.45:5).

"For thus saith the LORD that created the heavens; God himself that formed the earth and made it; he hath established it, he created it not in vain, he formed it to be inhabited: I am the LORD; and there is none else" (Is.45:18).

"Remember the former things of old: for I am God, and there is none else; I am God, and there is none like me" (Is.46:9).

"One God and Father of all, who is above all, and through all, and in you all" (Eph.4:6).

"For there is one God, and one mediator between God and men, the man Christ Jesus" (1 Tim.2:5).

2. Jesus Christ declared that God exists by proclaiming that He Himself is the Son of God.

"He that believeth on him is not condemned: but he that believeth not is condemned already, because he hath not believed in the name of the only begotten Son of God" (Jn.3:18).

> "Verily, verily, I say unto you, The hour is coming, and now is, when the dead shall hear the voice of the Son of God: and they that hear shall live" (Jn.5:25).
>
> "But these are written, that ye might believe that Jesus is the Christ, the Son of God; and that believing ye might have life through his name" (Jn.20:31).

3. Jesus Christ declared that God exists by proclaiming that He was One with the Father.

> "I and my Father are one" (Jn.10:30).

Thought.

The only way to have a relationship with the Father is to believe in the Son of God, the Lord Jesus Christ Himself. We must trust Christ and believe His Word: He and the Father are One.

> "If I do not the works of my Father, believe me not. But if I do, though ye believe not me, believe the works: that ye may know, and believe, that the Father is in me, and I in him" (Jn.10:37-38).
>
> "Believest thou not that I am in the Father, and the Father in me? the words that I speak unto you I speak not of myself: but the Father that dwelleth in me, he doeth the works" (Jn.14:10).
>
> "And now I am no more in the world, but these are in the world, and I come to thee. Holy Father, keep through thine own name those whom thou hast given me, that they may be one, as we are" (Jn.17:11).
>
> "And the glory which thou gavest me I have given them; that they may be one, even as we are one" (Jn.17:22).

4. Jesus Christ declared that God exists by proclaiming His own pre-existence with the Father.

> "Jesus said unto them, Verily, verily, I say unto you, Before Abraham was, I am" (Jn.8:58).
>
> "And now, O Father, glorify thou me with thine own self with the glory which I had with thee before the world was" (Jn.17:5).

Thought.

Note two lessons:
a) Because Jesus Christ is God, the believer must...
   - worship Christ as he would worship God
   - obey Christ as he would obey God
   - serve Christ as he would serve God
   - honor Christ as he would honor God
   - believe Christ as he would believe God

b) Because Jesus Christ is God, we have a God who is our...

- Lord
- Savior
- Master
- Creator
- Provider

- Great High Priest
- Intercessor
- Sacrificial Lamb of God
- Coming King and LORD of Lords

> "In the beginning was the Word, and the Word was with God, and the Word was God. The same was in the beginning with God. All things were made by him; and without him was not any thing made that was made" (Jn.1:1-3).
>
> "I am Alpha and Omega, the beginning and the end, the first and the last" (Rev.22:13).

5. Jesus Christ declared that God exists by proclaiming the love of God.

> "For God so loved the world, that he gave his only begotten Son, that whosoever believeth in him should not perish, but have everlasting life" (Jn.3:16).

Thought.

The most glorious truth is that God gave His one and only Son, His only begotten Son. This is the most remarkable proof of God's love. It magnifies and shows how great His love really is.

> "Then they that were in the ship came and worshipped him, saying, Of a truth thou art the Son of God" (Mt.14:33).
>
> "While he yet spake, behold, a bright cloud overshadowed them: and behold a voice out of the cloud, which said, This is my beloved Son, in whom I am well pleased; hear ye him" (Mt.17:5).
>
> "The beginning of the gospel of Jesus Christ, the Son of God" (Mk.1:1).
>
> "And I saw, and bare record that this is the Son of God" (Jn.1:34).
>
> "Say ye of him, whom the Father hath sanctified, and sent into the world, Thou Blasphemest; because I said, I am the Son of God?" (Jn.10:36).
>
> "She saith unto him, Yea, Lord: I believe that thou art the Christ, the Son of God, which should come into the world" (Jn.11:27).
>
> "Whosoever shall confess that Jesus is the Son of God, God dwelleth in him, and he in God" (1Jn.4:15).

6. Jesus Christ declared that God exists by proclaiming that a person can live eternally with God.

> "For God so loved the world, that he gave his only begotten Son, that whosoever believeth in him should not perish, but have everlasting life" (Jn.3:16).

> "Verily, verily, I say unto you, He that heareth my word, and believeth on him [God] that sent me, hath everlasting life, and shall not come into condemnation; but is passed from death unto life" (Jn.5:24).

Thought.

God was willing to give the thing most dear to His heart, His Son, in order to save the world. Note this: God had even planned to give His Son throughout eternity.

> "Him, being delivered by the determinate counsel and foreknowledge of God, ye have taken, and by wicked hands have crucified and slain: Whom God hath raised up, having loosed the pains of death: because it was not possible that he should be holden of it" (Acts 2:23-24).
>
> "And was there until the death of Herod: that it might be fulfilled which was spoken of the Lord by the prophet, saying, Out of Egypt have I called my son" (Mt.2:15).
>
> "And the angel answered and said unto her, The Holy Ghost shall come upon thee, and the power of the Highest shall overshadow thee: therefore also that holy thing which shall be born of thee shall be called the Son of God" (Lk.1:35)

7. Jesus Christ declared that God exists by teaching that the person who rejects the Son of God will bear the terrible judgment and wrath of God.

> "But whosoever shall deny me before men, him will I also deny before my Father which is in heaven" (Mt.10:33).
>
> "But he that denieth me before men shall be denied before the angels of God" (Lk.12:9).
>
> "He that believeth on the Son hath everlasting life: and he that believeth not the Son shall not see life; but the wrath of God abideth on him" (Jn.3:36).
>
> "He that believeth on him is not condemned: but he that believeth not is condemned already, because he hath not believed in the name of the only begotten Son of God" (Jn.3:18).

Thought.

Note two facts:

a) We must believe on the Son in order to guarantee everlasting life.

> "Verily, verily, I say unto you, He that heareth my word, and believeth on him that sent me, hath everlasting life, and shall not come into condemnation; but is passed from death unto life" (Jn.5:24).
>
> "Jesus said unto her, I am the resurrection, and the life: he that believeth in me, though he were dead, yet shall he live" (Jn.11:25).
>
> "But these are written, that ye might believe that Jesus is the Christ, the Son of God; and that believing ye might have life through his name" (Jn.20:31).

"And that from a child thou hast known the holy scriptures, which are able to make thee wise unto salvation through faith which is in Christ Jesus" (2 Tim.3:15).

"Whosoever believeth that Jesus is the Christ is born of God: and every one that loveth him that begat loveth him also that is begotten of him" (1 Jn.5:1).

b) We must not reject Jesus Christ nor ever be ashamed of our relationship with Him. Christ has done far too much for us to deny Him, to ever be ashamed of Him.

"For I am not ashamed of the gospel of Christ: for it is the power of God unto salvation to every one that believeth; to the Jew first, and also to the Greek" (Ro.1:16).

"As it is written, Behold, I lay in Sion a stumblingstone and rock of offence: and whosoever believeth on him shall not be ashamed" (Ro.9:33).

"According to my earnest expectation and my hope, that in nothing I shall be ashamed, but that with all boldness, as always, so now also Christ shall be magnified in my body, whether it be by life, or by death" (Ph.1:20).

"Yet if any man suffer as a Christian, let him not be ashamed; but let him glorify God on this behalf" (1 Pt.4:16).

"And now, little children, abide in him; that, when he shall appear, we may have confidence, and not be ashamed before him at his coming" (1 Jn.2:28).

8. Jesus Christ declared the existence of God by praying to His Father, the LORD God Himself (Jehovah, Yahweh).

"These words spake Jesus, and lifted up his eyes to heaven, and said, Father, the hour is come; glorify thy Son, that thy Son also may glorify thee" (Jn.17:1).

"And now, O Father, glorify thou me with thine own self with the glory which I had with thee before the world was" (Jn.17:5).

"And now I am no more in the world, but these are in the world, and I come to thee. Holy Father, keep through thine own name those whom thou hast given me, that they may be one, as we are" (Jn.17:11).

"Father, I will that they also, whom thou hast given me, be with me where I am; that they may behold my glory, which thou hast given me: for thou lovedst me before the foundation of the world. O righteous Father, the world hath not known thee: but I have known thee, and these have known that thou hast sent me" (Jn.17:24-25).

Thought.

We must focus and direct our prayers to the only living and true God, to the Father of the Lord Jesus Christ, to Him and Him alone. We must never pray nor seek help from other gods, gods that are nothing more than the imaginations of men.

> "At that time Jesus answered and said, I thank thee, O Father, Lord of heaven and earth, because thou hast hid these things from the wise and prudent, and hast revealed them unto babes" (Mt.11:25).
>
> "Then said Jesus, Father, forgive them; for they know not what they do. And they parted his raiment, and cast lots" (Lk.23:34).
>
> "Then they took away the stone from the place where the dead was laid. And Jesus lifted up his eyes, and said, Father, I thank thee that thou hast heard me" (Jn.11:41).
>
> "Ye have not chosen me, but I have chosen you, and ordained you, that ye should go and bring forth fruit, and that your fruit should remain: that whatsoever ye shall ask of the Father in my name, he may give it you" (Jn.15:16).
>
> "And in that day ye shall ask me nothing. Verily, verily, I say unto you, Whatsoever ye shall ask the Father in my name, he will give it you. Hitherto have ye asked nothing in my name: ask, and ye shall receive, that your joy may be full" (Jn.16:23-24).

VII. What Is the Decision Required by This Commandment?

1. The decision can be stated positively:
   a. We must acknowledge that there is only one living and true God and serve Him with our whole hearts.

   > "And thou, Solomon my son, know thou the God of thy father, and serve him with a perfect heart and with a willing mind: for the LORD searcheth all hearts, and understandeth all the imaginations of the thoughts: if thou seek him, he will be found of thee; but if thou forsake him, he will cast thee off for ever" (1 Chron. 28:9).
   >
   > "Thou hast avouched the LORD this day to be thy God, and to walk in his ways, and to keep his statutes, and his commandments, and his judgments, and to hearken unto his voice" (Dt.26:17).
   >
   > "For though there be that are called gods, whether in heaven or in earth, (as there be gods many, and lords many,) But to us there is but one God, the Father, of whom are all things, and we in him; and one Lord Jesus Christ, by whom are all things, and we by him. Howbeit there is not in every man that knowledge" (1 Cor.8:5-7).

   b. We must turn to the LORD and be saved, for He alone is God.

   > "Look unto me, and be ye saved, all the ends of the earth: for I am God, and there is none else" (Is.45:22).

c. We must love the LORD our God (Jehovah, Yahweh) with all our hearts.

> "Hear, O Israel: The LORD our God is one LORD: And thou shalt love the LORD thy God with all thine heart, and with all thy soul, and with all thy might" (Dt.6:4-5).

d. We must seek to walk before God and be blameless.

> "And when Abram was ninety years old and nine, the LORD appeared to Abram, and said unto him, I am the Almighty God; walk before me, and be thou perfect" (Gen.17:1).
> "But this thing commanded I them, saying, Obey my voice, and I will be your God, and ye shall be my people: and walk ye in all the ways that I have commanded you, that it may be well unto you" (Jer.7:23).

e. We must sanctify the LORD in our hearts, set Him apart as holy and fear Him.

> "Sanctify the LORD of hosts himself; and let him be your fear, and let him be your dread" (Is.8:13).
> "But sanctify the Lord God in your hearts: and be ready always to give an answer to every man that asketh you a reason of the hope that is in you with meekness and fear" (1 Pt.3:15).

f. We must realize that we cannot serve two masters; we cannot serve God and money.

> "No man can serve two masters: for either he will hate the one, and love the other; or else he will hold to the one, and despise the other. Ye cannot serve God and mammon" (Mt.6:24).

2. The decision can be stated negatively: we must have no other gods whatsoever; we must never believe in other gods, none whatsoever.

> "Thou shalt have no other gods before me" (Ex.20:3).
> "Take heed to yourselves, that your heart be not deceived, and ye turn aside, and serve other gods, and worship them" (Dt.11:16).
> "Little children, keep yourselves from idols. Amen" (1 Jn.5:21).

The decision demanded by God is clear: we are not to have any other gods, none whatsoever. There is only one true and living God, the Father of our Lord Jesus Christ. We are to believe *in Him and in Him alone.*

> "And he believed in the LORD; and he counted it to him for righteousness" (Gen.15:6).
> "And they rose early in the morning, and went forth into the wilderness of Tekoa: and as they went forth, Jehoshaphat stood and said,

Hear me, O Judah, and ye inhabitants of Jerusalem; Believe in the LORD your God, so shall ye be established; believe his prophets, so shall ye prosper" (2 Chron.20:20).

"For God so loved the world, that he gave his only begotten Son, that whosoever believeth in him should not perish, but have everlasting life" (Jn.3:16).

"Then said they unto him, What shall we do, that we might work the works of God? Jesus answered and said unto them, This is the work of God, that ye believe on him whom he [God] hath sent" (Jn.6:28-29).

"And this is his commandment, That we should believe on the name of his Son Jesus Christ, and love one another, as he gave us commandment" (1 Jn.3:23).

"Commandment Two..."

Commandment Two Concerns The Worship of God—Never Make Nor Worship Other Gods Exodus 20:4-6

Contents

Commandment Two Concerns
The Worship of God—Never Make
Nor Worship Other Gods
Exodus 20:4-6

COMMANDMENT 2:	4 Thou shalt not make unto thee any graven image, or any likeness of any thing that is in heaven above, or that is in the earth beneath, or that is in the water under the earth:
1. **Who is to obey this commandment? You**	
2. **How long was this commandment to be in force? Forever**	
3. **What is forbidden by this commandment?**	
a. Prohibits the making of idols	
b. Prohibits the worship of idols	
c. Prohibits covetousness (cp. Col.3:5)	5 Thou shalt not bow down thyself to them, nor serve them: for I the LORD thy God am a jealous God, visiting the iniquity of the fathers upon the children unto the third and fourth generation of them that hate me;
4. **Why did God give this commandment?**	
a. Because God is a jealous God	
b. Because the influence of idolatry is passed down from parents to children	
c. Because the influence of loving God lasts for generations	6 And showing mercy unto thousands of them that love me, and keep my commandments.
5. **What is the decision required by this commandment? Obedience**	

There is only one true and living God, the Sovereign LORD and Majesty of the universe. Commandment one established this wonderful fact. He is the great Creator and Sustainer of the universe. He is the LORD God (Jehovah, Yahweh) of heaven, the Father of the Lord Jesus Christ. As the Lord God, the Creator of all people, He has one major concern: how people worship Him. This is the concern of this commandment: the worship of God by man. Every person upon earth worships something. The great tragedy is that most people worship falsely. They worship something other than the only true and living God. They worship false gods...

- the false gods created by the imagination of people

- the false gods of science and technology

- the false gods made of wood, stone, metal, and other materials—all formed into the image of idols

- the false gods of self, money, sex, pleasure, houses, lands, and the other possessions of this earth

- the false gods of the state and government, of its power to feed, protect, and take care of man

- the false gods of natural law, of the basic forces of the universe, of believing that energy or force itself is the controlling power of the universe and of life

The false gods worshipped by people are innumerable. Every person has an image of what the *supreme* authority of the universe is, an image of the supreme being of the universe, an image of that to which he should give his life. To what should we give our lives? What should we be worshipping? The demand of this commandment is that we give our lives to the only true and living God, that we worship Him and Him alone.

Note what worship is:

⇒ Worship is the heart's reaching out to God (drawing near God for His love and care) and the giving of one's heart to God in praise, thanksgiving, service, and witness.

This is exactly what God demands:

⇒ that we reach out to Him, draw near Him for His love and care.

⇒ that we give ourselves (sacrificially) to God in praise, thanksgiving, service, and witness.

This is the subject of this great commandment: *Commandment Two Concerns The Worship of God—Never Make Nor Worship Other Gods*, 20:4-6.

    I.   Who is to obey this commandment (v.4)?

    II.   How long was this commandment to be in force (v.4)?

   III.   What is forbidden by this commandment (v.4-5)?

   IV.   Why did God give this commandment (v.5-6)?

    V.   What are the Biblical consequences of breaking this commandment?

   VI.   What are the Biblical benefits of keeping this commandment?

  VII.   What is the teaching of Jesus Christ concerning this commandment?

 VIII.   What is the decision required by this commandment (v.6)?

I. Who Is to Obey This Commandment?

Note the very first word of the commandment: "You" (v.4). God addresses this commandment to "you." "You" are personally responsible to Him, responsible to obey His commandment. But you are not only *responsible* to obey: you are held *accountable* to obey by God. The idea is just this: If you disobey God, you will be held accountable and judged by God.

Now, who is to obey this commandment?

⇒ "You," you personally.

⇒ "You" are *responsible* to obey this commandment.

⇒ "You" are held *accountable* to obey. And if you disobey the commandment, you will be judged.

> "This day the LORD thy God hath commanded thee to do these statutes and judgments: thou shalt therefore keep and do them with all thine heart, and with all thy soul" (Dt.26:16).

II. How Long Was This Commandment to Be in Force?

Was it given to Israel alone, or was it given through Israel to all people of all generations? Note the commandment: You shall not make nor worship any idol whatsoever (v.4-5). God Himself spoke these words (v.1), a commandment that forbids—absolutely forbids—the making and worshipping of anything other than God Himself.

God is the great Creator, the Sovereign Lord and Majesty of the universe. This means that He and He alone is to be *acknowledged and worshipped* by His creation. In fact, the Creator would never tolerate His subjects (creation) worshipping anything or anyone other than Himself.

How long is this commandment in force? It is in force as long as God's creation stands, as long as the universe exists. This commandment was in force when it was first given by God, and the commandment is still in force today. It will be in force throughout all eternity. No person is ever to worship anything other than the Lord God Himself.

You and your descendants are under the force of this commandment. All people of all generations are to obey this commandment.

> "Take heed to yourselves, that your heart be not deceived, and ye turn aside, and serve other gods, and worship them" (Dt.11:16).
> "O worship the LORD in the beauty of holiness: fear before him, all the earth" (Ps.96:9).
> "I am the LORD: that is my name: and my glory will I not give to another, neither my praise to graven images" (Is.42:8).

"Then saith Jesus unto him, Get thee hence, Satan: for it is written, Thou shalt worship the LORD thy God, and him only shalt thou serve" (Mt.4:10).

III. What Is Forbidden by This Commandment?

"You shall not make any idol nor worship any other god—none whatsoever." How is this commandment broken? How is it violated? Scripture says that this commandment forbids at least three things.

1. This commandment prohibits the *making* of any idol whatsoever; therefore, the commandment is broken and violated by making idols (v.4).
   a. To make an image of anything for worship is wrong. Note the verse: We must not build an image of anything for worship, not an image of anything in the sky above nor that is in the earth beneath, nor that is in the water upon the earth. Nothing in the universe is ever to have an image made of it, not for worship.
   Note that the entire universe is covered; even the unseen world of heaven is covered. No idol of anything is ever to be made...
   - not heavenly creatures: angels, demons, devils, or imaginary gods
   - not heavenly bodies such as the sun, moon, or stars
   - not earthly creatures such as cows, elephants, or man
   - not water creatures such as fish, crocodiles, or sea animals

   The making of any idol whatsoever is forbidden—absolutely forbidden. God emphatically declares, "You shall never make an idol of anything, not ever—not of anything."
   b. This commandment also forbids the making of an image of God Himself; He is an heavenly being (v.4). Note that "no image or form or likeness of anything in heaven is to be made" (v.4). God is in heaven, in the spiritual world or dimension of being; therefore, no image is to be made of God.
   c. A question needs to be asked at this point: What about images such as pictures, crucifixes, statues, and other symbols that are used to stir our memory to pray and worship? Is this commandment speaking against such images? There is a tendency within human nature to focus upon that which is seen instead of upon the unseen, a tendency to fix our attention upon the seen object (the picture, the crucifix, etc.) instead of upon God. Reason and honesty—especially *honesty*—demand that we acknowledge this fact. Consequently, if we use visible objects to arouse us to pray and worship, there is great danger...
   - that a pure and spiritual worship of God will fade, deteriorate, and be degraded.

- that the physical object will become more valued and receive more of our attention than God. Why? Because God is spiritual and unseen, and the physical object is seen.

William Barclay has an excellent statement on idolatry. Note carefully what he says:

"[Idolatry] began because men found it difficult to worship a god they could not see. So they said to themselves, 'We will make something which will represent the god and that will make it easier to think of the god.' In the first instance the idol was never meant to be the god; it was meant only to stand for the god.

"We can perhaps understand it, if we think of it this way. Suppose we have a friend whom we have not seen for a very long time, and suppose we sit down to write a letter to that friend, and suppose we find the letter hard to write, because we have been separated for so long. In such a situation it might well help if we took a photograph of the friend and put it where we could see it, and wrote, as it were, looking at the photograph. The photograph would bring our friend nearer to our mind. At first that is what an idol was meant to do.

"The trouble was that men began to worship the idol instead of the god it stood for; men began to worship the symbol instead of the reality it was supposed to represent. It is not really difficult to see how idolatry began, and it is not really so silly as it looks. For all that, we may well be saying, 'I am not likely to do a thing like that.' But perhaps we are more likely to do it than we think.

"Take a very small thing first of all. Quite a lot of people carry some kind of lucky mascot, some kind of charm. Some carry a lucky penny or a lucky sign of the zodiac, or, for instance, if they go on a journey, they take a St. Christopher sign to avoid accidents. That is really idolatry, for it is believing that in some way the carrying of a little bit of metal or plastic can have an effect on their lives.

"But there is something much more serious than that. The real essence of idolatry is that a man worships a thing instead of God.

"There is no doubt at all that there is a great deal of that today. People assess their success in life by the number of things which they possess. We think a man a success if he has a big motor car, or an elaborate television set or record-player, or if he can go every year for a Continental holiday.

"This is obviously wrong."[1]

---

[1] William Barclay. *The Old Law and the New Law.* (Philadelphia, PA: The Westminster Press, 1972), p.11-13.

Arthur W. Pink gives a thought-provoking statement on idolatry that is well worth quoting:

> "This commandment strikes against a desire, or should we say a disease, which is deeply rooted in the human heart, namely, to bring in some aids to the worship of God, beyond those which He has appointed—material aids, things which can be perceived by the senses. Nor is the reason for this difficult to find: God is incorporeal, invisible, and can be realized only by a spiritual principle, and since that principle is dead in fallen man, he naturally seeks that which accords with his carnality. But how different is it with those who have been quickened by the Holy Spirit. No one who truly knows God as a living reality needs any images to aid his devotions; none who enjoys daily communion with Christ requires any pictures of Him to help him to pray and adore, for he conceives of Him by faith and not by fancy."[2]

Now, having said this, the commandment does not forbid artistic talent, that is, the making of sculptures, pictures, statues, and crucifixes for the purpose of the fine arts. The commandment strikes against making and using images and idols...
- for the purpose of worship
- for the purpose of controlling our lives and looking after us

This steals our hearts away from the only living and true God.

Thought 1.

Adrian Rogers has an excellent illustration dealing with making an image or likeness of God for the purpose of worship and prayer:

> "Idolatry is wrong because it gives a distorted or false picture of God. An idol is a material thing, and no idol can represent the invisible, spiritual God. Jesus said in John 4:24, 'God is a Spirit.' I know the King James Version includes the indefinite article, but the literal translation is, God is spirit.' That is, spirit is His very essence.
>
> "No wonder, then, that Jesus went on to say, 'They that worship him must worship him in spirit and in truth.' What material thing could possibly represent spirit? God is a circle whose center is everywhere and whose circumference is nowhere. God is spirit. There is nowhere where God is not, and no material thing can represent Him.
>
> "There's nothing you can compare God to or with. There's nothing that says, 'This is what God is totally like.' God Himself asked, 'To whom then will ye liken me, or shall I be equal?' (Isaiah 40:25).

---

[2] Arthur W. Pink. *The Ten Commandments*. (Grand Rapids, MI: Baker Books, 1994), p.21-22.

We can say one man is like another man, one chair is like another chair, one piano like another piano, and so on. But there's only one God. You can't compare Him to anything or anyone....

"Suppose a woman walks into a room and finds her husband embracing another woman. He sees his wife out of the corner of his eye and says, 'Now wait a minute, honey. Don't get the wrong idea here. Let me tell you what I was doing. This woman is so beautiful, she reminded me of you. I was really just thinking of you when I was embracing her.'

"There's not a woman in America who would buy that, including my wife, Joyce! And God doesn't buy it either when we worship something else and say, 'Now, LORD, wait a minute. Don't get the wrong idea here. I was only worshiping this thing because it reminds me of You. I'm really worshiping You.'

"No, you really aren't. That's what the Second Commandment is all about."[3]

Thought 2.

There is only one true image of God, only one *image* that is acceptable to God.[4]

a) Jesus Christ is the visible image of the invisible God.

> **"In whom [Christ] we have redemption through his blood, even the forgiveness of sins: Who is the image of the invisible God, the firstborn of every creature" (Col.1:14-15).**

b) Jesus Christ is the express image, the exact representation, of God's person.

> **"[Christ] who being the brightness of his [God's] glory, and the express image of his person, and upholding all things by the word of his power, when he had by himself purged our sins, sat down on the right hand of the Majesty on high" (Heb.1:3).**

c) Jesus Christ is the very form, the very nature, of God.

> **"Who, being in the form of God, thought it not robbery to be equal with God" (Ph.2:6).**

---

[3] Adrian Rogers. *Ten Secrets For A Successful Family*. (Wheaton, IL: Crossway Books, 1996), p.44-45.

[4] These points are taken from the Sunday School material: *Ten Overlooked Principles in Building Successful Families* which is derived from Adrian Rogers' *Ten Secrets For A Successful Family*.

d) Jesus Christ is the fulness of the Godhead bodily.

> **"For in him dwelleth all the fulness of the Godhead bodily. And ye are complete in him, which is the head of all principality and power" (Col.2:9-10).**

e) Jesus Christ is the image to whom we are to be conformed.

> **"For whom he did foreknow, he also did predestinate to be conformed to the image [likeness, NIV] of his Son, that he might be the firstborn among many brethren" (Ro.8:29).**

f) Jesus Christ is the image to which we shall be gloriously and eternally made (transformed).

> **"Beloved, now are we the sons of God, and it doth not yet appear what we shall be: but we know that, when he shall appear, we shall be like him; for we shall see him as he is" (1 Jn.3:2).**

g) Jesus Christ is the very nature and revelation of God Himself.

> **"If ye had known me, ye should have known my Father also: and from henceforth ye know him, and have seen him. Philip saith unto him, Lord, show us the Father, and it sufficeth us. Jesus saith unto him, Have I been so long time with you, and yet hast thou not known me, Philip? he that hath seen me hath seen the Father; and how sayest thou [then], Show us the Father? Believest thou not that I am in the Father, and the Father in me? the words that I speak unto you I speak not of myself: but the Father that dwelleth in me, he doeth the works" (Jn.14:7-10).**

2. This commandment prohibits the *worship* of any other god whatsoever, prohibits the worship of anything other than God Himself (v.5).

a. This strikes a death blow against one of the most common ideas and claims of people: that all religions worship the same god, that no matter what we may call god and no matter what religion we follow, we all worship the same *supreme being*.

Remember the first commandment: there are no other gods; there is only one true and living God (v.5). Therefore, if we create a god within our own minds—if we worship something else, some other so-called god, if we treat something else as a god—we misrepresent the truth. No matter how large our religion may become, even if billions of people followed, our worship would be a lie. It would be wrong; it would be sinful behavior. Our idea of God would be inaccurate, incomplete, and false. And false worship is a gross insult to the *only* living and true God, to the *only* Sovereign LORD and Majesty of the universe.

⇒ It is wrong to worship things in the sky such as the sun, moon, and stars; wrong to trust and use the zodiac and other so-called *fortune-tellers* to guide one's life.

⇒ It is wrong to worship things in the earth such as man, cows, elephants, and other animals.

⇒ It is wrong to worship things in the water such as fish, crocodiles, and so-called sea creatures.

⇒ It is wrong to worship false messiahs and saviors.

⇒ It is wrong to engage in the worship of anything other than the LORD God Himself.

Simply stated, it is wrong to worship the image of God created by man's imagination, wrong to picture what we think God is like and wrong to worship that image of God. God has revealed Himself, revealed exactly who He is and what He is like, in the Lord Jesus Christ and in the Holy Scripture. It is the Lord God revealed by Jesus Christ and the Holy Scripture that we are to picture and worship. We are to worship the *LORD God of revelation*—the LORD God *revealed by Jesus Christ*—worship Him and Him alone.

b. This commandment also strikes a death blow against what was mentioned earlier, that of using images of heavenly beings for worship and prayer (v.5). God does not accept any worship that comes to Him through an idol. God is Spirit, not physical and material. God is invisible, not visible to the naked eye. Therefore, to worship an image of God is to misrepresent God, and misrepresentation of God is a lie, is sinful behavior. It is a gross insult to the Sovereign LORD of the universe.

⇒ It is wrong to worship any physical or visible image of God, wrong to worship any idol or anything else upon earth, even wrong to worship an invisible image of God created within the imagination of man.

⇒ It is even wrong to worship religious rituals; our worship and passion should be only for God Himself.

"To whom then will ye liken me, or shall I be equal? saith the Holy One" (Is.40:25)

God is Spirit. He has no physical form that can be seen with the human eye. Therefore, God is not to be worshipped through physical, visible objects. When God is worshipped in some visible form, the glory of the invisible God is degraded. Why? Because God is Spirit, omnipotent and omnipresent Spirit, the all-powerful and all-knowing Sovereign of the Universe, the Creator of all things that are in heaven and earth, both visible and invisible. God cannot be bottled up; His glory cannot be formed and sculpted into any image whatsoever. No imagination of man can picture God. Man's thoughts, descriptions, and images of God are totally incomplete and inadequate. As Spirit, He is out beyond the universe, surrounding and embracing the universe. No planet or star—no heavenly body—extends out beyond God's presence and knowledge.

As stated, God is Spirit; and they that worship Him must worship Him in Spirit and in truth. The Scripture emphatically declares:

> **"God [is] a Spirit: and they that worship him must worship [him] in spirit and in truth" (Jn.4:24).**
>
> **"For the invisible things of him from the creation of the world are clearly seen, being understood by the things that are made, even his eternal power and Godhead; so that they are without excuse: Because that, when they knew God, they glorified him not as God, neither were thankful; but became vain in their imaginations, and their foolish heart was darkened. Professing themselves to be wise, they became fools, And changed the glory of the uncorruptible God into an image made like to corruptible man, and to birds, and fourfooted beasts, and creeping things. Wherefore God also gave them up to uncleanness through the lusts of their own hearts, to dishonour their own bodies between themselves: Who changed the truth of God into a lie, and worshipped and served the creature more than the Creator, who is blessed for ever. Amen" (Ro.1:20-25).**
>
> **"Little children, keep yourselves from idols. Amen" (1 Jn.5:21).**
>
> **"Take heed to yourselves, that your heart be not deceived, and ye turn aside, and serve other gods, and worship them" (Dt.11:16).**

3. This commandment prohibits *covetousness*, prohibits craving and seeking anything more than we crave and seek God (v.5, cp. Col.3:5). Scripture emphatically declares...

- "Covetousness...is idolatry" (Col.3:5; cp. Eph.5:5).

Covetousness is craving and desiring something so much that a person makes it the primary thing in his life. The object becomes the first thing in a person's life, the major craving, the longing desire of the person's heart and life. A person can covet and make an idol out of anything:

⇒ sex	⇒ boyfriend	⇒ business	⇒ fame
⇒ drugs	⇒ girlfriend	⇒ job	⇒ ceremony
⇒ alcohol	⇒ country	⇒ power	⇒ ritual
⇒ pornography	⇒ recreation	⇒ money	⇒ the cross
⇒ family	⇒ sports	⇒ position	

A person's god or idol is that which he puts first in his life, that which he desires and craves the most, that to which he gives his life: his primary thoughts, energy, time, and money. Note what God said about man during the last days of human history:

- ⇒ they would be lovers of selves (2 Tim.3:2).
- ⇒ they would be lovers of pleasure (2 Tim.3:4).
- ⇒ their god would be their stomachs (Ph.3:19).

"(For many walk, of whom I have told you often, and now tell you even weeping, that they are the enemies of the cross of Christ: Whose end is destruction, whose God is their belly, and whose glory is in their shame, who mind earthly things)" (Ph.3:18-19).

"This know also, that in the last days perilous times shall come. For men shall be lovers of their own selves, covetous, boasters, proud, blasphemers, disobedient to parents, unthankful, unholy, Without natural affection, trucebreakers, false accusers, incontinent, fierce, despisers of those that are good, Traitors, heady, highminded, lovers of pleasures more than lovers of God; Having a form of godliness, but denying the power thereof: from such turn away" (2 Tim.3:1-5).

Thought 1.

Maxie Dunnam has a practical comment on this commandment that is well worth quoting at length:

"God is unseen, a Spirit and Power invisible to our eyes. So, we need settings, symbols, places of worship to be vivid reminders of God. The problem comes when the symbol, the reminder, becomes a substitute, when it becomes an idol and takes the place of God.

"There's a dramatic story of this in Numbers 21. In their wandering through the wilderness, the people of Israel were attacked and tortured by fiery serpents. Moses, on the instruction of God, made a bronze serpent and set it up on a pole. Those who had been bitten looked at the bronze serpent and were healed. Not much is made of that story as it is found in Numbers 21:6-9, but centuries later we find that bronze serpent making another brief appearance. This time, we find King Hezekiah breaking the serpent in pieces, because the people had been burning incense to it (2 Kings 18:4). What had happened? What Moses had used as a reminder of God's power prevailing over the poison of the serpents, bit by bit, had become a god itself.

"This has happened in Christian history in relation to the cross and the crucifix. That which is to be a reminder of the love of the cross, meant to help men and women in looking at it to fix their hearts and minds on the One who bled and died there, becomes regarded with superstitious reverence. The cross, or the crucifix, becomes a holy thing. The symbol is identified and confused with the reality for which it stands.

"The core lesson is this: whenever anyone or anything usurps the place that God should have in our lives, we're guilty of idolatry.

"For most of us, that would not be a graven image such as a cross or a crucifix. But how easily money becomes an idol. We allow money—how we get it and how we use it—to edge God out of the number one place in our lives.

"I've seen love in marriage distorted to the point that it usurps God's place in our lives. I've certainly seen love of country distorted to the point that it blinds people to God's call to justice and righteousness.

"The making of idols usually means making the means an end. This happens all the time in the church. I know some people who do that with the Bible. The Bible itself becomes an idol. Listen carefully to people who passionately crusade, in their words, to 'save the Bible.' Look at their lives. We can angrily wage a war to protect the inerrancy of the Bible, and appear to be righteous in the cause, and still lose our souls. That's the problem Jesus was addressing when He said, 'Not everyone who says to Me, "Lord, Lord," will enter the Kingdom of Heaven, but those who do the will of My heavenly Father.'

"In all sorts of ways, we have committed the sin of idolatry by making the means an end. Even in our worship, we turn the liturgy, our means of worshipping God, into an end itself, so that the means and methods of worship become more important than the worship itself. We need to even look at...our spiritual disciplines. Spiritual discipline is for the purpose of facilitating our relationship to God. We pray and worship and study Scripture, sometimes we fast, to be open to God, to cultivate Christ's presence. But to make these disciplines ends in themselves, to make them the measurement of how holy we are, is making discipline a fetish. Not only are we in danger of turning others off when we zealously exaggerate these disciplines, they become idols."[5]

Thought 2.

J. Vernon McGee also has an excellent application on this commandment.

"Some people may feel that this passage does not apply to us today. Colossians 3:5 tells us that '...covetousness...is idolatry.' Anything that you give yourself to, especially in abandonment, becomes your 'god.' Many people do not worship Bacchus, the cloven-footed Greek and Roman god of wine and revelry of long ago, but they worship the bottle just the same. There are millions of alcoholics in our country right now. The liquor interests like to tell us about how much of the tax burden they carry, when actually they do not pay a fraction of the bill for the casualties they cause by their product. A lot of propaganda is being fed to this generation and large groups of people are being brainwashed. Whether or not folk recognize it, they worship the god Bacchus.

"Other people worship Aphrodite, that is, the goddess of sex. Some people worship money. Anything to which you give your time, heart, and soul, becomes your God. God says that we are not to have any gods before Him."[6]

---

5   Maxie Dunnam. *Mastering the Old Testament, Volume 2: Exodus*, p.255-256.
6   J. Vernon McGee. *Thru The Bible*, Vol.1. (Nashville, TN: Thomas Nelson Publishers, 1981), p.267.

"Wherefore should the heathen say, Where is now their God? But our God is in the heavens: he hath done whatsoever he hath pleased. Their idols are silver and gold, the work of men's hands. They have mouths, but they speak not: eyes have they, but they see not: They have ears, but they hear not: noses have they, but they smell not: They have hands, but they handle not: feet have they, but they walk not: neither speak they through their throat. They that make them are like unto them; so is every one that trusteth in them" (Ps.115:2-8).

"They [idols] are upright as the palm tree, but speak not: they must needs be borne, because they cannot go. Be not afraid of them; for they cannot do evil, neither also is it in them to do good" (Jer.10:5).

IV. Why Did God Give This Commandment?

God gave this commandment for at least three reasons (v.5-6).

1. First, God prohibits the worship of idols because He is a jealous God (v.5). The Hebrew word for *jealous* means to be red in the face. God loves and cares for man. God does not want people living in error and following false gods that can do absolutely nothing to help them throughout life. Therefore, God is jealous—hot in the face—against anything that turns people away from the truth and from God Himself.

Note this fact: Scripture declares that idolatry is *spiritual adultery*; therefore, the displeasure of God against idolatry is rightly called jealous.[7] Jealousy means that God has a sensitive nature, a nature of love. God is jealous of anything or anyone who threatens to take away the honor, recognition, or reverence that is due Him. Therefore, if a person gives his primary devotion, his primary attention, honor, time, energy, effort, or money to anything other than God Himself, he commits spiritual adultery against God. He turns away from God to something else. The result: God becomes jealous, red-hot against any person who is unfaithful to Him. Man must never forget: God does not tolerate unfaithfulness; He will never allow a rival to replace Him. Note what Scripture says:

a. God's jealousy will not allow His glory and honor to be transferred to another.

"I am the LORD: that is my name: and my glory will I not give to another, neither my praise to graven images" (Is.42:8).

---

7   Matthew Henry. *Matthew Henry's Commentary*, Vol. 1. (Old Tappan, NJ: Fleming H. Revell Co., A Division of Baker Book House, No date given), p.359.

"For mine own sake, even for mine own sake, will I do it: for how should my name be polluted? and I will not give my glory unto another" (Is.48:11).

b. God declares that His very name is *Jealous*; therefore, He absolutely will not tolerate the worship of any other god.

"But ye shall destroy their altars, break their images, and cut down their groves: For thou shalt worship no other god: for the LORD, whose name is Jealous, is a jealous God" (Ex.34:13-14).

c. God's jealousy arouses His anger against those who deny and hate Him.

"(For the LORD thy God is a jealous God among you) lest the anger of the LORD thy God be kindled against thee, and destroy thee from off the face of the earth" (Dt.6:15).

d. God's jealousy will judge all those who oppose Him.

"The LORD will not spare him [the idolater], but then the anger of the LORD and his jealousy shall smoke against that man, and all the curses that are written in this book shall lie upon him, and the LORD shall blot out his name from under heaven" (Dt.29:20; cp. 1 Ki.14:22; Ps.79:5; Is.42:13; Is.59:17; Ezk.5:13; 16:38; 23:25; 36:5).
"God is jealous, and the LORD revengeth; the LORD revengeth, and is furious; the LORD will take vengeance on his adversaries, and he reserveth wrath for his enemies" (Nah.1:2).
"Neither their silver nor their gold shall be able to deliver them in the day of the LORD'S wrath; but the whole land shall be devoured by the fire of his jealousy: for he shall make even a speedy riddance of all them that dwell in the land" (Zeph.1:18; cp. Zeph.3:8).
"He that overcometh shall inherit all things; and I will be his God, and he shall be my son. But the fearful, and unbelieving, and the abominable, and murderers, and whoremongers, and sorcerers, and idolaters, and all liars, shall have their part in the lake which burneth with fire and brimstone: which is the second death" (Rev.21:7-8).

e. God's jealousy, His zeal, will vindicate His true people, His true followers.

"For out of Jerusalem shall go forth a remnant, and they that escape out of mount Zion: the zeal of the LORD of hosts shall do this" (2 Ki.19:31).
"Of the increase of his government and peace there shall be no end, upon the throne of David, and upon his kingdom, to order it, and to establish it with judgment and with justice from henceforth even

for ever. The zeal of the LORD of hosts will perform this" (Is.9:7; cp. Is.26:11).

"Therefore thus saith the LORD GOD; Now will I bring again the captivity of Jacob, and have mercy upon the whole house of Israel, and will be jealous for my holy name" (Ezk.39:25).

"Then will the LORD be jealous for his land, and pity his people" (Joel 2:18; Zech.1:14).

"Thus saith the LORD of hosts; I was jealous for Zion with great jealousy, and I was jealous for her with great fury" (Zech.8:2).

f.   God's jealousy demands total allegiance, loyalty, and devotion.

"For thou shalt worship no other god: for the LORD, whose name is Jealous, is a jealous God" (Ex.34:14).

"And Joshua said unto the people, Ye cannot serve the LORD: for he is an holy God; he is a jealous God; he will not forgive your transgressions nor your sins" (Josh.24:19).

2. Second, God prohibits the worship of idols because the influence of idolatry is passed down from the parents to their children (v.5). If a person's worship is false, he leads his children and grandchildren into false worship. What he does greatly influences and affects his family.

We must never forget this one fact: the human race is a living organism. What one person does affects other persons. This is clearly seen in acts of love, care, benevolence, war, lawlessness, drunkenness, drugs, immorality—in all acts of behavior. The closer a person is to others, the more the person's actions affect them. People influence people, and the point of this verse is that parents influence children, greatly influence them. A mother who is a drug addict is likely to lead her children to use drugs. A father who loves and puts sports before God leads his children to love and put things before God.

Note that Scripture uses the word "hate" (v.5). If parents deny and *hate* God and worship idols, the children will be greatly influenced to deny and *hate* God and worship idols. Consequently, God's judgment falls upon the children for generations. The result and consequences of idolatry are terrible. The worship of idols, just like all other behavior, influences the children of a family. Children are conditioned, heavily influenced by the behavior of their parents and their surroundings. Therefore, if a parent worships idols, most likely the children will worship idols. And all idolaters shall be judged by God. Therefore, the sin of idolatry and the judgment upon idolatry are passed down from generation to generation. Terrible consequences! All due to the *sins of the fathers and mothers*, especially the evil sin of idolatry.

This is what is known as the *judicial judgment of God*, a judgment that is justly deserved. If a parent sows the seed of idolatry, he is usually going to bear children who will be greatly influenced by his behavior. The children will deny and hate God and worship the idols of man. But note: this does not mean that God holds a child guilty for the sins of his parents. God is not talking about the guilt of sin. He is talking about the results, the consequences of sin. Every person shall bear the judgment and punishment for his own sin. No person will ever be judged and punished for the sins of others.

> **"The fathers shall not be put to death for the children, neither shall the children be put to death for the fathers: every man shall be put to death for his own sin" (Dt.24:16).**

Thought 1.

God punishes sin, the sins of all people for all generations. God executes justice upon the sins of the fathers and the sins of the children. No generation of sin ever escapes the judgment of God.

> **"[God] now commandeth all men every where to repent: Because he hath appointed a day, in the which he will judge the world in righteousness by that man whom he hath ordained; whereof he hath given assurance unto all men, in that he hath raised him from the dead" (Acts 17:30-31).**

> **"And to you who are troubled rest with us, when the LORD Jesus shall be revealed from heaven with his mighty angels, In flaming fire taking vengeance on them that know not God, and that obey not the gospel of our Lord Jesus Christ: Who shall be punished with everlasting destruction from the presence of the LORD, and from the glory of his power" (2 Th.1:7-9).**

> **"Behold, the LORD cometh with ten thousands of his saints, To execute judgment upon all, and to convince all that are ungodly among them of all their ungodly deeds which they have ungodly committed, and of all their hard speeches which ungodly sinners have spoken against him" (Jude 14-15).**

> **"Then shalt thou say unto them, Because your fathers have forsaken me, saith the LORD, and have walked after other gods, and have served them, and have worshipped them, and have forsaken me, and have not kept my law; And ye have done worse than your fathers; for, behold, ye walk every one after the imagination of his evil heart, that they may not hearken unto me: Therefore will I cast you out of this land into a land that ye know not, neither ye nor your fathers; and there shall ye serve other gods day and night; where I will not show you favour" (Jer.16:11-13; cp. Is.65:7).**

> **"I the LORD search the heart, I try the reins, even to give every man according to his ways, and according to the fruit of his doings" (Jer.17:10).**

> **"Behold, all souls are mine; as the soul of the father, so also the soul of the son is mine: the soul that sinneth, it shall die" (Ezk.18:4).**

3. Third, God prohibits the worship of idols because the influence of a loving and obedient parent lasts forever, for a thousand generations (v.6). Note that the sin and punishment of idolatry are passed down for three or four generations, but the love and obedience of parents are passed down to their children for *thousands of generations*. This is what is known as Hebrew parallelism: it does not mean thousands of people, but thousands of generations. Note exactly what the verse says: God's mercy is shown to thousands of those who love and obey Him, shown for thousands of generations. Parents who love God and keep God's commandments...

- will influence their children for thousands of generations
- will have the mercy of God showered upon thousands of their children for thousands of generations

This shows the awesome influence of parents upon their children and the absolute necessity for loving and obeying God. Judgment will fall upon those who disobey this commandment—fall upon both the parents and their children for three or four generations. But God's mercy will be showered upon those who obey this commandment, be showered upon thousands of children for thousands of generations.

However, note a most significant fact: God's mercy is showered only upon the obedient, only upon those who love God and keep His commandments, the very commandments He is spelling out in this passage.

> "Train up a child in the way he should go: and when he is old, he will not depart from it" (Pr.22:6).
> "When I call to remembrance the unfeigned faith that is in thee [Timothy], which dwelt first in thy grandmother Lois, and thy mother Eunice; and I am persuaded that in thee also" (2 Tim.1:5).
> "And the LORD was with Jehoshaphat, because he walked in the first ways of his father David, and sought not unto Baalim" (2 Chron.17:3).
> "And he [Uzziah] did that which was right in the sight of the LORD, according to all that his father Amaziah did" (2 Chron. 26:4).

V. What Are the Consequences of Breaking This Commandment?

1. The person who follows a false worship will not inherit the kingdom of God.

> "Now the works of the flesh are manifest, which are these; Adultery, fornication, uncleanness, lasciviousness, Idolatry, witchcraft, hatred, variance, emulations, wrath, strife, seditions, heresies, Envyings, murders, drunkenness, revellings, and such like: of the which I tell you before, as I have also told you in time past, that they which do such things shall not inherit the kingdom of God" (Gal.5:19-21).

> "Know ye not that the unrighteous shall not inherit the kingdom
> of God? Be not deceived: neither fornicators, nor idolaters, nor adul-
> terers, nor effeminate, nor abusers of themselves with mankind, Nor
> thieves, nor covetous, nor drunkards, nor revilers, nor extortioners,
> shall inherit the kingdom of God" (1 Cor.6:9-10).

2. The person who follows a false worship is an idolater.

> "Now these things [the Old Testament] were our examples, to the
> intent we should not lust after evil things, as they also lusted. Neither
> be ye idolaters, as were some of them; as it is written, The people sat
> down to eat and drink, and rose up to play. Neither let us commit
> fornication, as some of them committed, and fell in one day three and
> twenty thousand. Neither let us tempt Christ, as some of them also
> tempted, and were destroyed of serpents. Neither murmur ye, as
> some of them also murmured, and were destroyed of the destroyer"
> (1 Cor.10:6-10).

3. The person who follows a false worship serves a false religion or god.

> "For all the gods of the people are idols: but the LORD made the
> heavens" (1 Chron. 16:26).
> "For they served idols, whereof the LORD had said unto them, Ye
> shall not do this thing" (2 Ki.17:12).

4. The person who follows a false worship is only worshipping the work of
his own hands.

> "Their land also is full of idols; they worship the work of their
> own hands, that which their own fingers have made" (Is.2:8).
> "To whom will ye liken me, and make me equal, and compare me,
> that we may be like? They lavish gold out of the bag, and weigh sil-
> ver in the balance, and hire a goldsmith; and he maketh it a god: they
> fall down, yea, they worship. They bear him upon the shoulder, they
> carry him, and set him in his place, and he standeth; from his place
> shall he not remove: yea, one shall cry unto him, yet can he not an-
> swer, nor save him out of his trouble" (Is.46:5-7).

5. The person who follows a false worship is only following the rituals and
teachings of men.

> "He answered and said unto them, Well hath Esaias prophesied
> of you hypocrites, as it is written, This people honoureth me with
> their lips, but their heart is far from me. Howbeit in vain do they
> worship me, teaching for doctrines the commandments of men. For
> laying aside the commandment of God, ye hold the tradition of men,
> as the washing of pots and cups: and many other such like things ye

do. And he said unto them, Full well ye reject the commandment of God, that ye may keep your own tradition" (Mk.7:6-9).

6. The person who follows a false worship fails to experience the power of God.

"[People] having a form of godliness, but denying the power thereof: from such turn away" (2 Tim.3:5).

7. The person who follows a false worship is detestable to God and unfit for doing anything good.

"They profess that they know God; but in works they deny him, being abominable [detestable], and disobedient, and unto every good work reprobate" (Tit.1:16).

8. The person who follows a false worship is seduced and carried away.

"Ye know that ye were Gentiles, carried away unto these dumb idols, even as ye were led" (1 Cor.12:2).

"For false Christs and false prophets shall rise, and shall show signs and wonders, to seduce, if it were possible, even the elect" (Mk.13:22).

9. The person who follows a false worship will cry out for help, but there will be no help.

"They that make a graven image are all of them vanity; and their delectable things shall not profit; and they are their own witnesses; they see not, nor know; that they may be ashamed. Who hath formed a god, or molten a graven image that is profitable for nothing? Behold, all his fellows shall be ashamed: and the workmen, they are of men: let them all be gathered together, let them stand up; yet they shall fear, and they shall be ashamed together. The smith with the tongs both worketh in the coals, and fashioneth it with hammers, and worketh it with the strength of his arms: yea, he is hungry, and his strength faileth: he drinketh no water, and is faint. The carpenter stretcheth out his rule; he marketh it out with a line; he fitteth it with planes, and he marketh it out with the compass, and maketh it after the figure of a man, according to the beauty of a man; that it may remain in the house. He heweth him down cedars, and taketh the cypress and the oak, which he strengtheneth for himself among the trees of the forest: he planteth an ash, and the rain doth nourish it. Then shall it be for a man to burn: for he will take thereof, and warm himself; yea, he kindleth it, and baketh bread; yea, he maketh a god, and worshippeth it; he maketh it a graven image, and falleth down thereto. He burneth part thereof in the fire; with part thereof he eateth flesh; he roasteth roast, and is satisfied: yea, he warmeth himself, and saith, Aha, I am warm, I have seen the fire: And the residue thereof he maketh a god, even his graven image: he falleth down unto it, and worshippeth it, and prayeth unto it, and saith, <u>Deliver me; for thou art my god</u>. They have not known nor understood: for he hath shut their eyes, that they cannot see; and their hearts, that they cannot understand. And none considereth in his heart, neither is there knowledge nor understanding to say, I have burned part of it in the fire; yea, also I have baked bread upon the coals thereof; I have roasted flesh, and eaten it: and shall I make the residue thereof an abomination? shall I fall down to the stock of a tree? He feedeth on ashes: a deceived heart hath turned him aside, that <u>he cannot deliver his soul</u>, nor say, Is there not a lie in my right hand?" (Is.44:9-20).

"Then shall the cities of Judah and inhabitants of Jerusalem go, and cry unto the gods unto whom they offer incense: but they shall not save them at all in the time of their trouble" (Jer.11:12).

10. The person who follows a false worship becomes a hater of God.

"And even as they did not like to retain God in their knowledge, God gave them over to a reprobate mind, to do those things which are not convenient; Being filled with all unrighteousness, fornication, wickedness, covetousness, maliciousness; full of envy, murder, debate, deceit, malignity; whisperers, Backbiters, <u>haters of God</u>, despiteful, proud, boasters, inventors of evil things, disobedient to parents, Without understanding, covenantbreakers, without natural affection, implacable, unmerciful" (Ro.1:28-31).

11. The person who follows a false worship will face severe punishment.

"And to you who are troubled rest with us, when the Lord Jesus shall be revealed from heaven with his mighty angels, In flaming fire taking vengeance on them that know not God, and that obey not the gospel of our Lord Jesus Christ: Who shall be punished with everlasting destruction from the presence of the Lord, and from the glory of his power" (2 Th.1:7-9).

12. The person who follows a false worship will face the judicial judgment of God.

"Wherefore God also gave them up to uncleanness through the lusts of their own hearts, to dishonour their own bodies between themselves: Who changed the truth of God into a lie, and worshipped and served the creature more than the Creator, who is blessed for ever. Amen"(Ro. 1:24-25, cp. 18-25).

13. The person who follows a false worship will turn people away from the truth.

"For the time will come when they will not endure sound doctrine; but after their own lusts shall they heap to themselves teachers, having itching ears; And they shall turn away their ears from the truth, and shall be turned unto fables" (2 Tim.4:3-4).

14. The person who follows a false worship dishonors God and brings shame upon the witness of God.

"Thou that makest thy boast of the law, through breaking the law dishonourest thou God? For the name of God is blasphemed among the Gentiles through you, as it is written" (Ro.2:23-24).

"Many will say to me in that day, Lord, Lord, have we not prophesied in thy name? and in thy name have cast out devils? and in thy name done many wonderful works? And then will I profess unto them, I never knew you: depart from me, ye that work iniquity" (Mt.7:22-23).

"Therefore by the deeds of the law there shall no flesh be justified in his sight: for by the law is the knowledge of sin" (Ro.3:20).

"Knowing that a man is not justified by the works of the law, but by the faith of Jesus Christ, even we have believed in Jesus Christ, that we might be justified by the faith of Christ, and not by the works of the law: for by the works of the law shall no flesh be justified" (Gal.2:16).

15. The person who follows a false worship will face God's wrath.

"Mortify therefore your members which are upon the earth; fornication, uncleanness, inordinate affection, evil concupiscence, and covetousness [greed], which is idolatry: For which things' sake the wrath of God cometh on the children of disobedience" (Col.3:5-6).

16. The person who follows a false worship has no hope and is without God in this world, without His care.

"That at that time ye were without Christ, being aliens from the commonwealth of Israel, and strangers from the covenants of promise, having no hope, and without God in the world" (Eph.2:12).

17. The person who follows a false worship turns away from the LORD, the only living and true God, and shows himself to be a fool: he shows that his thinking is futile, his mind confused, and his heart darkened.

"For the wrath of God is revealed from heaven against all ungodliness and unrighteousness of men, who hold the truth in unrighteousness; Because that which may be known of God is manifest in them; for God hath showed it unto them. For the invisible things of him from the creation of the world are clearly seen, being understood by the things that are made, even his eternal power and Godhead; so that they are without excuse: Because that, when they knew God, they glorified him not as God, neither were thankful; but became vain in their imaginations, and their foolish heart was darkened....Who changed the truth of God into a lie, and worshipped and served the creature more than the Creator, who is blessed for ever. Amen" (Ro.1:18-21, 25).

18. The person who follows a false worship will be sentenced to hell.

"But the fearful, and unbelieving, and the abominable, and murderers, and whoremongers, and sorcerers, and idolaters, and all liars, shall have their part in the lake which burneth with fire and brimstone: which is the second death" (Rev.21:8).

VI. What are the Benefits of Keeping This Commandment?

The greatest blessings imaginable are heaped upon the person who worships the LORD God and Him alone.

1. The person who worships God—truly worships Him—will worship God in spirit and in truth and be saved.

"Ye worship ye know not what: we know what we worship: for salvation is of the Jews. But the hour cometh, and now is, when the true worshippers shall worship the Father in spirit and in truth: for the Father seeketh such to worship him. God [is] a Spirit: and they that worship him must worship [him] in spirit and in truth" (Jn.4:22-24).
"Jesus saith unto him, I am the way, the truth, and the life: no man cometh unto the Father, but by me" (Jn.14:6).
"For we are the circumcision, which worship God in the spirit, and rejoice in Christ Jesus, and have no confidence in the flesh" (Ph.3:3).

2. The person who worships God—truly worships Him—will escape the judgment of God.

"Not forsaking the assembling of ourselves together, as the manner of some is; but exhorting one another: and so much the more, as ye see the day approaching. For if we sin wilfully after that we have received the knowledge of the truth, there remaineth no more sacrifice for sins, But a certain fearful looking for of judgment and fiery indignation, which shall devour the adversaries" (Heb.10:25-27).

3. The person who worships God—truly worships Him—will receive the peace of God that passes all understanding.

> "Be careful for nothing; but in every thing by prayer and supplication with thanksgiving [worship] let your requests be made known unto God. And the peace of God, which passeth all understanding, shall keep your hearts and minds through Christ Jesus" (Ph.4:6-7).
>
> "Thou wilt keep him in perfect peace, whose mind is stayed on thee: because he trusteth in thee [an unbroken spirit of worship]" (Is.26:3).

4. The person who worships God—truly worships Him—will receive the *spiritual rest* of God.

> "O come, let us worship and bow down: let us kneel before the LORD our maker. For he is our God; and we are the people of his pasture, and the sheep of his hand. To day if ye will hear his voice, Harden not your heart, as in the provocation, and as in the day of temptation in the wilderness: When your fathers tempted me, proved me, and saw my work. Forty years long was I grieved with this generation, and said, It is a people that do err in their heart, and they have not known my ways: Unto whom I sware in my wrath that they should not enter into my rest" (Ps.95:6-11).
>
> "There remaineth therefore a rest to the people of God. For he that is entered into his rest, he also hath ceased from his own works, as God did from his. Let us labour therefore to enter into that rest, lest any man fall after the same example of unbelief" (Heb.4:9-11).

5. The person who worships God—truly worships Him—is filled with the joy of life.

> "And they worshipped him, and returned to Jerusalem with great joy" (Lk.24:52).
>
> "Speaking to yourselves in psalms and hymns and spiritual songs, singing and making melody in your heart to the Lord; Giving thanks always for all things unto God and the Father in the name of our Lord Jesus Christ" (Eph.5:19-20).
>
> "Thou wilt show me the path of life: in thy presence is fulness of joy; at thy right hand there are pleasures for evermore" (Ps.16:11).

6. The person who worships God—truly worships Him—will enjoy and abide in the presence of the LORD.

> "Surely goodness and mercy shall follow me all the days of my life: and I will dwell in the house of the LORD for ever" (Ps.23:6).
>
> "LORD, I have loved the habitation of thy house, and the place where thine honour dwelleth" (Ps.26:8).

"One thing have I desired of the LORD, that will I seek after; that I may dwell in the house of the LORD all the days of my life, to behold the beauty of the LORD, and to enquire in his temple" (Ps.27:4).

"Blessed is the man whom thou choosest, and causest to approach unto thee, that he may dwell in thy courts: we shall be satisfied with the goodness of thy house, even of thy holy temple" (Ps.65:4).

"My soul longeth, yea, even fainteth for the courts of the LORD: my heart and my flesh crieth out for the living God" (Ps.84:2; cp. Ps.84:10; 122:1).

7. The person who worships God—truly worships Him—will receive the desires of his heart.

"Delight thyself also in the LORD; and he shall give thee the desires of thine heart" (Ps.37:4).

8. The person who worships God—truly worships Him—will be delivered from sorrow and trouble and surrounded by mercy.

"Many sorrows shall be to the wicked: but he that trusteth in the LORD, mercy shall compass him about. Be glad in the LORD, and rejoice, ye righteous: and shout for joy, all ye that are upright in heart" (Ps.32:10-11).

9. The person who worships God—truly worships Him—will be delivered through the temptations and trials of this life.

"Wherefore in all things it behoved him to be made like unto his brethren, that he might be a merciful and faithful high priest in things pertaining to God, to make reconciliation for the sins of the people. For in that he himself hath suffered being tempted, he is able to succour them that are tempted" (Heb.2:17-18).

"For we have not an high priest which cannot be touched with the feeling of our infirmities; but was in all points tempted like as we are, yet without sin. Let us therefore come boldly unto the throne of grace, that we may obtain mercy, and find grace to help in time of need" (Heb.4:15-16).

10. The person who worships God—truly worships Him—will be assured of God's resurrection power.

"And Abraham said unto his young men, Abide ye here with the ass; and I and the lad will go yonder and worship, and come again to you....And it came to pass after these things, that God did tempt Abraham, and said unto him, Abraham: and he said, Behold, here I am. And he said, Take now thy son, thine only son Isaac, whom thou lovest, and get thee into the land of Moriah; and offer him there for a burnt offering upon one of the mountains which I will tell thee of. And Abraham rose up early in the morning, and saddled his ass, and took two of his young men with him, and Isaac his son, and clave the wood for the burnt offering, and rose up, and went unto the place of which God had told him. Then on the third day Abraham lifted up his eyes, and saw the place afar off. And Abraham said unto his young men, Abide ye here with the ass; and I and the lad will go yonder and worship, and come again to you, And Abraham took the wood of the burnt offering, and laid it upon Isaac his son; and he took the fire in his hand, and a knife; and they went both of them together. And Isaac spake unto Abraham his father, and said, My father: and he said, Here am I, my son. And he said, Behold the fire and the wood: but where is the lamb for a burnt offering? And Abraham said, My son, God will provide himself a lamb for a burnt offering: so they went both of them together. And they came to the place which God had told him of; and Abraham built an altar there, and laid the wood in order, and bound Isaac his son, and laid him on the altar upon the wood. And Abraham stretched forth his hand, and took the knife to slay his son. And the angel of the LORD called unto him out of heaven, and said, Abraham, Abraham: and he said, Here am I. And he said, Lay not thine hand upon the lad, neither do thou any thing unto him: for now I know that thou fearest God, seeing thou hast not withheld thy son, thine only son from me. And Abraham lifted up his eyes, and looked, and behold behind him a ram caught in a thicket by his horns: and Abraham went and took the ram, and offered him up for a burnt offering in the stead of his son. And Abraham called the name of that place Jehovah-jireh: as it is said to this day, In the mount of the LORD it shall be seen" (Gen.22:5; 22:1-14).

"By faith Abraham, when he was tried, offered up Isaac: and he that had received the promises offered up his only begotten son, Of whom it was said, That in Isaac shall thy seed be called: <u>Accounting that God was able to raise him up</u>, even from the dead; from whence also he received him in a figure" (Heb.11:17-19).

"For if we believe that Jesus died and rose again, even so them also which sleep in Jesus will God bring with him" (1 Th.4:14).

11. The person who worships God—truly worships Him—will remember God's deliverance and salvation.

"But the LORD, who brought you up out of the land of Egypt with great power and a stretched out arm, him shall ye fear, and him shall ye worship, and to him shall ye do sacrifice" (2 Ki.17:36).

"And you hath he quickened, who were dead in trespasses and sins; Wherein in time past ye walked according to the course of this world, according to the prince of the power of the air, the spirit that now worketh in the children of disobedience: Among whom also we all had our conversation in times past in the lusts of our flesh, fulfilling the desires of the flesh and of the mind; and were by nature the children of wrath, even as others. But God, who is rich in mercy, for his great love wherewith he loved us, Even when we were dead in sins, hath quickened us together with Christ, (by grace ye are saved;)" (Eph.2:1-5).

"Wherefore remember, that ye being in time past Gentiles in the flesh, who are called Uncircumcision by that which is called the Circumcision in the flesh made by hands; That at that time ye were without Christ, being aliens from the commonwealth of Israel, and strangers from the covenants of promise, having no hope, and without God in the world: But now in Christ Jesus ye who sometimes were far off are made nigh by the blood of Christ" (Eph.2:11-13).

12. The person who worships God—truly worships Him—will be used by God to bring the lost to Christ.

"And when the day of Pentecost was fully come, they were all with one accord in one place [worshipping, praying]. And suddenly there came a sound from heaven as of a rushing mighty wind, and it filled all the house where they were sitting. And there appeared unto them cloven tongues like as of fire, and it sat upon each of them. And they were all filled with the Holy Ghost, and began to speak with other tongues, as the Spirit gave them utterance. And there were dwelling at Jerusalem Jews, devout men, out of every nation under heaven....But Peter, standing up with the eleven, lifted up his voice, and said unto them, Ye men of Judaea, and all ye that dwell at Jerusalem, be this known unto you, and hearken to my words....Then they that gladly received his word were baptized: and the same day there were added unto them about three thousand souls" (Acts 2:1-5, 14, 41).

"Go, stand and speak in the temple to the people all the words of this life" (Acts 5:20).

"And at midnight Paul and Silas prayed, and sang praises unto God: and the prisoners heard them. And suddenly there was a great earthquake, so that the foundations of the prison were shaken: and immediately all the doors were opened, and every one's bands were loosed. And the keeper of the prison awaking out of his sleep, and seeing the prison doors open, he drew out his sword, and would have killed himself, supposing that the prisoners had been fled. But Paul cried with a loud voice, saying, Do thyself no harm: for we are all here. Then he called for a light, and sprang in, and came trembling, and fell down before Paul and Silas, And brought them out, and said, Sirs, what must I do to be saved? And they said, Believe on the Lord Jesus Christ, and thou shalt be saved, and thy house" (Acts 16:25-31).

"Come and hear, all ye that fear God, and I will declare what he hath done for my soul" (Ps.66:16).

"I will mention the lovingkindnesses of the LORD, and the praises of the LORD, according to all that the LORD hath bestowed on us, and the great goodness toward the house of Israel, which he hath be-

stowed on them according to his mercies, and according to the multitude of his lovingkindnesses" (Is.63:7).

"Then they that feared the LORD spake often one to another: and
the LORD hearkened, and heard it, and a book of remembrance was
written before him for them that feared the LORD, and that thought
upon his name" (Mal.3:16).

13. The person who worships God—truly worships Him—can worship God
in spirit no matter where he is, any time and any place.

"Our fathers worshipped in this mountain; and ye say, that in Jerusalem is the place where men ought to worship. Jesus saith unto
her, Woman, believe me, the hour cometh, when ye shall neither in
this mountain, nor yet at Jerusalem, worship the Father. Ye worship
ye know not what: we know what we worship: for salvation is of the
Jews. But the hour cometh, and now is, when the true worshippers
shall worship the Father in spirit and in truth: for the Father seeketh
such to worship him. God is a Spirit: and they that worship him must
worship him in spirit and in truth" (Jn.4:20-24).

14. The person who worships God—truly worships Him—will have the
wonderful opportunity of laying his crown at the feet of Christ, his Lord
and Savior.

"The four and twenty elders [a symbol of believers] fall down before him that sat on the throne, and worship him that liveth for ever
and ever, and cast their crowns before the throne, saying, Thou art
worthy, O Lord, to receive glory and honour and power: for thou
hast created all things, and for thy pleasure they are and were created" (Rev.4:10-11).

15. The person who worships God—truly worships Him—will experience a
strong bond and fellowship with other believers.

"And they continued stedfastly in the apostles' doctrine and fellowship, and in breaking of bread, and in prayers" (Acts 2:42).

"And they, continuing daily with one accord in the temple, and
breaking bread from house to house, did eat their meat with gladness
and singleness of heart" (Acts 2:46)

"That which we have seen and heard declare we unto you, that ye
also may have fellowship with us: and truly our fellowship is with the
Father, and with his Son Jesus Christ" (1 Jn.1:3).

VII. What Is the Teaching of Jesus Christ Concerning This Commandment?

1. Jesus Christ declared that He would worship only the LORD God, Him and Him alone. Christ refused to engage in false worship.

> "If thou therefore wilt worship me [the devil], all shall be thine. And Jesus answered and said unto him, Get thee behind me, Satan: for it is written, Thou shalt worship the LORD thy God, and him only shalt thou serve" (Lk.4:7-8).

<u>Thought.</u>
a) The believer must worship the LORD God, Him and Him alone.

> "Give unto the LORD the glory due unto his name: bring an offering, and come before him: worship the LORD in the beauty of holiness" (1 Chron.16:29).
> "My soul longeth, yea, even fainteth for the courts of the LORD: my heart and my flesh crieth out for the living God" (Ps.84:2).
> "O come, let us worship and bow down: let us kneel before the LORD our maker" (Ps.95:6).
> "O worship the LORD in the beauty of holiness: fear before him, all the earth" (Ps.96:9).
> "Exalt ye the LORD our God, and worship at his footstool; for he is holy" (Ps.99:5).

b) The believer absolutely must never engage in false worship.

> "Turn ye not unto idols, nor make to yourselves molten gods: I am the LORD your God" (Lev.19:4).
> "Ye shall make you no idols nor graven image, neither rear you up a standing image, neither shall ye set up any image of stone in your land, to bow down unto it: for I am the LORD your God" (Lev.26:1).
> "For all the gods of the nations are idols: but the LORD made the heavens" (Ps.96:5).
> "What profiteth the graven image that the maker thereof hath graven it; the molten image, and a teacher of lies, that the maker of his work trusteth therein, to make dumb idols?" (Hab.2:18).
> "Wherefore, my dearly beloved, flee from idolatry" (1 Cor.10:14).
> "Little children, keep yourselves from idols. Amen" (1 Jn.5:21).
> "Mortify [put to death] therefore your members which are upon the earth; fornication, uncleanness, inordinate affection, evil concupiscence, and covetousness, which is idolatry" (Col.3:5).
> "For they themselves show of us what manner of entering in we had unto you, and how ye turned to God from idols to serve the living and true God" (1 Th.1:9).

"Notwithstanding I have a few things against thee, because thou sufferest that woman Jezebel, which calleth herself a prophetess, to teach and to seduce my servants to commit fornication, and to eat things sacrificed unto idols" (Rev.2:20).

2. Jesus Christ declared that the Father seeks true worshippers, those who worship Him in spirit and in truth.

"Our fathers worshipped in this mountain; and ye say, that in Jerusalem is the place where men ought to worship. Jesus saith unto her, Woman, believe me, the hour cometh, when ye shall neither in this mountain, nor yet at Jerusalem, worship the Father. Ye worship ye know not what: we know what we worship: for salvation is of the Jews. But the hour cometh, and now is, when the true worshippers shall worship the Father in spirit and in truth: for the Father seeketh such to worship him. God is a Spirit: and they that worship him must worship him in spirit and in truth" (Jn.4:20-24).

Thought.

Note several points:

a)   Our worship of God must be true and genuine, not fake nor hypocritical.

"My little children, let us not love [nor worship] in word, neither in tongue; but in deed and in truth. And hereby we know that we are of the truth, and shall assure our hearts before him" (1 Jn.3:18-19).

"He answered and said unto them, Well hath Esaias prophesied of you hypocrites, as it is written, This people honoureth me with their lips, but their heart is far from me" (Mk.7:6).

b)   We must worship God in the fulness of His Spirit.

"And be not drunk with wine, wherein is excess; but be filled with the Spirit; Speaking to yourselves in psalms and hymns and spiritual songs, singing and making melody in your heart to the Lord" (Eph.5:18-19).

c)   We must worship God in truth.

"The LORD is nigh unto all them that call upon him, to all that call upon him in truth" (Ps.145:18).

"Jesus saith unto him, I am the way, the truth, and the life: no man cometh unto the Father, but by me" (Jn.14:6).

"And I will pray the Father, and he shall give you another Comforter, that he may abide with you for ever; Even the Spirit of truth; whom the world cannot receive, because it seeth him not, neither knoweth him: but ye know him; for he dwelleth with you, and shall be in you" (Jn.14:16-17).

d) We must worship God continually and consistently.

> "**Praying always with all prayer and supplication in the Spirit, and watching thereunto with all perseverance and supplication for all saints**" (Eph.6:18).
> "**Rejoice in the Lord alway: and again I say, Rejoice**" (Ph.4:4).
> "**...I will bless the LORD at all times: his praise shall continually be in my mouth**" (Ps.34:1).

3. Jesus Christ declared that there is only one true image of God, only one *image* that is acceptable to God: Jesus Christ, the very Image and Revelation of God Himself:

> "**If ye had known me, ye should have known my Father also: and from henceforth ye know him, and have seen him. Philip saith unto him, Lord, show us the Father, and it sufficeth us. Jesus saith unto him, Have I been so long time with you, and yet hast thou not known me, Philip? he that hath seen me hath seen the Father; and how sayest thou then, Show us the Father? Believest thou not that I am in the Father, and the Father in me? the words that I speak unto you I speak not of myself: but the Father that dwelleth in me, he doeth the works**" (Jn.14:7-10).

Thought.

a) We must believe that Jesus Christ is the visible image, the very nature, of the invisible God.

> "**In whom [Christ] we have redemption through his blood, even the forgiveness of sins: Who is the image of the invisible God, the first-born of every creature**" (Col.1:14-15).

b) We must believe that Jesus Christ is the express image, the exact representation, of God's person.

> "**[Christ] who being the brightness of his glory, and the express image of his person, and upholding all things by the word of his power, when he had by himself purged our sins, sat down on the right hand of the Majesty on high**" (Heb.1:3).

c) We must believe that Jesus Christ is God: the very form, the very nature, of God.

> "**Who, being in the form of God, thought it not robbery to be equal with God**" (Ph.2:6).

d) We must believe that Jesus Christ is the fulness of the Godhead, the fulness of God in a human body.

> **"For in him dwelleth all the fulness of the Godhead bodily. And ye are complete in him, which is the head of all principality and power" (Col.2:9-10).**

e) We must believe that Jesus Christ is the image to whom we are to be conformed.

> **"For whom he did foreknow, he also did predestinate to be conformed to the image of his Son, that he might be the firstborn among many brethren" (Ro.8:29).**

f) We must believe that Jesus Christ is the image to which we shall be gloriously and eternally made (transformed).

> **"Beloved, now are we the sons of God, and it doth not yet appear what we shall be: but we know that, when he shall appear, we shall be like him; for we shall see him as he is" (1 Jn.3:2).**

4. Jesus Christ displayed great humility in His worship of God, falling on His face before His Heavenly Father.

> **"And he went a little farther, and fell on his face, and prayed, saying, O my Father, if it be possible, let this cup pass from me: nevertheless not as I will, but as thou wilt" (Mt.26:39).**

Thought.
a) We must approach God with great humility, acknowledging that we have nothing to offer Him yet need everything from Him.

> **"For I know that in me (that is, in my flesh,) dwelleth no good thing: for to will is present with me; but how to perform that which is good I find not" (Ro.7:18).**

b) We must be willing to put aside all pride and humble ourselves before God's mighty hand.

> **"Wherefore God also hath highly exalted him, and given him a name which is above every name: That at the name of Jesus every knee should bow, of things in heaven, and things in earth, and things under the earth; And that every tongue should confess that Jesus Christ is Lord, to the glory of God the Father" (Ph.2:9-11).**
> **"And Moses and Aaron went from the presence of the assembly unto the door of the tabernacle of the congregation, and they fell**

upon their faces: and the glory of the LORD appeared unto them" (Num.20:6).

"And he said, Nay; but as captain of the host of the LORD am I now come. And Joshua fell on his face to the earth, and did worship, and said unto him, What saith my lord unto his servant?" (Josh.5:14).

"So Ahab went up to eat and to drink. And Elijah went up to the top of Carmel; and he cast himself down upon the earth, and put his face between his knees" (1 Ki.18:42).

"And Jehoshaphat bowed his head with his face to the ground: and all Judah and the inhabitants of Jerusalem fell before the LORD, worshipping the LORD" (2 Chron. 20:18).

c) We must humble ourselves before God and cast our care upon Him, trusting that He has our greatest good in mind.

"Likewise, ye younger, submit yourselves unto the elder. Yea, all of you be subject one to another, and be clothed with humility: for God resisteth the proud, and giveth grace to the humble. Humble yourselves therefore under the mighty hand of God, that he may exalt you in due time: Casting all your care upon him; for he careth for you" (1 Pt.5:5-7).

5. Jesus Christ made it His custom to worship God with other believers on the Sabbath.

"And he came to Nazareth, where he had been brought up: and, as his custom was, he went into the synagogue on the sabbath day, and stood up for to read" (Lk.4:16).

"Now about the midst of the feast Jesus went up into the temple, and taught" (Jn.7:14).

Thought.

a) We must never forsake our worship of God, not even for a brief time.

"And they worshipped him, and returned to Jerusalem with great joy: And were continually in the temple, praising and blessing God. Amen" (Lk.24:52-53).

"And they, continuing daily with one accord in the temple, and breaking bread from house to house, did eat their meat with gladness and singleness of heart" (Acts 2:46).

b) We must assemble together...
- for worship
- for prayer
- for the study of God's Word
- for ministry and witnessing

"And when he was departed thence, he went into their synagogue" (Mt.12:9).

"And they went into Capernaum; and straightway on the sabbath day he entered into the synagogue, and taught" (Mk.1:21).

"But when they departed from Perga, they came to Antioch in Pisidia, and went into the synagogue on the sabbath day, and sat down" (Acts 13:14).

"Now Peter and John went up together into the temple at the hour of prayer, being the ninth hour" (Acts 3:1).

c) We must assemble together often and never forsake our coming together. Genuine believers need each other—the presence, fellowship, strength, encouragement, care, and love of one another.

"Not forsaking the assembling of ourselves together, as the manner of some is; but exhorting one another: and so much the more, as ye see the day approaching" (Heb.10:25).

"Blessed are they that dwell in thy house: they will be still praising thee. Selah" (Ps.84:4).

VIII. What Is the Decision Required by This Commandment?

Obedience. God accepts all who love Him and keep His commandments.

"He that hath my commandments, and keepeth them, he it is that loveth me: and he that loveth me shall be loved of my Father, and I will manifest myself to him" (Jn.14:21).

"If ye keep my commandments, ye shall abide in my love; even as I have kept my Father's commandments, and abide in his love....Ye are my friends, if ye do whatsoever I command you" (Jn.15:10, 14).

1. The commandment can be stated positively:
   a. We must choose this day whom we will serve, the false gods of this earth or the LORD Himself (Jehovah, Yahweh).

"Now therefore fear the LORD, and serve him in sincerity and in truth: and put away the gods which your fathers served on the other side of the flood, and in Egypt; and serve ye the LORD. And if it seem evil unto you to serve the LORD, choose you this day whom ye will serve; whether the gods which your fathers served that were on the other side of the flood, or the gods of the Amorites, in whose land ye dwell: but as for me and my house, we will serve the LORD" (Josh.24:14-15).

"And Elijah came unto all the people, and said, How long halt ye between two opinions? if the LORD be God, follow him: but if Baal [false god], then follow him" (1 Ki.18:21).

b. We must remember this day the LORD our Creator, bow down and worship Him and Him alone as our Maker.

> "O come, let us worship and bow down: let us kneel before the LORD our maker. For he is our God; and we are the people of his pasture, and the sheep of his hand" (Ps.95:6-7).
>
> "Remember now thy Creator in the days of thy youth, while the evil days come not, nor the years draw nigh, when thou shalt say, I have no pleasure in them" (Eccl.12:1).

c. We must honor the LORD as our Father.

> "Wherefore come out from among them, and be ye separate, saith the Lord, and touch not the unclean thing; and I will receive you, And will be a Father unto you, and ye shall be my sons and daughters, saith the Lord Almighty" (2 Cor.6:17-18).

d. We must worship God in Spirit and in truth.

> "God [is] a Spirit: and they that worship him must worship [him] in spirit and in truth" (Jn.4:24).

e. We must trust the LORD and keep our minds upon the LORD.

> "Thou wilt keep him in perfect peace, whose mind is stayed on thee: because he trusteth in thee. Trust ye in the LORD for ever: for in the LORD JEHOVAH is everlasting strength" (Is.26:3-4).

f. We must meditate upon the LORD.

> "When I remember thee upon my bed, and meditate on thee in the night watches" (Ps.63:6).

g. We must pray and rejoice in everything.

> "Be careful for nothing; but in every thing by prayer and supplication with thanksgiving let your requests be made known unto God. And the peace of God, which passeth all understanding, shall keep your hearts and minds through Christ Jesus" (Ph.4:6-7).

h. We must give thanks in the name of Christ for everything.

> "Giving thanks always for all things unto God and the Father in the name of our Lord Jesus Christ" (Eph.5:20).

"Be careful for nothing; but in every thing by prayer and supplication with thanksgiving let your requests be made known unto God" (Ph.4:6).

i. We must rejoice in the LORD and be glad.

"Be glad in the LORD, and rejoice, ye righteous: and shout for joy, all ye that are upright in heart" (Ps.32:11).

j. We must delight ourselves in the LORD.

"Delight thyself also in the LORD; and he shall give thee the desires of thine heart" (Ps.37:4).

k. We must assemble ourselves together to worship the LORD.

"Not forsaking the assembling of ourselves together, as the manner of some is; but exhorting one another: and so much the more, as ye see the day approaching" (Heb.10:25).

l. We must guard our steps when we go to the house of God, guard ourselves and make sure we listen.

"Keep thy foot when thou goest to the house of God, and be more ready to hear, than to give the sacrifice of fools: for they consider not that they do evil" (Eccl.5:1).
"And ye shall know the truth, and the truth shall make you free" (Jn.8:32).
"Sanctify them through thy truth: thy word is truth" (Jn.17:17).

m. We must continue to study, teach, and preach God's Word; to pray, observe the Lord's Supper, and fellowship together.

"And they continued stedfastly in the apostles' doctrine and fellowship, and in breaking of bread, and in prayers" (Acts 2:42).
"Preach the word; be instant in season, out of season; reprove, rebuke, exhort with all longsuffering and doctrine" (2 Tim.4:2).

n. We must baptize all new believers in the name of the Father.

"Go ye therefore, and teach all nations, baptizing them in the name of the Father, and of the Son, and of the Holy Ghost" (Mt.28:19).

2. The commandment can be stated negatively:

   a. We must not make nor worship any other god, no other god whatsoever. We must never worship anything other than the LORD God Himself, the only living and true God.

> "Thou shalt not make unto thee any graven image, or any likeness of any thing that is in heaven above, or that is in the earth beneath, or that is in the water under the earth" (Ex.20:4).
>
> "Take heed to yourselves, that your heart be not deceived, and ye turn aside, and serve other gods, and worship them" (Dt.11:16).
>
> "Wherefore, my dearly beloved, flee from idolatry" (1 Cor.10:14).
>
> "Little children, keep yourselves from idols. Amen" (1 Jn.5:21).

   b. We must not set the poor example of a false worship for our children. We must not mislead our children into the worship of false religion and false idols; we must not lead our children to worship anything other than the LORD God Himself, the only living and true God.

> "Only take heed to thyself, and keep thy soul diligently, lest thou forget the things which thine eyes have seen, and lest they depart from thy heart all the days of thy life: but teach them thy sons, and thy sons' sons" (Dt.4:9).
>
> "And he did evil in the sight of the LORD, and walked in the way of his father, and in the way of his mother, and in the way of Jeroboam the son of Nebat, who made Israel to sin" (1 Ki.22:52).
>
> "And thou, Solomon my son, know thou the God of thy father, and serve him with a perfect heart and with a willing mind: for the LORD searcheth all hearts, and understandeth all the imaginations of the thoughts: if thou seek him, he will be found of thee; but if thou forsake him, he will cast thee off for ever" (1 Chron.28:9).
>
> "He also walked in the ways of the house of Ahab: for his mother was his counseller to do wickedly" (2 Chron.22:3).
>
> "Train up a child in the way he should go: and when he is old, he will not depart from it" (Pr.22:6).
>
> "But have walked after the imagination of their own heart, and after Baalim, which their fathers taught them" (Jer.9:14).
>
> "And she, being before instructed of her mother, said, Give me here John Baptist's head in a charger" (Mt.14:8).

   c. We must remove and destroy all false worship.

> "But thus shall ye deal with them; ye shall destroy their altars, and break down their images, and cut down their groves, and burn their graven images with fire" (Dt.7:5).
>
> "Ye shall defile also the covering of thy graven images of silver, and the ornament of thy molten images of gold: thou shalt cast them away as a menstruous cloth; thou shalt say unto it, Get thee hence" (Is.30:22).

d. We must mortify, put to death, all false worship.

> "Mortify therefore your members which are upon the earth; fornication, uncleanness, inordinate affection, evil concupiscence, and covetousness, which is idolatry" (Col.3:5).

e. We must recognize that an idol is nothing, that there is only one true and living God.

> "As concerning therefore the eating of those things that are offered in sacrifice unto idols, we know that an idol is nothing in the world, and that there is none other God but one. For though there be that are called gods, whether in heaven or in earth, (as there be gods many, and lords many,) But to us there is but one God, the Father, of whom are all things, and we in him; and one Lord Jesus Christ, by whom are all things, and we by him" (1 Cor.8:4-6).

"Commandment Three...

Commandment Three Concerns God's Name—Never Misuse God's Name; Never Use Profanity or Vulgarity Exodus 20:7

Contents

Commandment Three Concerns God's Name—Never Misuse God's Name; Never Use Profanity or Vulgarity Exodus 20:7

Commandment 3: **Never dishonor God's name; never use profanity or vulgarity** a. He is the LORD your God b. He will hold you accountable	7 Thou shalt not take the name of the LORD thy God in vain; for the LORD will not hold him guiltless that taketh his name in vain.

Profanity and vulgarity are sweeping the earth. Cursing, swearing, foul and filthy talk, polluted and distasteful language—even using God's name in vain—all forms of profanity and vulgarity are flowing from the mouth of man. Words that expose a prejudicial and disrespectful heart and that degrade others are even peppering the daily conversation of people.

Unfortunately, man's language has always included *gutter talk*. But today, *gutter talk*—profanity—seems to be running rampant. Profanity is becoming more and more accepted by society. Profanity is becoming one of the most prevailing sins and 'popular' vices of the world. This is the subject covered by this commandment, a subject that must be heeded or else the very foundation of society—human language with all the emotions it arouses—will collapse. Simply stated, profanity is a creeping paralysis that will destroy civilization. How could profanity and vulgarity possibly have such a devastating effect upon society? Because civilization is bound together by the civility and decency of human language and by God's grace being poured out upon mankind. Profanity will cause civilization to disintegrate into verbal attacks that lead to personal violence and lawlessness. Profanity—foul, dirty cursing and indecent, prejudicial, and damning talk—destroys human language and arouses emotions and reactions that cause people to strike out against fellow citizens. Thereby civil and decent societies are corrupted and civilizations destroyed—all because human language lost its decency and civility; all because profanity paralyzed the growth and development of human relationships. This is the subject of this great commandment: *Commandment Three Concerns God's Name—Never Misuse God's Name; Never Use Profanity or Vulgarity, 20:7.*

    I.   Who is to obey this commandment (v.7)?

   II.   How long was this commandment to be in force (v.7)?

  III.   What is forbidden by this commandment (v.7)?

  IV.   Why did God give this commandment (v.7)?

   V.   What are the Biblical consequences of breaking this commandment?

  VI.   What are the Biblical benefits of keeping this commandment?

 VII.   What is the teaching of Jesus Christ concerning this commandment?

VIII.   What is the decision required by this commandment (v.7)?

I.   Who Is to Obey This Commandment?

It is a *personal* commandment: a commandment given to you individually. How you use God's name—how you treat God's name—is of vital concern to God. He is the great Creator, the Sovereign LORD and Majesty, the Supreme Ruler and Judge of the universe; therefore, His name is always to be honored, praised, and worshipped. Because of His person—who He is—God demands and insists that you never—no, never—misuse His name.

⇒ *You* must never curse nor abuse His name.

⇒ *You* must never use His name in a frivolous or insincere way.

⇒ *You* must never take the name of the LORD God in vain.

This commandment is directed to *you*. It is directed to me. It is directed to every human being upon the earth.

> **"But above all things, my brethren, swear not, neither by heaven, neither by the earth, neither by any other oath: but let your yea be yea; and your nay, nay; lest ye fall into condemnation" (Jas.5:12).**

II.   How Long Was This Commandment to Be in Force?

As long as people live. No person who has ever lived, who is living now, or who ever will live is ever to misuse God's name. The true and living God is *God Almighty*, the Sovereign LORD and Majesty of the universe, the *Ruler and Judge* of all people. Therefore, any person is a fool to misuse God's name...

- a fool to curse God
- a fool to use God's name in an abusive way or in a frivolous or insincere way

No person of any generation or period of history—as long as God lives, as long as God exists, from everlasting to everlasting—is to misuse or take God's name in vain. This is what God demands; this is one of the ways we are to relate to God. This commandment is in force as long as we live and as long as God exists, forever.

> **"And all people of the earth shall see that thou art called by the name of the LORD; and they shall be afraid of thee" (Dt.28:10).**
> **"Sanctify [set apart] the LORD of hosts himself; and let him be your fear, and let him be your dread" (Is.8:13).**

III. What Is Forbidden by the Third Commandment? How Is This Commandment Broken Or Violated?

The Hebrew word "vain" (lassaw) means empty, meaningless, thoughtless, senseless, frivolous, worthless, groundless. It means using God's name in a thoughtless and insincere way. The root of the word (shawu) has the idea of a vapor that fades and vanishes away, a vapor that is meaningless and worthless.[1] It also has the idea of a tempest, a storm, a tornado that is erratic, that jumps here and there, that causes destruction and devastation, that is totally senseless and destructive.[2]

How does a person misuse the Lord's name or takes God's name in vain? There are at least four ways:

1. A person misuses God's name or takes God's name in vain by *profanity and vulgarity*. This commandment forbids profanity.

   a. Profanity is the cursing, abusive, bitter, blasphemous use of God's name or of any of God's creation. By creation is meant everything within the universe. Thus taking God's name in vain, misusing God's name, includes all uses of vulgarity and profanity: the use of foul, distasteful slang words, and even words such as damn, hell, darn, and other such words.

   What do such words have to do with misusing God's name? Very simply, when we use profanity, we are profaning and cursing something in creation. And no person has the right to profane and curse anything in God's creation. We must never forget this one fact:

   ⇒ The earth is the Lord's: He is the great Creator and Sustainer of everything within the universe. He is the Sovereign LORD and Majesty of the universe itself and of everything within the universe. All creation exists because of God, and all creation stands to the praise of God's name. Therefore, to profane or curse anything in creation is to take God's name in vain. To use profanity—to

---

[1] William Wilson. *Wilson's Old Testament Word Studies.* (McLean, VA: MacDonald Publishing Company, No date given), p.465.

[2] James Strong. *Strong's Exhaustive Concordance of the Bible.* (Nashville, TN: Thomas Nelson, Inc., 1990), 7723.

profane or curse anything—is destructive, totally senseless and worthless.

b. Profanity is a terrible thing when it curses God Himself or uses His name to swear. Using God's name is an insult cast in His face and will result in terrible judgment upon the profane curser.

Remember, a person's name stands for the person. When a person's name is mentioned, if we know the person, our thoughts immediately picture him: who he is and what he is, his nature, character, behavior, and beliefs. We have an immediate image of the person, the kind of person he is.

This is especially true with God. God is holy and righteous. He is loving, kind, and gracious. God is the great Creator and Sustainer of the universe, the sovereign LORD and Majesty of all. Moreover, God is the great Redeemer, the Savior of mankind. He is God Almighty, the Most High God, the LORD God of the universe, whose name is set above the heavens, and whose name is called Wonderful, Counselor, the Mighty God, the Everlasting Father, the Prince of Peace (Is.9:6).

God's name is holy. God's name is different from all other names, set apart from all other names. God's name is above, before, and over all other names. God's name is higher than the heavens, far above every name that is named, in both heaven and earth, visible and invisible.

The point is this: God's holy name should arouse us to stand in awe before Him, never to curse Him. God's holy name should stir us to reverence and adore Him, even fear and tremble before Him. The last thing any person should ever do is misuse God's name:

⇒ use His name as a curse word
⇒ use His name in a vulgar, disgusting way
⇒ use His name in a profane way

Thought 1.

Profanity is like a storm, a terrible, terrifying tempest that is destructive, totally senseless, and worthless. Profanity is a prevailing sin that is sweeping our nation and world today. Profanity is rapidly becoming so acceptable that it is a part of everyday conversation. The terrible danger of profanity has been forgotten. The danger is tragically ignored and even denied. Nevertheless, the danger is a true fact: profanity is a creeping paralysis...

• that destroys the source of respect between people, between the citizens of a diverse society and nation
• that destroys the moral strength and esteem of a people for one another and for their nation
• that corrupts the language of a nation and people

- that destroys the ability of a people to continue to grow, build, advance, enhance, enlarge, and increase the quality of their lives, society, and nation

Profanity will destroy a nation by corrupting the language and respect of people for one another. Over time, profanity will attack and destroy everything held dear by society. Note how a foul mouth destroys:

> **"His mouth is full of cursing and deceit and fraud: under his tongue is mischief and vanity. He sitteth in the lurking places of the villages: in the secret places doth he murder the innocent: his eyes are privily set against the poor....He hath said in his heart, God hath forgotten: he hideth his face; he will never see it" (Ps.10:7-8, 11).**
>
> **"Their throat is an open sepulchre; with their tongues they have used deceit; the poison of asps is under their lips: Whose mouth is full of cursing and bitterness: Their feet are swift to shed blood: Destruction and misery are in their ways: And the way of peace have they not known: There is no fear of God before their eyes" (Ro.3:13-18).**

2. A person misuses God's name by *false swearing*. Perjury—lying under oath—is wrong. Calling upon God to witness to a lie is misusing God's name. False swearing may take place before a neighbor, a business partner, a wife or husband, a judge or jury. Tragically, when we are called upon to swear or take an oath to verify that we are telling the truth, far too often we lie: we swear falsely.

> **"Again, ye have heard that it hath been said by them of old time, Thou shalt not forswear thyself, but shalt perform unto the Lord thine oaths: But I say unto you, Swear not at all; neither by heaven; for it is God's throne: Nor by the earth; for it is his footstool: neither by Jerusalem; for it is the city of the great King. Neither shalt thou swear by thy head, because thou canst not make one hair white or black. But let your communication be, Yea, yea; Nay, nay: for whatsoever is more than these cometh of evil" (Mt.5:33-37).**
>
> **"If a soul sin, and commit a trespass against the LORD, and lie unto his neighbour in that which was delivered him to keep, or in fellowship, or in a thing taken away by violence, or hath deceived his neighbour; Or have found that which was lost, and lieth concerning it, and sweareth falsely; in any of all these that a man doeth, sinning therein" (Lev.6:2-3).**

3. A person misuses God's name by using His name in some *irreverent way*, in some frivolous, dishonoring, or light way. How does a person do this? *Reverence* is the key word. When God's name is used, it is always to be in a reverent way. God's name is never to be used in any irreverent way whatsoever.

   a. All the sayings that use God's name in an irreverent or careless way
are wrong:

⇒ God Almighty   ⇒ Oh God   ⇒ God or Jesus Christ or
⇒ Sweet Jesus   ⇒ Somebody up there   Christ (by themselves,
⇒ God damn this   ⇒ The Man upstairs   spoken carelessly)
   or that   ⇒ Lord have mercy

Any use of God's name that is not reverent—that is not in prayer,
praise, witness, or worship—is wrong.

   b. All the flippant joking about God, the frivolous, humorous stories that
use God's name, are wrong.

   c. All the prayers that carelessly and repetitiously use God's name in a
thoughtless and *meaningless* way are wrong: "Lord do this; Lord do that,"
"God bless" and "God help."

   God's name is sacred: it is holy, righteous, and pure. God's name is the
name of the Omnipresent, Omnipotent, Omniscient God. God's name
is to be worshipped and praised—always reverenced—never used in a
thoughtless, meaningless, flippant, frivolous way; never used in a dishonoring or light way. God's name is never to be misused, never to be
taken in vain.

> **"But fornication, and all uncleanness, or covetousness, let it not be
> once named among you, as becometh saints; Neither filthiness, nor
> foolish talking, nor jesting [crude, rude, foul, dirty, joking], which are
> not convenient: but rather giving of thanks" (Eph.5:3-4).**

Thought 1.

Adrian Rogers, in his book Ten Secrets for a Successful Family, says this:
"When you use...profanity, it shows two things: an empty head and a
wicked heart. You see, profanity reveals a feeble mind trying to express itself. But it also reveals a wicked heart truly expressing itself. 'Out of the
abundance of the heart the mouth speaketh,' Jesus said in Matthew
12:34....A profane mouth reveals a profane heart!"[3]

   Or as the excellent preacher Vance Havner once said, "What's down in
the well comes up in the bucket!"

4. A person misuses God's name by *hypocrisy*. This commandment prohibits
using God's name hypocritically, forbids claiming the name of the Lord in a
hypocritical way. A hypocrite....

- is a person who professes the name of God but lives for self and the world
- is a person who uses God's name to manipulate people (to get what he
wants)
- is a person who uses God's name to secure support for projects that are
not necessarily God's will (for example, politicians or religious leaders)
- is a person who uses God's name to secure followers, to deceive people

---

[3]   Adrian Rogers. *Ten Secrets For A Successful Family*, p.60.

"Not every one that saith unto me, Lord, Lord, shall enter into the kingdom of heaven; but he that doeth the will of my Father which is in heaven. Many will say to me in that day, Lord, Lord, have we not prophesied in thy name? and in thy name have cast out devils? and in thy name done many wonderful works? And then will I profess unto them, I never knew you: depart from me, ye that work iniquity" (Mt.7:21-23).

"And why call ye me, Lord, Lord, and do not the things which I say?" (Lk.6:46).

"Hear ye this, O house of Jacob, which are called by the name of Israel, and are come forth out of the waters of Judah, which swear by the name of the LORD, and make mention of the God of Israel, but not in truth, nor in righteousness" (Is.48:1).

Thought 1.

In the early days of American history, the great general George Washington took a strong stand against profanity. He wrote in his orderly book of August 3, 1776: "The General is sorry to be informed that the foolish and wicked practice of profane swearing, a vice hitherto little known in the American army, is growing into fashion...He hopes the officers will, by example as well as influence, endeavor to check it, and that both they and the men will reflect that we can have little hope of the blessing of heaven on our arms if we insult it by our impiety and profanity."[4]

IV. Why Did God Give This Ccommandment?

Why does God forbid vulgarity? Why must we never misuse God's name, never swear, curse, nor damn anything upon earth, never damn anything in creation? Two reasons are given within the commandment itself.

1. First, you must not use vulgarity or misuse God's name for a very clear reason: because the LORD is *your* God (v.2, 7). If you have accepted Christ as your Savior, then the LORD has saved you from Egypt, from the enslavements and bondages of this earth (v.2). He has saved you from sin, shame, and death. He has saved you from the bondages of the flesh, from...

- adultery and immorality
- drunkenness and carousing
- false worship and idolatry
- hatred and strife
- jealousy and envy

- wild living and sensuality
- cursing and lying
- sorcery and witchcraft
- anger and division
- selfish ambition and greed

---

[4] J. Vernon McGee. *Love, Liberation and the Law.* (Nashville, TN: Thomas Nelson Publishers, 1995), p.38-39.

And on and on. God has saved you from all this to a life of love, joy, and peace. Moreover, He has saved you from death and the judgment to come. He has saved you from hell itself. You are going to live forever, eternally with Him. The LORD is now your God. How could you ever misuse His name?

Now note: if you have never accepted Christ, then all the above can be yours. God will save you from the enslavements and bondages of this earth and give you life eternal. The point is this: the drive and energy of your heart must be not to misuse the name of the LORD God, the Savior of the world. The drive and energy of your life must be to stand in awe of His name: to praise, worship, serve, and bear testimony to His name.

> "Enter into his gates with thanksgiving, and into his courts with praise: be thankful unto him, and bless his name" (Ps.100:4).

> "Sanctify the LORD of hosts himself; and let him be your fear, and let him be your dread" (Is.8:13).

> "For thus saith the high and lofty One that inhabiteth eternity, whose name is Holy; I dwell in the high and holy place, with him also that is of a contrite and humble spirit, to revive the spirit of the humble, and to revive the heart of the contrite ones" (Is.57:15).

> "And being found in fashion as a man, he humbled himself, and became obedient unto death, even the death of the cross. Wherefore God also hath highly exalted him, and given him a name which is above every name: That at the name of Jesus every knee should bow, of things in heaven, and things in earth, and things under the earth: And that every tongue should confess that Jesus Christ is Lord, to the glory of God the Father" (Ph.2:8-11).

> "By him therefore let us offer the sacrifice of praise to God continually, that is, the fruit of our lips giving thanks to his name" (Heb.13:15).

> "But ye are a chosen generation, a royal priesthood, an holy nation, a peculiar people; that ye should show forth the praises of him who hath called you out of darkness into his marvellous light" (1 Pt.2:9).

2. Second, you must not use vulgarity or misuse God's name for a terrifying reason: because the LORD holds you accountable if you misuse His name. The word "guiltless" (waqah) means that God will not count us clear or free from blame. He will not count us clean or pure, innocent or guiltless. God will not acquit us, not let us go unpunished.

A man may curse God or swear falsely to his wife or neighbor or even to some jury, and he may not be corrected or punished. But God knows that the man cursed His name or lied, and Scripture is clear: God will punish him. God will avenge the person who insulted His great and glorious name. In fact, note what Scripture says: the person who curses and misuses God's name stands as an *enemy of God*.

> "Thine enemies take thy name in vain" (Ps.139:20).

⇒ The person who uses profanity openly declares that he is the sworn enemy of the high and holy God. This person is condemned; God shall avenge His name and judge the *curser*.

⇒ The person who swears falsely deliberately declares that he is the sworn enemy of the true and righteous God. The person is condemned; God shall avenge His name and judge the *false swearer*.

⇒ The person who uses God's name in an irreverent way, who is careless and thoughtless in the use of God's name, will not be guiltless. He shall be condemned. God shall avenge His name and judge the *irreverent person*.

⇒ The person who uses God's name hypocritically stands as the sworn enemy of God. The hypocrite is condemned. God shall avenge His name and severely judge the *hypocrite*.

⇒ The bold sinner—the person who misuses God's name—must appear before God to give an account for his cursing and lying and for his irreverent use of God's holy name. If a person curses God, he curses the name of the high and lofty One, the name of the LORD God Himself, the only living and true God, the only holy name that could have saved him from death and judgment to come. God shall avenge His name and judge the *bold sinner*.

> "As he loved cursing, so let it come unto him: as he delighted not in blessing, so let it be far from him" (Ps.109:17).
> "And I will come near to you to judgment; and I will be a swift witness against the sorcerers, and against the adulterers, and against false swearers, and against those that oppress the hireling [hired laborer] in his wages, the widow, and the fatherless, and that turn aside the stranger from his right, and fear not me, saith the LORD of hosts" (Mal.3:5).
> "And to you who are troubled rest with us, when the Lord Jesus shall be revealed from heaven with his mighty angels, In flaming fire taking vengeance on them that know not God, and that obey not the gospel of our Lord Jesus Christ" (2 Th.1:7-8).
> "And as it is appointed unto men once to die, but after this the judgment" (Heb.9:27).
> "But the heavens and the earth, which are now, by the same word are kept in store, reserved unto fire against the day of judgment and perdition of ungodly men" (2 Pt.3:7).
> "And Enoch also, the seventh from Adam, prophesied of these, saying, Behold, the Lord cometh with ten thousands of his saints, To execute judgment upon all, and to convince all that are ungodly among them of all their ungodly deeds which they have ungodly committed,

and of all their hard speeches which ungodly sinners have spoken against him" (Jude 14-15).

"But the fearful, and unbelieving, and the abominable, and murderers, and whore-mongers, and sorcerers, and idolaters, and all liars [cursers, false swearers], shall have their part in the lake which burneth with fire and brimstone: which is the second death" (Rev.21:8).

V. What Are the Consequences of Breaking This Commandment, the Consequences of Misusing God's Name?

What happens to the person who uses profanity and blasphemes God? What happens to the person who damns things and curses things to hell, who has a foul, filthy, degrading and distasteful mouth? God's name is holy, and it must be treated as such. No foul mouthed person, no person who misuses God's name, can escape these terrible consequences.

1. There are the consequences upon God.
   a. The person who misuses God's name, who uses profanity, blasphemes the name of the LORD.

   "Do not they blaspheme that worthy name by the which ye are called?" (Jas.2:7).
   "And the Israelitish woman's son blasphemed the name of the LORD, and cursed. And they brought him unto Moses: (and his mother's name was Shelomith, the daughter of Dibri, of the tribe of Dan:)" (Lev.24:11).

   b. The person who misuses God's name, who uses profanity, profanes or abuses God's name.

   "And I will sanctify my great name, which was profaned among the heathen, which ye have profaned in the midst of them; and the heathen shall know that I am the LORD, saith the Lord GOD, when I shall be sanctified in you before their eyes" (Ezk.36:23).

2. There are the consequences upon oneself, the day-to-day consequences.
   a. The person who misuses God's name, who uses profanity, shows that he does not know God, that he is wicked and unrighteous.

   "As it is written, There is none righteous, no, not one: There is none that understandeth, there is none that seeketh after God. They are all gone out of the way, they are together become unprofitable; there is none that doeth good, no, not one. Their throat is an open sepulchre; with their tongues they have used deceit; the poison of asps is under their lips: Whose mouth is full of cursing and bitterness" (Ro.3:10-14).

"The wicked in his pride doth persecute the poor: let them be taken in the devices that they have imagined....His mouth is full of cursing and deceit and fraud: under his tongue is mischief and vanity" (Ps.10:2, 7).

"But unto the wicked God saith, What hast thou to do to declare my statutes, or that thou shouldest take my covenant in thy mouth? Seeing thou hatest instruction, and castest my words behind thee....Thou givest thy mouth to evil, and thy tongue frameth deceit. Thou sittest and speakest against thy brother; thou slanderest thine own mother's son" (Ps.50:16-17, 19-20).

b. The person who misuses God's name, who uses profanity, shows that he is a hypocrite.

"Then began he [Peter] to curse and to swear, saying, I know not the man. And immediately the cock crew" (Mt.26:74).

"Therewith bless we God, even the Father; and therewith curse we men, which are made after the similitude of God. Out of the same mouth proceedeth blessing and cursing. My brethren, these things ought not so to be" (Jas.3:9-10).

c. The person who misuses God's name, who uses profanity, is a fool.

"He that hideth hatred with lying lips, and he that uttereth a slander, is a fool" (Pr.10:18).

d. The person who misuses God's name, who uses profanity, has a throat like an open grave, a throat that bears the stinking smell of death.

"For there is no faithfulness in their mouth; their inward part is very wickedness; their throat is an open sepulchre; they flatter with their tongue" (Ps.5:9).

"Their throat is an open sepulchre; with their tongues they have used deceit; the poison of asps is under their lips" (Ro.3:13).

e. The person who misuses God's name, who uses profanity, shows that he has an evil heart.

"O generation of vipers, how can ye, being evil, speak good things? for out of the abundance of the heart the mouth speaketh" (Mt.12:34).

"The words of his mouth were smoother than butter, but war was in his heart: his words were softer than oil, yet were they drawn swords" (Ps.55:21).

f. The person who misuses God's name, who uses profanity, will have a testimony, a reputation, that is marked by malice and deception.

> "Let all bitterness, and wrath, and anger, and clamour, and evil speaking, be put away from you, with all malice" (Eph.4:31).
> "Wherefore laying aside all malice, and all guile, and hypocrisies, and envies, and all evil speakings" (1 Pt.2:1).
> "For he that will love life, and see good days, let him refrain his tongue from evil, and his lips that they speak no guile" (1 Pt.3:10).

g. The person who misuses God's name, who uses profanity, will be deceived and have a vain, useless, empty religion.

> "If any man among you seem to be religious, and bridleth not his tongue, but deceiveth his own heart, this man's religion is vain" (Jas.1:26).

h. The person who misuses God's name, who uses profanity, will defile his body.

> "And the tongue is a fire, a world of iniquity: so is the tongue among our members, that it defileth the whole body, and setteth on fire the course of nature; and it is set on fire of hell" (Jas.3:6).

i. The person who misuses God's name, who uses profanity, will be found out, he will be exposed, even though he took every caution to be discreet and secretive.

> "Curse not the king, no not in thy thought; and curse not the rich in thy bedchamber: for a bird of the air shall carry the voice, and that which hath wings shall tell the matter" (Eccl. 10:20).

j. The person who misuses God's name, who uses profanity, curses people who are made in God's image.

> "For oftentimes also thine own heart knoweth that thou thyself likewise hast cursed others" (Eccl.7:22).
> "Therewith bless we God, even the Father; and therewith curse we men, which are made after the similitude [likeness] of God. Out of the same mouth proceedeth blessing and cursing. My brethren, these things ought not so to be" (Jas.3:9-10).
> "An hypocrite with his mouth destroyeth his neighbour: but through knowledge shall the just be delivered" (Pr.11:9).
> "Take ye heed every one of his neighbour, and trust ye not in any brother: for every brother will utterly supplant, and every neighbour will walk with slanders" (Jer.9:4).

"Speak not evil one of another, brethren. He that speaketh evil of his brother, and judgeth his brother, speaketh evil of the law, and judgeth the law: but if thou judge the law, thou art not a doer of the law, but a judge" (Jas.4:11).

k. The person who misuses God's name, who uses profanity, will be held accountable for every idle word in the day of judgment.

"O generation of vipers, how can ye, being evil, speak good things? for out of the abundance of the heart the mouth speaketh. A good man out of the good treasure of the heart bringeth forth good things: and an evil man out of the evil treasure bringeth forth evil things. But I say unto you, That every idle word that men shall speak, they shall give account thereof in the day of judgment" (Mt.12:34-36).

l. The person who misuses God's name, who uses profanity, will suffer the reciprocal judgment of God: suffer the very curse he pronounced and uttered.

"As he loved cursing, so let it come unto him: as he delighted not in blessing, so let it be far from him. As he clothed himself with cursing like as with his garment, so let it come into his bowels like water, and like oil into his bones" (Ps.109:17-18).

3. There are the consequences of judgment.
    a. The person who misuses God's name, who uses profanity, will face the judgment of God and not inherit the kingdom of God.

"Neither filthiness [obsenity], nor foolish talking, nor jesting [coarse joking], which are not convenient: but rather giving of thanks. For this ye know, that no whoremonger, nor unclean person, nor covetous man, who is an idolater, hath any inheritance in the kingdom of Christ and of God" (Eph.5:4-5).
"Whoso privily slandereth his neighbour, him will I cut off: him that hath an high look and a proud heart will not I suffer" (Ps.101:5).
"Behold, ye trust in lying words, that cannot profit. Will ye steal, murder, and commit adultery, and swear falsely, and burn incense unto Baal, and walk after other gods whom ye know not....And I will cast you out of my sight, as I have cast out all your brethren, even the whole seed of Ephraim" (Jer.7:8-9, 15).
"For the land is full of adulterers; for because of swearing the land mourneth; the pleasant places of the wilderness are dried up, and their course is evil, and their force is not right. For both prophet and priest are profane; yea, in my house have I found their wickedness, saith the LORD. Wherefore their way shall be unto them as slippery ways in the darkness: they shall be driven on, and fall therein: for I will bring evil

upon them, even the year of their visitation, saith the LORD" (Jer.23:10-12).

b. The person who misuses God's name, who uses profanity, will be declared guilty and condemned.

> "Thou shalt not take the name of the LORD thy God in vain; for the LORD will not hold him guiltless that taketh his name in vain" (Ex.20:7).
> "But above all things, my brethren, swear not, neither by heaven, neither by the earth, neither by any other oath: but let your yea be yea; and your nay, nay; lest ye fall into condemnation" (Jas.5:12).

c. The person who misuses God's name, who uses profanity, will bear the curse of his profanity and be destroyed by his very own words.

> "As he loved cursing, so let it come unto him: as he delighted not in blessing, so let it be far from him" (Ps.109:17).
> "He that keepeth his mouth keepeth his life: but he that openeth wide his lips shall have destruction" (Pr.13:3).
> "Whoso keepeth his mouth and his tongue keepeth his soul from troubles" (Pr.21:23).

d. The person who curses his father or mother shows that he is not cleansed and will be condemned and face the terrible wrath of God.

> "Whoso curseth his father or his mother, his lamp shall be put out in obscure darkness" (Pr.20:20).
> "There is a generation that curseth their father, and doth not bless their mother. There is a generation that are pure in their own eyes, and yet is not washed from their filthiness" (Pr.30:11-12).
> "For the sin of their mouth and the words of their lips let them even be taken in their pride: and for cursing and lying which they speak. Consume them in wrath, consume them, that they may not be: and let them know that God ruleth in Jacob unto the ends of the earth. Selah" (Ps.59:12-13).

VI. What are the Benefits of Keeping This Commandment?

What happens to the person who does not misuse nor take God's name in vain? The person who uses God's name correctly will be greatly blessed.

1. The person who uses God's name correctly will be saved.

> "For whosoever shall call upon the name of the Lord shall be saved" (Ro.10:13).

"But as many as received him, to them gave he power to become the sons of God, even to them that believe on his name" (Jn.1:12).

"Seek ye the LORD while he may be found, call ye upon him while he is near: Let the wicked forsake his way, and the unrighteous man his thoughts: and let him return unto the LORD, and he will have mercy upon him; and to our God, for he will abundantly pardon" (Is.55:6-7).

2. The person who uses God's name correctly will confess and bow at the name of His Son, Jesus Christ.

"Wherefore God also hath highly exalted him, and given him a name which is above every name: That at the name of Jesus every knee should bow, of things in heaven, and things in earth, and things under the earth; And that every tongue should confess that Jesus Christ is Lord, to the glory of God the Father" (Ph.2:9-11).

3. The person who uses God's name correctly will be filled with God's Spirit, walking about with joy.

"And be not drunk with wine, wherein is excess; but be filled with the Spirit; Speaking to yourselves in psalms and hymns and spiritual songs, singing and making melody in your heart to the Lord" (Eph.5:18-19).

4. The person who uses God's name correctly will walk in light.

"Who is among you that feareth the LORD, that obeyeth the voice of his servant, that walketh in darkness, and hath no light? let him trust in the name of the LORD, and stay upon his God" (Is.50:10).

5. The person who uses God's name correctly will be heard, helped, and strengthened in the day of trouble.

"The LORD hear thee in the day of trouble; the name of the God of Jacob defend thee; Send thee help from the sanctuary, and strengthen thee out of Zion; Remember all thy offerings, and accept thy burnt sacrifice; Selah" (Ps.20:1-3).

"The LORD is nigh unto all them that call upon him, to all that call upon him in truth. He will fulfil the desire of them that fear him: he also will hear their cry, and will save them" (Ps.145:18-19).

"For there is no difference between the Jew and the Greek: for the same Lord over all is rich unto all that call upon him" (Ro.10:12).

6. The person who uses God's name correctly will be safe and secure.

"The name of the LORD is a strong tower: the righteous runneth into it, and is safe" (Pr.18:10).

7. The person who uses God's name correctly will have his prayers answered.

> "After this manner therefore pray ye: Our Father which art in heaven, Hallowed be thy name" (Mt.6:9).
> "Call unto me, and I will answer thee, and show thee great and mighty things, which thou knowest not" (Jer.33:3).

8. The person who uses God's name correctly will have a mouth filled with praise and honor.

> "Let my mouth be filled with thy praise and with thy honour all the day" (Ps.71:8).

9. The person who uses God's name correctly will know how to help others with a special word of encouragement.

> "The LORD God hath given me the tongue of the learned, that I should know how to speak a word in season to him that is weary: he wakeneth morning by morning, he wakeneth mine ear to hear as the learned" (Is.50:4).

VII.   What Is the Teaching of Jesus Christ Concerning This Commandment?

1. Jesus Christ declared that a person misuses God's name by false swearing.

> "Again, ye have heard that it hath been said by them of old time, Thou shalt not forswear thyself, but shalt perform unto the Lord thine oaths: But I say unto you, Swear not at all; neither by heaven; for it is God's throne: Nor by the earth; for it is his footstool: neither by Jerusalem; for it is the city of the great King. Neither shalt thou swear by thy head, because thou canst not make one hair white or black. But let your communication be, Yea, yea; Nay, nay: for whatsoever is more than these cometh of evil" (Mt.5:33-37).

Thought.

We must never swear to make a promise we cannot keep. Perjury—lying under oath—is wrong. All misuse of God's name that calls upon Him to witness to a lie is misusing God's name. The false swearing may take place...

- before a wife or husband
- before a neighbor
- before a business partner
- before a judge or jury
- before any person

> "But above all things, my brethren, swear not, neither by heaven, neither by the earth, neither by any other oath: but let your yea be yea; and your nay, nay; lest ye fall into condemnation" (Jas.5:12).

"If a man vow a vow unto the LORD, or swear an oath to bind his soul with a bond; he shall not break his word, he shall do according to all that proceedeth out of his mouth" (Num.30:2).

"When thou shalt vow a vow unto the LORD thy God, thou shalt not slack to pay it: for the LORD thy God will surely require it of thee; and it would be sin in thee" (Dt.23:21).

"Thou shalt make thy prayer unto him, and he shall hear thee, and thou shalt pay thy vows" (Job 22:27).

"Offer unto God thanksgiving; and pay thy vows unto the most High" (Ps.50:14).

"Vow, and pay unto the LORD your God: let all that be round about him bring presents unto him that ought to be feared" (Ps.76:11).

"When thou vowest a vow unto God, defer not to pay it; for he hath no pleasure in fools: pay that which thou hast vowed" (Eccl.5:4).

2. Jesus Christ declared that God's Name is holy, set apart from all other names.

"After this manner therefore pray ye: Our Father which art in heaven, Hallowed be thy name" (Mt.6:9).

Thought 1.

Note several points.

a) God's name is much too precious to be used flippantly. His name is a *refuge for man*, not a cesspool to be filled with foul language.

"I will say of the LORD, He is my refuge and my fortress: my God; in him will I trust" (Ps.91:2).

"Wherefore God also hath highly exalted him, and given him a name which is above every name: That at the name of Jesus every knee should bow, of things in heaven, and things in earth, and things under the earth; And that every tongue should confess that Jesus Christ is Lord, to the glory of God the Father" (Ph. 2:9-11).

b) God's name is to be hallowed, set apart as holy.

"And he said unto them, When ye pray, say, Our Father which art in heaven, Hallowed be thy name. Thy kingdom come. Thy will be done, as in heaven, so in earth" (Lk.11:2).

"Speak unto Aaron and to his sons, that they separate themselves from the holy things of the children of Israel, and that they profane not my holy name in those things which they hallow unto me: I am the LORD" (Lev.22:2).

c) God's name is to be feared.

"If thou wilt not observe to do all the words of this law that are written in this book, that thou mayest fear this glorious and fearful name, THE LORD THY GOD" (Dt.28:58).

d) God's name is a strong tower into which the believer can run.

> "The name of the LORD is a strong tower: the righteous runneth into it, and is safe" (Pr.18:10).

3. Jesus Christ declared that God's name must be glorified and honored.

> "Father, glorify thy name. Then came there a voice from heaven, saying, I have both glorified it, and will glorify it again" (Jn.12:28).

Thought.

We must always seek to glorify and honor God's name...
- in everything we do
- in everything we say
- in everything we think

> "Let your light so shine before men, that they may see your good works, and glorify your Father which is in heaven" (Mt.5:16).
> "And call upon me in the day of trouble: I will deliver thee, and thou shalt glorify me" (Ps.50:15).
> "Now the God of patience and consolation grant you to be like-minded one toward another according to Christ Jesus: That ye may with one mind and one mouth glorify God, even the Father of our Lord Jesus Christ" (Ro.15:5-6).
> "Ye that fear the LORD, praise him; all ye the seed of Jacob, glorify him; and fear him, all ye the seed of Israel" (Ps.22:23).
> "I will praise thee, O LORD my God, with all my heart: and I will glorify thy name for evermore" (Ps.86:12).
> "What? know ye not that your body is the temple of the Holy Ghost which is in you, which ye have of God, and ye are not your own? For ye are bought with a price: therefore glorify God in your body, and in your spirit, which are God's" (1 Cor.6:19-20).

4. Jesus Christ declared that God's name must not be abused by the hypocrisy of self-righteous men [professing believers].

> "Even so ye also outwardly appear righteous unto men, but within ye are full of hypocrisy and iniquity" (Mt.23:28).

Thought.

God's name must never be misused.

a) We must not misuse God's name by professing (blessing) God and then using profanity.

> "Out of the same mouth proceedeth blessing and cursing. My brethren, these things ought not so to be" (Jas. 3:10).

b) We must not misuse God's name by living a hypocritical life, claiming to know God but refusing to obey Him.

"He that saith, I know him, and keepeth not his commandments, is a liar, and the truth is not in him" (1 Jn.2:4).

"They profess that they know God; but in works they deny him, being abominable, and disobedient, and unto every good work reprobate" (Tit.1:16).

c. We must not misuse God's name by judging others in the name of God when we are ever so short ourselves.

"Either how canst thou say to thy brother, Brother, let me pull out the mote that is in thine eye, when thou thyself beholdest not the beam that is in thine own eye? Thou hypocrite, cast out first the beam out of thine own eye, and then shalt thou see clearly to pull out the mote that is in thy brother's eye" (Lk.6:42).

VIII. What Is the Decision Required by This Commandment?

Simply stated, we must obey God's commandments.

1. Note that the commandment can be stated positively: Honor God's name— always. This was exactly what Christ Himself said. In fact, He said that we were to pray every day for God's name to be *hallowed* (Mt.6:9).

2. Note also that the commandment can be stated negatively: you shall not misuse God's name, shall not take His name in vain.

What decision is demanded by this commandment? We must not curse or swear; we must turn to God for salvation and forgiveness. We must...

• quit cursing and swearing
• quit using God's name in irreverent and thoughtless ways
• quit using God's name hypocritically

3. Note what Scripture says about this commandment and God's name.
    a. We must not misuse God's name, never take God's name in vain. This is one of the Ten great Commandments.

"Thou shalt not take the name of the LORD thy God in vain; for the LORD will not hold him guiltless that taketh his name in vain" (Ex.20:7).

b. We must never swear falsely, not by God's name: we must not profane His name.

"And ye shall not swear by my name falsely, neither shalt thou profane the name of thy God: I am the LORD" (Lev.19:12).

c. We must fear God's name.

> "If thou wilt not observe to do all the words of this law that are written in this book, that thou mayest fear this glorious and fearful name, THE LORD THY GOD; Then the LORD will make thy plagues wonderful [fearful]" (Dt.28:58-59).

d. We must not use God's name hypocritically nor have a hypocritical tongue.

> "Hear ye this, O house of Jacob, which are called by the name of Israel, and are come forth out of the waters of Judah, which swear by the name of the LORD, and make mention of the God of Israel, but not in truth, nor in righteousness" (Is.48:1).
>
> "Therewith bless we God, even the Father; and therewith curse we men, which are made after the similitude of God. Out of the same mouth proceedeth blessing and cursing. My brethren, these things ought not so to be. Doth a fountain send forth at the same place sweet water and bitter? Can the fig tree, my brethren, bear olive berries? either a vine, figs? so can no fountain both yield salt water and fresh" (Jas.3:9-12).

e. We must not love false oaths.

> "And let none of you imagine evil in your hearts against his neighbour; and love no false oath: for all these are things that I hate, saith the LORD" (Zech.8:17).

f. We must never swear; rather we must speak directly, never swearing nor using oaths.

> "But I say unto you, Swear not at all; neither by heaven; for it is God's throne: Nor by the earth; for it is his footstool: neither by Jerusalem; for it is the city of the great King. Neither shalt thou swear by thy head, because thou canst not make one hair white or black. But let your communication be, Yea, yea; Nay, nay: for whatsoever is more than these cometh of evil" (Mt.5:34-37).
>
> "But above all things, my brethren, swear not, neither by heaven, neither by the earth, neither by any other oath: but let your yea be yea; and your nay, nay; lest ye fall into condemnation" (Jas.5:12).

g. We must swear only by the God of Truth.

> "That he who blesseth himself in the earth shall bless himself in the God of truth; and he that sweareth in the earth shall swear by the God of truth" (Is.65:16).

h. We are to believe on God's name, not curse His name.

> "But as many as received him, to them gave he power to become the sons of God, even to them that believe on his name" (Jn.1:12).
> "For whosoever shall call upon the name of the Lord shall be saved" (Ro.10:13).

i. We are to walk in the name of the LORD our God, not curse Him.

> "For all people will walk every one in the name of his god, and we will walk in the name of the LORD our God for ever and ever" (Mic.4:5).

j. We are to proclaim the name of God to people, bear testimony to His name.

> "But sanctify the Lord God in your hearts: and be ready always to give an answer to every man that asketh you a reason of the hope that is in you with meekness and fear" (1 Pt.3:15).
> "Ye are my witnesses, saith the LORD, and my servant whom I have chosen: that ye may know and believe me, and understand that I am he: before me there was no God formed, neither shall there be after me" (Is.43:10).
> "Then I said, I will not make mention of him, nor speak any more in his name. But his word was in mine heart as a burning fire shut up in my bones, and I was weary with forbearing, and I could not stay" (Jer.20:9).

k. We must praise God's name not curse His name.

> "Praise the LORD; for the LORD is good: sing praises unto his name; for it is pleasant" (Ps.135:3).

l. We must hallow God's name, set God's name far above all names.

> "After this manner therefore pray ye: Our Father which art in heaven, Hallowed be thy name" (Mt.6:9).
> "Sanctify them through thy truth: thy word is truth" (Jn.17:17).

m. We must not misuse God's name by making a false, hypocritical profession.

> "Not every one that saith unto me, Lord, Lord, shall enter into the kingdom of heaven; but he that doeth the will of my Father which is in heaven. Many will say to me in that day, Lord, Lord, have we not

prophesied in thy name? and in thy name have cast out devils? and in thy name done many wonderful works? And then will I profess unto them, I never knew you: depart from me, ye that work iniquity" (Mt.7:21-23).

"And why call ye me, Lord, Lord, and do not the things which I say?" (Lk.6:46).

Commandment Four Concerns God's Day—Never Fail to Observe the Sabbath, to Keep it Holy Exodus 20:8-11

Contents

Commandment Four Concerns God's Day—Never Fail to Observe the Sabbath, to Keep it Holy
Exodus 20:8-11

COMMANDMENT 4:	
1. **Who is to obey this commandment?**	8 Remember the Sabbath day, to keep it holy.
2. **What is the charge of this commandment?**	9 Six days shalt thou labor, and do all thy work:
a. You *shall work* for six days	10 But the seventh day is the Sabbath of the LORD thy God: in it thou shalt not do any work, thou, nor thy son, nor thy daughter, thy manservant, nor thy maidservant, nor thy cattle, nor thy stranger that is within thy gates:
b. You *shall not do any work* on the Sabbath: No work whatsoever is to be done on the Sabbath, not by anyone under your authority, including animals and strangers	
3. **Why did God give this commandment?**	11 For in six days the LORD made heaven and earth, the sea, and all that in them is, and rested the seventh day: wherefore the LORD blessed the Sabbath day, and hallowed it.
a. Because the 7th day is to be a day of rest: The LORD's example	
b. Because the 7th day is to be a day of worship: The LORD blessed it & made it holy	

Work, rest, and worship—these are three of the basic essentials of human life. Listen to them again:

⇒ work

⇒ rest

⇒ worship

Man needs all three. God made man to work, to rest, and to worship. This is what the Sabbath is all about. God Himself divided time into seven days. Holy Scripture declares that God created the universe in six days and then rested on the seventh day (Gen.2:1-3).

133

Man is to follow God's example: work for six days and then rest and worship on the seventh day. God Himself set the day aside for us. God loves and cares for us, and He knows what we need. We need a full day every week for rest and relaxation and for worship—so much so that God made it one of the ten great laws that are to govern human life. This is the subject of this great commandment: *Commandment Four Concerns God's Day—Never Fail to Observe the Sabbath, to Keep it Holy*, 20:8-11.

    I.   Who is to obey this commandment? How long was this commandment to be in force (v.8)?

    II.   What is the charge of this commandment (v.9-10)?

   III. Why did God give this commandment (v.11)?

   IV. What are the Biblical consequences of breaking this commandment?

    V.   What are the Biblical benefits of keeping this commandment?

   VI. What is the teaching of Jesus Christ concerning this commandment?

  VII. What is the decision required by this commandment (v.11)?

I.   Who Is to Obey This Commandment?

This is the longest of the Ten Commandments, four verses, almost one-third of the fifteen verses that cover the Ten Commandments (v.3-17). And note: all four verses dealing with the Sabbath declare that it is *you* who is to keep this commandment. Note the emphasis and the force of the language toward *you*:

⇒ Verse 8: the imperative *you*—*You* are to remember the Sabbath day, to keep it holy.

⇒ Verse 9: *You* are to labor and do all your work in six days.

⇒ Verse 10: *You* are not to do any work on the Sabbath day, nor is your family, nor is any slave or employee for whom you are responsible.

⇒ Verse 11: the understood *you*—*You* are to follow God's example in setting the Sabbath day aside, using it as a day of rest and worship.

How long was this commandment to be in force? Note the word "remember" (zakar). God is charging us to remember something that had taken place in the past. What? Long before the Sabbath was included in the Ten Commandments, the Sabbath day had been instituted as a day of rest and worship. Verse 11 tells us when: at creation, right after God had created the universe.

The point is this: the Sabbath day was not given to Israel alone; the Sabbath day was given to every nation and people upon earth. The Sabbath day was instituted by God at creation, long before the Ten Commandments were ever given, long before Israel was ever formed as a people or nation. The Sabbath day was given to all people for rest and worship. A day of rest and worship— one day out of every seven—is the God-given right of every man, woman, and child upon earth. This commandment applies to every generation of people, to every person, so long as the earth stands.

> **"And he said unto them, The Sabbath was made for man, and not man for the Sabbath" (Mk.2:27).**
>
> **"Not forsaking the assembling of ourselves together, as the manner of some is; but exhorting one another: and so much the more, as ye see the day approaching" (Heb.10:25).**
>
> **"For in six days the LORD made heaven and earth, the sea, and all that in them is, and rested the seventh day: wherefore the LORD blessed the Sabbath day, and hallowed it [for all people]" (Ex.20:11).**

II.   What Is the Charge of This Commandment?

"Remember the Sabbath day, to keep it holy." Several facts need to be noted.

1. The word "remember" (zakar) is imperative, a strong, strong imperative: "You must remember—remember to the point of *keeping* and *observing*—the day of rest and worship." When the Ten Commandments are repeated in Deuteronomy, the Hebrew word is translated "keep" or "observe":

> **"Keep the Sabbath day to sanctify it, as the LORD thy God hath commanded thee" (Dt.5:12).**

2. The Hebrew word "Sabbath" does not mean the seventh day (Saturday) as so many people think. The word "Sabbath" (shabbath) means to rest, to repose, to cease. It means to cease from work, to rest from work.

This is significant, for God is charging us to keep the Sabbath, the day of rest and worship. He is not specifying a particular day of the week when man is to worship and rest. God simply says, work six days and then rest on the seventh day.

  a. This fact is important for industrialized and technological societies. Why? Because so many people *have* to work on Saturday or on Sunday, on the day set aside by their religion as the day of worship and rest. In many cases, factories cannot shut down their huge furnaces, boilers, and machines without damaging them mechanically. They have to be operated continually; therefore, thousands upon thousands of people have to work on Saturday and Sunday. The same is true with many service industries and other businesses.

Thought. When businesses have to operate seven days a week, what are the employees of these businesses to do about worship and rest? Two very practical things must be done throughout the remaining generations of history:
⇒ The church must provide other services through the week for worship and rest, provide them for people who have to work on Saturday or Sunday.
⇒ People who work on the regular day of worship and rest must still worship God and rest at the alternate services and days scheduled by the church.

> **"Not forsaking the assembling of ourselves together, as the manner of some is; but exhorting one another: and so much the more, as ye see the day approaching" (Heb.10:25).**
> **"And they went into Capernaum; and straightway on the sabbath day he [Jesus Christ] entered into the synagogue, and taught" (Mk.1:21).**
> **"And he came to Nazareth, where he had been brought up: and, as his <u>custom</u> was, he went into the synagogue on the sabbath day, and stood up for to read" (Lk.4:16).**
> **"But when they departed from Perga, they came to Antioch in Pisidia, and went into the synagogue on the sabbath day, and sat down" (Acts 13:14).**

b. When the law was given by Moses, the Jews set aside the seventh day, Saturday, as their day of worship and rest. Today, others follow their practice. But the largest body of Christian believers have switched their day of worship and rest from the last day of the week to the first day of the week, from Saturday to Sunday. Why?
⇒ Because Jesus Christ burst loose from the bonds of death on the first day of the week. Believers wish to celebrate His glorious resurrection and the great hope of their salvation on the very day He arose.
⇒ Because the first day of the week is called "the Lord's day" (Rev.1:10). Believers wish to worship on the Lord's day.
⇒ Because the early followers of Christ switched their day of worship and rest to the first day of the week. The tradition has continued down through the centuries.

> **"And upon the first day of the week, when the disciples came together to break bread, Paul preached unto them, ready to depart on the morrow; and continued his speech until midnight" (Acts 20:7).**

> **"Upon the first day of the week let every one of you lay by him in store, as God hath prospered him, that there be no gatherings when I come" (1 Cor.16:2).**

3.   The Sabbath, the day of rest and worship, is to be kept *holy*. The Sabbath...
*   is to be a day sanctified, set apart, devoted, dedicated, and consecrated to God for worship and rest.
*   is to be a day hallowed, honored, and made sacred in obedience to God and His command.
*   is to be a day that *focuses our minds* upon living pure and clean lives, lives that are free from all pollution and defilement, lives that are totally free from sin and evil.
*   is to be a day that is totally different and distinct from all other days of the world and their busy schedules.

Thought.

Holy means sanctified, separated, set apart, devoted, dedicated, consecrated, hallowed, honored, made sacred. It means to be pure, clean, and free from all pollution and defilement, totally free from sin and evil. It means to be totally different and distinct from anything else, from all that is in the world with all its corruption.[1]

> **"Exalt the LORD our God, and worship at his holy hill; for the LORD our God is holy" (Ps.99:9).**
> **"Wherefore come out from among them, and be ye separate, saith the Lord, and touch not the unclean thing; and I will receive you, And will be a Father unto you, and ye shall be my sons and daughters, saith the Lord Almighty. Having therefore these promises, dearly beloved, let us cleanse ourselves from all filthiness of the flesh and spirit, perfecting holiness in the fear of God" (2 Cor.6:17-7:1).**
> **"Follow peace with all men, and holiness, without which no man shall see the Lord" (Heb.12:14).**
> **"Because it is written, Be ye holy; for I am holy" (1 Pt.1:16).**
> **"Who shall not fear thee, O Lord, and glorify thy name? for thou only art holy: for all nations shall come and worship before thee; for thy judgments are made manifest" (Rev.15:4).**

4.   Note that two clear instructions are given by God, two demands, two "you shalls" concerning the Sabbath commandment:
⇒ You *shall* work six days, but only for six days (v.9).
⇒ You *shall not* do any work on the seventh day (v.10).

---

[1]   Harris, Archer, Waltke. *Theological Wordbook of the New Testament.* (Chicago, IL: Moody Bible Institute of Chicago, 1980), p.786-789.
Vine, Unger, White. *Vine's Complete Expository Dictionary of Old and New Testament Words.* (Nashville, TN: Thomas Nelson Publishers, 1985), p.113-114.
Francis Brown. *The New Brown-Driver-Briggs-Gesenius Hebrew-English Lexicon.* (Peabody, MA: Hendrickson Publishers, 1979), p.872-873.

a. **You shall work six days a week, but *only* six days (v.9).** This commandment declares that man is to work, to work diligently. From the very beginning of creation, God commanded man to work.

⇒ God told Adam (man) to dress and keep the Garden of Eden, to develop and maintain it.

> **"And the LORD God took the man, and put him into the garden of Eden to dress it and to keep it" (Gen.2:15).**

⇒ Scripture clearly says that a man must work if he is to eat and meet his needs.

> **"For even when we were with you, this we commanded you, that if any would not work, neither should he eat. For we hear that there are some which walk among you disorderly, working not at all, but are busybodies. Now them that are such we command and exhort by our Lord Jesus Christ, that with quietness they work, and eat their own bread" (2 Th.3:10-12).**

⇒ Scripture also says that a person should look after his own affairs and work with his own hands.

> **"And that ye study to be quiet, and to do your own business, and to work with your own hands, as we commanded you" (1 Th.4:11).**

What about people who have enough money, so much that they do not have to work? They have worked hard and earned huge amounts of money, or have inherited large estates, or won a large sum. Does this commandment apply to them? Yes. No person is ever to sit idle nor live an extravagant lifestyle, wasting and hoarding wealth. Scripture warns us: we are responsible to meet the needs of the world. Every person is to work as long as he lives, helping to conquer the evils of this earth—all the ravaging and destructive forces that bring suffering and destruction to man:

⇒ hunger   ⇒ loneliness
⇒ thirst   ⇒ emptiness
⇒ disease   ⇒ death, both physical and spiritual

> **"Jesus said unto him, If thou wilt be perfect, go [and] sell that thou hast, and give to the poor, and thou shalt have treasure in heaven: and come [and] follow me. But when the young man heard that saying, he went away sorrowful: for he had great possessions. Then said Jesus unto his disciples, Verily I say unto you, That a rich man shall hardly enter into the kingdom of heaven. And again I say unto you, It is eas-**

ier for a camel to go through the eye of a needle, than for a rich man
to enter into the kingdom of God" (Mt.19:21-24).

"And he spake a parable unto them, saying, The ground of a certain rich man brought forth plentifully: And he thought within himself, saying, What shall I do, because I have no room where to bestow
my fruits? And he said, This will I do: I will pull down my barns, and
build greater; and there will I bestow all my fruits and my goods.
And I will say to my soul, Soul, thou hast much goods laid up for
many years; take thine ease, eat, drink, [and] be merry. But God said
unto him, [Thou] fool, this night thy soul shall be required of thee:
then whose shall those things be, which thou hast provided? So [is] he
that layeth up treasure for himself, and is not rich toward God"
(Lk.12:16-21).

What about the people who are lazy and slothful, people who do not
give an honest day's work or else shun work altogether? Again, Scripture warns the lazy and slothful.

"Yet a little sleep, a little slumber, a little folding of the hands to
sleep: So shall thy poverty come as one that travelleth, and thy want
as an armed man" (Pr.6:10-11).
"For the drunkard and the glutton shall come to poverty: and
drowsiness shall clothe a man with rags" (Pr.23:21).
"He that tilleth his land shall have plenty of bread: but he that fol-
loweth after vain [unproductive] persons shall have poverty enough"
(Pr.28:19).

Man is to work six days a week. God created man with a nature that
must work. There is within man a restlessness, a drive, an energy to be
active, to work and achieve and conquer. Man never experiences complete fulfillment and satisfaction unless he works and senses that he
achieves something worthwhile. If man does not direct his energy into
profitable work, then he directs it to worthless or even destructive ac-
tivities: to lawlessness, gangs, mobs, war, sex, alcohol, drugs, over-
eating—all to the damage of others or himself. It is this—a lack of work
and a lack of sensing fulfillment and satisfaction—that causes so much
lawlessness and problems for society.

But note this fact: man is to work six days a week, but *only* six days
a week.

b. You shall not do any work on the seventh day, none whatsoever (v.10).
Note how strongly God expects this commandment to be obeyed: no
person is to work seven days a week...

- not you (male or female)
- not your son or daughter
- not your slaves (employees)
- not your animals
- not even a stranger

<u>Thought</u>.

The fourth commandment was given for our good. Without the Sabbath rest, we would soon break our bodies down. We would be constantly weary, worn out, and burned out. Productivity would soon decline. This has been proven time and again in dictatorial nations and slave markets that have demanded constant, unbroken work with no rest for its labor force. Productivity declined sharply, as well as health, physical strength, and mental alertness and ability.

Resting one day a week is an absolute essential for the human body. Business and labor, individuals and groups—we all must protect our bodies and the productivity of our society and economies. How? By obeying God's fourth commandment: Remember the Sabbath day; keep it holy—do not work on the Sabbath. Allow our bodies and minds to rest one day a week.

> "For in six days the LORD made heaven and earth, the sea, and all that in them is, and rested the seventh day: wherefore the LORD blessed the sabbath day, and hallowed it" (Ex.20:11).
>
> "Six days thou shalt do thy work, and on the seventh day thou shalt rest: that thine ox and thine ass may rest, and the son of thy handmaid, and the stranger, may be refreshed" (Ex.23:12).
>
> "Ye shall keep the sabbath therefore; for it is holy unto you" (Ex.31:14).

III. Why Did God Give This Commandment?

God gives two strong reasons why the Sabbath is to be kept.

1. Man needs a day of rest: he needs to rest and relax one day out of every seven (v.11^a). The LORD Himself created the earth in six days and then rested on the seventh day (Gen.2:1-3). The LORD showed man that there is a natural flow to life. For example, there is the natural flow of birth and growth, aging and dying, inhaling and exhaling air. On and on the list could go. But for the present point, there is the natural flow of day and night, of work and sleep. God knows this; He created the natural flow to life. Therefore, He knows that man must by nature rest as well as work. He knows that a person cannot just go on working day after day and week after week without a break from the routine. The human body could never stand up under such pressure. This is one of the major reasons for the Sabbath, that man might have a break in his normal work routine, that he might have a day given over to rest and relaxation.

2. Now note why the seventh day is to be a day of worship (v.11^b): because the LORD Himself blessed the Sabbath day and made it holy. He Himself set it apart as a special day, as a day when man would focus upon worshipping and honoring God.

Thought.

The Sabbath day is only a shadow—a picture, a type, a symbol—of the Lord Jesus Christ. This is exactly what Scripture says:

> **"Let no man therefore judge you in meat, or in drink, or in respect of an holyday, or of the new moon, or of the sabbath day: Which are a shadow of things to come; but the body is of Christ" (Col.2:16-17).**

The Sabbath rest and worship point to the Lord Jesus Christ; the Sabbath is a picture of the perfect rest and worship that Jesus Christ brings to man. The Sabbath gives man a day to rest and worship, but Jesus Christ gives man rest itself, a complete and perfect rest and a perfect worship, the perfect assurance that we are acceptable to God.

a) Jesus Christ gives us the rest of salvation and deliverance, rest from the burden of sin—the rest of the human soul.

> **"Come unto me, all [ye] that labour and are heavy laden, and I will give you rest. Take my yoke upon you, and learn of me; for I am meek and lowly in heart: and ye shall find rest unto your souls" (Mt.11:28-29).**

b) Jesus Christ gives us the rest of freedom, rest from the bondages and enslavements to sin.

> **"Who his own self bare our sins in his own body on the tree, that we, being dead to sins, should live unto righteousness: by whose stripes ye were healed" (1 Pt.2:24).**

c) Jesus Christ gives us rest from condemnation.

> **"There is therefore now no condemnation to them which are in Christ Jesus, who walk not after the flesh, but after the Spirit....For what the law could not do, in that it was weak through the flesh, God sending his own Son in the likeness of sinful flesh, and for sin, condemned sin in the flesh" (Ro.8:1, 3).**

d) Jesus Christ gives us the rest of conquest and victory, the glorious liberty of living a life above the terrible trials and sufferings of this world.

> **"Now thanks be unto God, which always causeth us to triumph in Christ, and maketh manifest the savour of his knowledge by us in every place" (2 Cor.2:14).**
>
> **"For whatsoever is born of God overcometh the world: and this is the victory that overcometh the world, even our faith. Who is he that**

overcometh the world, but he that believeth that Jesus is the Son of God?" (1 Jn.5:4-5).

e) Jesus Christ gives us the rest of guidance.

"Lo, I am with you alway, [even] unto the end of the world. Amen" (Mt.28:20).

"Howbeit when he, the Spirit of truth, is come, he will guide you into all truth" (Jn.16:13).

f) Jesus Christ gives us the rest of provision.

"But seek ye first the kingdom of God, and his righteousness; and all these things shall be added unto you" (Mt.6:33).

"The LORD is my shepherd; I shall not want. He maketh me to lie down in green pastures: he leadeth me beside the still waters. He restoreth my soul: he leadeth me in the paths of righteousness for his name's sake. Yea, though I walk through the valley of the shadow of death, I will fear no evil: for thou art with me; thy rod and thy staff they comfort me. Thou preparest a table before me in the presence of mine enemies: thou anointest my head with oil; my cup runneth over. Surely goodness and mercy shall follow me all the days of my life: and I will dwell in the house of the LORD for ever" (Ps.23:1-6).

g) Jesus Christ gives us the rest of assurance, the assurance of security and protection.

"Who shall separate us from the love of Christ? shall tribulation, or distress, or persecution, or famine, or nakedness, or peril, or sword?...Nay, in all these things we are more than conquerors through him that loved us. For I am persuaded, that neither death, nor life, nor angels, nor principalities, nor powers, nor things present, nor things to come, Nor height, nor depth, nor any other creature, shall be able to separate us from the love of God, which is in Christ Jesus our Lord" (Ro.8:35, 37-39).

h) Jesus Christ gives us the rest of a fruitful life, the rest of satisfaction and fulfillment.

"I am come that they might have life, and that they might have [it] more abundantly" (Jn.10:10).

i) Jesus Christ gives us the rest of eternal life.

"In my Father's house are many mansions: if [it were] not [so], I would have told you. I go to prepare a place for you. And if I go and prepare a place for you, I will come again, and receive you unto myself; that where I am, [there] ye may be also" (Jn.14:2-3).

j) Jesus Christ gives us the rest of peace and rest from anxiety.

> "Peace I leave with you, my peace I give unto you: not as the world giveth, give I unto you. Let not your heart be troubled, neither let it be afraid" (Jn.14:27).
>
> "These things I have spoken unto you, that in me ye might have peace. In the world ye shall have tribulation: but be of good cheer; I have overcome the world" (Jn.16:33).
>
> "Be careful for nothing; but in every thing by prayer and supplication with thanksgiving let your requests be made known unto God. And the peace of God, which passeth all understanding, shall keep your hearts and minds through Christ Jesus" (Ph.4:6-7).
>
> "Casting all your care [anxiety] upon him; for he careth for you" (1 Pt.5:7).

IV. What Are the Consequences of Breaking This Commandment?

After creating the world in six days, God rested. He did not rest because He was tired and needed relaxation. God spent the seventh day resting in order to establish the Sabbath as a day of rest and worship for man. God set the pattern: man is to follow God's pattern, to obey His commandment, to remember the Sabbath day and to keep it holy. The very fact that God Himself rested on the Sabbath means that the day is of major importance: God expects man to observe the Sabbath, to keep it holy. God, in His infinite wisdom, knew that those who were made in His image needed to rest and worship one day a week. This is a commandment that God fully expects His people to obey. This is made perfectly clear throughout Scripture. Severe consequences fall upon people who do not keep the Sabbath, the day of rest and worship.

1.   The person who willingly does not keep the Sabbath disobeys God, stubbornly refuses to do what God has commanded. The man who *consistently* breaks this commandment, who never keeps the Sabbath (never worships God nor rests) puts his soul in grave, eternal danger. This person shows that he does not really believe God; therefore, he will not inherit the kingdom of God.

> "And let us consider one another to provoke unto love and to good works: <u>Not forsaking the assembling of ourselves together</u>, as the manner of some is; but exhorting one another: and so much the more, as ye see the day approaching. For if we sin wilfully after that we have received the knowledge of the truth, there remaineth no more sacrifice for sins, But a certain fearful looking for of judgment and fiery indignation, which shall devour the adversaries. He that despised Moses'

law died without mercy under two or three witnesses: Of how much sorer punishment, suppose ye, shall he be thought worthy, who hath trodden under foot the Son of God, and hath counted the blood of the covenant, wherewith he was sanctified, an unholy thing, and hath done despite unto the Spirit of grace? For we know him that hath said, Vengeance belongeth unto me, I will recompense, saith the Lord. And again, The Lord shall judge his people. It is a fearful thing to fall into the hands of the living God" (Heb.10:24-31).

"But the house of Israel rebelled against me in the wilderness: they walked not in my statutes, and they despised my judgments, which if a man do, he shall even live in them; and my sabbaths they greatly polluted: then I said, I would pour out my fury upon them in the wilderness, to consume them" (Ezk.20:13).

2. The person who does not keep the Sabbath displeases God and shall face the judgment of God.

a. The violators of the Sabbath faced the judgment of God in the Old Testament.

"Ye shall keep the sabbath therefore; for it is holy unto you: every one that defileth it shall surely be put to death: for whosoever doeth any work therein, that soul shall be cut off from among his people" (Ex.31:14).

"And while the children of Israel were in the wilderness, they found a man that gathered sticks upon the sabbath day. And they that found him gathering sticks brought him unto Moses and Aaron, and unto all the congregation. And they put him in ward [jail], because it was not declared what should be done to him. And the LORD said unto Moses, The man shall be surely put to death: all the congregation shall stone him with stones without the camp" (Num.15:32-35).

"Thou hast despised mine holy things, and hast profaned my sabbaths....And I will scatter thee among the heathen, and disperse thee in the countries, and will consume thy filthiness out of thee" (Ezk.22:8, 15).

b. The violators of the Sabbath will face the judgment of God according to the New Testament.

"Not forsaking the assembling of ourselves together, as the manner of some is; but exhorting one another: and so much the more, as ye see the day approaching. For if we sin wilfully after that we have received the knowledge of the truth, there remaineth no more sacrifice for sins, But a certain fearful looking for of judgment and fiery indignation, which shall devour the adversaries. He that despised Moses' law died without mercy under two or three witnesses: Of how much sorer punishment, suppose ye, shall he be thought worthy, who hath trodden under foot the Son of God, and hath counted the blood of the covenant, wherewith he was sanctified, an unholy thing, and hath done despite unto the Spirit of grace?" (Heb.10:25-29).

3. The person who does not keep the Sabbath breaks the clear commandment of God.

> "And it came to pass, that there went out some of the people on the seventh day for to gather [manna], and they found none. And the LORD said unto Moses, How long refuse ye to keep my commandments and my laws?" (Ex.16:27-28).
>
> "Remember the sabbath day, to keep it holy" (Ex.20:8).
>
> "Not forsaking the assembling of ourselves together, as the manner of some is; but exhorting one another: and so much the more, as ye see the day approaching" (Heb.10:25).

4. The person who does not keep the Sabbath profanes, desecrates, violates, and even ignores what God has called holy.

> "Ye shall keep the sabbath therefore; for it is holy unto you" (Ex.31:14).
>
> "Thou hast despised mine holy things, and hast profaned my sabbaths" (Ezk.22:8).
>
> "Then I contended with the nobles of Judah, and said unto them, What evil thing is this that ye do, and profane the sabbath day? Did not your fathers thus, and did not our God bring all this evil upon us, and upon this city? yet ye bring more wrath upon Israel by profaning the sabbath" (Neh.13:15-19).

5. The person who does not keep the Sabbath pollutes or desecrates the worship of God.

> "Little children, keep yourselves from idols. Amen" (1 Jn.5:21).
>
> "Because they had not executed my judgments, but had despised my statutes, and had polluted my sabbaths, and their eyes were after their fathers' idols" (Ezk.20:24).
>
> "Moreover this they have done unto me: they have defiled my sanctuary in the same day, and have profaned my sabbaths" (Ezk.23:38).

6. The person who does not keep the Sabbath loses out on the worship and fellowship with other believers.

> "And they continued stedfastly in the apostles' doctrine and fellowship, and in breaking of bread, and in prayers" (Acts 2:42).
>
> "Not forsaking the assembling of ourselves together, as the manner of some is; but exhorting one another: and so much the more, as ye see the day approaching" (Heb.10:25).

> "But if we <u>walk in the light</u>, as he is in the light, we have fellowship one with another, and the blood of Jesus Christ his Son cleanseth us from all sin" (1 Jn.1:7).
>
> "I am a companion of all them that fear thee, and of them that <u>keep thy precepts</u>" (Ps.119:63).

7. The person who does not keep the Sabbath gives occasion for others to judge and criticize him.

> "Let no man therefore judge you in meat, or in drink, or in respect of an holyday, or of the new moon, or of the sabbath days: Which are a shadow of things to come; but the body is of Christ" (Col.2:16-17).
>
> "Who art thou that judgest another man's servant? to his own master he standeth or falleth. Yea, he shall be holden up: for God is able to make him stand. One man esteemeth one day above another: another esteemeth every day alike. Let every man be fully persuaded in his own mind. He that regardeth the day, regardeth it unto the Lord; and he that regardeth not the day, to the Lord he doth not regard it....For whether we live, we live unto the Lord; and whether we die, we die unto the Lord: whether we live therefore, or die, we are the Lord's" (Ro.14:4-6, 8).
>
> "Let us not therefore judge one another any more: but judge this rather, that no man put a stumblingblock or an occasion to fall in his brother's way" (Ro.14:13).

8. The person who observes the Sabbath and stresses the keeping of the Sabbath over meeting the needs of people becomes *legalistic and rigid.* The legalist shall be judged and condemned by his own actions.

> "And, behold, there was a man which had [his] hand withered. And they asked him, saying, Is it lawful to heal on the sabbath days? that they might accuse him. And he said unto them, What man shall there be among you, that shall have one sheep, and if it fall into a pit on the sabbath day, will he not lay hold on it, and lift [it] out? How much then is a man better than a sheep? Wherefore it is lawful to do well on the sabbath days. Then saith he to the man, Stretch forth thine hand. And he stretched [it] forth; and it was restored whole, like as the other" (Mt.12:10-13).
>
> "And the ruler of the synagogue answered with indignation, because that Jesus had healed on the sabbath day, and said unto the people, There are six days in which men ought to work: in them therefore come and be healed, and not on the sabbath day. The Lord then answered him, and said, [Thou] hypocrite, doth not each one of you on the sabbath loose his ox or [his] ass from the stall, and lead [him] away to watering? And ought not this woman, being a daughter of Abraham, whom Satan hath bound, lo, these eighteen years, be loosed from this bond on the sabbath day?" (Lk.13:14-16).

> "For as many as are of the works of the law are under the curse: for it is written, Cursed is every one that continueth not in all things which are written in the book of the law to do them" (Gal.3:10).

V.   What Are the Benefits of Keeping This Commandment?

When God requires something of His people, it is always for their good. Always. The same is true concerning the Sabbath. For our own good we are to remember the Sabbath and keep it holy.

1.   The person who keeps the Sabbath and trusts God will find rest, both *physical and spiritual rest*.

> "Six days thou shalt do thy work, and on the seventh day thou shalt rest: that thine ox and thine ass may rest, and the son of thy handmaid, and the stranger, may be refreshed" (Ex.23:12).
> "There remaineth therefore a rest to the people of God. For he that is entered into his rest, he also hath ceased from his own works, as God did from his. Let us labour therefore to enter into that rest, lest any man fall after the same example of unbelief" (Heb.4:9-11).

2.   The person who follows God will keep the Sabbath and live a sanctified life, a life set apart by God.

> "Speak thou also unto the children of Israel, saying, Verily my sabbaths ye shall keep: for it is a sign between me and you throughout your generations; that ye may know that I am the LORD that doth sanctify you" (Ex.31:13).

3.   The person who obeys God by keeping the Sabbath will be given an everlasting name.

> "For thus saith the LORD unto the eunuchs [committed believers] that keep my sabbaths, and choose the things that please me, and take hold of my covenant; Even unto them will I give in mine house and within my walls a place and a name better than of sons and of daughters: I will give them an everlasting name, that shall not be cut off" (Is.56:4-5).

4.   The person who loves the LORD and keeps the Sabbath will inherit God's holy mountain (a symbol of heaven) and experience the joy of having his prayers answered.

> "Also the sons of the stranger, that join themselves to the LORD, to serve him, and to love the name of the LORD, to be his servants, every one that keepeth the sabbath from polluting it, and taketh hold of my

covenant; Even them will I bring to my holy mountain, and make them joyful in my house of prayer: their burnt offerings and their sacrifices shall be accepted upon mine altar; for mine house shall be called an house of prayer for all people" (Is.56:6-7).

5.   The person who follows the LORD and keeps the true spirit of the Sabbath will do acts of mercy and good on the Sabbath day.

"And, behold, there was a man which had his hand withered. And they asked him, saying, Is it lawful to heal on the sabbath days? that they might accuse him. And he said unto them, What man shall there be among you, that shall have one sheep, and if it fall into a pit on the sabbath day, will he not lay hold on it, and lift it out? How much then is a man better than a sheep? Wherefore it is lawful to do well on the sabbath days. Then saith he to the man, Stretch forth thine hand. And he stretched it forth; and it was restored whole, like as the other" (Mt.12:10-13).

"And Jesus answering spake unto the lawyers and Pharisees, saying, Is it lawful to heal on the sabbath day? And they held their peace. And he took him, and healed him, and let him go; And answered them, saying, Which of you shall have an ass or an ox fallen into a pit, and will not straightway pull him out on the sabbath day? And they could not answer him again to these things" (Lk.14:3-6).

6.   The person who keeps the Sabbath will be able to enjoy the special day that was made for him.

"And he said unto them, The sabbath was made for man, and not man for the sabbath: Therefore the Son of man is Lord also of the sabbath" (Mk.2:27-28).

7.   The person who truly follows the LORD and keeps the Sabbath will be filled with joy and be victorious throughout life.

"If thou turn away thy foot from the sabbath, from doing thy pleasure on my holy day; and call the sabbath a delight, the holy of the LORD, honourable; and shalt honour him, not doing thine own ways, nor finding thine own pleasure, nor speaking thine own words: Then shalt thou delight thyself in the LORD; and I will cause thee to ride upon the high places of the earth, and feed thee with the heritage of Jacob thy father: for the mouth of the LORD hath spoken it" (Is.58:13-14).

VI. What Is the Teaching of Jesus Christ Concerning This Commandment?

1.   Jesus Christ declared that He is the LORD of the Sabbath.

> "For the Son of man is Lord even of the sabbath day" (Mt.12:8).
> "Therefore the Son of man is Lord also of the sabbath" (Mk.2:28).

Thought.

Jesus Christ is the Source and LORD of the Sabbath. As the Source and LORD of the Sabbath, Jesus Christ wants us to know that He and He alone has the right...

*   to determine how the Sabbath is to be used
*   to determine how we are to rest on the Sabbath
*   to determine how we are to worship God on the Sabbath

> "For in six days the LORD made heaven and earth, the sea, and all that in them is, and rested the seventh day: wherefore the LORD blessed the sabbath day, and hallowed it" (Ex.20:11).
> "But I say unto you, That in this place is [one] greater than the temple. But if ye had known what [this] meaneth, I will have mercy, and not sacrifice, ye would not have condemned the guiltless. For the Son of man is Lord even of the sabbath day" (Mt.12:6-8).
> "And the ruler of the synagogue answered with indignation, because that Jesus had healed on the sabbath day, and said unto the people, There are six days in which men ought to work: in them therefore come and be healed, and not on the sabbath day. The Lord then answered him, and said, [Thou] hypocrite, doth not each one of you on the sabbath loose his ox or [his] ass from the stall, and lead [him] away to watering? And ought not this woman, being a daughter of Abraham, whom Satan hath bound, lo, these eighteen years, be loosed from this bond on the sabbath day? And when he had said these things, all his adversaries were ashamed: and all the people rejoiced for all the glorious things that were done by him" (Lk.13:14-17).
> "And it came to pass, as he went into the house of one of the chief Pharisees to eat bread on the sabbath day, that they watched him. And, behold, there was a certain man before him which had the dropsy. And Jesus answering spake unto the lawyers and Pharisees, saying, Is it lawful to heal on the sabbath day? And they held their peace. And he took him, and healed him, and let him go; And answered them, saying, Which of you shall have an ass or an ox fallen into a pit, and will not straightway pull him out on the sabbath day?" (Lk.14:1-5).

2.   Jesus Christ declared that the Sabbath was made for man and not man for the Sabbath.

> "And it came to pass, that he went through the corn fields on the sabbath day; and his disciples began, as they went, to pluck the ears of

corn. And the Pharisees said unto him, Behold, why do they on the sabbath day that which is not lawful?...And he said unto them, The sabbath was made for man, and not man for the sabbath" (Mk.2:23-24, 27).

Thought.

We must never be rigid and inflexible in what we allow and disallow on the Sabbath, so rigid that we bind ourselves to a life of legalism instead of grace (cp. 1 Sam.6:1-6).

> "There is therefore now no condemnation to them which are in Christ Jesus, who walk not after the flesh, but after the Spirit" (Ro.8:1).
> "Stand fast therefore in the liberty wherewith Christ hath made us free, and be not entangled again with the yoke of bondage" (Gal.5:1).

3.   Jesus Christ declared that it is sometimes a necessity to work on the Sabbath.

> "And it came to pass on the second sabbath after the first, that he went through the corn fields; and his disciples plucked the ears of corn, and did eat, rubbing them in their hands" (Lk.6:1).
> "Then said Jesus unto them, I will ask you one thing; Is it lawful on the sabbath days to do good, or to do evil? to save life, or to destroy it? And looking round about upon them all, he said unto the man, Stretch forth thy hand. And he did so: and his hand was restored whole as the other" (Lk.6:9-10).

Thought 1.

When businesses have to operate seven days a week, what are the employees of these businesses to do about worship and rest? Two very practical things must be done throughout the remaining generations of history:
a)   The church must provide other services through the week for worship and rest, provide them for people who have to work Saturday or Sunday.
b)   People who work on the regular day of worship and rest must still worship God and rest at the alternative services and days scheduled by the church.

> "Not forsaking the assembling of ourselves together, as the manner of some is; but exhorting one another: and so much the more, as ye see the day approaching" (Heb.10:25).
> "And he came to Nazareth, where he had been brought up: and, as his custom was, he went into the synagogue on the sabbath day, and stood up for to read" (Lk.4:16).
> "But when they departed from Perga, they came to Antioch in Pisidia, and went into the synagogue on the sabbath day, and sat down" (Acts 13:14).

Thought 2.

There are many people who have to work on Sunday:

⇒ medical workers   ⇒ pastors   ⇒ media personnel (tele-
⇒ policemen   ⇒ missionaries   vision, radio, etc.)
⇒ firemen   ⇒ maintenance workers   ⇒ professional athletes

As demanding as these and other professions are, every person *still needs* a day in the week for worship and rest. We must never get so busy that we forget the LORD. God knows us better than we do; therefore He knows how easily we slip into bad habits. God will not strike us down and kill us if we fail to keep the Sabbath, but we will be destroying ourselves.

> "And it came to pass, that there went out some of the people on the seventh day for to gather, and they found none. And the LORD said unto Moses, How long refuse ye to keep my commandments and my laws?" (Ex.16:27-28).
>
> "Ye shall keep the sabbath therefore; for it is holy unto you: every one that defileth it shall surely be put to death: for whosoever doeth any work therein, that soul shall be cut off from among his people" (Ex.31:14).
>
> "But the house of Israel rebelled against me in the wilderness: they walked not in my statutes, and they despised my judgments, which if a man do, he shall even live in them; and my sabbaths they greatly polluted: then I said, I would pour out my fury upon them in the wilderness, to consume them" (Ezk.20:13).
>
> "Thou hast despised mine holy things, and hast profaned my sabbaths" (Ezk.22:8).

4.   Jesus Christ taught that a person should worship on the day of rest, taught the truth by example.

> "And he came to Nazareth, where he had been brought up: and, as his <u>custom</u> was, he went into the synagogue on the sabbath day, and stood up for to read" (Lk.4:16).

Thought.

We must obey God and follow the example of the Lord Jesus Christ. In fact, we must be diligent and strict in following Christ: we must worship on the day of rest, worship the LORD our God.

> "And when the sabbath day was come, he began to teach in the synagogue: and many hearing him were astonished, saying, From whence hath this man these things? and what wisdom is this which is given unto him, that even such mighty works are wrought by his hands?" (Mk.6:2).

"And came down to Capernaum, a city of Galilee, and taught them on the sabbath days" (Lk.4:31).

"But when they [Paul and his company] departed from Perga, they came to Antioch in Pisidia, and went into the synagogue on the sabbath day, and sat down" (Acts 13:14).

"And when the Jews were gone out of the synagogue, the Gentiles besought that these words might be preached to them the next sabbath" (Acts 13:42).

"And the next sabbath day came almost the whole city together to hear the word of God" (Acts 13:44).

"For Moses of old time hath in every city them that preach him, being read in the synagogues every sabbath day" (Acts 15:21).

"And on the sabbath we went out of the city by a river side, where prayer was wont to be made; and we sat down, and spake unto the women which resorted thither" (Acts 16:13).

"And Paul, as his manner was, went in unto them, and three sabbath days reasoned with them out of the scriptures" (Acts 17:2).

"And he reasoned in the synagogue every sabbath, and persuaded the Jews and the Greeks" (Acts 18:4).

5. Jesus Christ gives us rest. The word "sabbath" means rest; therefore, the Sabbath is a symbol of the rest that comes only from having a relationship with Jesus Christ.

a. Jesus Christ gives us the rest of *SALVATION AND DELIVERANCE*.

"Behold, God is my salvation; I will trust, and not be afraid: for the LORD Jehovah is my strength and my song; he also is become my salvation" (Is.12:2).

"The LORD is my light and my salvation; whom shall I fear? the LORD is the strength of my life; of whom shall I be afraid?" (Ps.27:1).

"But the salvation of the righteous is of the LORD: he is their strength in the time of trouble" (Ps.37:39).

"For the Son of man is come to seek and to save that which was lost" (Lk.19:10).

"Who gave himself for our sins, that he might deliver us from this present evil world, according to the will of God and our Father" (Gal.1:4).

"Wherefore he is able also to save them to the uttermost that come unto God by him, seeing he ever liveth to make intercession for them" (Heb.7:25).

b. Jesus Christ gives us the rest of *ASSURANCE*.

"My sheep hear my voice, and I know them, and they follow me: And I give unto them eternal life; and they shall never perish, neither shall any [man] pluck them out of my hand. My Father, which gave

[them] me, is greater than all; and no [man] is able to pluck [them] out of my Father's hand" (Jn.10:27-29).

"Being confident of this very thing, that he which hath begun a good work in you will perform it until the day of Jesus Christ" (Ph.1:6).

"For I know whom I have believed, and am persuaded that he is able to keep that which I have committed unto him against that day" (2 Tim.1:12).

"Let us draw near with a true heart in full assurance of faith, having our hearts sprinkled from an evil conscience, and our bodies washed with pure water" (Heb.10:22).

"Now unto him that is able to keep you from falling, and to present you faultless before the presence of his glory with exceeding joy, To the only wise God our Saviour, be glory and majesty, dominion and power, both now and ever. Amen" (Jude 1:24-25).

c. Jesus Christ gives us the rest of *SECURITY*.

"When thou liest down, thou shalt not be afraid: yea, thou shalt lie down, and thy sleep shall be sweet" (Pr.3:24).

"When thou passest through the waters, I will be with thee; and through the rivers, they shall not overflow thee: when thou walkest through the fire, thou shalt not be burned; neither shall the flame kindle upon thee" (Is.43:2).

"Who shall separate us from the love of Christ? shall tribulation, or distress, or persecution, or famine, or nakedness, or peril, or sword?...Nay, in all these things we are more than conquerors through him that loved us. For I am persuaded, that neither death, nor life, nor angels, nor principalities, nor powers, nor things present, nor things to come, Nor height, nor depth, nor any other creature, shall be able to separate us from the love of God, which is in Christ Jesus our Lord" (Ro.8:35, 37-39).

"Nevertheless the foundation of God standeth sure, having this seal, The Lord knoweth them that are his. And, Let every one that nameth the name of Christ depart from iniquity" (2 Tim.2:19).

"So that we may boldly say, The Lord is my helper, and I will not fear what man shall do unto me" (Heb.13:6).

d. Jesus Christ gives us the rest of *PROVISION*, of daily bread and every other human need.

"Behold the fowls of the air: for they sow not, neither do they reap, nor gather into barns; yet your heavenly Father feedeth them. Are ye not much better than they?" (Mt.6:26).

"But seek ye first the kingdom of God, and his righteousness; and all these things shall be added unto you" (Mt.6:33).

"But my God shall supply all your need according to his riches in glory by Christ Jesus" (Ph. 4:19).

"Thou preparest a table before me in the presence of mine enemies: thou anointest my head with oil; my cup runneth over" (Ps.23:5).

"For since the beginning of the world men have not heard, nor perceived by the ear, neither hath the eye seen, O God, beside thee, what he hath prepared for him that waiteth for him" (Is.64:4).

e. Jesus Christ gives us the rest of *CONQUEST AND VICTORY* over sin and death.

"These things I have spoken unto you, that in me ye might have peace. In the world ye shall have tribulation: but be of good cheer; I have overcome the world" (Jn.16:33).

"Nay, in all these things we are more than conquerors through him that loved us" (Ro.8:37).

"There hath no temptation taken you but such as is common to man: but God is faithful, who will not suffer you to be tempted above that ye are able; but will with the temptation also make a way to escape, that ye may be able to bear it" (1 Cor.10:13).

"Now thanks be unto God, which always causeth us to triumph in Christ, and maketh manifest the savour of his knowledge by us in every place" (2 Cor.2:14).

"(For the weapons of our warfare are not carnal, but mighty through God to the pulling down of strong holds;) Casting down imaginations, and every high thing that exalteth itself against the knowledge of God, and bringing into captivity every thought to the obedience of Christ" (2 Cor.10:4-5).

"For whatsoever is born of God overcometh the world: and this is the victory that overcometh the world, even our faith. Who is he that overcometh the world, but he that believeth that Jesus is the Son of God?" (1 Jn.5:4-5).

f. Jesus Christ gives us the rest of *A FULFILLED LIFE.*

"...I am come that they might have life, and that they might have it more abundantly" (Jn.10:10).

"And God is able to make all grace abound toward you; that ye, always having all sufficiency in all things, may abound to every good work" (2 Cor.9:8).

"Now unto him that is able to do exceeding abundantly above all that we ask or think, according to the power that worketh in us" (Eph.3:20).

"For I am now ready to be offered, and the time of my departure is at hand. I have fought a good fight, I have finished my course, I have kept the faith: Henceforth there is laid up for me a crown of righteousness, which the Lord, the righteous judge, shall give me at that day: and not to me only, but unto all them also that love his appearing" (2 Tim.4:6-8).

"And God gave Solomon wisdom and understanding exceeding much, and largeness of heart, even as the sand that is on the sea shore" (1 Ki.4:29).

g. Jesus Christ gives us the rest of *ETERNAL LIFE.*

"Then shall the King say unto them on his right hand, Come, ye blessed of my Father, inherit the kingdom prepared for you from the foundation of the world" (Mt.25:34).

"For God so loved the world, that he gave his only begotten Son, that whosoever believeth in him should not perish, but have everlasting life" (Jn.3:16).

"Labour not for the meat which perisheth, but for that meat which endureth unto everlasting life, which the Son of man shall give unto you: for him hath God the Father sealed" (Jn.6:27).

"And I give unto them eternal life; and they shall never perish, neither shall any man pluck them out of my hand" (Jn.10:28).

"In hope of eternal life, which God, that cannot lie, promised before the world began" (Tit.1:2).

"Keep yourselves in the love of God, looking for the mercy of our Lord Jesus Christ unto eternal life" (Jude 1:21).

"Surely goodness and mercy shall follow me all the days of my life: and I will dwell in the house of the LORD for ever" (Ps.23:6).

h. Jesus Christ gives us the rest of *THE HUMAN SOUL.*

"And fear not them which kill the body, but are not able to kill the soul: but rather fear him which is able to destroy both soul and body in hell" (Mt.10:28).

"Take my yoke upon you, and learn of me; for I am meek and lowly in heart: and ye shall find rest unto your souls" (Mt.11:29).

"In a moment, in the twinkling of an eye, at the last trump: for the trumpet shall sound, and the dead shall be raised incorruptible, and we shall be changed. For this corruptible must put on incorruption, and this mortal must put on immortality. So when this corruptible shall have put on incorruption, and this mortal shall have put on immortality, then shall be brought to pass the saying that is written, Death is swallowed up in victory. O death, where is thy sting? O grave, where is thy victory? The sting of death is sin; and the strength of sin is the law. But thanks be to God, which giveth us the victory through our Lord Jesus Christ" (1 Cor.15:52-57).

"And I saw thrones, and they sat upon them, and judgment was given unto them: and I saw the souls of them that were beheaded for the witness of Jesus, and for the word of God, and which had not worshipped the beast, neither his image, neither had received his mark upon their foreheads, or in their hands; and they lived and reigned with Christ a thousand years" (Rev.20:4).

i. Jesus Christ gives us the rest of *PEACE, THE REST FROM ANXIETY*.

> "Peace I leave with you, my peace I give unto you: not as the world giveth, give I unto you. Let not your heart be troubled, neither let it be afraid" (Jn.14:27).
>
> "These things I have spoken unto you, that in me ye might have peace. In the world ye shall have tribulation: but be of good cheer; I have overcome the world" (Jn.16:33).
>
> "But the fruit of the Spirit is love, joy, peace, longsuffering, gentleness, goodness, faith" (Gal.5:22).
>
> "Grace and peace be multiplied unto you through the knowledge of God, and of Jesus our Lord" (2 Pt.1:2).
>
> "For he [Jesus Christ] is our peace, who hath made both one, and hath broken down the middle wall of partition between us" (Eph.2:14).
>
> "Be careful for nothing; but in every thing by prayer and supplication with thanksgiving let your requests be made known unto God. And the peace of God, which passeth all understanding, shall keep your hearts and minds through Christ Jesus" (Ph.4:6-7).
>
> "And let the peace of God rule in your hearts, to the which also ye are called in one body; and be ye thankful" (Col.3:15).
>
> "Therefore being justified by faith, we have peace with God through our Lord Jesus Christ" (Ro.5:1).
>
> "And the very God of peace sanctify you wholly; and I pray God your whole spirit and soul and body be preserved blameless unto the coming of our Lord Jesus Christ" (1 Th.5:23).
>
> "Casting all your care upon him; for he careth for you" (1 Pt.5:7).
>
> "Thou wilt keep him in perfect peace, whose mind is stayed on thee: because he trusteth in thee" (Is.26:3).

Thought.

The Sabbath is a picture of the perfect rest that Jesus Christ brings to a person. The Sabbath gives a person a day to rest and worship, but...

- Jesus Christ gives a person rest itself, a complete rest, a perfect rest of mind and soul.
- Jesus Christ gives a person the perfect assurance that we are acceptable to God.

A person is to be faithful to worship and rest on the Sabbath, as God has ordained. It is only through obedience to God's command that we are able to receive the perfect rest that only God can give.

> "Remember the sabbath day, to keep it holy. Six days shalt thou labour, and do all thy work: But the seventh day is the sabbath of the LORD thy God: in it thou shalt not do any work, thou, nor thy son, nor thy daughter, thy manservant, nor thy maidservant, nor thy cattle, nor thy stranger that is within thy gates: For in six days the LORD made heaven and earth, the sea, and all that in them is, and rested the sev-

enth day: wherefore the LORD blessed the sabbath day, and hallowed it" (Ex.20:8-11).

"There remaineth therefore a rest to the people of God. For he that is entered into his rest, he also hath ceased from his own works, as God did from his. Let us labour therefore to enter into that rest, lest any man fall after the same example of unbelief" (Heb.4:9-11).

"Come unto me, all ye that labour and are heavy laden, and I will give you rest" (Mt.11:28).

"But they that wait upon the LORD shall renew their strength; they shall mount up with wings as eagles; they shall run, and not be weary; and they shall walk, and not faint" (Is.40:31).

"For the Son of man is Lord even of the sabbath day" (Mt.12:8; cp. Mk. 2:27-28).

VII. What Is the Decision Required by This Commandment?

People from every nation must obey the charge to remember the Sabbath and to keep the Sabbath holy. The fourth commandment is stated positively: we are to...

- remember the Sabbath day
- keep it holy
- work for six days of the week
- rest on the seventh day
- follow God's example of setting the Sabbath day aside, using it as a day of rest and worship

The fourth commandment requires a personal choice, a choice that will greatly improve our lives if we will obey God and keep the commandment. Note the teaching of Scripture, the decisions demanded by this commandment:

1.   We must follow the Lord's example of worshipping one day a week, consistently and regularly.

> "And he [Jesus Christ] came to Nazareth, where he had been brought up: and, as his custom was, he went into the synagogue on the sabbath day, and stood up for to read" (Lk.4:16).

2.   We must not forsake our worship, the assembling together with other believers.

> "Not forsaking the assembling of ourselves together, as the manner of some is; but exhorting one another: and so much the more, as ye see the day approaching" (Heb.10:25).

3.   We are to bring our offerings to the LORD on the day of worship.

> "Upon the first day of the week let every one of you lay by him in store, as God hath prospered him, that there be no gatherings when I come" (1 Cor.16:2).

4.   We must not fail to worship regularly lest others criticize our testimony for Christ.

> "One man esteemeth one day above another: another esteemeth every day alike. Let every man be fully persuaded in his own mind. He that regardeth the day, regardeth it unto the Lord; and he that regardeth not the day, to the Lord he doth not regard it. He that eateth, eateth to the Lord, for he giveth God thanks; and he that eateth not, to the Lord he eateth not, and giveth God thanks" (Ro.14:5-6).

5.   We must work six days and then rest and worship on the Sabbath.

> "Remember the sabbath day, to keep it holy. Six days shalt thou labour, and do all thy work: But the seventh day is the sabbath of the LORD thy God: in it thou shalt not do any work, thou, nor thy son, nor thy daughter, thy manservant, nor thy maidservant, nor thy cattle, nor thy stranger that is within thy gates" (Ex.20:8-10).

6.   We must keep the Sabbath, not just do what we want to do or feel like doing on the Sabbath.

> "Ye shall fear every man his mother, and his father, and keep my sabbaths: I am the LORD your God" (Lev.19:3).
> "If thou turn away thy foot from the sabbath, from doing thy pleasure on my holy day; and call the sabbath a delight, the holy of the LORD, honourable; and shalt honour him, not doing thine own ways, nor finding thine own pleasure, nor speaking thine own words: Then shalt thou delight thyself in the LORD; and I will cause thee to ride upon the high places of the earth, and feed thee with the heritage of Jacob thy father: for the mouth of the LORD hath spoken it" (Is.58:13-14).

7.   We must rejoice and be glad on the Sabbath, for it is the day the LORD has made.

> "This is the day which the LORD hath made; we will rejoice and be glad in it" (Ps.118:24).

Part Two: The Laws Governing Man's Duty to Others

"Commandment
Five...

Commandment Five Concerns the Family—Never Dishonor Parents Exodus 20:12

Contents

Commandment Five Concerns the Family—Never Dishonor Parents
Exodus 20:12

COMMANDMENT 5: Concerns *man's family*: Honor your father & mother	12 Honour thy father and thy mother: that thy days may be long upon the land which the LORD thy God giveth thee.

The family is of vital importance, for the family was the *first institution* formed upon earth. God created the first man and woman, Adam and Eve, and they became man and wife; then Eve bore a son. Thereby, the first family was formed, created as the most important institution, as the foundation of all human life and development that was to follow. It is the family that forms the community, society, and government of nations. It is not enough for men and women to exist. Men and women must become fathers and mothers. They must give birth to children or else everything human eventually ceases to exist:

⇒ Human life would stop.

⇒ Human society would stop.

⇒ Human government would stop.

The family—father, mother, and child—is the most important institution, the very foundation of society, communities, and nations. As goes the family, so goes society.

The point: every generation must give attention to the family and strengthen it if the human race is to survive. We are fools if we do not strengthen our families, do not strengthen them for our generation and for future generations. The very survival of society and civilization depends upon strong families, upon fathers, mothers, and children who honor and respect one another. For this reason, we must give attention and fight against the evils of men, the evils that destroy us all...

- selfishness & greed
- disrespect
- disobedience
- rebellion
- withdrawal & coldness
- bitterness
- revenge
- hatred
- hostility
- abuse
- murder
- adultery
- immorality
- ungodliness
- indulgence & license
- alcohol, drugs
- gambling
- irresponsibility
- materialism
- unbelief
- lawlessness

God established the primacy and importance of the family forever when He created the first man and the first woman. He reinforces the primacy of the family with this great commandment: "Honor your father and your mother" (v.12). This is the subject of the present commandment: *Commandment Five Concerns the Family—Never Dishonor Parents*, 20:12.

I. Who Is to Obey This Commandment?

Who is to obey his father and his mother? Everyone of us. Just think for a moment: every person upon earth has, or has had in the past, a father and mother! God commands us—everyone of us—to honor and respect our fathers and mothers. What about abusive parents? They will be discussed in a later point, but for now the point is this: God expects us, He commands us, to honor and respect our fathers and mothers.

How long was this commandment to be in force? Was it meant for Israel alone, meant only for the ancient world? Or has there always been a need for children to honor and respect their parents? How about today? Is there a need today for us to honor our fathers and mothers?

The answer is obvious. In fact, each of the Ten Commandments meets a very specific need of man, a desperate need that has to be met or else man and society will be destroyed. Glance quickly at each of the commandments and this fact is clearly seen.

The point is just this: God loves man and has determined that man must be saved not destroyed. Therefore, God has reached out to man in giving man the Ten Commandments to govern his life and community.

If the family disintegrated, then all the great virtues of life to keep him from destroying himself would soon disappear: honor, respect, concern, responsibility, decency, love, joy, peace—true love, joy, and peace. When the great virtues are weakened, community and society are weakened. How long then is the fifth commandment to be in force? How many generations of people are to honor their parents? As long as men and women and children live upon earth, we are to honor and obey our parents.

> "Children, obey your parents in the Lord: for this is right. Honour thy father and mother; (which is the first commandment with promise;) That it may be well with thee, and thou mayest live long on the earth" (Eph.6:1-3).

II.   What Is the Charge of This Commandment?

The first four commandments covered our duty to God. But once we have done our duty to God, note what our very next duty is: to honor our parents.
⇒ The divine order is just this: God first, then our parents.

Note six points about the charge of this commandment.
1.   The Hebrew word "honor" (kabed) means that we are to respect, esteem, and highly regard our parents. There is even the idea of reverence in the word *honor*: we are to *reverence* our parents. The Greek word for "honor" (timao) pictures exactly what is meant: it means that we are to esteem and value our parents as precious (Amplified Bible); to show them respect, reverence, kindness, and obedience. Matthew Henry says that in practical terms, the commandment means we are to...
  * respect our parents and reverence them
  * obey our parents
  * submit to the rebukes, instructions, and corrections of our parents
  * listen to our parents' advice, direction, and concern
  * comfort our parents[1]

Thought.
What does God mean by *honoring our parents*? Scripture tells us:

a)   To honor means to obey and respect our parents.

> "For Moses said, Honour thy father and thy mother; and, Whoso curseth father or mother, let him die the death" (Mk.7:10).
> "Children, obey your parents in the Lord: for this is right. Honour thy father and mother; (which is the first commandment with

---
[1]   Matthew Henry. *Matthew Henry's Commentary*, p. 361-362.

promise;) That it may be well with thee, and thou mayest live long on the earth" (Eph.6:1-3).

"Children, obey your parents in all things: for this is well pleasing unto the Lord" (Col.3:20).

"Honour thy father and thy mother: that thy days may be long upon the land which the LORD thy God giveth thee" (Ex.20:12).

"Honour thy father and thy mother, as the LORD thy God hath commanded thee; that thy days may be prolonged, and that it may go well with thee, in the land which the LORD thy God giveth thee" (Dt.5:16).

"For God commanded, saying, Honour thy father and mother: and, He that curseth father or mother, let him die the death" (Mt.15:4).

b) To honor means to listen to the instructions of our parents; to obey the instructions, never forsaking them.

"My son, hear the instruction of thy father, and forsake not the law of thy mother" (Pr.1:8).

"Hear, ye children, the instruction of a father, and attend to know understanding....Hear, O my son, and receive my sayings; and the years of thy life shall be many. I have taught thee in the way of wisdom; I have led thee in right paths. When thou goest, thy steps shall not be straitened [hampered, NIV]; and when thou runnest, thou shalt not stumble. Take fast hold of instruction; let her not go: keep her; for she is thy life" (Pr.4:1, 10-13).

"My son, keep thy father's commandment, and forsake not the law of thy mother" (Pr.6:20).

c) To honor means to listen to our parents and never despise them when they are old.

"Hearken unto thy father that begat thee, and despise not thy mother when she is old" (Pr.23:22).

d) To honor means to be wise, never foolish.

"A wise son maketh a glad father: but a foolish son is the heaviness of his mother" (Pr.10:1).

"A wise son maketh a glad father: but a foolish man despiseth his mother" (Pr.15:20).

e) To honor means to have a testimony of pure and right behavior.

"Even a child is known by his doings, whether his work [behavior, conduct] be pure, and whether it be right" (Pr.20:11).

f) To honor means to respect and reverence our parents when they are elderly.

> "Ye shall fear every man his mother, and his father, and keep my sabbaths: I am the LORD your God" (Lev.19:3).
>
> "Thou shalt rise up before the hoary [gray] head, and honour the face of the old man, and fear thy God: I am the LORD" (Lev.19:32).
>
> "And Elihu the son of Barachel the Buzite answered and said, I am young, and ye are very old; wherefore I was afraid, and durst not show you mine opinion" (Job 32:6).
>
> "Hearken unto thy father that begat thee, and despise not thy mother when she is old" (Pr.23:22).

g) To honor means to accept the true faith of our parents, their belief in God's Son, the Lord Jesus Christ.

> "When I call to remembrance the unfeigned faith that is in thee, which dwelt first in thy grandmother Lois, and thy mother Eunice; and I am persuaded that in thee also" (2 Tim.1:5).
>
> "And that from a child thou hast known the holy scriptures, which are able to make thee wise unto salvation through faith which is in Christ Jesus" (2 Tim.3:15).

h) To honor means to respect our parents so much that it carries over to others, honoring and respecting all persons.

> "Rebuke not an elder, but intreat him as a father; and the younger men as brethren" (1 Tim.5:1).

2. Note that mothers are to be honored just as much as fathers, and fathers just as much as mothers: "[Children] honor your father and your mother" (v.12). Mothers and fathers are placed on equal footing. God Himself honors and respects mothers as much as fathers and charges all children to honor each equally.

3. Note that every person within the family is mentioned: the child, the mother, and the father. If our mothers and fathers are living, we are to honor and respect them. But note this fact as well: every person in the world, whether young or old (adult), is the child of some father and mother. Thus if every child showed honor and respect to his parents, then the very air of honor and respect would likely carry over to others. Honor and respect would catch aflame and spread throughout the world.

The implication is clear: the families of the earth and the world as a whole are to be filled with honor and respect. Honor and respect are to flood the hearts and lives of our families. If this will take place, then honor and respect will flow out and flood society and civilization. Subsequently, the whole world would be filled with honor and respect. This is God's will; this is one of the main reasons God has given this commandment.

Note: the family is the basic unit of society, the very foundation of society. If honor and respect control the behavior of the family, it will help to control the behavior of our communities and society. God wants *honor and respect* to be the prevailing force flowing out from the hearts of people to one another. God knows:

⇒ if we honor and respect one another, then peace and love will prevail upon the earth.

⇒ if we honor and respect one another, then the behavior of men will be controlled.

⇒ if we honor and respect one another, there will be no lawlessness and selfishness. There will be only honor and respect for all people—for all the parents and children of the earth.

Thought.

William Barclay makes three points that should stir us to keep this commandment, to always honor our parents:

"With the fifth commandment we come right home, for the fifth commandment is 'Honour your father and your mother' (Exodus 20:12). Of all the commandments this should be the easiest to obey.

"i. It should be easy to obey this commandment because it is natural to do so. This commandment is, as it were, built into the very structure of life. It is not a commandment which we find only in the Bible. There never was a society of any kind in which this commandment was not accepted as binding. In ancient Greece, for instance, Solon the great lawgiver laid it down that, if a son did not support his parents in their old age, when they needed support, he should lose his rights as a citizen. The Greeks believed that to honour parents is part of the basic duty of every citizen of the state. Anyone who has good parents and who does not realise the duty of honouring them is an unnatural person. Nature itself demands that we keep this commandment.

"ii. It is a duty of gratitude to keep this commandment. It was our parents who brought us into this world, and we owe them our lives. Of all living creatures man takes longest to become able to support and look after himself.

"There is a long time when we cannot get ourselves a home or food or clothes, and when we are entirely dependent on our parents; and there is a considerable part of that time when we are so helpless, that a blow would kill us, and, even if nothing was done to us, and we were just alone, we would certainly die. We ought to find it easy to keep this commandment, if only as a matter of gratitude to those to whom we literally owe the fact that we came into the world, and that we survived through the years when we were quite unable to help ourselves, or to get the things necessary to keep body and soul together.

"Apart from that purely physical side of life, many of us owe a great deal to the care and the love and even to the sacrifice of our parents to give us a good start in life....We ought to be grateful that in many, many homes the parents do without things and plan and save so that their children should have a chance to do well in life. Of all faults, ingratitude is the ugliest and the most hurting, and not to keep this commandment is to be guilty of ingratitude.

"iii.   To honour our parents is a matter of common sense. They have walked the journey of life before us, and therefore they know the dangers and the pitfalls in the way. If you are going on a journey through what is to you an unknown country, a map and a guide-book will be very useful, but most useful of all will be the advice and the experience of one who has already travelled that way.

"When parents advise their child to do or not to do something, he should understand that it is not because they wish to show their authority or because they are killjoys or because they are old-fashioned, it is because out of their experience they know that the thing is right or wrong, safe or dangerous.

"The man who will not listen to the voice of experience will certainly end in trouble—and he will deserve all that is coming to him....

"It is sensible to listen to what our parents tell us, because they have an experience of life that we do not yet possess."[2]

4.   Note that this commandment emphasizes one of the great lessons of life, that we learn by example. Children are to learn to honor their parents. How? By the parents showing honor to their parents. The commandment charges all children to honor their parents. Even if they are adults and parents themselves, the adult child is to honor and respect his parents. Parents are to create an atmosphere of honor and respect in the home. By so doing, the parent teaches— sets an example—for his child to honor him. This commandment stresses the awesome importance of parents setting the right example before their children.

> **"In all things showing thyself a pattern of good works: in doctrine showing uncorruptness, gravity, sincerity" (Tit.2:7).**
> **"Train up a child in the way he should go: and when he is old, he will not depart from it" (Pr.22:6).**

God makes it clear: parents have the obligation to teach this commandment and all the other commandments to their children.

---

[2]   William Barclay. *The Old Law & The New Law*, p.24-26.

"And thou shalt teach them [the commandments] diligently unto thy children, and shalt talk of them when thou sittest in thine house, and when thou walkest by the way, and when thou liest down, and when thou risest up" (Dt.6:7).

"And, ye fathers, provoke not your children to wrath: but bring them up in the nurture and admonition of the Lord" (Eph.6:4).

5.   What about parents who neglect their children or who abuse their children? Are children to honor and respect parents who are evil, who live in sin and abuse them? The Preacher's Outline & Sermon Bible® (N.T. Vol.9) has an excellent comment on this point that is quoted at length because of its importance:

"Children obey your parents in the Lord: for this is right" (Eph.6:1).

"Children are to obey their parents. The word 'obey' (hupakouo) means to submit to; to comply with; to hearken; to heed; to follow the directions or guidance of some instruction. When a parent guides and directs a child, the child is to obey the parent. But what about the problems that are so repulsively evident in society: the problems of parental abuse—the problems of physical abuse, sexual abuse, and mental abuse? Is a child to obey a parent when the parent is so devilishly wrong? No! A thousand times no!

"To obey means to obey *in the Lord*. Note the command again: 'Children, obey your parents in the Lord.' The phrase 'in the Lord' means at least two things.

a. "There is a limit to the child's obedience. When a parent is not acting in the Lord, he is not to be obeyed. The Lord has nothing whatsoever to do with the filth of unrighteousness and abuse of precious children. If a child can break away and free himself from such parental corruption, he has every right to be freed from his parent. The Lord came to set men free from the abuse and the filth of sin, not to enslave men to it, and especially not to enslave children to it.

"One of the most severe warnings ever issued in all of history was issued by the Lord Jesus to adults who abuse children:

"And whosoever shall offend one of these little ones that believe in me, it is better for him that a millstone were hanged about his neck, and he were cast into the sea. And if thy hand offend thee [by abusing a child], cut it off: it is better for thee to enter into life maimed, than having two hands to go into hell, into the fire that never shall be quenched: where their worm dieth not, and the fire is not quenched. And if thy foot offend thee [by abusing a child], cut it off: it is better for thee to enter halt into life, than having two feet to be cast into hell, into the fire that never shall be quenched: where their worm dieth not, and the fire is not quenched. And if thine eye offend thee [by lusting after a child], pluck it out: it is better for thee

to enter into the kingdom of God with one eye, than having two eyes to be cast into hell fire: where their worm dieth not, and the fire is not quenched" (Mk.9:42-48).

"The abusing parent had better heed, for one of the things that God will not tolerate—absolutely not tolerate—is the abuse of a child. We must proclaim the Word of God: children are to obey their parents, but they are to obey only if the parents' desire and instructions are *in the Lord*. If a parent is beating a child black and blue or sexually abusing a child, the child should go to some other adult he feels close to and ask for help. And ministers of the Lord—ministers who are called to proclaim Christ and to do what they can to bring His righteousness to earth—must teach the truth from the pulpits of the world.

b. "The phrase 'in the Lord' also tells why the child is to obey his parents. 'Children, obey your parents in the Lord'—obeying your parents is right; it is of the Lord; it pleases the Lord; therefore, obey them. When they guide and instruct you, follow them (cp. Col.3:20).

"Lehman Strauss points out that obedience is the first law of the universe—that the law of obedience regulates everything in the world: the stars, the planets, the seasons. Even man himself tries to govern the world by the law of obedience. He wants obedience in the state, at work, at play, and at home.[3] The point is simply this: the law of obedience is the very nature of things, at the very core of the universe and of man's life and behavior upon earth. Therefore, it is to be expected that God would command children to obey their parents. Children are to obey—obey because it pleases the Lord and it is the right thing to do.

"Note the emphasis here; it is striking. Children are not told to obey parents because it pleases the parent, but because it pleases the Lord. Pleasing one's parents is, of course, a reason for obeying them. But the *first* reason for obeying parents is that it pleases the Lord. The child is to know the Lord to such a degree that he is continually thinking about the Lord and about pleasing Him. The child is to walk so closely with the Lord that his mind is constantly upon the Lord—upon what he can do to please the Lord. When the child so knows the Lord, then obeying his parents will become an automatic response."[4]

"For Moses said, Honour thy father and thy mother; and, Whoso curseth father or mother, let him die the death" (Mk.7:10).
"Children, obey your parents in the Lord: for this is right" (Eph.6:1).

---

3 Lehman Strauss. *Devotional Studies in Galatians & Ephesians*. (Neptune, NJ: Loizeaux Brothers, 1957), p.212.
4 *Galatians, Ephesians, Philippians, Colossians*, Vol.9. "The Preacher's Outline & Sermon Bible"®. (Chattanooga, TN: Leadership Ministries Worldwide, 1991), p.219-220.

"Children, obey your parents in all things: for this is well pleasing unto the Lord" (Col.3:20).

"My son, hear the instruction of thy father, and forsake not the law of thy mother" (Pr.1:8; cp. Pr.6:20; 23:22).

"My son keep my words, and lay up my commandments with thee" (Pr.7:1).

"A wise son maketh a glad father: but a foolish son is the heaviness of his mother" (Pr.10:1).

"Even a child is known by his doings, whether his work be pure, and whether it be right" (Pr.20:11).

"Remember now thy Creator in the days of thy youth, while the evil days come not, nor the years draw nigh, when thou shalt say, I have no pleasure in them" (Eccl.12:1).

6.   What about abusive children, children who abuse their parents? Again, The Preacher's Outline & Sermon Bible® (N.T. Vol.9) has an excellent statement covering this point:

"To obey parents means to honor one's father and mother. The word 'honor' (timao) means to 'esteem and value as precious' (The Amplified New Testament); to show respect, reverence, kindness, courtesy, and obedience.[5] Scripture is not speaking to any certain age child. It is speaking to all of us who are children with parents still living. We are to honor our fathers and mothers: *to esteem and value them as precious*—to respect and reverence them. Tragically, this is a rarity today. Too often a child's response to his parent is that of...

- talking back
- cutting the parent
- ignoring the parent
- grumbling
- disregarding instructions

- not listening
- speaking disrespectfully
- acting like a 'know it all'
- calling the parent a cute but *disrespectful* name

"In addition to these, there is the dishonor of delinquency, crime, drugs, alcohol, and the abuse of property; and the list could go on and on. And when it comes to adult children with aged parents, there is the dishonor of neglect, the ignoring of their needs and the shuffling of them to the side and failing to adequately care for them. Too many adult children forget how much their parents have done for them—bringing them into the world and taking care of them for years. Too many children forget the rich experience and knowledge that their parents have gained through the years and that could be put to great use in meeting community and world needs. And even if the parents failed to be and to do all they should have, we as Christian

---

[5]   Kenneth S. Wuest. *Ephesians and Colossians*. "Word Studies in the Greek New Testament," Vol.1. (Grand Rapids, MI: Eerdmans Publishing Co., 1966), p.136.

children are instructed to honor them as followers of the Lord Jesus Christ."[6]

> **"Children, obey your parents in the Lord: for this is right" (Eph.6:1).**
>
> **"But if any widow have children or nephews, let them learn first to show piety at home, and to requite [repay, pay back] their parents: for that is good and acceptable before God....But if any provide not for his own, and specially for those of his own house, he hath denied the faith, and is worse than an infidel" (1 Tim.5:4, 8).**
>
> **"Whoso curseth his father or his mother, his lamp shall be put out in obscure darkness" (Pr.20:20).**
>
> **"The eye that mocketh at his father, and despiseth to obey his mother, the ravens of the valley shall pick it out, and the young eagles shall eat it" (Pr.30:17).**
>
> **"Honour thy father and thy mother: that thy days may be long upon the land which the LORD thy God giveth thee" (Ex.20:12).**
>
> **"Ye shall fear every man his mother, and his father, and keep my sabbaths: I am the LORD your God" (Lev.19:3).**
>
> **"Thou shalt rise up before the hoary [gray] head, and honor the face of the old man, and fear thy God: I am the LORD" (Lev.19:32).**
>
> **"Cursed be he that setteth light by his father or his mother: and all the people shall say, Amen" (Dt.27:16).**

Thought.

Maxie Dunnam warns us about making a "cult of the child" within society, showing how this attitude teaches children to be disrespectful and disobedient.

> "I'm concerned about the extreme to which we have gone with the cult of the child during the past thirty or forty years in the United States. To be sure, we needed to give more attention to children. The adage 'Children are to be seen and not heard' was a caricature of children treated as wards and, in the extreme in many cultures, as chattel. So we needed to get away from that. But as is so often the case, the pendulum swung too far. We reared our children to be self-centered. We ordered our worlds around not only their needs, but their whims. Our thinking about discipline was distorted. We spared the rod and spoiled the child. There was no center of authority around which the child could order his life, no clear guidelines or directions, no well-defined values. And so respect was diminished, especially at the point of children listening and being obedient. This was not so much the child's fault as the parent's default."[7]

---

[6] *Galatians, Ephesians, Philippians, Colossians*, Vol.9. "The Preacher's Outline & Sermon Bible"®, p.219-220.

[7] Maxie Dunnam. *Mastering the Old Testament, Volume 2: Exodus*, p.261-262.

III. What Are the Two Great Promises Attached to This Commandment?

Every person should seek diligently to lay hold of these two very specific promises covered by this Scripture.

1. The person who honors his parents will live an extended life upon earth (v.12b). Common sense tells us this. A tension-filled home—a home full of arguments, bickering, abuse, and divisiveness—causes all kinds of physical and emotional problems, shortening the life of family members. Whereas a home filled with love, joy, and peace strengthens the health and emotional stability of a person, thereby adding years to a person's life.

God knows what He is talking about; He knows exactly what He is promising. If the Israelites would teach their children to honor their parents, then generations of Israelite homes would be filled with love, joy, and peace. Maxie Dunnam has an excellent thought on the importance of the family to Israel that sets a dynamic example for every civilization:

> "I believe one of the primary reasons Judaism has survived across the years is precisely its family structure. The Jews survived the Holocaust and thousands of years of anti-Semitism because the Jewish family had a sense of identity and a sense of order. It doesn't matter where the family is on the Sabbath, when the Sabbath comes, they stop and pray. It didn't matter what Hitler and all the powers of Nazism said, when Passover came it was time to tell the story, even if the family was gathered in a concentration camp and there were no candles to light. There was a sense of order and identity that gave them roots and strength and perspective and discipline. At the heart of that family structure was a reverence for parents, a high regard, a respect, an esteem for the older members of the family. The elderly were honored and cared for."[8]

2. The person who honors his parents will inherit *the promised land* (v.12c). This was a glorious promise to the Israelites: if they would honor their parents, they would have a long reign in *the promised land*. But the converse is implied as well: if they dishonored their parents, they would live for only a short time in *the promised land*.

Note how *the promised land* is tied to honoring one's parents. This does not mean that a person who honors his parents will necessarily inherit eternal life. God does not use this commandment (to honor our parents) to set up a merit system to reach the promised land of heaven. What God means is this: a person who truly follows and honors God will obey God: he will keep this com-

---

8   Maxie Dunnam. *Mastering the Old Testament, Volume 2: Exodus*, p.261.

mandment; he will honor his parents. And because he believes and obeys God, he will inherit the promised land.

Thought.
In practical terms, Scripture tells us exactly what God means by this commandment.
a) To honor our parents means to respect and to reverence our parents.
b) To honor our parents means to obey our parents.

> "Children, obey your parents in the Lord: for this is right. Honour thy father and mother; (which is the first commandment with promise;) That it may be well with thee, and thou mayest live long on the earth" (Eph.6:1-3).
>
> "Children, obey your parents in all things: for this is well pleasing unto the Lord" (Col.3:20).

IV.   What Are the Consequences of Breaking This Commandment?

> "Honour thy father and thy mother" (Ex.20:12).

This commandment is stated in the positive: it is a gracious invitation by God to obey. If a person obeys, God promises to bless him mightily. But if the person breaks this commandment, he faces terrible consequences.

1.   A person who does not honor his parents—*consistently*, over the course of time—is in serious jeopardy of affecting his eternal destiny. The man who is marked by the deeds of the sinful nature cannot and will not honor his parents. Scripture says this person will not inherit the kingdom of God.

> "Now the works of the flesh are manifest, which are these; Adultery, fornication, uncleanness, lasciviousness, Idolatry, witchcraft, hatred, variance, emulations, wrath, strife, seditions, heresies, Envyings, murders, drunkenness, revellings, and such like: of the which I tell you before, as I have also told you in time past, that they which do such things shall not inherit the kingdom of God" (Gal.5:19-21).
>
> "And even as they did not like to retain God in their knowledge, God gave them over to a reprobate mind, to do those things which are not convenient; Being filled with all unrighteousness, fornication, wickedness, covetousness, maliciousness; full of envy, murder, debate, deceit, malignity; whisperers, Backbiters, haters of God, despiteful, proud, boasters, inventors of evil things, disobedient to parents, Without understanding, covenantbreakers, without natural affection, implacable, unmerciful: Who knowing the judgment of God, that they which commit such things are worthy of death, not only do the same, but have pleasure in them that do them" (Ro.1:28-32).

"This know also, that in the last days perilous times shall come. For men shall be lovers of their own selves, covetous, boasters, proud, blasphemers, <u>disobedient to parents</u>, unthankful, unholy, Without natural affection, trucebreakers, false accusers, incontinent, fierce, despisers of those that are good, Traitors, heady, highminded, lovers of pleasures more than lovers of God; Having a form of godliness, but denying the power thereof: from such turn away. For of this sort are they which creep into houses, and lead captive silly women laden with sins, led away with divers lusts, Ever learning, and never able to come to the knowledge of the truth. Now as Jannes and Jambres withstood Moses, so do these also resist the truth: men of corrupt minds, reprobate concerning the faith" (2 Tim.3:1-8).

2. A person who does not honor his parents brings the full judgment of God upon himself.

"And he that smiteth his father, or his mother, shall be surely put to death" (Ex.21:15).

"The eye that mocketh at his father, and despiseth to obey his mother, the ravens of the valley shall pick it out, and the young eagles shall eat it" (Pr.30:17).

"For every one that curseth his father or his mother shall be surely put to death: he hath cursed his father or his mother; his blood shall be upon him" (Lev.20:9).

"Not every one that saith unto me, Lord, Lord, shall enter into the kingdom of heaven; but he that doeth the will of my Father which is in heaven" (Mt.7:21).

3. A person who does not honor his parents fills the home with hatred.

"For the son dishonoureth the father, the daughter riseth up against her mother, the daughter in law against her mother in law; a man's enemies are the men of his own house" (Mic.7:6).

"Better is a dry morsel, and quietness therewith, than an house full of sacrifices with strife. A wise servant shall have rule over a son that causeth shame, and shall have part of the inheritance among the brethren" (Pr.17:1-2).

"As coals are to burning coals, and wood to fire; so is a contentious man to kindle strife" (Pr.26:21).

4. A person who does not honor his parents causes his parents to become heavy in spirit and broken-hearted.

"And the king [David] was much moved, and went up to the chamber over the gate, and wept: and as he went, thus he said, O my son Absalom, my son, my son Absalom! would God I had died for thee, O Absalom, my son, my son!" (2 Sam.18:33. Absalom had committed insurrection against his father and been killed.)

"A wise son maketh a glad father: but a foolish son is the heaviness of his mother" (Pr.10:1).

5. A person who does not honor his parents shames and disgraces his parents.

"He that wasteth his father, and chaseth away his mother, is a son that causeth shame, and bringeth reproach" (Pr.19:26).

"The rod and reproof give wisdom: but a child left to himself bringeth his mother to shame" (Pr.29:15).

6. A person who does not honor his parents will cause his parents to suffer great sorrow and regret, losing their joy.

"He that begetteth a fool doeth it to his sorrow: and the father of a fool hath no joy" (Pr.17:21).

7. A person who does not honor his parents is marked by destruction.

"Whoso robbeth his father or his mother, and saith, It is no transgression; the same is the companion of a destroyer" (Pr.28:24).

8. A person who does not honor his parents has the haunting testimony of a fool.

"He that begetteth a fool doeth it to his sorrow: and the father of a fool hath no joy" (Pr.17:21).

"A foolish son is the calamity of his father: and the contentions of a wife are a continual dropping" (Pr.19:13).

9. A person who curses his father and mother is not cleansed from his filth.

"There is a generation that curseth their father, and doth not bless their mother....[those who] are pure in their own eyes, and yet is not washed from their filthiness" (Pr.30:11-12).

V.   What Are the Benefits of Keeping This Commandment?

There are wonderful blessings in store for those who keep this commandment.

1. A person who honors his parents will make his father glad.

"A wise son maketh a glad father: but a foolish man despiseth his mother" (Pr.15:20).

2. A person who honors his parents helps to extend his life and makes things go better (far better than a tension-filled home).

> "Honour thy father and thy mother, as the LORD thy God hath commanded thee; that thy days may be prolonged, and that it may go well with thee, in the land which the LORD thy God giveth thee" (Dt.5:16).
> "That it may be well with thee, and thou mayest live long on the earth" (Eph.6:3).

3. A person who honors his parents will greatly influence his own children to do what is right.

> "And he did that which was right in the sight of the LORD, and walked in all the way of David his father, and turned not aside to the right hand or to the left" (2 Ki.22:2).
> "When I call to remembrance the unfeigned faith that is in thee, which dwelt first in thy grandmother Lois, and thy mother Eunice; and I am persuaded that in thee also" (2 Tim.1:5).

4. A person who honors his parents will gain wisdom and understanding from parents who have experienced life.

> "Hear, ye children, the instruction of a father, and attend to know understanding" (Pr.4:1).

5. A person who honors his parents will learn how to discern between good and bad company.

> "Whoso keepeth the law is a wise son: but he that is a companion of riotous men shameth his father" (Pr.28:7).

6. A person who honors his parents will appreciate the discipline his parents applied during his childhood.

> "The rod and reproof give wisdom: but a child left to himself bringeth his mother to shame" (Pr.29:15).

7. A person who honors his parents will have a good testimony to show the world.

> "Even a child is known by his doings, whether his work be pure, and whether it be right" (Pr.20:11).

8.   A person who honors his parents will be in a right relationship with God and man.

> **"Children, obey your parents in the Lord: for this is right" (Eph.6:1).**

9.   A person who honors his parents will inherit the promised land of heaven.

> **"Honour thy father and thy mother: that thy days may be long upon the land [promised land, a symbol of heaven] which the Lord thy God giveth thee" (Ex.20:12).**
>
> **"Honour thy father and mother; (which is the first commandment with promise)" (Eph.6:2).**

10. A person who honors his parents will always have God's care, even if his parents fail him.

> **"When my father and my mother forsake me, then the Lord will take me up" (Ps.27:10).**

11. A person who honors his parents will be blessed as he keeps God's commandments.

> **"Now therefore hearken unto me, O ye children: for blessed are they that keep my ways" (Pr.8:32).**

12. A person who honors his parents will be more likely to come to know Christ and the truth of the Scriptures.

> **"When I call to remembrance the unfeigned faith that is in thee, which dwelt first in thy grandmother Lois, and thy mother Eunice; and I am persuaded that in thee also" (2 Tim.1:5).**
>
> **"And that from a child thou hast known the holy scriptures, which are able to make thee wise unto salvation through faith which is in Christ Jesus"(2 Tim.3:15).**

VI.   What Is the Teaching of Jesus Christ Concerning This Commandment?

1.   Jesus Christ declared that children are to honor their parents.

> **"For God commanded, saying, Honour thy father and mother: and, He that curseth father or mother, let him die the death" (Mt.15:4).**
>
> **"Thou knowest the commandments, Do not commit adultery, Do not kill, Do not steal, Do not bear false witness, Honour thy father and thy mother" (Lk.18:20).**

Thought.

Scripture is clear. There should be no misunderstanding: we are to honor and obey our parents.

> "Children, obey your parents in the Lord: for this is right" (Eph.6:1).
> "Children, obey your parents in all things: for this is well pleasing unto the Lord" (Col.3:20).

2. Jesus Christ declared that it is wrong to break God's commandment (honor your father and mother).

> "But he answered and said unto them, Why do ye also transgress the commandment of God by your tradition? For God commanded, saying, Honour thy father and mother: and, He that curseth father or mother, let him die the death. But ye say, Whosoever shall say to [his] father or [his] mother, [It is] a gift, by whatsoever thou mightest be profited by me; And honour not his father or his mother, [he shall be free]. Thus have ye made the commandment of God of none effect by your tradition. [Ye] hypocrites, well did Esaias prophesy of you, saying, This people draweth nigh unto me with their mouth, and honoureth me with [their] lips; but their heart is far from me. But in vain they do worship me, teaching [for] doctrines the commandments of men" (Mt.15:3-9).

Thought.

We must never twist God's Word to excuse us from our duty to take care of our parents. We must never ignore our parents. We must pledge total obedience to God's Word and honor our parents...
- no matter how unpopular it is to do so
- no matter how much it goes against the grain of society
- no matter how much help and care they need

> "He answered and said unto them, Well hath Esaias prophesied of you hypocrites, as it is written, This people honoureth me with [their] lips, but their heart is far from me. Howbeit in vain do they worship me, teaching [for] doctrines the commandments of men. For laying aside the commandment of God, ye hold the tradition of men, [as] the washing of pots and cups: and many other such like things ye do" (Mk.7:6-8).
> "Making the word of God of none effect through your tradition, which ye have delivered: and many such like things do ye" (Mk.7:13).
> "Children, obey your parents in the Lord: for this is right. Honour thy father and mother; (which is the first commandment with promise;) That it may be well with thee, and thou mayest live long on the earth" (Eph.6:1-3).

"But whoso looketh into the perfect law of liberty, and continueth therein, he being not a forgetful hearer, but a doer of the work, this man shall be blessed in his deed" (Jas.1:25).

"Thou shalt rise up before the hoary [gray] head, and honour the face of the old man, and fear thy God: I am the LORD" (Lev.19:32).

"O that there were such an heart in them, that they would fear me, and keep all my commandments always, that it might be well with them, and with their children for ever!" (Dt.5:29).

"And if thou wilt walk in my ways, to keep my statutes and my commandments, as thy father David did walk, then I will lengthen thy days" (1 Ki.3:14).

"Hearken unto thy father that begat thee, and despise not thy mother when she is old" (Pr.23:22).

3.   Jesus Christ declared that in the case of marriage, a man must leave his parents and cleave to his wife.

"For this cause [starting another home] shall a man leave his father and mother, and cleave to his wife" (Mk.10:7).

Thought.
A man leaves his father and mother and cleaves to his wife, creating a new family distinct from the family of his parents. The union between husband and wife is to gain primacy over the union between parent and child. *Leaving* is a permanent act; *cleaving* is also a permanent act.

"Therefore shall a man leave his father and his mother, and shall cleave unto his wife: and they shall be one flesh" (Gen.2:24).

"What therefore God hath joined together, let not man put asunder" (Mk.10:9).

"For the woman which hath an husband is bound by the law to her husband so long as he liveth; but if the husband be dead, she is loosed from the law of her husband" (Ro.7:2).

"And unto the married I command, yet not I, but the Lord, Let not the wife depart from her husband: But and if she depart, let her remain unmarried, or be reconciled to her husband: and let not the husband put away his wife" (1 Cor.7:10-11).

4.   Jesus Christ declared that the person who loved his parents or anyone else in his family more than Christ was not worthy of Christ.

"He that loveth father or mother more than me is not worthy of me: and he that loveth son or daughter more than me is not worthy of me" (Mt.10:37).

<u>**Thought.**</u>

We must love God supremely, putting Him before all others, even before our families (cp. Mt.6:33). A man's decision to follow Christ, no matter the sacrifice to his family, is a wise decision; in fact, it is the only reasonable decision (Ro.12:1-2).

> "If any man come to me, and hate not his father, and mother, and wife, and children, and brethren, and sisters, yea, and his own life also, he cannot be my disciple" (Lk.14:26).
>
> "Anyone who wants to be my follower must love me far more than he does his own father, mother, wife, children, brothers, or sisters—yes, more than his own life—otherwise he cannot be my disciple" (Lk.14:26, LIVING BIBLE).
>
> "Jesus said unto him, Thou shalt love the Lord thy God with all thy heart, and with all thy soul, and with all thy mind. This is the first and great commandment" (Mt.22:37-38).
>
> "I beseech you therefore, brethren, by the mercies of God, that ye present your bodies a living sacrifice, holy, acceptable unto God, which is your reasonable service. And be not conformed to this world: but be ye transformed by the renewing of your mind, that ye may prove what is that good, and acceptable, and perfect, will of God" (Ro.12:1-2).

VII. What Is the Decision Required by This Commandment?

Simply stated, obedience. Without a doubt, many of the world's problems—perhaps most—would be solved if the fifth commandment were obeyed. The fifth commandment is stated positively: we are to honor our fathers and our mothers. Note the teaching of Scripture, the decisions demanded by this commandment:

1. We are to honor our parents because it is the right thing to do.

> "Children, obey your parents in the Lord: for this is right" (Eph.6:1).
> "Children, obey your parents in all things: for this is well pleasing unto the Lord" (Col.3:20).

2. We are to honor our parents because it helps to extend our lives and makes things go better (far better than a tension-filled home).

> "Honour thy father and thy mother, as the LORD thy God hath commanded thee; that thy days may be prolonged, and that it may go well with thee, in the land which the LORD thy God giveth thee" (Dt.5:16; cp. 1 Pt.3:10-12).

3. We are to honor our parents because it is one of God's Ten great Commandments.

> "Honour thy father and thy mother: that thy days may be long upon the land which the LORD thy God giveth thee" (Ex.20:12).

4. We are to fear, reverence, and respect our parents.

> "Ye shall fear every man his mother, and his father, and keep my sabbaths: I am the LORD your God" (Lev.19:3).

5. We are to obey our parents "in the Lord."

> "Children, obey your parents in the Lord: for this is right" (Eph.6:1).

6. We are to keep and follow the teaching of our parents.

> "My son, keep thy father's commandment, and forsake not the law of thy mother: Bind them continually upon thine heart, and tie them about thy neck. When thou goest, it shall lead thee; when thou sleepest, it shall keep thee; and when thou awakest, it shall talk with thee. For the commandment is a lamp; and the law is light; and reproofs of instruction are the way of life: To keep thee from the evil woman, from the flattery of the tongue of a strange woman" (Pr.6:20-24).

7. We are to heed the Christian witness of our parents.

> "When I call to remembrance the unfeigned faith that is in thee, which dwelt first in thy grandmother Lois, and thy mother Eunice; and I am persuaded that in thee also" (2 Tim.1:5).
> "And that from a child thou hast known the holy scriptures, which are able to make thee wise unto salvation through faith which is in Christ Jesus" (2 Tim.3:15).

8. We are to honor our parents even when we become adults.

> "And Joseph brought them [his father and brothers] out from between his knees, and he bowed himself with his face to the earth" (Gen.48:12).
> "Bath-sheba therefore went unto king Solomon, to speak unto him for Adonijah. And the king rose up to meet her, and bowed himself unto her, and sat down on his throne, and caused a seat to be set for the king's mother; and she sat on his right hand" (1 Ki.2:19).
> "Hearken unto thy father that begat thee, and despise not thy mother when she is old" (Pr.23:22).

9. We are to follow the example of Christ in obeying and subjecting ourselves to our parents.

> "And he went down with them, and came to Nazareth, and was subject unto them: but his mother kept all these sayings in her heart" (Lk.2:51).

10. We are to provide for our parents when they become aged.

> "If any man or woman that believeth have widows, let them relieve them, and let not the church be charged; that it may relieve them that are widows indeed" (1 Tim.5:16).

11. We are not to deify our parents or family.

> "He that loveth father or mother more than me is not worthy of me: and he that loveth son or daughter more than me is not worthy of me" (Mt.10:37).

12. We must not follow in the steps of evil parents as some have done in the past.

> "Ahaziah the son of Ahab began to reign over Israel in Samaria the seventeenth year of Jehoshaphat king of Judah, and reigned two years over Israel. And he did evil in the sight of the LORD, and walked in the way of his father, and in the way of his mother, and in the way of Jeroboam the son of Nebat, who made Israel to sin" (1 Ki.22:51-52).
>
> "Forty and two years old was Ahaziah when he began to reign, and he reigned one year in Jerusalem. His mother's name also was Athaliah the daughter of Omri. He also walked in the ways of the house of Ahab: for his mother was his counseller to do wickedly" (2 Chron.22:2-3).
>
> "And she, being before instructed of her mother [Herodias], said, Give me here John Baptist's head in a charger" (Mt.14:8).

"Commandment Six...

Commandment Six Concerns Man's Life—Never Kill Exodus 20:13

Contents

Commandment Six Concerns Man's Life—Never Kill, Ex.20:13

COMMANDMENT 6: Concerns *man's life*—Never kill	13 Thou shalt not kill.

Murder, lawlessness, and violence are sweeping the earth. Hundreds of thousands of people are being murdered and slaughtered year after year. The dignity of man—man as the most glorious being, as the most honorable being and summit of creation—has been lost. The value of human life is almost worthless in some societies.

- Society after society considers human beings, even young children, to be nothing more than chattel property, laborers existing only for the ruling class and the wealthy.
- Society after society allows the constant barrage of violence and lawlessness to be shown in films and other media, shown even to small children—despite the undeniable impression printed upon the human mind and its terrible consequences.

People have become desensitized and hardened to lawlessness, violence, and killing. The front pages of newspapers and news reports of television and radio are usually filled with terrible crimes. In addition, the entertainment industry—television, movies, video games, music, books, magazines—focuses upon lawlessness, violence, and killing as well as immorality. The nobility of man—man as the most excellent creature—is being dragged through the mud and degraded by the corrupt minds of sinful and evil people.

The point is this: life is pictured as cheap by both the media and the entertainment industry of society. The mind of a person is bombarded by act after act of lawlessness, violence, and killing every day of his life—if he reads the newspaper, watches television, listens to the radio, or picks up a magazine.

Think about what has just been said: every day of a person's life is filled with images and thoughts of lawlessness, violence, and killing if he reads the newspaper, watches television, listens to the radio, or picks up a magazine.

No wonder we have become desensitized and hardened to violence and murder. No wonder life is so cheap and means so little to so many people. No wonder so many have become lawless and violent. No wonder so many assault and kill. We just see and hear so much about violence and killing every day of our lives.

This is the important subject of this commandment, a commandment so desperately needed: *Commandment Six Concerns Man's Life—Never Kill*, 20:13.

I. Who is to obey this commandment? How long was this commandment to be in force (v.13)?

II. What is forbidden by this commandment (v.13)?

III. What are the Biblical consequences of breaking this commandment?

IV. What are the Biblical benefits of keeping this commandment?

V. What is the teaching of Jesus Christ concerning this commandment?

VI. What is the decision required by this commandment (v.13)?

I. Who Is to Obey This Commandment? How Long Was This Commandment to Be in Force?

Was this commandment only to govern Israel and the ancient world? Was murder—lawlessness and violence—only a problem in the ancient world? The answer is obvious. One of the most terrible social ills down through history has been murder and the lawlessness and violence that surround murder. God gave this commandment to govern civilization, the societies of every generation of man. God gave this commandment to make communities and streets safe, our homes and businesses secure.

Now, who is to keep this commandment: "You shall not murder" (v.13)? *You*! The commandment is forceful; it is directed to *you* personally, to every person upon this earth: "*You* shall not murder." The motives and emotions that arouse a person to murder—the desires, passions, greed, anger, wrath, revenge—are all to be put down and controlled. *You*—all of us—are responsible to obey this commandment. *You* are to control the anger, passions, and greed of your flesh when they are aroused. *You* are to obey the sixth great commandment of God: "*You* shall not murder" (v.13).

II. What Is Forbidden by This Commandment?

How is this commandment broken or violated? Before actually looking at what the commandment forbids, note why God gave the commandment.

1.   The purpose for this commandment is to preserve life: to teach people the sanctity of human life, that they are to honor and hold human life in the highest esteem. Man is created in the image and likeness of God; therefore, man's life is of infinite value to God (Gen.1:26-27). Man is...

- God's *master creation*
- God's *royal masterpiece*
- God's *precious possession*
- God's *priceless property*

Why is man to be so highly esteemed? As stated, because man is created in the *image and likeness* of God. God demands that human life be valued above all the wealth in the world (Mt.16:26; Mk.8:36). The sanctity of human life is to be honored above all else.

> "And God said, Let us make man in our image, after our like-ness: and let them have dominion over the fish of the sea, and over the fowl of the air, and over the cattle, and over all the earth, and over every creeping thing that creepeth upon the earth. So God cre-ated man in his own image, in the image of God created he him; male and female created he them" (Gen.1:26-27).
> "And surely your blood of your lives will I require; at the hand of every beast will I require it, and at the hand of man; at the hand of every man's brother will I require the life of man. Whoso sheddeth man's blood, by man shall his blood be shed: for in the image of God made he man. And you, be ye fruitful, and multiply; bring forth abundantly in the earth, and multiply therein" (Gen.9:5-7).
> "For what shall it profit a man, if he shall <u>gain the whole world</u>, and lose his own soul?" (Mk.8:36; cp. Mt.16:26).

2.   Now, what is forbidden by this commandment: "You shall not murder" (v.13)? The Hebrew word for "kill" or "killing" (rasah) means premeditated, planned, deliberate, intentional, unauthorized murder.

This commandment is broken either by a planned murderous attack upon a person(s) or by a rash, reckless attack. This commandment forbids the taking of a life because a person is...

- angry
- passionate
- lusting
- bitter
- vengeful
- coveting
- violent
- selfish
- rebelling
- uncontrolled
- stealing

Murder for such reasons as these is wrong and must always be counted wrong. This is the only way to make our community, society, and civilization safe and secure. The terrifying evils of this earth—lawlessness, violence, and murder—must not be allowed. We must always agree with God's Holy Word: murder for such reasons as anger, robbery, and violence must always be counted wrong and be punished.

But there are also other forms of murder that are just as wrong as lifting one's own hand to kill another person. All over the world, there are people who commit murder...

- by forcing people to work in conditions that will injure or eventually kill them, that lead to their premature death
- by forcing people to live in horrible conditions, so horrible that the environment or lack of basic necessities eventually kills them
- by selling and hooking people on drugs, drugs that eventually enslave and kill the addicts

Man must control and punish the lawless, the violent, and the murderers who roam his streets and in many cases sit in the plush offices of authority and rule. Evil men must be stopped and taught to obey this commandment or else our civilization can never survive. Lawlessness, violence, and murder must be stamped out. We can have safe streets and parks, unlocked doors, and the freedom to move about at night only if we obey this commandment. We will have a satisfying and fruitful life only if we heed this commandment: "You shall not murder [live lawless and violent lives]" (v.13).

But even the above are not the only kinds of murder forbidden by God. The spirit of lawlessness, violence, and murder so sweeps through the societies and history of man that at least two other types of murder need to be discussed: abortion and suicide (see point 7, pages 192-200 for discussion).

3.   Note this fact: this commandment is not a blanket commandment against all killing. God's Word clearly says that the taking of life is justified, understandable, and allowed...

- as capital punishment (Gen.9:6)
- in a justified war (Dt.13:15; 1 Sam.15:3; 2 Sam.10:1f)
- in cases of adultery (Lev.20:10). This may seem harsh to society today, but this commandment and penalty were given to protect and preserve the family. The very survival of Israel depended upon the family being preserved as the basic unit of society. Loyalty to the family taught the Israelites to be loyal to the nation as a whole.
- in the defense of ourselves, for example, when a thief breaks into our home (Ex.22:2)
- in accidental killing (Dt.19:5)
- in killing animals for food (Gen.9:3)

4.   What is the ultimate cause, the basic source, of murder? Scripture says that the underlying cause and source of murder is twofold:
  a. Satan, the devil, is the arch-enemy of God and man: he seeks to tempt and arouse people to live greedy and selfish lives, lives of lawlessness, violence, and murder.

"Ye are of [your] father the devil, and the lusts of your father ye will do. He was a murderer from the beginning, and abode not in the truth, because there is no truth in him. When he speaketh a lie, he speaketh of his own: for he is a liar, and the father of it" (Jn.8:44).

b. Lust—the unregulated urges of man's heart—drives some people to rob, assault, and kill. Some people allow the lust of their soul—greed and covetousness—to drive them to lawlessness, violence, and murder.

"But every man is tempted, when he is drawn away of his own lust, and enticed. Then when lust hath conceived, it bringeth forth sin: and sin, when it is finished, bringeth forth death" (Jas.1:14-15).

"From whence come wars and fightings among you? come they not hence, even of your lusts that war in your members? Ye lust, and have not: ye kill, and desire to have, and cannot obtain: ye fight and war, yet ye have not, because ye ask not. Ye ask, and receive not, because ye ask amiss, that ye may consume it upon your lusts" (Jas.4:1-3).

5. What will be the eternal judgment of God upon the murderer? Death, spiritual and eternal death.

"For the wages of sin is death" (Ro.6:23).

"For to be carnally minded is death" (Ro.8:6).

"Now the works of the flesh are manifest, which are these; Adultery, fornication, uncleanness, lasciviousness, Idolatry, witchcraft, hatred, variance, emulations, wrath, strife, seditions, heresies, Envyings, murders, drunkenness, revellings, and such like: of the which I tell you before, as I have also told you in time past, that they which do such things shall not inherit the kingdom of God" (Gal.5:19-21).

"But every man is tempted, when he is drawn away of his own lust, and enticed. Then when lust hath conceived, it bringeth forth sin: and sin, when it is finished, bringeth forth death" (Jas.1:14-15).

"But the fearful, and unbelieving, and the abominable, and murderers, and whoremongers, and sorcerers, and idolaters, and all liars, shall have their part in the lake which burneth with fire and brimstone: which is the second death" (Rev.21:8).

"The soul that sinneth, it shall die" (Ezk.18:4).

6. Can a murderer be saved and forgiven for his sin of murder? Scripture says "yes," a resounding "yes!" But the murderer must confess his sin and repent, turning away from his life of sin. He must genuinely give his heart and life to Jesus Christ and live for Jesus Christ.

"I tell you, Nay: but, except ye repent, ye shall all likewise perish" (Lk.13:3).

> "Repent ye therefore, and be converted, that your sins may be blotted out, when the times of refreshing shall come from the presence of the Lord" (Acts 3:19).
>
> "Let the wicked forsake his way, and the unrighteous man his thoughts: and let him return unto the LORD, and he will have mercy upon him; and to our God, for he will abundantly pardon" (Is.55:7).
>
> "But if the wicked will turn from all his sins that he hath committed, and keep all my statutes, and do that which is lawful and right, he shall surely live, he shall not die" (Ezk.18:21).
>
> "Then Peter said unto them, Repent, and be baptized every one of you in the name of Jesus Christ for the remission of sins, and ye shall receive the gift of the Holy Ghost" (Acts 2:38).
>
> "For the wages of sin is death; but the gift of God is eternal life through Jesus Christ our Lord" (Ro.6:23).
>
> "For to be carnally minded is death; but to be spiritually minded is life and peace" (Ro.8:6).

7.   Jesus Christ taught that this commandment means far more than just prohibiting the killing of people. He enlarged the meaning to include both the anger that is aroused within the heart and the lawless motives that drive a person to kill others.

> "Ye have heard that it was said by them of old time, Thou shalt not kill; and whosoever shall kill shall be in danger of the judgment: But I say unto you, That whosoever is angry with his brother without a cause shall be in danger of the judgment: and whosoever shall say to his brother, Raca, shall be in danger of the council: but whosoever shall say, Thou fool, shall be in danger of hell fire" (Mt.5:21-22).

Note what Christ is saying: He is saying that man has a problem. Man misreads God's law. Man interprets God's law to say what he wishes it to say. Man applies it only to the outward act, in this case to the act of murder. Man fails to look inward—within himself—to the cause.

Murder is deeper than just an outward act. It is an inward act: an act of anger, bitterness, enmity. Murder is born from within, from an uncontrolled spirit, from an unregulated urge, from an inner anger. Anger itself is the root sin, the sin that first breaks the law of God. Anger is...

- bitterness and enmity
- indignation and wrath
- striking out against a person
- rage and fury
- an uncontrolled spirit
- desiring a person's hurt
- a disappointment or hatred of oneself
- envying and killing a person's happiness
- slandering and destroying a person's image (who is created in God's image)

The growth of anger is dangerous. Unresolved anger will fester. It can become uncontrolled and give birth to murder. There are three steps in the growth of anger given by Christ.

a. The anger that broods, that is selfish. It harbors malice; it will not forget; it lingers; it broods; it wills revenge and sometimes seeks revenge.
b. The anger that holds contempt (raca). It despises; it ridicules; it arrogantly exalts self and calls another person empty and useless. This is an anger that is full of malice. It despises and scorns (raca). It arises from pride—a proud wrath (Pr.21:24). Such feelings or anger walk over and trample a person. It says that whatever ill comes upon a person is deserved.
c. The anger that curses. It seeks to destroy a man and his reputation morally, intellectually, and spiritually.

There is a justified anger. In fact, the believer must be an angry person—angry with those who sin and do wrong, who are unjust and selfish in their behavior. However, a justified anger is always disciplined and controlled; it is always limited to those who do wrong either against God or against others. The distinguishing mark between justified and unjustified anger is that a justified anger is never selfish; it is never shown because of what has happened to oneself. It is an anger that is purposeful. The believer knows that he is angry for a legitimate reason, and he seeks to correct the situation in the most peaceful way possible.

> "Be ye angry, and sin not: let not the sun go down upon your wrath" (Eph.4:26).
> "If it be possible, as much as lieth in you, live peaceably with all men" (Ro.12:18).
> "And the Jews' passover was at hand, and Jesus went up to Jerusalem, and found in the temple those that sold oxen and sheep and doves, and the changers of money sitting: and when he had made a scourge of small cords, he drove them all out of the temple, and the sheep, and the oxen; and poured out the changer's money, and overthrew the tables [all a justified anger]" (Jn.2:13-16).

Thought 1.

Anger is cast against many. Too often hurt feelings exist between those who are supposed to be the closest: husband and wife, parent and child, neighbor and friend, employer and employee. The Lord is clear about the matter: we must never allow anger to take hold of us without just cause.

> "But now ye also put off all these; anger, wrath, malice, blasphemy, filthy communication out of your mouth" (Col.3:8).
> "Wherefore, my beloved brethren, let every man be swift to hear, slow to speak, slow to wrath" (Jas.1:19).
> "Whosoever hateth his brother is a murderer: and ye know that no murderer hath eternal life abiding in him" (1 Jn.3:15).
> "Cease from anger, and forsake wrath: fret not thyself in any wise to do evil" (Ps.37:8).

"He that is soon angry dealeth foolishly; and a man of wicked devices is hated" (Pr.14:17).

"He that is slow to anger is better than the mighty; and he that ruleth his spirit than he that taketh a city" (Pr.16:32).

"The discretion of a man deferreth his anger; and it is his glory to pass over a transgression" (Pr.19:11).

"Be not hasty in thy spirit to be angry: for anger resteth in the bosom of fools" (Eccl.7:9).

Thought 2.

There are many reasons why people get angry and develop feelings against others:

⇒ To seek revenge and to hurt

⇒ To express disagreement or displeasure

⇒ To reveal passion or secure some end

⇒ To give warning

⇒ To show ego or authority

⇒ To show hurt, resentment, or bitterness

⇒ To correct a wrong (a justified anger)

Thought 3.

Abortion, the killing of unborn babies, is one of the major indictments against the human race down through the centuries. The sanctity of life has been and still is under lethal attack. Tragically, the tide of public opinion usually runs counter to the clear commandment of God, "You shall not kill." Because abortion is legal in so many societies and is so prevalent, it is being discussed at length here.

a) What does the Bible say about the creation of man and the fetus or unborn baby in the womb?

"So God created man in his own image, in the image of God created he him; male and female created he them" (Gen.1:27).

"This is the book of the generations of Adam. In the day that God created man, in the likeness of God made he him" (Gen.5:1).

"Did not he that made me in the womb make him? and did not one fashion us in the womb?" (Job 31:15).

"Thy hands have made me and fashioned me: give me understanding, that I may learn thy commandments" (Ps.119:73).

"For thou hast possessed my reins: thou hast covered me in my mother's womb. I will praise thee; for I am fearfully and wonderfully made: marvellous are thy works; and that my soul knoweth right well. My substance was not hid from thee, when I was made in secret, and curiously wrought in the lowest parts of the earth. Thine eyes did see my substance, yet being unperfect; and in thy book all my members were written, which in continuance were fashioned, when as yet there was none of them" (Ps.139:13-16).

"As thou knowest not what is the way of the spirit, nor how the bones do grow in the womb of her that is with child: even so thou knowest not the works of God who maketh all" (Eccl.11:5).

"Then the word of the LORD came unto me, saying, Before I formed thee in the belly I knew thee; and before thou camest forth out of the womb I sanctified thee, and I ordained thee a prophet unto the nations" (Jer.1:4-5).

"Now the birth of Jesus Christ was on this wise: When as his mother Mary was espoused to Joseph, before they came together, she was found with child of the Holy Ghost. Then Joseph her husband, being a just man, and not willing to make her a public example, was minded to put her away privily [secretly]. But while he thought on these things, behold, the angel of the Lord appeared unto him in a dream, saying, Joseph, thou son of David, fear not to take unto thee Mary thy wife: for that which is conceived in her is of the Holy Ghost" (Mt.1:18-20).

b) What does the medical profession say about the fetus or unborn child in the mother's womb? The excellent Bible teacher Stuart Briscoe says this:

"Physicians have given us a wide variety of suggestions about when the fetus becomes human. Seven of them are outlined by Oliver O'Donavan and quoted in Norman Anderson's *Issues of Life and Death*.[1]

"1. The first group says the fetus becomes fully human at the point of conception. Among those some would say 'the point of conception' rather unguardedly, while others would describe it not as a moment, but a process that we cannot accurately measure. But both would agree that, whenever it takes place, the child becomes invested with the divine image.

"2. Others claim that the problem with the first theory is that 50 percent of all impregnated ova disappear in the natural course of events. If that is the case, then 50 percent of unborn, unformed, unimplanted ova have the divine image and simply drift off into eternity without having existed in any sense that is meaningful to us. These people state that the person starts to be formed at implantation; before that it has no meaningful existence at all.

"3. A third group says the fetus becomes human when it takes human shape. They say it will measure at least three centimeters, which will happen between forty-five and forty-nine days after conception.

"4. Still another group claims the fetus becomes human at animation. Old-time theologians used to try to figure out when the body got

[1] Stuart Briscoe. *The Ten Commandments*. (Wheaton, IL: Harold Shaw Publishers, 1986), p.96-98.

the soul and when the soul left. They thought of the body having a soul, as opposed to thinking that humans are body, soul, and spirit. When it came to animation, people believed—and in some circumstances still do believe—that a time exists when the fetus becomes 'ensouled'. To give you an idea how things have changed, Aristotle said that took place twenty-five to forty days after conception for the male, but fifty to eighty days after conception for the female.

"5. A fifth way of thinking says the fetus becomes human at viability—the point at which it could survive without its mother. We have a problem with this today because with our rapidly advancing technology the fetus's viability point changes all the time. Supreme Court Justice Sandra Day O'Connor said, 'Fetal viability in the first trimester of pregnancy may be possible in the not too distant future.' If that happens, it will make the Supreme Court's ruling palpable nonsense.

"6. Another set of people would try to get the problem out of the way simply by declaring the fetus human at birth, not before. If so, how do you take into account the biblical passages we've considered?

"7. Finally, some would claim that the fetus becomes fully human one year after birth. They say that at this stage the human child is comparable to all other animals at the moment of birth, because human children are much more helpless than other animals."[2]

c) Now, when does the unborn child become a human being? When is the fetus made in the image of God? Having looked at what the Bible says and at what different people in the medical profession say, when does the fetus actually become human? Stuart Briscoe gives an excellent discussion of this question as well.

"All this speculation leaves us in a great, big fog—because when we look at Scripture, medical science, and our knowledge, we find it very difficult to pinpoint the moment the unborn becomes a human made in the image of God.

"Because of this difficulty, people argue about whether the fetus is a person, is fully human, is subhuman, or is potentially human. Those in favor of aborting call it subhuman. They would compare it to an appendix—simply a pile of useless tissue, lacking importance. In the light of Scripture, we cannot accept this position under any circumstances.

"Despite the complexity of the issue and the degree of uncertainty that surrounds it, if we allow the fetus to go full term, it will become a human being. Therefore under no circumstances should we feel comfortable in agreeing to any callous or careless interference with that. If I

---

[2] Norman Anderson. *Issues of Life and Death.* (Downers Grove, IL: InterVarsity Press, 1977).

cannot categorically say when something is made in God's image, I'm not even going to get close to tampering with it. It would seem we need to take that minimal position at the very least."[3]

d) What about the mother whose life is in danger if she bears the child? Or whose unborn child is due to rape or incest? Or who had an abortion without any knowledge of what God says about the mother? Are we as believers to minister to them? Again, Stuart Briscoe's discussion of this point is so excellent that it is well worth quoting at length:

"If we are in favor of life, we must favor not only the life of the unborn, but also that of the mother. We need to express concern for the mother, her physical well-being, her emotional situation, and her spiritual state.

"We need to care for the young woman whom we tell, 'In having an abortion, you murdered something made in the image of God.'
⇒ "What will that do to her emotions?
⇒ "How does that affect her spiritually?
⇒ "How can she look the world in the face again?

"If we aggressively go after women who have had abortions, we may well drive them to the point of emotional breakdown or even suicide. Among those who have experienced abortions, there exists a high incidence of depression and an increasingly high level of suicide. It seems to me that if we call ourselves pro-life, we must be pro-life for the unborn and the born as well. We've got to be for the fetus and for the mother, which complicates the abortion issue quite dramatically.

"In some cases that means we must balance out the rights of the unborn against those of the living.
⇒ "The Roman Catholics have arrived at a simple answer for this: They see the rights of the fetus as the primary ones.
⇒ "Those in the feminist tradition and with more liberal thinking call that nonsense, saying the rights of the living are far more important than the rights of the potentially living.
⇒ "Others who grapple with the Word of God ask, 'How do we put these together?'

"Can we countenance abortion on demand? Emphatically no! Can we ban abortion, period, for all circumstances and conditions? It would seem to me that by doing so we could get ourselves in situations where we cannot adequately deal with the needs for the life of the mother and the life of the unborn. Some people would probably agree that if the mother has a very major medical problem, and carrying the

---

[3] Stuart Briscoe. *The Ten Commandments*, p.98.

child threatens her life, action needs to be taken. To balance this out, let me quote a British physician: 'In forty years of gynecological and obstetric practice, I can only remember a handful of occasions in which the mother's life was in danger because of the birth of the fetus.' We need to bear that in mind.

"I believe we must uphold the sanctity of life for both the born and the unborn. I believe we must take that position. If we wish to take a stand for the rights of the unborn, potentially made in the image of God, we must be ready at the same time to care for those who have had abortions and feel depression and overwhelming guilt and who might commit suicide. We need to cultivate compassion for both. When we persuade women not to abort the unborn, we should be prepared to help with the steps of the pregnancy that follow. But we also need to aid those who need forgiveness—we must help human lives in many dimensions, not only in the right to be born"[4]

Thought 4.

Suicide is viewed differently by different people and societies. For example...

- Can a Christian believer commit suicide? Become so despondent, depressed, and discouraged that he takes his own life?
- Can a person be justified if he is so heroic that he undertakes a suicide mission for his nation or for some great cause? This has happened often down through history. The Japanese kamikaze pilots of the Second World War are a prime example. In fact, many of the surviving men who have fought in war would know of men who gave themselves to undertake suicidal missions.

One thing is sure: a deliberate suicide *to escape* this life with all its trials and problems is a desperate crime, a crime that should never be committed. Suicide happens, happens far too often, but it is never the answer. God has stamped His image upon every human life, and no person should ever destroy himself. There are three strong reasons why a person should never commit suicide.

a) God forbids murder, and suicide is the murdering of oneself.

> **"Thou shalt not kill" (Ex.20:13).**
> **"For this, Thou shalt not commit adultery, Thou shalt not kill, Thou shalt not steal, Thou shalt not bear false witness, Thou shalt not covet; and if there be any other commandment, it is briefly comprehended in this saying, namely, Thou shalt love thy neighbor as thyself" (Ro.13:9).**

---

[4]   Stuart Briscoe. *The Ten Commandments*, p.98-100.

"But let none of you suffer as a murderer, or as a thief, or as an evildoer, or as a busybody in other men's matters" (1 Pt.4:15).

b) The person destroys the very image of God that is stamped upon his or her life.

"So God created man in his own image, in the image of God created he him; male and female created he them" (Gen.1:27).

c) Jesus Christ, God's very own Son, loves and cares for us. He helps us *conquer* and *overcome* whatever problems confront us, no matter how terrible. He will give us wisdom and show us how to *conquer* the problem.

"For in that he himself hath suffered being tempted, he is able to succour them that are tempted" (Heb.2:18).
"For we have not an high priest which cannot be touched with the feeling of our infirmities; but was in all points tempted like as we are, yet without sin. Let us therefore come boldly unto the throne of grace, that we may obtain mercy, and find grace to help in time of need" (Heb.4:15-16).
"There hath no temptation taken you but such as is common to man: but God is faithful, who will not suffer you to be tempted above that ye are able; but will with the temptation also make a way to escape, that ye may be able to bear it" (1 Cor.10:13).
"If any of you lack wisdom, let him ask of God, that giveth to all men liberally, and upbraideth not; and it shall be given him" (Jas.1:5).

Now, having said the above, what should our attitude (and the church's attitude) be toward suicidal people and their families? To the genuine Christian believer, the answer is obvious: we are to minister to them. We are to seek out and help all who hurt and face desperate problems and circumstances. Note what has just been said: we are not to sit around waiting for hurting people to cross our paths. We are to actively seek out, find, and help hurting people. This is the call of every Christian believer and the mission of the church. Christ made this perfectly clear.

"Even as the Son of man came not to be ministered unto, but to minister, and to give his life a ransom for many" (Mt.20:28; cp. Lk.4:18).
"Let this mind be in you, which was also in Christ Jesus: Who, being in the form of God, thought it not robbery to be equal with God: But made himself of no reputation, and took upon him the form of a servant, and was made in the likeness of men" (Ph.2:5-7; cp. Lk.4:18).

"For the Son of man is come to seek and to save that which was lost" (Lk.19:10; cp. Jn.20:21).

"Peace [be] unto you: as [my] Father hath sent me, even so send I you" (Jn.20:21).

III. What Are the Consequences of Breaking This Commandment?

"Thou shalt not kill."

These four words have behind them the eternal force of the One who is the Author of life. Life is sacred. The sanctity of life has and always will remain unchanged in the eyes of God. Those who break this commandment will face the Righteous Judge who will hold them completely accountable for murder. No murderer can escape these terrible consequences.

1. The person who murders another person will suffer the wrath of God.

"For the wrath of God is revealed from heaven against all ungodliness and unrighteousness of men, who hold the truth in unrighteousness....Being filled with all unrighteousness, fornication, wickedness, covetousness, maliciousness; full of envy, murder, debate, deceit, malignity; whisperers" (Ro.1:18, 29).

2. The person who murders another person will be judged and will not inherit the kingdom of God. He will not inherit eternal life.

"Now the works of the flesh are manifest, which are these; Adultery, fornication, uncleanness, lasciviousness, Idolatry, witchcraft, hatred, variance, emulations, wrath, strife, seditions, heresies, Envyings, murders, drunkenness, revellings, and such like: of the which I tell you before, as I have also told you in time past, that they which do such things shall not inherit the kingdom of God" (Gal.5:19-21).

"Whosoever hateth his brother is a murderer: and ye know that no murderer hath eternal life abiding in him" (1 Jn.3:15).

3. The person who kills another person is to face civil court: the sentencing, imprisonment, death penalty, or some other form of retribution.

"For rulers are not a terror to good works, but to the evil. Wilt thou then not be afraid of the power? do that which is good, and thou shalt have praise of the same: For he is the minister of God to thee for good. But if thou do that which is evil, be afraid; for he beareth not the sword in vain: for he is the minister of God, a revenger to execute wrath upon him that doeth evil" (Ro.13:3-4).

"And he that killeth any man shall surely be put to death" (Lev.24:17).

"Then ye shall appoint you cities to be cities of refuge for you; that the slayer may flee thither, which killeth any person at unawares" (Num. 35:11).

"The revenger of blood himself shall slay the murderer: when he meeteth him, he shall slay him. But if he thrust him of hatred, or hurl at him by laying of wait, that he die; Or in enmity smite him with his hand, that he die: he that smote him shall surely be put to death; for he is a murderer: the revenger of blood shall slay the murderer, when he meeteth him. But if he thrust him suddenly without enmity, or have cast upon him any thing without laying of wait, Or with any stone, wherewith a man may die, seeing him not, and cast it upon him, that he die, and was not his enemy, neither sought his harm: Then the congregation shall judge between the slayer and the revenger of blood according to these judgments: And the congregation shall deliver the slayer out of the hand of the revenger of blood, and the congregation shall restore him to the city of his refuge, whither he was fled: and he shall abide in it unto the death of the high priest, which was anointed with the holy oil" (Num.35:19-25).

4. The person who kills another person destroys an individual made in the image of God.

"Whoso sheddeth man's blood, by man shall his blood be shed: for in the image of God made he man" (Gen.9:6).

5. The person who deliberately kills another person shows that he is defiled and has an evil heart.

"For out of the heart proceed evil thoughts, murders, adulteries, fornications, thefts, false witness, blasphemies: These are [the things] which defile a man" (Mt.15:19-20).

6. The person who murders another person causes the loss of someone's loved one—a mother, father, sister, brother, son, daughter, or close friend.

"Then Herod, when he saw that he was mocked of the wise men, was exceeding wroth, and sent forth, and slew all the children that were in Bethlehem, and in all the coasts thereof, from two years old and under, according to the time which he had diligently inquired of the wise men. Then was fulfilled that which was spoken by Jeremy the prophet, saying, In Rama was there a voice heard, lamentation, and weeping, and great mourning, Rachel weeping [for] her children, and would not be comforted, because they are not" (Mt.2:16-18).

"And they stoned Stephen, calling upon God, and saying, Lord Jesus, receive my spirit. And he kneeled down, and cried with a loud voice, Lord, lay not this sin to their charge. And when he had said this, he fell asleep....And devout men carried Stephen to his burial, and made great lamentation over him" (Acts 7:59-60; 8:2).

IV. What Are the Benefits of Keeping This Commandment?

The person who obeys this commandment and does not kill another person has made a decision to value life. The contrast is stark between a culture that allows or executes the innocent and helpless and a culture that honors and protects the sacredness of human life. Those who really love, defend, and protect life benefit an entire community, nation, and world. What are the benefits when God's people speak out against murder? What are the benefits to believers who respect the sanctity of life?

1.   The person who belongs to the LORD and respects the sanctity of life will not kill but will walk in the Spirit and bear the fruit of the Spirit.

> "Now the works of the flesh are manifest, which are these; Adultery, fornication, uncleanness, lasciviousness, Idolatry, witchcraft, hatred, variance, emulations, wrath, strife, seditions, heresies, Envyings, murders, drunkenness, revellings, and such like: of the which I tell you before, as I have also told you in time past, that they which do such things shall not inherit the kingdom of God. But the fruit of the Spirit is love, joy, peace, longsuffering, gentleness, goodness, faith, Meekness, temperance: against such there is no law. And they that are Christ's have crucified the flesh with the affections and lusts. If we live in the Spirit, let us also walk in the Spirit" (Gal.5:19-25).

2.   The person who follows God and respects the sanctity of life will have a sacrificial love for his brother.

> "We know that we have passed from death unto life, because we love the brethren. He that loveth not his brother abideth in death. Whosoever hateth his brother is a murderer: and ye know that no murderer hath eternal life abiding in him. Hereby perceive we the love of God, because he laid down his life for us: and we ought to lay down our lives for the brethren" (1 Jn.3:14-16).

3.   The person who belongs to the LORD and respects the sanctity of life will have great love for his friends, willing to die if necessary.

> "Greater love hath no man than this, that a man lay down his life for his friends" (Jn.15:13).

4.   The person who shares in the glorious salvation of God and respects the sanctity of life will experience a true urgency, a keen sense of the times, a sober perspective, an understanding about how fragile life can be.

> "Whereas ye know not what shall be on the morrow. For what is your life? It is even a vapour, that appeareth for a little time, and then vanisheth away" (Jas.4:14).
>
> "As for man, his days are as grass: as a flower of the field, so he flourisheth. For the wind passeth over it, and it is gone; and the place thereof shall know it no more" (Ps.103:15-16).
>
> "The voice said, Cry. And he said, What shall I cry? All flesh is grass, and all the goodliness thereof is as the flower of the field: The grass withereth, the flower fadeth: because the spirit of the LORD bloweth upon it: surely the people is grass" (Is.40:6-7).
>
> "I, even I, am he that comforteth you: who art thou, that thou shouldest be afraid of a man that shall die, and of the son of man which shall be made as grass" (Is.51:12).
>
> "For all flesh is as grass, and all the glory of man as the flower of grass. The grass withereth, and the flower thereof falleth away" (1 Pt.1:24).

5.   The person who knows the truth and respects the sanctity of life will live in the truth and not be deceived by the original murderer, Satan.

> "Ye are of your father the devil, and the lusts of your father ye will do. He was a murderer from the beginning, and abode not in the truth, because there is no truth in him. When he speaketh a lie, he speaketh of his own: for he is a liar, and the father of it" (Jn.8:44).

6.   The person who truly respects the sanctity of life will understand that the only way to save his life is to give it away to Christ.

> "For whosoever will save his life shall lose it: but whosoever will lose his life for my sake, the same shall save it. For what is a man advantaged, if he gain the whole world, and lose himself, or be cast away [eternally]?" (Lk.9:24-25).

7.   The person who follows God and respects the sanctity of life will enjoy abundant life, life in Jesus Christ.

> "The thief [Satan] cometh not, but for to steal, and to kill, and to destroy: I am come that they might have life, and that they might have it more abundantly" (Jn.10:10).

8.   The person who respects the sanctity of life will be saved from doing Satan's will (to destroy human life).

"The thief [Satan] cometh not, but for to steal, and to kill, and to destroy: I am come that they might have life, and that they might have it more abundantly" (Jn.10:10).

9.　The person who fully and completely respects the sanctity of life respects the life of the baby who is still in the womb of the mother.

"For thou hast possessed my reins: thou hast covered me in my mother's womb. I will praise thee; for I am fearfully and wonderfully made: marvellous are thy works; and that my soul knoweth right well. My substance was not hid from thee, when I was made in secret, and curiously wrought in the lowest parts of the earth. Thine eyes did see my substance, yet being unperfect; and in thy book all my members were written, which in continuance were fashioned, when as yet there was none of them" (Ps.139:13-16).

"Before I formed thee in the belly I knew thee; and before thou camest forth out of the womb I sanctified thee, and I ordained thee a prophet unto the nations" (Jer.1:5).

"And it came to pass, that, when Elisabeth heard the salutation of Mary, the babe leaped in her womb; and Elisabeth was filled with the Holy Ghost: And she spake out with a loud voice, and said, Blessed art thou among women, and blessed is the fruit of thy womb" (Lk.1:41-42).

V.　What Is the Teaching of Jesus Christ Concerning This Commandment?

1.　Jesus Christ declared that murder is not only an outward act but also an attitude. Murder occurs within the hearts of men.

"Ye have heard that it was said by them of old time, Thou shalt not kill; and whosoever shall kill shall be in danger of the judgment: But I say unto you, That whosoever is angry with his brother without a cause shall be in danger of the judgment: and whosoever shall say to his brother, Raca, shall be in danger of the council: but whosoever shall say, Thou fool, shall be in danger of hell fire" (Mt.5:21-22).

Thought.

Murder is not only an outward act; it is also inward. It is born within a person's heart and mind. It is...

- anger
- bitterness
- enmity

We must never allow anger to take hold of us without just cause. Reconciliation is urgent while there is still time. We must not allow our relationships to sour beyond repair. Life is far too short to allow our anger to make us bitter and unforgiving. We must forgive others.

Anger that goes unresolved will allow a spirit of murder to enter the human heart.

> **"Be ye angry, and sin not: let not the sun go down upon your wrath" (Eph.4:26).**
>
> **"If a man say, I love God, and hateth his brother, he is a liar: for he that loveth not his brother whom he hath seen, how can he love God whom he hath not seen? And this commandment have we from him, That he who loveth God love his brother also" (1 Jn.4:20-21).**
>
> **"For out of the heart proceed evil thoughts, murders, adulteries, fornications, thefts, false witness, blasphemies" (Mt.15:19).**
>
> **"For from within, out of the heart of men, proceed evil thoughts, adulteries, fornications, murders" (Mk.7:21).**

2.   Jesus Christ declared that Satan is the source of murder, that he is the arch-enemy of God and man, that he was a murderer from the beginning.

> **"Ye are of your father the devil, and the lusts of your father ye will do. He was a murderer from the beginning, and abode not in the truth, because there is no truth in him. When he speaketh a lie, he speaketh of his own: for he is a liar, and the father of it" (Jn.8:44).**

Thought.

We must not reject the truth and follow in the murderous steps of Satan. Satan is a murderer in three senses:

a) He was behind the first murder: the man Cain killing his brother (Gen.4:8).

b) He was behind the sin of Adam, which brought death to the whole human race. He is the murderer, the one who caused the death of men (Ro.5:12).

c) He is behind the murder of human life and behind the loss of man's experiencing real life here on earth. The devil destroys life and all abundant living when he can: all love, joy, peace, patience, gentleness, goodness, faith, meekness, and discipline.

> **"The thief cometh not, but for to steal, and to kill, and to destroy..." (Jn.10:10).**
>
> **"But let none of you suffer as a murderer, or as a thief, or as an evil doer, or as a busybody in other men's matters" (1 Pt.4:15).**
>
> **"Whosoever hateth his brother is a murderer: and ye know that no murderer hath eternal life abiding in him" (1 Jn.3:15).**
>
> **"Be sober, be vigilant; because your adversary the devil, as a roaring lion, walketh about, seeking whom he may devour" (1 Pt.5:8).**
>
> **"Then Satan answered the Lord, and said, Doth Job fear God for nought? Hast not thou made an hedge about him, and about his house, and about all that he hath on every side? thou hast blessed the**

work of his hands, and his substance is increased in the land. But put forth thine hand now, and touch all that he hath, and he will curse thee to thy face" (Job 1:9-11).

3. Jesus Christ declared that some of His disciples would be murdered by family members because of their allegiance to Him.

"And the brother shall deliver up the brother to death, and the father the child: and the children shall rise up against their parents, and cause them to be put to death. And ye shall be hated of all men for my name's sake: but he that endureth to the end shall be saved" (Mt.10:21-22).

Thought.

A believer's own family can become his greatest persecutor, even his murderer. Why? There are three reasons:
a) Because of the believer's commitment to Christ and His righteousness.
b) Because of the family's orthodox religion or church.
c) Because of the believer's commitment to live for Christ. Such an active witness is sometimes an embarrassment to a family.

Nothing hurts more than having our own family oppose us when we make a decision to follow Christ. When our families oppose and persecute us, it hurts deeply.

"If the world hate you, ye know that it hated me before it hated you. If ye were of the world, the world would love his own: but because ye are not of the world, but I have chosen you out of the world, therefore the world hateth you. Remember the word that I said unto you, The servant is not greater than his lord. If they have persecuted me, they will also persecute you; if they have kept my saying, they will keep yours also" (Jn.15:18-20).

"And he said unto them, Verily I say unto you, There is no man that hath left house, or parents, or brethren, or wife, or children, for the kingdom of God's sake, Who shall not receive manifold more in this present time, and in the world to come life everlasting" (Lk.18:29-30).

4. Jesus Christ declared that evil men will kill believers, *thinking* that they are doing God a service.

"They shall put you out of the synagogues: yea, the time cometh, that whosoever killeth you will think that he doeth God service" (Jn.16:2).

Thought.

The believer is warned that people, even some religionists, will persecute and murder the followers of Christ. The believer can stumble and fall over persecution. Persecution can...

- cause a believer to question his beliefs
- cause a believer to weaken and return to the way of false religion
- silence a believer and his witness
- cause a believer to deny Jesus

The believer must take comfort in God's great promises to His persecuted people.

> "Blessed are ye, when men shall revile you, and persecute you, and shall say all manner of evil against you falsely, for my sake. Rejoice, and be exceeding glad: for great is your reward in heaven: for so persecuted they the prophets which were before you" (Mt.5:11-12).
>
> "And they departed from the presence of the council, rejoicing that they were counted worthy to suffer shame for his name" (Acts 5:41).
>
> "Choosing rather to suffer affliction with the people of God, than to enjoy the pleasures of sin for a season" (Heb.11:25).
>
> "Yea, and all that will live godly in Christ Jesus shall suffer persecution. But evil men and seducers shall wax worse and worse, deceiving, and being deceived" (2 Tim.3:12-13).

5.   Jesus Christ declared that His people would be the victims of great violence and murder in the last days.

> "For nation shall rise against nation, and kingdom against kingdom: and there shall be famines, and pestilences, and earthquakes, in divers places. All these are the beginning of sorrows. Then shall they deliver you up to be afflicted, and shall kill you: and ye shall be hated of all nations for my name's sake. And then shall many be offended, and shall betray one another, and shall hate one another. And many false prophets shall rise, and shall deceive many. And because iniquity shall abound, the love of many shall wax cold. But he that shall endure unto the end, the same shall be saved. And this gospel of the kingdom shall be preached in all the world for a witness unto all nations; and then shall the end come" (Mt.24:7-14).

Thought.

The believer must expect persecution. He must remember that Christ foretold that he would be persecuted. Remembering keeps the believer from being caught off guard and stumbling. The believer is to *prepare* for persecution by *thinking through* what he will do when he is...

• ridiculed	• slandered	• questioned	• abused
• attacked	• opposed	• imprisoned	• martyred
• criticized	• tortured		

"Remember the word that I said unto you, The servant is not greater than his lord. If they have persecuted me, they will also persecute you; if they have kept my saying, they will keep yours also" (Jn.15:20).

"But these things have I told you, that when the time shall come, ye may remember that I told you of them. And these things I said not unto you at the beginning, because I was with you" (Jn.16:4).

"But the God of all grace, who hath called us unto his eternal glory by Christ Jesus, after that ye have suffered a while, make you perfect, stablish, strengthen, settle you. To him be glory and dominion for ever and ever. Amen" (1 Pt.5:10-11).

6. Jesus Christ declared that religious hypocrites are related to the sons of those who murdered God's prophets.

"Woe unto you, scribes and Pharisees, hypocrites! because ye build the tombs of the prophets, and garnish the sepulchres of the righteous, And say, If we had been in the days of our fathers, we would not have been partakers with them in the blood of the prophets. Wherefore ye be witnesses unto yourselves, that ye are the children of them which killed the prophets. Fill ye up then the measure of your fathers...how can ye escape the damnation of hell? Wherefore, behold, I send unto you prophets, and wise men, and scribes: and some of them ye shall kill and crucify; and some of them shall ye scourge in your synagogues, and persecute them from city to city: That upon you may come all the righteous blood shed upon the earth, from the blood of righteous Abel unto the blood of Zacharias son of Barachias, whom ye slew between the temple and the altar. Verily I say unto you, All these things shall come upon this generation" (Mt.23:29-36).

Thought.

We must have no part in crucifying the Body of Christ all over again. We must not in any way be associated with verbal abuse against any of God's people, not with...

- slander
- gossip
- insults
- smearing
- scolding

"Saying, Touch not mine anointed, and do my prophets no harm" (Ps.105:15).

"Whoso privily [secretly] slandereth his neighbour, him will I cut off: him that hath an high look and a proud heart will not I suffer" (Ps.101:5).

"An hypocrite with his mouth destroyeth his neighbour: but through knowledge shall the just be delivered" (Pr.11:9).

"Thou shalt not go up and down as a talebearer among thy people: neither shalt thou stand against the blood of thy neighbour: I am the Lord" (Lev.19:16).

"A talebearer revealeth secrets: but he that is of a faithful spirit concealeth the matter" (Pr.11:13).

"He that covereth a transgression seeketh love; but he that repeateth a matter separateth very friends" (Pr.17:9).

"The words of a talebearer are as wounds, and they go down into the innermost parts of the belly" (Pr.18:8).

"He that goeth about as a talebearer revealeth secrets: therefore meddle not with him that flattereth with his lips" (Pr.20:19).

"Where no wood is, there the fire goeth out: so where there is no talebearer, the strife ceaseth" (Pr.26:20).

VI. What Is the Decision Required by This Commandment?

How can lawlessness, violence, and murder be eliminated from society? What can we do to make our streets and homes safe, to feel free and secure to walk about in a neighborhood?

1. We must not live a life of hypocrisy: we must hate what is evil and cleave to what is good; we must become actively involved in stamping out violence, lawlessness, and murder.

> "Let love be without dissimulation [hypocrisy]. Abhor that which is evil; cleave to that which is good" (Ro.12:9).

2. We must teach the sanctity of life and the brotherhood of man:
   a. Teach that we are all created in the image of God and that we all bear that image.

> "So God created man in his own image, in the image of God created he him; male and female created he them" (Gen.1:27).

   b. Teach that we are to love our neighbor as ourselves.

> "And the second [is] like unto it, Thou shalt love thy neighbor as thyself" (Mt.22:39).
> "This is my commandment, That ye love one another, as I have loved you" (Jn.15:12).
> "For this, Thou shalt not commit adultery, Thou shalt not kill, Thou shalt not steal, Thou shalt not bear false witness, Thou shalt not covet; and if there be any other commandment, it is briefly comprehended in this saying, namely, Thou shalt love thy neighbor as thyself. Love worketh no ill to his neighbor: therefore love is the fulfilling of the law" (Ro.13:9-10).

> "Seeing ye have purified your souls in obeying the truth through the Spirit unto unfeigned love of the brethren, see that ye love one another with a pure heart fervently" (1 Pt.1:22).

3. We must conquer anger when it first arises within our hearts and minds:
   a. By not giving way to a vicious, vengeful anger.

   > "Ye have heard that it was said by them of old time, Thou shalt not kill; and whosoever shall kill shall be in danger of the judgment: But I say unto you, That whosoever is angry with his brother without a cause shall be in danger of the judgment: and whosoever shall say to his brother, Raca, shall be in danger of the council: but whosoever shall say, Thou fool, shall be in danger of hell fire" (Mt.5:21-22).
   > "Be ye angry, and sin not: let not the sun go down upon your wrath: Neither give place to the devil" (Eph.4:26-27).

   b. By not allowing egotistical pride to take a foothold in our lives, for pride breeds contention (anger).

   > "Only by pride cometh contention: but with the well advised is wisdom" (Pr.13:10).

   c. By not making friends with a hot-tempered person, a person who is easily angered.

   > "Make no friendship with an angry man; and with a furious man thou shalt not go: Lest thou learn his ways, and get a snare to thy soul" (Pr.22:24-25).

4. We must make sure that justice is executed, that the lawless, violent, and murderous are justly punished.

   > "Whoso sheddeth man's blood, by man shall his blood be shed: for in the image of God made he man" (Gen.9:6).
   > "And thine eye shall not pity; but life shall go for life, eye for eye, tooth for tooth, hand for hand, foot for foot" (Dt.19:21).
   > "He that smiteth a man, so that he die, shall be surely put to death" (Ex.21:12).

"Commandment
Seven...

Commandment Seven Concerns Man's Family—Never Commit Adultery or Immorality Exodus 20:14

Contents

Commandment Seven Concerns Man's Family—Never Commit Adultery or Immorality Exodus 20:14

COMMANDMENT 7: Concerns *man's family*: Forbids adultery	14 Thou shalt not commit adultery.

How serious a problem is adultery? In just a moment we shall see that this commandment refers to all forms of immorality. In light of that, how serious a problem is immorality in our society? Most authorities and polls tell us that...

- adultery is prevalent
- pregnancy among unwed mothers is on a sharp rise
- premarital sex is commonplace in many societies, the accepted practice among the young
- sex among unmarried adults—young and old alike—is accepted and even expected by the vast majority of people

Is there a cesspool of immorality in society today? Most honest and thinking observers of history would say that immorality is a very serious problem today. Why? Because it threatens the family, the very foundation of society and civilization. The family is the primary place where trust, loyalty, and love are to be taught and demonstrated. If a person will not be faithful and loyal to his family, how can he be trusted to be faithful and loyal to his nation, society, and civilization? It is far easier to be loyal to that which can be physically seen, such as one's family, than for that which is only an ideal such as a nation, society, and civilization. Immorality strikes at the very foundation of society, the family. It tears apart the family and causes hurt, suffering, strain, shame, guilt, secrecy, destitution, distrust, disloyalty, and unfaithfulness. Moreover, immorality and adultery teach that certain behavior is acceptable: selfishness, unfaithfulness, distrust, disloyalty, secrecy, irresponsibility, and on and on.

This is the reason God gave us this commandment: to preserve our lives; to preserve the great qualities that bring peace, love, and trust to our lives, qualities that build a healthy mind and heart. This is the great subject of this commandment, a much needed subject: *Commandment Seven Concerns Man's Family—Never Commit Adultery or Immorality*, 20:14.

I.   Who is to obey this commandment? How long was this commandment to be in force (v.14)?

II.   What is forbidden by this commandment (v.14)?

III.   What are the Biblical consequences of breaking this commandment?

IV.   What are the Biblical benefits of keeping this commandment?

V.   What is the teaching of Jesus Christ concerning this commandment?

VI.   What is the decision required by this commandment (v.14)?

I.   Who Is to Obey This Commandment? How Long Is This Commandment to Be in Force?

Was this commandment to govern only the ancient world or is there still a need for the commandment: "You shall not commit adultery or immorality"? It is almost ridiculous to ask if this commandment governing immorality is needed today. Keep in mind that this is one of the Ten great Commandments of God. God has created man, and God knows that man has some very basic needs, needs that have to be controlled or else they will run wild and destroy man and his world. One of these needs is the need for sex. God created man as a sexual being primarily to build a close bond between husband and wife (holding the family together) and to repopulate the earth. God knows that man's sexual drive is strong, very strong. God has created the drive to be strong to make sure the great qualities of life are nourished (love, joy, peace, trust, faithfulness, unity) and that the earth is always repopulated. But God also knows that man has to control his drive: man has to keep his drive within bounds, within very specific limits. Therefore, God commands man: "You shall not commit adultery; you shall not commit acts of immorality against marriage and the family."

Who is to obey this commandment? And how long is this commandment to be in force? You are to obey, and the commandment is in force as long as man lives, as long as man is to repopulate the earth.

> "Thou shalt not commit adultery" (Ex.20:14).
>
> "Flee fornication [all forms of sex outside of marriage]. Every sin that a man doeth is without the body; but he that committeth fornication sinneth against his own body" (1 Cor.6:18).
>
> "For this is the will of God, even your sanctification, that ye should abstain from fornication: That every one of you should know how to possess his vessel in sanctification and honour; Not in the lust of concupiscence, even as the Gentiles which know not God" (1 Th.4:3-5).

II.   What Is Forbidden by This Commandment?

1. Adultery (naap) or *adulterate* means to debase, to corrupt oneself sexually, to make oneself impure sexually, to have sex outside of marriage. What God is saying is simple, unqualified, and irrevocable: "You shall not commit adultery: you shall not debase yourself, corrupt yourself, nor make yourself impure sexually. You shall not have sex outside of marriage."

   a. Scripture teaches that a person becomes sexually impure in at least three ways:

     ⇒ A person has sex with someone other than his or her spouse. This is what is commonly called *adultery*.

     ⇒ A person has sex before marriage. This is called *fornication*. Fornication refers to any sexual immorality, either before marriage or after marriage.

     ⇒ A person fantasizes and lusts after a person other than his or her spouse, allows his mind and heart to be set upon another person.

   b. Note that the sin of adultery embraces all that leads up to the act of sex, not just the sexual act itself. Adultery is far more than just being sexually unfaithful in marriage. This commandment forbids any immoral thought or act...

- that makes a person impure for marriage
- that spots or dirties a person's marriage
- that causes a person to lose his or her virginity
- that keeps a person from being able to offer himself or herself as a pure virgin when married

     Illicit sex is a violation against the marriage to be. Illicit sex dirties, corrupts, spots, and makes a person impure either before or after marriage.

   c. The thought life of a person is important when dealing with adultery. Adultery is committed in the heart long before the act is committed. Always keep in mind that God's law is spiritual as well as physical; therefore His law also deals with the thoughts of the mind and heart. This commandment forbids committing adultery in the heart. A person is...

- not to prostitute his thoughts and imaginations
- not to allow impure, lustful thoughts
- not to indulge in illicit fantasies

2. The meaning of adultery was expanded by the Lord Jesus Christ, by God's Son Himself. Christ taught that this commandment means far more than just committing the act of adultery. He enlarged the commandment to include thoughts and lusts, to include the second look at a person who is dressed to sexually attract or expose his or her body.

> **"Ye have heard that it was said by them of old time, Thou shalt not commit adultery: But I say unto you, That whosoever looketh on a woman to lust after her hath committed adultery with her already in his heart. And if thy right eye offend thee, pluck it out, and cast [it] from thee: for it is profitable for thee that one of thy members should perish, and not [that] thy whole body should be cast into hell. And if thy right hand offend thee, cut it off, and cast [it] from thee: for it is profitable for thee that one of thy members should perish, and not [that] thy whole body should be cast into hell" (Mt.5:27-30).**

3. Now, what causes adultery and immorality? There are no doubt many causes, but we can perhaps summarize them all under the following five categories.
   a. Immorality is caused by corrupt moral standards or a lack of moral standards.
      ⇒ Some people have never been taught nor are they aware that sex outside of marriage is wrong in the sight of God. Their society has become so corrupted down through the ages that belief in the true and living God has been lost as well as the sanctity of sex and marriage.
   b. Immorality is caused by lax or liberal moral standards, or by a selfish, worldly, immoral lifestyle. These people either ignore or deny God's commandment, choosing to live as they wish.
   c. Immorality is caused by the need for companionship, attention, or love or by the need for appreciation or fulfillment. Many people reach out to others because of these very basic needs. This is especially true during marriage when a husband or wife fails to meet these needs in his or her spouse.
   d. Immorality is caused by anger, hostility, or the seeking of revenge. A host of behaviors can anger a person and arouse him to commit adultery, such things as coldness, indifference, neglect, a biting tongue, harshness, selfishness.
   e. Immorality is caused by poor ego strength or by an inflated ego, by a lack of self-esteem or self-worth, by a need to feel important, or by the challenge and conquest of the affair. The most intimate thing a person can give to another is his or her body. Therefore, sex is a challenge or conquest for many people; it is an ego booster, an act that either builds a person's feelings of importance or adds to his or her trophy case of conquests.

Sex is a very normal, natural act, a most precious and cherished act given by God. God has built the desire for sex into the very nature of man. In fact, sex is the most intimate experience God has chosen for man to nourish the great virtues of life and to propagate the human race. But the depraved, sinful heart of man has corrupted sex, so much so that man has developed a sex-crazed society. In very practical terms, immorality is caused...

- by ignoring or denying God and His Word
- by ignoring right vs. wrong
- by lack of teaching and training
- by unsatisfying, inadequate sex with a spouse
- by coldness, the alienation of husband or wife
- by living in a dream or fantasy world due to such things as pornography, films, or suggestive music
- by not guarding relationships, by getting too close and becoming attracted to a person
- by not guarding against loneliness, emptiness, or disappointment in one's spouse or loved one

4. Now, why does God forbid adultery? Prohibit immorality? What is God's purpose, His reason for giving this commandment? Keep in mind what is stated above: the experience of sex is a gift to man, a gift given by God. God created sex for man, and even went so far as to make sex...

- a part of man's very nature
- the very way man is to propagate the human race

Note what this means: if man failed to have sex, the human race would cease to be. Human life would become extinct within a few generations. God so intertwined sex within man's nature that man must have sex. All this is to say one thing: sex is of critical importance to God. God not only approves of sex: He is the Giver and Creator of the experience of sex. But He put boundaries and limits around sex. Sex was created for marriage, for the home, and only for marriage and the home. This leads us to the purposes for sex, the reasons why God gave this seventh commandment.

a. God gave the seventh commandment to preserve man, to protect and safeguard the value of the individual, the sanctity of man's body and spirit. When a man and woman lie together, they are never more vulnerable, never more exposed. Lying together, their bodies and spirits are more exposed than at any other time. God intended sex to be one of the most intimate, warm, precious, and growing experiences of human life. Sex was created so that two people could grow together, could nourish and nurture each other in...

• love	• attractiveness
• joy	• attention
• peace	• care
• trust	• security
• loyalty	• self-esteem
• perseverance	• a sense of fulfillment

On and on the list could go; but note all the wonderful, positive, and strong qualities that sex is supposed to bring between two people. This is the reason God gave the seventh commandment: "You shall not commit adultery" (v.13). These things are so important for a healthy personality that God did something: He ordained that one man and one woman were to give their lives to one another, that they were to focus upon sharing and developing the wonderful qualities in the other. God ordained marriage. Sex outside marriage never develops these qualities. Illicit sex always causes problems...

- guilt
- jealousy
- unhappiness
- broken trust
- disease
- selfishness
- disloyalty
- dissolution of the family
- problem children
- broken marriages
- loss of self-esteem
- loss of respect for others
- loss of respect by others
- loss of affection and relationships
- insecurity
- emotional problems
- a sense of being used
- unwanted pregnancies
- a cheapening of sex
- a lack of fulfillment
- a false sense of security

The point: God gave the seventh commandment to preserve the value of human life, the sanctity of man's body and spirit.

b. God gave the seventh commandment to preserve the family and the human race, society itself. The family is the basic unit of any society; therefore, the family has to be protected and preserved for society to survive. This was true for Israel and it is true for us, no matter what our generation. When husbands and wives are living in love and are faithful to each other, the great qualities of life are learned and taught: loyalty, trust, commitment, love, joy, and peace. These are the very qualities that grow and develop fruitful lives, families, and nations. No family, society, or nation can survive without these great qualities.

God demands the *sanctity of marriage*. God demands that husbands and wives be pure and faithful to one another, that they love one another and never commit adultery: "You shall never commit adultery, never commit any act of immorality."

> "Thou shalt not commit adultery" (Ex.20:14).
> "Flee fornication [all forms of sex outside of marriage]. Every sin that a man doeth is without the body; but he that commiteth fornication sinneth against his own body" (1 Cor.6:18).
> "Abstain from fornication" (1 Th.4:3).
> "Abstain from fleshly lusts, which war against the soul" (1 Pt.2:11).

III. What Are the Consequences of Breaking This Commandment?

It is clear that there is no such thing as a private sin. The sins of one man will affect the lives of many. This is especially true when adultery is committed. Adultery is a gross act of betrayal; adultery or immorality is a hideous crime against everyone: God, oneself, and others. Those who commit adultery (immorality) will face severe judgment, both now and in the future. The consequences should cause any man or woman contemplating this sin to seriously weigh the pleasure of the fleeting experience against the terrible harm it causes.

1. The person who commits adultery (sexual immorality) and never repents will forfeit eternal life; he will not inherit the kingdom of God.

> **"Know ye not that the unrighteous shall not inherit the kingdom of God? Be not deceived: neither fornicators, nor idolaters, nor adulterers, nor effeminate, nor abusers of themselves with mankind, Nor thieves, nor covetous, nor drunkards, nor revilers, nor extortioners, shall inherit the kingdom of God. And such were some of you: but ye are washed, but ye are sanctified, but ye are justified in the name of the Lord Jesus, and by the Spirit of our God" (1 Cor.6:9-11).**

2. The person who commits adultery (sexual immorality) and never repents will eventually die in his sin and face the severe judgment of God.

> **"Marriage is honourable in all, and the bed undefiled: but whoremongers and adulterers God will judge" (Heb.13:4).**
> **"But the fearful, and unbelieving, and the abominable, and murderers, and whoremongers, and sorcerers, and idolaters, and all liars, shall have their part in the lake which burneth with fire and brimstone: which is the second death" (Rev.21:8).**
> **"And the man that committeth adultery with another man's wife, even he that committeth adultery with his neighbour's wife, the adulterer and the adulteress shall surely be put to death" (Lev.20:10).**

3. The person who commits adultery (sexual immorality) and never repents destroys his soul.

> **"But whoso committeth adultery with a woman lacketh understanding: he that doeth it destroyeth his own soul" (Pr.6:32).**

4. The person who commits adultery (sexual immorality) and never repents loses the battle for his soul.

> **"Dearly beloved, I beseech you as strangers and pilgrims, abstain from fleshly lusts, which war against the soul" (1 Pt.2:11).**

5.   The person who commits adultery (sexual immorality) and never repents will suffer the judicial judgment of God.

> "Wherefore God also gave them up to uncleanness through the lusts of their own hearts, to dishonour their own bodies between themselves....For this cause God gave them up unto vile affections: for even their women did change the natural use into that which is against nature: And likewise also the men, leaving the natural use of the woman, burned in their lust one toward another; men with men working that which is unseemly, and receiving in themselves that recompence of their error which was meet. And even as they did not like to retain God in their knowledge, God gave them over to a reprobate mind, to do those things which are not convenient" (Ro.1:24, 26-28).

6.   The person who committed adultery under the law of the Old Testament was put to death.

> "And the man that committeth adultery with another man's wife, even he that committeth adultery with his neighbour's wife, the adulterer and the adulteress shall surely be put to death" (Lev.20:10).

7.   The person who commits adultery (sexual immorality) and never repents injures and devastates people, destroys the unity of a family.

> "And it came to pass in an eveningtide, that David arose from off his bed, and walked upon the roof of the king's house: and from the roof he saw a woman washing herself; and the woman was very beautiful to look upon. And David sent and inquired after the woman. And one said, Is not this Bath-sheba, the daughter of Eliam, the wife of Uriah the Hittite? And David sent messengers, and took her; and she came in unto him, and he lay with her; for she was purified from her uncleanness: and she returned unto her house. And the woman conceived, and sent and told David, and said, I am with child....And it came to pass in the morning, that David wrote a letter to Joab, and sent it by the hand of Uriah. And he wrote in the letter, saying, Set ye Uriah in the forefront of the hottest battle, and retire ye from him, that he may be smitten, and die. And it came to pass, when Joab observed the city, that he assigned Uriah unto a place where he knew that valiant men were. And the men of the city went out, and fought with Joab: and there fell some of the people of the servants of David; and Uriah the Hittite died also....And when the wife of Uriah heard that Uriah her husband was dead, she mourned for her husband. And when the mourning was past, David sent and fetched her to his house, and she became his wife, and bare him a son. But the thing that David had done displeased the LORD" (2 Sam.11:2-5, 14-17, 26-27; cp. 2 Sam.12:1f).

8. The person who commits adultery (sexual immorality) and never repents lives a worldly, fleshly life, not a spiritual life.

> **"Love not the world, neither the things that are in the world. If any man love the world, the love of the Father is not in him. For all that is in the world, the lust of the flesh, and the lust of the eyes, and the pride of life, is not of the Father, but is of the world" (1 Jn.2:15-16).**

9. The person who commits adultery (sexual immorality) and never repents shows that he has a corrupted heart [thought-life] and that he lacks self-control.

> **"But I say unto you, That whosoever looketh on a woman to lust after her hath committed adultery with her already in his heart" (Mt.5:28).**
>
> **"Lust not after her beauty in thine heart; neither let her take thee with her eyelids" (Pr.6:25).**

10. The person who commits adultery (sexual immorality) and never repents becomes enslaved to a sinful lifestyle.

> **"Know ye not, that to whom ye yield yourselves servants to obey, his servants ye are to whom ye obey; whether of sin unto death, or of obedience unto righteousness?" (Ro.6:16).**
>
> **"For they that are after the flesh do mind the things of the flesh; but they that are after the Spirit the things of the Spirit" (Ro.8:5).**
>
> **"Having eyes full of adultery, and that cannot cease from sin; beguiling unstable souls: an heart they have exercised with covetous practices; cursed children" (2 Pt.2:14).**

11. The person who commits adultery (sexual immorality) and never repents sins against his own body. The person creates all kinds of problems for himself—emotionally, mentally, and physically.

> **"Flee fornication. Every sin that a man doeth is without the body; but he that committeth fornication <u>sinneth against his own body</u>" (1Cor.6:18).**

12. The person who commits adultery (sexual immorality) and never repents lives a secretive life.

> **"The eye also of the adulterer waiteth for the twilight, saying, No eye shall see me: and disguiseth his face" (Job 24:15).**

13. The person who commits adultery (sexual immorality) and never repents attacks the precious symbolism between Christ and His bride, the church.

"For as a young man marrieth a virgin, so shall thy sons marry thee: and as the bridegroom rejoiceth over the bride, so shall thy God rejoice over thee" (Is.62:5).

"Husbands, love your wives, even as Christ also loved the church, and gave himself for it" (Eph.5:25).

"For I am jealous over you with godly jealousy: for I have espoused you to one husband, that I may present you as a chaste virgin to Christ" (2 Cor.11:2).

"Let us be glad and rejoice, and give honour to him: for the marriage of the Lamb is come, and his wife hath made herself ready" (Rev.19:7).

"And I John saw the holy city, new Jerusalem, coming down from God out of heaven, prepared as a bride adorned for her husband" (Rev.21:2).

"And the Spirit and the bride say, Come. And let him that heareth say, Come. And let him that is athirst come. And whosoever will, let him take the water of life freely" (Rev.22:17).

IV. What Are the Benefits of Keeping This Commandment?

There are many wonderful benefits for those who keep this commandment.

1.   A person who is sexually faithful and who trusts Jesus Christ as his Savior will have a life that is washed, sanctified, and justified in the name of Jesus Christ.

"Know ye not that the unrighteous shall not inherit the kingdom of God? Be not deceived: neither fornicators, nor idolaters, nor adulterers, nor effeminate, nor abusers of themselves with mankind....And such were some of you: but ye are washed, but ye are sanctified, but ye are justified in the name of the Lord Jesus, and by the Spirit of our God" (1Cor. 6:9, 11).

2.   A person who has a pure heart is sexually faithful and will see God.

"Blessed are the pure in heart: for they shall see God" (Mt.5:8).

3.   A person who is sexually faithful gains the wonderful experience of being joined together as one flesh, of being spiritually united to one husband or wife.

"Therefore shall a man leave his father and his mother, and shall cleave unto his wife: and they shall be one flesh" (Gen.2:24).

"For this cause shall a man leave his father and mother, and cleave to his wife" (Mk.10:7).

"What therefore God hath joined together, let not man put asunder" (Mk.10:9).

4. A person who is sexually faithful and who follows God will never lose the presence of God (*David's prayer after committing adultery*).

"Cast me not away from thy presence; and take not thy holy spirit from me" (Ps.51:11).

5. A person who is sexually faithful and shares in the glorious salvation of God will have his prayers answered.

"Likewise, ye husbands, dwell with them according to knowledge, giving honour unto the wife, as unto the weaker vessel, and as being heirs together of the grace of life; that your prayers be not hindered" (1 Pt.3:7).

6. A person who knows the Lord and is sexually faithful receives the very special favor of the Lord.

"Whoso findeth a wife findeth a good thing, and obtaineth favour of the Lord" (Pr.18:22).

7. A person who is sexually faithful protects his body from certain emotional, mental, and physical problems.

"Flee fornication. Every sin that a man doeth is without the body; but he that commiteth fornication sinneth against his own body" (1 Cor.6:18).

8. A person who is sexually faithful gains self-control, the control over his body.

"But the fruit of the Spirit is love, joy, peace, longsuffering, gentleness, goodness, faith, Meekness, temperance [self-control]: against such there is no law" (Gal.5:22-23).
"But the fruit of the Spirit is love, joy, peace, patience, kindness, goodness, faithfulness, gentleness, self-control; against such things there is no law" (Gal.5:22-23, NASB).
"But I keep under my body, and bring it into subjection [from all forms of sin]: lest that by any means, when I have preached to others, I myself should be a castaway" (1 Cor.9:27).

9. A person who knows God and is sexually faithful protects his body as the temple of God's Spirit and glorifies God.

"What? know ye not that your body is the temple of the Holy Ghost which is in you, which ye have of God, and ye are not your own? For ye are bought with a price: therefore glorify God in your body, and in your spirit, which are God's" (1 Cor.6:19-20).

10. A person who is sexually faithful will win the war that is going on in his soul.

"Dearly beloved, I beseech you as strangers and pilgrims, abstain from fleshly lusts, which war against the soul" (1 Pt. 2:11).

11. A person who is sexually faithful has integrity before God and man.

"I made a covenant with mine eyes; why then should I think upon a maid?" (Job 31:1).

12. A person who is sexually faithful enjoys a commitment that lasts for a lifetime.

"For the woman which hath an husband is bound by the law to her husband so long as he liveth; but if the husband be dead, she is loosed from the law of her husband" (Ro.7:2).
"And unto the married I command, yet not I, but the Lord, Let not the wife depart from her husband: But and if she depart, let her remain unmarried, or be reconciled to her husband: and let not the husband put away his wife" (1Cor.7:10-11).

13. A person who is sexually faithful will have an honorable and undefiled marriage.

"Marriage is honourable in all, and the bed undefiled: but whoremongers and adulterers God will judge" (Heb.13:4).

14. A person who is sexually faithful enjoys giving and receiving love.

"Let the husband render unto the wife due benevolence [his marital duty]: and likewise also the wife unto the husband [her marital duty]. The wife hath not power of her own body, but the husband: and likewise also the husband hath not power of his own body, but the wife" (1 Cor.7:3-4).

15. A person who knows God and is sexually faithful has a most glorious experience, that of walking in *Biblical* submission to the LORD.

"Wives, submit yourselves unto your own husbands, as unto the Lord" (Eph.5:22).

> "Likewise, ye wives, be in subjection to your own husbands; that, if any obey not the word, they also may without the word be won by the conversation of the wives" (1 Pt.3:1).

16. A person who gives his life to Christ and is sexually faithful enjoys a most wonderful experience, that of sharing in the sacrificial love of Christ Himself.

> "Husbands, love your wives, even as Christ also loved the church, and gave himself for it" (Eph.5:25).

17. A person who is sexually faithful helps to preserve the unity and spirit of the family.

> "Therefore shall a man leave his father and his mother, and shall cleave unto his wife: and they shall be one flesh" (Gen.2:24).
> "What therefore God hath joined together, let not man put asunder" (Mk.10:9).
> "For this cause shall a man leave his father and mother, and shall be joined unto his wife, and they two shall be one flesh" (Eph.5:31).

18. A person who is sexually faithful will always be given a way of escape.

> "There hath no temptation taken you but such as is common to man: but God is faithful, who will not suffer you to be tempted above that ye are able; but will with the temptation also make a way to escape, that ye may be able to bear it" (1 Cor.10:13).

V. What Is the Teaching of Jesus Christ Concerning This Commandment?

1. Jesus Christ declared that God commanded man not to commit adultery.

> "He saith unto him, Which? Jesus said, Thou shalt do no murder, Thou shalt not commit adultery, Thou shalt not steal, Thou shalt not bear false witness" (Mt.19:18; cp. Mk.10:19; Lk.18:20).

<u>Thought.</u>
Scripture is forceful: no person is to commit adultery nor any other immoral act.

> "Thou shalt not commit adultery" (Ex.20:14).
> "Flee fornication [all forms of sex outside marriage]" (1 Cor.6:18).
> "For this is the will of God, even your sanctification, that ye should abstain from fornication: That every one of you should know how to possess his vessel in sanctification and honour; Not in the lust of concupiscence, even as the Gentiles which know not God" (1 Th.4:3-5).

2. Jesus Christ declared that the real meaning of adultery and of all sexual immorality...
- is a deliberate look
- is a desire, a lust, a passion
- begins in the heart

> "Ye have heard that it was said by them of old time, Thou shalt not commit adultery: But I say unto you, That whosoever looketh on a woman to lust after her hath committed adultery with her already in his heart" (Mt.5:27-28).

Thought.
The wrong use of sex is sin. In the right context, sex is a part of man's nature...
- that nourishes and expresses an intimate love
- that creates life

The purpose for this law is threefold:

a) To assure respect and protection for families and neighbors. God will take vengeance upon those who destroy families through adultery.

> "Abstain from all appearance of evil" (1 Th.5:22).
> "For this is the will of God, even your sanctification, that ye should abstain from fornication: that every one of you should know how to possess his vessel in sanctification and honour; not in the lust of concupiscence, even as the Gentiles which know not God: that no man go beyond and defraud his brother in any matter: because that the Lord is the avenger of all such, as we also have forewarned you and testified" (1 Th.4:3-6).
> "And the man that committeth adultery with another man's wife, even he that committeth adultery with his neighbour's wife, the adulterer and the adulteress shall surely be put to death" (Lev.20:10).

b) To protect a man from eternal judgment, the judgment of perishing in hell.

> "Know ye not that the unrighteous shall not inherit the kingdom of God? Be not deceived: neither fornicators, nor idolaters, nor adulterers, nor effeminate, nor abusers of themselves with mankind, Nor thieves, nor covetous, nor drunkards, nor revilers, nor extortioners, shall inherit the kingdom of God" (1 Cor.6:9-10).
> "Now the works of the flesh are manifest, which are these; Adultery, fornication, uncleanness, lasciviousness, Idolatry, witchcraft, hatred, variance, emulations, wrath, strife, seditions, heresies, Envyings, murders, drunkenness, revellings, and such like: of the which I

tell you before, as I have also told you in time past, that they which do such things shall not inherit the kingdom of God" (Gal.5:19-21).

"But the fearful, and unbelieving, and the abominable, and murderers, and whoremongers, and sorcerers, and idolaters, and all liars, shall have their part in the lake which burneth with fire and brimstone: which is the second death" (Rev.21:8).

"But whoso committeth adultery with a woman lacketh understanding: he that doeth it destroyeth his own soul" (Pr.6:32).

"Marriage is honourable in all, and the bed undefiled: but whoremongers and adulterers God will judge" (Heb.13:4).

c) To protect a man from sinning against his own body, from damaging his body emotionally, mentally, and physically.

"Flee fornication [all forms of illicit sex]. Every sin that a man doeth is without the body; but he that committeth fornication sinneth against his own body" (1 Cor.6:18).

"For this is the will of God, even your sanctification, that ye should abstain from fornication [all forms of illicit sex]: That every one of you should know how to possess his vessel [body] in sanctification and honour; Not in the lust of concupiscence, even as the Gentiles which know not God" (1 Th.4:3-5).

3. Jesus Christ declared that the source of adultery and sexual immorality is the human heart.

"For out of the heart proceed evil thoughts, murders, adulteries, fornications, thefts, false witness, blasphemies" (Mt.15:19).

Thought.

Adultery and all sexual immorality is an affliction that arises within the human heart. Men and women are powerless to resist this destructive sin unless they walk in the Spirit of God. And the spiritual walk must last for a lifetime, for sex is exalted throughout society as the summit of human experience. Sex is looked upon as acceptable even outside marriage.

When a person is tempted to commit a sexual sin, that person...
- must control the eyes: look away; never look a second time (Job 31:1)
- must control the mind: focus on something else
- must walk or even run away: flee from the temptation
- must whisper a prayer for strength
- must consider the consequences

"Know ye not that the unrighteous shall not inherit the kingdom of God? Be not deceived: neither fornicators, nor idolaters, nor adulterers, nor effeminate, nor abusers of themselves with mankind, Nor thieves, nor covetous, nor drunkards, nor revilers, nor extortioners, shall inherit the kingdom of God" (1 Cor.6:9-10).

"But I say unto you, That whosoever looketh on a woman to lust after her hath committed adultery with her already in his heart" (Mt.5: 28).

"Keep thy heart with all diligence; for out of it are the issues of life" (Pr.4:23).

"For as he thinketh in his heart, so is he: Eat and drink, saith he to thee; but his heart is not with thee" (Pr.23:7).

"A good man out of the good treasure of his heart bringeth forth that which is good; and an evil man out of the evil treasure of his heart bringeth forth that which is evil: for of the abundance of the heart his mouth speaketh" (Lk.6:45).

4.   Jesus Christ declared that the sin of divorce may cause others to fall into adultery and sexual immorality.

"But I say unto you, That whosoever shall put away his wife, saving for the cause of fornication [sexual immorality], causeth her to commit adultery: and whosoever shall marry her that is divorced committeth adultery" (Mt.5:32).

"And I say unto you, Whosoever shall put away his wife, except it be for fornication, and shall marry another, committeth adultery: and whoso marrieth her which is put away doth commit adultery" (Mt.19:9).

Thought.

The great tragedy of fornication (sexual immorality) or adultery is that it breaks the union and attachment between husband and wife. The union and attachment and all that goes with it—faith, hope, love, trust, assurance, confidence, and strength—are broken. If the husband and wife are not believers, then the physical and mental union of the marriage are broken. If they are believers, then all three unions are broken: the physical, mental, *and spiritual*.

"What therefore God hath joined together, let not man put asunder" (Mk.10:9).

"And unto the married I command, yet not I, but the Lord, Let not the wife depart from her husband: But and if she depart, let her remain unmarried, or be reconciled to her husband: and let not the husband put away his wife" (1 Cor.7:10-11).

"Let thy fountain be blessed: and rejoice with the wife of thy youth" (Pr.5:18).

"Husbands, love your wives, even as Christ also loved the church, and gave himself for it" (Eph.5:25).

"Likewise, ye wives, be in subjection to your own husbands; that, if any obey not the word, they also may without the word be won by the conversation [behavior, conduct] of the wives" (1 Pt.3:1).

"Marriage is honourable in all, and the bed undefiled: but whoremongers and adulterers God will judge" (Heb.13:4).

"Dearly beloved, I beseech you as strangers and pilgrims, abstain from fleshly lusts, which war against the soul" (1 Pt.2:11).

"Let thy fountain be blessed: and rejoice with the wife of thy youth" (Pr.5:18).

"Let the husband render unto the wife due benevolence: and likewise also the wife unto the husband. The wife hath not power of her own body, but the husband: and likewise also the husband hath not power of his own body, but the wife" (1 Cor.7:3-4).

5.   Jesus Christ declared that adultery and sexual immorality are not unforgivable sins and that people can turn away from a life of sin.

"And the scribes and Pharisees brought unto him a woman taken in adultery; and when they had set her in the midst, They say unto him, Master, this woman was taken in adultery, in the very act. Now Moses in the law commanded us, that such should be stoned: but what sayest thou? This they said, tempting him, that they might have to accuse him. But Jesus stooped down, and with his finger wrote on the ground, as though he heard them not. So when they continued asking him, he lifted up himself, and said unto them, He that is without sin among you, let him first cast a stone at her. And again he stooped down, and wrote on the ground. And they which heard it, being convicted by their own conscience, went out one by one, beginning at the eldest, even unto the last: and Jesus was left alone, and the woman standing in the midst. When Jesus had lifted up himself, and saw none but the woman, he said unto her, Woman, where are those thine accusers? hath no man condemned thee? She said, No man, Lord. And Jesus said unto her, Neither do I condemn thee: go, and sin no more" (Jn.8:3-11).

Thought.

a)   We must always confess and repent of our sins.

"Repent therefore of this thy wickedness, and pray God, if perhaps the thought of thine heart may be forgiven thee" (Acts 8:22).

"If we confess our sins, he is faithful and just to forgive us our sins, and to cleanse us from all unrighteousness" (1 Jn.1:9).

"Let the wicked forsake his way, and the unrighteous man his thoughts: and let him return unto the LORD, and he will have mercy upon him; and to our God, for he will abundantly pardon" (Is.55:7).

"But if the wicked will turn from all his sins that he hath committed, and keep all my statutes, and do that which is lawful and right, he shall surely live, he shall not die" (Ezk.18:21).

b) We must never lose hope that Jesus Christ will lift us out of sin. He will
    wash us, sanctify us, and justify us.

> "For he hath made him to be sin for us, who knew no sin; that we
> might be made the righteousness of God in him" (2 Cor.5:21).
>
> "Know ye not that the unrighteous shall not inherit the kingdom
> of God? Be not deceived: neither fornicators, nor idolaters, nor adul-
> terers, nor effeminate, nor abusers of themselves with mankind, Nor
> thieves, nor covetous, nor drunkards, nor revilers, nor extortioners,
> shall inherit the kingdom of God. And such were some of you: but ye
> are washed, but ye are sanctified, but ye are justified in the name of
> the Lord Jesus, and by the Spirit of our God" (1 Cor.6:9-11).
>
> "Who his own self bare our sins in his own body on the tree, that
> we, being dead to sins, should live unto righteousness: by whose
> stripes ye were healed" (1 Pt.2:24).
>
> "And he is the propitiation [sacrifice, covering] for our sins: and
> not for ours only, but also for the sins of the whole world" (1 Jn.2:2).
>
> "Herein is love, not that we loved God, but that he loved us, and
> sent his Son to be the propitiation for our sins" (1 Jn.4:10).

c) We must not accept Satan's condemnation, for God forgives the repen-
    tant sinner, forgives us no matter how terrible our sin.

> "There is therefore now no condemnation to them which are in
> Christ Jesus, who walk not after the flesh, but after the Spirit. For
> the law of the Spirit of life in Christ Jesus hath made me free from
> the law of sin and death" (Ro.8:1-2).
>
> "He hath not dealt with us after our sins; nor rewarded us ac-
> cording to our iniquities. For as the heaven is high above the earth,
> so great is his mercy toward them that fear him. As far as the east is
> from the west, so far hath he removed our transgressions from us.
> Like as a father pitieth his children, so the Lord pitieth them that
> fear him. For he knoweth our frame; he remembereth that we are
> dust" (Ps.103:10-14).
>
> "Who forgiveth all thine iniquities; who healeth all thy diseases"
> (Ps.103:3).

d) We must not abuse God's grace, must not fall back into a lifestyle of sin.

> "What shall we say then? Shall we continue in sin, that grace
> may abound? God forbid. How shall we, that are dead to sin, live
> any longer therein?" (Ro.6:1-2).
>
> "For if after they have escaped the pollutions of the world
> through the knowledge of the Lord and Saviour Jesus Christ, they
> are again entangled therein, and overcome, the latter end is worse
> with them than the beginning. For it had been better for them not to
> have known the way of righteousness, than, after they have known it,

to turn from the holy commandment delivered unto them. But it is happened unto them according to the true proverb, The dog is turned to his own vomit again; and the sow that was washed to her wallowing in the mire" (2 Pt.2:20-22).

VI. What Is the Decision Required by This Commandment?

Very simply, we must never commit adultery, never commit an immoral act. We must live pure, holy lives. But how? How can we guard ourselves to keep from committing sexual sin in a sex-crazed society—a society that uses sex to sell products and to provide entertainment, pleasure, and recreation? Scripture says the following:

1.   Never take a second look. And if you can prevent the first look, *never* look. As someone has said, we cannot keep the birds from flying over our heads, but we can prevent them from roosting there.

> "But I say unto you, That whosoever looketh on a woman to lust after her hath committed adultery with her already in his heart" (Mt.5:28).
> "I made a covenant with mine eyes; why then should I think upon a maid?" (Job 31:1).

2.   Flee temptation; flee the very appearance of evil. We must always flee at the very first offer, the very first sight, the very first thought, the very first urge (desire).

> "Abstain from all appearance of evil" (1 Th.5:22).

3.   Flee immorality—abstain totally.

> "Flee fornication [all forms of illicit sex]" (1 Cor.6:18).
> "For this is the will of God, even your sanctification, that ye should abstain from fornication: That every one of you should know how to possess his vessel in sanctification and honour; Not in the lust of concupiscence, even as the Gentiles which know not God" (1 Th.4:3-5).

4.   Never touch the unclean thing.

> "Wherefore come out from among them, and be ye separate, saith the Lord, and touch not the unclean thing; and I will receive you, And will be a Father unto you, and ye shall be my sons and daughters, saith the Lord Almighty" (2 Cor.6:17-18).

5.   Never talk about immorality, not even once.

> "But fornication, and all uncleanness, or covetousness, let it not be once named among you, as becometh saints; Neither filthiness, nor foolish talking, nor jesting, which are not convenient: but rather giving of thanks" (Eph.5:3-4).

6.   Never give any part of your body over to sin.

> "Neither yield ye your members [body parts] as instruments of unrighteousness unto sin: but yield yourselves unto God, as those that are alive from the dead, and your members as instruments of righteousness unto God" (Ro.6:13).

7.   Never let sin control your body.

> "Let not sin therefore reign in your mortal body, that ye should obey it in the lusts thereof" (Ro.6:12, cp. v.11-13).

8.   Do not love the world nor the things of the world.

> "Love not the world, neither the things that are in the world. If any man love the world, the love of the Father is not in him. For all that is in the world, the lust of the flesh, and the lust of the eyes, and the pride of life, is not of the Father, but is of the world" (1 Jn.2:15-16).

9.   Live a crucified life, a life sacrificed totally to Christ.

> "I am crucified with Christ: nevertheless I live; yet not I, but Christ liveth in me: and the life which I now live in the flesh I live by the faith of the Son of God, who loved me, and gave himself for me" (Gal.2:20).
>
> "And he said to [them] all, If any [man] will come after me, let him deny himself, and take up his cross daily, and follow me" (Lk.9:23).

10.   Sacrifice and commit your body totally to Jesus Christ.

> "I beseech you therefore, brethren, by the mercies of God, that ye present your bodies a living sacrifice, holy, acceptable unto God, which is your reasonable service. And be not conformed to this world: but be ye transformed by the renewing of your mind, that ye may prove what is that good, and acceptable, and perfect, will of God" (Ro.12:1-2).

11. Put the sinful acts of the body to death.

> "Likewise reckon ye also yourselves to be dead indeed unto sin, but alive unto God through Jesus Christ our Lord" (Ro.6:11).
> "For if ye live after the flesh, ye shall die: but if ye through the Spirit do mortify [put to death] the deeds of the body, ye shall live" (Ro.8:13).

12. Discipline yourself—strenuously so—in order to control your body.

> "But I keep under my body, and bring it into subjection: lest that by any means, when I have preached to others, I myself should be a castaway" (1 Cor.9:27).

13. Be filled with the Spirit of God not with alcoholic drink nor with drugs.

> "And be not drunk with wine, wherein is excess; but be filled with the Spirit" (Eph.5:18).

14. Guard your spirit.

> "Take heed to your spirit, and let none deal treacherously against the wife of his youth" (Mal.2:15).

15. Glorify God in your body.

> "Flee fornication. Every sin that a man doeth is without the body; but he that commiteth fornication sinneth against his own body. What? know ye not that your body is the temple of the Holy Ghost which is in you, which ye have of God, and ye are not your own? For ye are bought with a price: therefore glorify God in your body, and in your spirit, which are God's" (1 Cor.6:18-20).

16. Captivate and subject every thought to obey Christ.

> "Casting down imaginations, and every high thing that exalteth itself against the knowledge of God, and bringing into captivity every thought to the obedience of Christ" (2 Cor.10:5).

17. Listen to God's Word: hide His Word in your heart and live by it.

> "Wherewithal shall a young man cleanse his way? by taking heed thereto according to thy word....Thy word have I hid in mine heart, that I might not sin against thee" (Ps.119:9, 11).

Commandment Eight Concerns Man's Property—Never Steal Exodus 20:15

Contents

Commandment Eight Concerns Man's Property—Never Steal
Exodus 20:15

COMMANDMENT 8 Concerns *man's property*— Never steal	15 Thou shalt not steal.

Think for a moment. What is *the crime* most often committed within your community? The nation? Around the world? Probably stealing. So many people steal that stealing has become a very commonplace crime of society. If the thief does not assault or kill the victim, he is simply called a *common thief*. Thievery, robbery, and swindling have become epidemic, contributing to the lawlessness within society. And stealing is such a terrible epidemic that it threatens the very foundation of society itself. Just think of...

- government leaders who steal and misuse funds
- employees who steal from their employer
- employers who steal through unfair prices and wages
- dishonest athletes and famous people who steal
- acquaintances and neighbors who steal and are dishonest
- people who steal by living extravagant and indulgent lifestyles, hoarding and banking when so many are in such desperate need throughout the world
- people who steal by taking so much of the earth's wealth and resources

Stealing shows a disrespect for property and for human life. Stealing leads to more and more lawlessness, sometimes even assault and murder. Stealing always creates some havoc, and it can cause devastation. Stealing can bankrupt families, companies, communities, and even nations. Stealing always causes loss, loss for both the victim and the thief. The victim, of course, loses whatever object (physical or otherwise) is stolen; but in addition, the loss can be very painful and sometimes irreplaceable. The thief, though frequently undetected by men, always loses his reputation, integrity, and character before God; and eventually, unless he repents and turns from his sin, he loses his soul.

This is the subject of this important commandment: *Commandment Eight Concerns Man's Property—Never Steal*, 20:15.

I.   Who is to obey this commandment? How long was this commandment to be in force (v.15)?

II.   What is forbidden by this commandment (v.15)?

III.   What are the Biblical consequences of breaking this commandment?

IV.   What are the Biblical benefits of keeping this commandment?

V.   What is the teaching of Jesus Christ concerning this commandment?

VI.   What is the decision required by this commandment (v.15)?

I.   Who Is to Obey This Commandment? How Long Was This Commandment to Be in Force?

Was it only for the people of ancient times, or is it for us today as well? Stealing has been a problem for society as long as man has been on the earth, a serious problem. God gave this commandment because He cares for man, so much so that He wants to protect everything that concerns man, both his life and his property. Frankly, it would be foolish to suggest that God was concerned for the people and property of the ancient world but is unconcerned with the people and property of our day.

Note the verse: "You shall not steal." This commandment is directed to you and to every person who will ever live. It was wrong to steal in the ancient world, a terrible violation against man and God; and it is wrong to steal today. This commandment is in force today as much as it was in force for Israel:

> **"Thou shalt not steal" (Ex.20:15).**
> **"Let him that stole steal no more" (Eph.4:28).**

II.   What Is Forbidden by This Commandment?

1. "Stealing" (ganab) means to take and keep something that belongs to another person. William Barclay says:

> "[Stealing] is a 'natural' sin. It is human nature to want what we have not got; and the desire may turn to action; and, when it does, a man may steal. We do not need to argue about the rightness of this commandment. Everyone agrees that stealing is wrong."[1]

God has made man a working being, a being who must work, produce, achieve, accomplish, and possess. The desire to move ahead and progress is

---

[1] William Barclay. *The Old & The New Law*, p.37.

planted within man by God. This is the reason we desire things that we do not have. The desire is normal and natural; it is God-given. But the legitimate way to fulfill that desire is to work for what we want and can achieve in life. The illegitimate way to fulfill the desire is to steal. When we act out our desire to take something that does not belong to us—take it either secretly or by force—it is stealing.

2. Note that stealing is a *heart problem*: the cause, the source of stealing, is found in the human heart. Stealing begins with a desire, a passion, a lust, an urge, a coveting within man. When the desire is planted—when it conceives and it is carried out—the person steals. This is exactly what God says:

> **"But every man is tempted, when he is drawn away of his own lust, and enticed. Then when lust hath conceived, it bringeth forth sin: and sin, when it is finished, bringeth forth death" (Jas.1:14-15).**

Thought 1.
Note an excellent example of coveting—of desiring and lusting—in Scripture.

> **"When I saw among the spoils a goodly Babylonish garment, and two hundred shekels of silver, and a wedge of gold of fifty shekels weight, then I coveted them, and took them; and, behold, they are hid in the earth in the midst of my tent, and the silver under it" (Josh.7:21).**

Thought 2.
Arthur W. Pink[2] points out the following:
a) Stealing was the first sin committed by the human race: Eve took of the forbidden fruit.

> **"And when the woman saw that the tree was good for food, and that it was pleasant to the eyes, and a tree to be desired to make one wise, she took of the fruit thereof, and did eat, and gave also unto her husband with her; and he did eat" (Gen.3:6).**

b) Stealing was the first recorded sin committed by Israel after entering Canaan: Achan stole the spoils of war.

> **"When I saw among the spoils a goodly Babylonish garment, and two hundred shekels of silver, and a wedge of gold of fifty shekels weight, then I coveted them, and took them; and, behold, they are hid in the earth in the midst of my tent, and the silver under it" (Josh.7:21).**

---

[2] Arthur W. Pink. *The Ten Commandments*, p.54.

c) Stealing was the first recorded sin to defile the early church: Ananias and Sapphira kept back some of the money from the sale of their property, money that was to be given to the church.

> "But a certain man named Ananias, with Sapphira his wife, sold a possession, And kept back part of the price, his wife also being privy to it, and brought a certain part, and laid it at the apostles' feet. But Peter said, Ananias, why hath Satan filled thine heart to lie to the Holy Ghost, and to keep back part of the price of the land?" (Acts 5:1-3).

3. God's purpose for commanding people not to steal can be simply stated: it is to protect a person's property and his right to own property, to preserve peace among neighbors and within society. Stealing causes loss—sometimes terrible loss—to the victim. And stealing always leads to hard feelings, broken relationships, and sometimes revenge. This commandment protects a person's right...

- to feed, house, clothe, and provide for himself and his family
- to own property
- to reap and keep the property and rewards of his labor
- to secure enough goods and money to help meet the desperate needs of the poor, the suffering, and the lost of this world

> "Let him that stole steal no more: but rather let him labour, working with his hands the thing which is good, that he may have to give to him that needeth" (Eph.4:28).
>
> "For even when we were with you, this we commanded you, that if any would not work, neither should he eat. For we hear that there are some which walk among you disorderly, working not at all, but are busybodies. Now them that are such we command and exhort by our Lord Jesus Christ, that with quietness they work, and eat their own bread" (2 Th.3:10-12).

4. Now, how is this commandment broken, violated? Stealing is so common and so costly to society that the way people go about stealing needs to be studied. Moreover, stealing is not only a sin against society and the people stolen from, stealing is a sin against God. Stealing condemns a person to death, eternal death—unless the person repents and turns to God. For this reason, the various forms of stealing need to be looked at in some detail. A person breaks God's commandment, a person steals...

- by robbing a person, store, company, organization, bank, etc.
- by shoplifting
- by loafing on the job
- by not paying bills
- by keeping something borrowed
- by failing to pay debts
- by not paying due taxes

- by stealing the reputation and character of another through lies, gossip, or rumor
- by taking away a person's right to justice (Is.10:1-3)
- by false or deceptive advertising
- by keeping an overpayment or excessive refund check, or over-shipment of goods
- by overcharging or price-gouging: charging unfair prices
- by not paying fair and just wages
- by not giving a full day's work on the job
- by taking things from one's employer
- by making unauthorized phone calls
- by padding expense reports
- by unjustly extending business trips at company expense
- by manipulating information or stocks for personal gain
- by abusing sick days
- by arriving at work late or leaving work early without permission
- by stealing and enslaving people for work and profit
- by breaking the rules or cheating to win something, a game or a prize

All acts of stealing are wrong, but there is one form of stealing that is most serious and damning, that of robbing God:

⇒ A person robs God by failing to pay his tithes and offerings to God.

> "Even from the days of your fathers ye are gone away from mine ordinances, and have not kept them. Return unto me, and I will re-turn unto you, saith the LORD of hosts. But ye said, Wherein shall we return? Will a man rob God? Yet ye have robbed me. But ye say, Wherein have we robbed thee? In tithes and offerings" (Mal.3:7-8).

⇒ A person robs God by living a hypocritical, inconsistent life. When a person professes to believe and follow God, then fails to follow through, he robs God and other men of a *godly testimony*.

> "What? know ye not that your body is the temple of the Holy Ghost which is in you, which ye have of God, and ye are not your own? For ye are bought with a price: therefore glorify God in your body, and in your spirit, which are God's" (1 Cor.6:19-20).

⇒ A person robs God by living for self and the world, by choosing not to live for God. God is the great Creator of man; therefore, man owes his life—all he is and has—to God. When a person chooses to live like he wants, he steals his life from God.

> "I beseech you therefore, brethren, by the mercies of God, that ye present your bodies a living sacrifice, holy, acceptable unto God, which is your reasonable service. And be not conformed to this world: but be ye transformed by the renewing of your mind, that ye

may prove what is that good, and acceptable, and perfect, will of God" (Ro.12:1-2).

"Love not the world, neither the things that are in the world. If any man love the world, the love of the Father is not in him. For all that is in the world, the lust of the flesh, and the lust of the eyes, and the pride of life, is not of the Father, but is of the world" (1 Jn.2:15-16).

Thought 1.

This commandment against stealing is broken when property is taken, no matter how little and insignificant the item may be. F.B. Huey again has an excellent comment on the breaking of this commandment.

"The spirit of this commandment can be broken in ways other than taking the property of another violently or covertly. The employee who takes paper clips, postage stamps, stationery, etc., from his employer for personal use, the taxpayer who falsifies his tax return, the friend who borrows money or even a cup of sugar without intent of returning it, the shopkeeper who uses dishonest scales or engages in any kind of fraudulent business practice, the student who takes credit for work that was done by someone else, the employee who loafs on the job but accepts full wages, or the nation that takes the land of another by war—all violate this commandment."[3]

Maxie Dunnam also has an excellent application on this commandment:

"One of the tragedies of our day is how the justice system treats crimes of stealing. Poor people, with no money to hire legal defense, waste away in prisons for stealing a car or a television, while officers of huge corporate organizations preside in posh board rooms, though it is proven they have manipulated the stock market. Television gives us almost daily reports of defense contract 'cost overrides' that steal millions of tax dollars....Ours is a society 'on the take,' and stealing is one of our most blatant sins....

"Apart from the obvious ways of seeing this commandment broken, we should think of the more subtle ways we break it.
- by not giving our employers a full day for the pay we receive
- by stealing the good name of another with malicious gossip
- by remaining silent, thus stealing from another the word that might preserve reputation and/or undergird character
- by failing to give to others the support, praise, and credit they're due."[4]

---

[3] F.B. Huey, Jr. *Exodus*, p.91.
[4] Maxie Dunnam, *Mastering the Old Testament, Volume 2: Exodus*, p.265-266.

III. What Are the Consequences of Breaking This Commandment?

We live in a world where people have little respect for the property of others. Even when devastating tragedies strike (such as hurricanes), people race each other to see how much they can steal before the authorities restore order. God hates the sin of stealing with a strong passion. Why? Because stealing identifies a person with the greatest thief of all, Satan himself. The Scriptures expose Satan for what he is, a thief.

> "The thief [Satan] cometh not, but for to steal, and to kill, and to destroy: I am come that they might have life, and that they might have it more abundantly" (Jn.10:10).

God has spared no judgment for the thief of all thieves. Likewise, God will give every thief his just due. Anyone who breaks this holy commandment will suffer serious consequences. A thief would do well to heed this strong warning, a warning that will punish any violator who dares to break this commandment.

1. The person who steals and is committed to a life of crime will not inherit the kingdom of God.

> "Know ye not that the unrighteous shall not inherit the kingdom of God? Be not deceived: neither fornicators, nor idolaters, nor adulterers, nor effeminate, nor abusers of themselves with mankind, Nor thieves, nor covetous, nor drunkards, nor revilers, nor extortioners, shall inherit the kingdom of God" (1 Cor.6:9-10).

2. The persons [Adam and Eve] who stole from God in the garden of Eden died.

> "And the Lord God commanded the man, saying, Of every tree of the garden thou mayest freely eat: But of the tree of the knowledge of good and evil, thou shalt not eat of it: for in the day that thou eatest thereof thou shalt surely die" (Gen.2:16-17).

3. The person who steals defiles himself, makes himself unclean.

> "For out of the heart proceed evil thoughts, murders, adulteries, fornications, thefts, false witness, blasphemies: These are the things which defile a man" (Mt.15:19-20).

4. The person who steals angers God and provokes His wrath.

> "But the children of Israel committed a trespass in the accursed thing: for Achan, the son of Carmi, the son of Zabdi, the son of Zerah, of the tribe of Judah, took of the accursed thing: and the anger of the Lord was kindled against the children of Israel" (Josh.7:1).

"A false balance is abomination to the Lord: but a just weight is his delight" (Pr.11:1).

"Divers [differing] weights, and divers [differing] measures, both of them are alike abomination to the Lord" (Pr.20:10).

"Woe unto him that buildeth his house by unrighteousness, and his chambers by wrong; that useth his neighbour's service without wages, and giveth him not for his work" (Jer.22:13).

"Nor thieves, nor covetous, nor drunkards, nor revilers, nor extortioners, shall inherit the kingdom of God" (1 Cor.6:10).

5. The person who steals places his life in mortal danger.

"The getting of treasures by a lying tongue is a vanity tossed to and fro of them that seek death" (Pr.21:6).

6. The person who steals shows that he has forgotten God.

"In thee have they taken gifts to shed blood; thou hast taken usury and increase, and thou hast greedily gained of thy neighbours by extortion, and hast forgotten me, saith the LORD God" (Ezk.22:12).

7. The person who steals follows in the steps of God's adversary, Satan himself.

"The thief [Satan] cometh not, but for to steal, and to kill, and to destroy: I am come that they might have life, and that they might have it more abundantly" (Jn.10:10).

8. The person who steals causes heartache and sometimes painful suffering for others.

"And it came to pass, when David and his men were come to Ziklag on the third day, that the Amalekites had invaded the south, and Ziklag, and smitten Ziklag, and burned it with fire; And had taken the women captives, that were therein: they slew not any, either great or small, but carried them away, and went on their way. So David and his men came to the city, and, behold, it was burned with fire; and their wives, and their sons, and their daughters, were taken captives. Then David and the people that were with him lifted up their voice and wept, until they had no more power to weep" (1 Sam.30:1-4).

9. The person who steals causes economic hardship for the victim.

"Thou shalt not defraud thy neighbour, neither rob him: the wages of him that is hired shall not abide with thee all night until the morning" (Lev.19:13).

10. The person who steals the wife or husband of another causes families to be torn apart.

> "A foolish woman is clamorous: she is simple, and knoweth nothing. For she sitteth at the door of her house, on a seat in the high places of the city, To call passengers who go right on their ways: Whoso is simple, let him turn in hither: and as for him that wanteth understanding, she saith to him, Stolen waters are sweet, and bread eaten in secret is pleasant. But he knoweth not that the dead are there; and that her guests are in the depths of hell" (Pr.9:13-18).

11. The person who steals will eventually lose everything and prove that he is a fool.

> "As the partridge sitteth on eggs, and hatcheth them not; so he that getteth riches, and not by right, shall leave them in the midst of his days, and at his end shall be a fool" (Jer.17:11).

12. The person who steals is to make restitution. He is held accountable by God to make restitution.

> "If a man shall steal an ox, or a sheep, and kill it, or sell it; he shall restore five oxen for an ox, and four sheep for a sheep" (Ex.22:1).
> "If a man shall deliver unto his neighbour money or stuff to keep, and it be stolen out of the man's house; if the thief be found, let him pay double" (Ex.22:7).
> "And if it be stolen from him, he shall make restitution unto the owner thereof" (Ex.22:12).

13. The person who steals from the poor will become poor himself.

> "He that oppresseth the poor to increase his riches, and he that giveth to the rich, shall surely come to want" (Pr.22:16).

14. The person who steals tithes and offerings—who does not give his tithes and offerings to God—robs God.

> "Will a man rob God? Yet ye have robbed me. But ye say, Wherein have we robbed thee? In tithes and offerings" (Mal.3:8).

IV.   What Are the Benefits of Keeping This Commandment?

What would the world be like if everyone kept this commandment? If there was no thievery upon earth? The benefits and blessings of honesty would be unlimited.

1. A person who is honest and lives for God will have the constant presence and care of God.

> "Let your conversation [behavior, conduct] be without covetousness; and be content with such things as ye have: for he hath said, I will never leave thee, nor forsake thee" (Heb.13:5).

2. A person who belongs to the LORD and is honest will walk in righteousness and live in security.

> "He that walketh uprightly walketh surely: but he that perverteth his ways [steals] shall be known" (Pr.10:9).

3. A person who follows God and is honest will learn to be content.

> "Not that I speak in respect of want: for I have learned, in whatsoever state I am, therewith to be content. I know both how to be abased, and I know how to abound: every where and in all things I am instructed both to be full and to be hungry, both to abound and to suffer need" (Ph.4:11-12).
>
> "But godliness with contentment is great gain. For we brought nothing into this world, and it is certain we can carry nothing out. And having food and raiment let us be therewith content" (1 Tim.6:6-8).

4. A person who is honest and fears the LORD will be better off than a person with great treasure.

> "Better is little with the fear of the LORD than great treasure and trouble therewith" (Pr.15:16).

5. A person who is honest will have labor that is profitable.

> "Wealth gotten by vanity [dishonest money] shall be diminished: but he that gathereth by labour shall increase" (Pr.13:11).

6. A person who is honest and knows the LORD labors with his own hands, helping those in need.

> "Let him that stole steal no more: but rather let him labour, working with his hands the thing which is good, that he may have to give to him that needeth" (Eph.4:28).

7. A person who lives a righteous life is honest and will be delivered from death.

> "Treasures of wickedness profit nothing: but righteousness delivereth from death" (Pr.10:2).
>
> "But they that will be rich fall into temptation and a snare, and into many foolish and hurtful lusts, which drown men in destruction and perdition....But thou, O man of God, flee these things; and follow after righteousness, godliness, faith, love, patience, meekness. Fight the good fight of faith, lay hold on eternal life, whereunto thou art also called, and hast professed a good profession before many witnesses" (1 Tim.6:9, 11-12).

8. A person who loves God is honest and earns eternal treasures that are safely stored in heaven.

> "Lay not up for yourselves treasures upon earth, where moth and rust doth corrupt, and where thieves break through and steal: But lay up for yourselves treasures in heaven, where neither moth nor rust doth corrupt, and where thieves do not break through nor steal" (Mt.6:19-20).

9. A person who belongs to the LORD and is honest bears a strong witness for the LORD.

> "Not purloining [stealing], but showing all good fidelity; that they may adorn the doctrine of God our Saviour in all things" (Tit.2:10).

V.   What Is the Teaching of Jesus Christ Concerning This Commandment?

1. Jesus Christ declared that God commanded man not to steal.

> "He saith unto him, Which? Jesus said, Thou shalt do no murder, Thou shalt not commit adultery, Thou shalt not steal, Thou shalt not bear false witness" (Mt.19:18; cp. Mk.10:19; Lk.18:20).

<u>Thought.</u>
Scripture is clear: stealing is wrong.

> "Thou shalt not steal" (Ex.20:15).
> "Thou shalt not defraud thy neighbour, neither rob him" (Lev.19:13).
> "Let him that stole steal no more" (Eph.4:28).

A person who steals and never repents by turning to God will not inherit the kingdom of God.

> "Know ye not that the unrighteous shall not inherit the kingdom of God? Be not deceived: neither fornicators, nor idolaters, nor adul-

terers, nor effeminate, nor abusers of themselves with mankind, Nor thieves, nor covetous, nor drunkards, nor revilers, nor extortioners, shall inherit the kingdom of God" (1 Cor.6:9-10).

2. Jesus Christ declared that Satan is a thief and the source behind all stealing.

"The thief [Satan] cometh not, but for to steal, and to kill, and to destroy..." (Jn.10:10).

Thought.

a) Satan is a subtle destroyer of God's people. Satan is the one who tempts men to steal what is not theirs.

"Now the serpent was more subtil than any beast of the field which the LORD God had made. And he said unto the woman, Yea, hath God said, Ye shall not eat of every tree of the garden? And the woman said unto the serpent, We may eat of the fruit of the trees of the garden: But of the fruit of the tree which is in the midst of the garden, God hath said, Ye shall not eat of it, neither shall ye touch it, lest ye die. And the serpent said unto the woman, Ye shall not surely die: For God doth know that in the day ye eat thereof, then your eyes shall be opened, and ye shall be as gods, knowing good and evil. And when the woman saw that the tree was good for food, and that it was pleasant to the eyes, and a tree to be desired to make one wise, she took of the fruit thereof, and did eat, and gave also unto her husband with her; and he did eat" (Gen.3:1-6).

b) Satan is crafty. He fills the hearts of careless and unprotected men with an unquenchable desire for more and more.

"But the children of Israel committed a trespass in the accursed thing: for Achan, the son of Carmi, the son of Zabdi, the son of Zerah, of the tribe of Judah, took of the accursed thing: and the anger of the LORD was kindled against the children of Israel" (Josh.7:1).

"And it came to pass, as we went to prayer, a certain damsel possessed with a spirit of divination met us, which brought her masters much gain by soothsaying: The same followed Paul and us, and cried, saying, These men are the servants of the most high God, which show unto us the way of salvation. And this did she many days. But Paul, being grieved, turned and said to the spirit, I command thee in the name of Jesus Christ to come out of her. And he came out the same hour. And when her masters saw that the hope of their gains was gone, they caught Paul and Silas, and drew them into the marketplace unto the rulers" (Acts 16:16-19).

"For Demas hath forsaken me, having loved this present world, and is departed unto Thessalonica; Crescens to Galatia, Titus unto Dalmatia" (2 Tim.4:10).

3. Jesus Christ declared that there is no security in storing the world's treasures because thieves steal them or else they waste away or decrease in value.

> **"Lay not up for yourselves treasures upon earth, where moth and rust doth corrupt, and where thieves break through and steal: But lay up for yourselves treasures in heaven, where neither moth nor rust doth corrupt, and where thieves do not break through nor steal"** (Mt.6:19-20).

Thought.
a)   We are to place no confidence in earthly riches: they will not last.
b)   We are to collect heavenly riches...
   * because they will give meaning and purpose to life
   * because they will escape corruption
   * because they cannot be stolen by anyone
c)   We are to have a pure heart in order...
   * to grasp the true treasure, the treasure in heaven
   * to protect ourselves from the consequences of greed and covetousness
d)   We are to love Christ with an undivided and uncompromising devotion.

> **"For what is a man profited, if he shall gain the whole world, and lose his own soul? or what shall a man give in exchange for his soul?"** (Mt.16:26).
> **"For the love of money is the root of all evil: which while some coveted after, they have erred from the faith, and pierced themselves through with many sorrows"** (1 Tim.6:10).
> **"Better is little with the fear of the Lord than great treasure and trouble therewith"** (Pr.15:16).
> **"But seek ye first the kingdom of God, and his righteousness; and all these things shall be added unto you. Take therefore no thought for the morrow: for the morrow shall take thought for the things of itself. Sufficient unto the day is the evil thereof"** (Mt.6:33-34).

4. Jesus Christ declared that man's craving for material possessions (the cares of this life and the lure of wealth) will leave him with an empty life, an unfruitful life.

> **"And some [seed] fell among thorns; and the thorns sprung up, and choked them....He also that received seed among the thorns is he that heareth the word; and the care of this world, and the deceitfulness of riches, choke the word, and he becometh unfruitful"** (Mt.13:7, 22).

<u>Thought.</u>

a) We must not be deceived and ensnared by the cares of the world. Note their effect on a person:

⇒ They prick and prick away at the Word.

⇒ They entangle a person in the world and the things of the world (2 Tim.2:3-4).

⇒ They irritate, aggravate, trouble, and hinder a person from pursuing his task.

⇒ They keep a person's mind on the cares of the world, not on God and the things of the Word or Spirit (Ro.8:5-8; 2 Cor.10:3-5).

b) We must not crave wealth or we will become deceived...

- by becoming self-confident and self-dependent
- by becoming overly comfortable, extravagant, and indulgent
- by becoming consumed with thoughts of keeping what we have and passionately finding more
- by becoming secure in a false idea of what it means to be blessed by God

"For we brought nothing into this world, and it is certain we can carry nothing out" (1 Tim.6:7).

"But they that will be rich fall into temptation and a snare, and into many foolish and hurtful lusts, which drown men in destruction and perdition" (1 Tim.6:9).

"And the cares of this world, and the deceitfulness of riches, and the lusts of other things entering in, choke the word, and it becometh unfruitful" (Mk.4:19).

"Then said Jesus unto his disciples, Verily I say unto you, That a rich man shall hardly enter into the kingdom of heaven. And Jesus looked round about, and saith unto his disciples, How hardly shall they that have riches enter into the kingdom of God! And the disciples were astonished at his words. But Jesus answereth again, and saith unto them, Children, how hard is it for them that trust in riches to enter into the kingdom of God! It is easier for a camel to go through the eye of a needle, than for a rich man to enter into the kingdom of God" (Mk.10:23-25).

"And again I say unto you, It is easier for a camel to go through the eye of a needle, than for a rich man to enter into the kingdom of God" (Mt.19:23-24).

"Your gold and silver is cankered; and the rust of them shall be a witness against you, and shall eat your flesh as it were fire. Ye have heaped treasure together for the last days" (Jas.5:3).

"Wilt thou set thine eyes upon that which is not? for riches certainly make themselves wings; they fly away as an eagle toward heaven" (Pr.23:5).

"As the partridge sitteth on eggs, and hatcheth them not; so he that getteth riches, and not by right, shall leave them in the midst of his days, and at his end shall be a fool" (Jer.17:11).

5. Jesus Christ declared the following:
  ⇒ If a man cheats a little, he will not be honest with greater responsibilities.
  ⇒ If a man is not faithful with the money of other people, he cannot be trusted with his own money.
  ⇒ If a man cannot be trusted with worldly wealth, he cannot be trusted with the true riches of heaven.
  ⇒ A man cannot serve God and money—he must chose whom he will serve.
  ⇒ Unless a man is faithful in small matters, he will not be faithful in large ones.

  "He that is faithful in that which is least is faithful also in much: and he that is unjust in the least is unjust also in much. If therefore ye have not been faithful in the unrighteous mammon, who will commit to your trust the true riches? And if ye have not been faithful in that which is another man's, who shall give you that which is your own? No servant can serve two masters: for either he will hate the one, and love the other; or else he will hold to the one, and despise the other. Ye cannot serve God and mammon" (Lk.16:10-13).

Thought.
a) We must be found faithful in handling possessions, for our faithfulness determines what we will be trusted with eternally.
b) Money and possessions are the least trust given to a person. They are nothing compared to spiritual riches, to true heavenly riches. We must desire true and lasting treasure more than anything else.
c) A person serves one of two masters, either God or the things and riches of the world. He gives himself either to one or the other:
  ⇒ He focuses himself upon the things and riches of the world or upon God.
  ⇒ He turns himself over to the things and riches of the world or to God.
  ⇒ He thinks primarily upon the things of the world or upon God.
  ⇒ He gives his time, energy, and effort to the things of the world or to God.
  ⇒ He allows his worldly pursuits to control him, or Christ to control his pursuits.

  "And if it seem evil unto you to serve the LORD, choose you this day whom ye will serve; whether the gods which your fathers served that were on the other side of the flood, or the gods of the Amorites, in whose land ye dwell: but as for me and my house, we will serve the LORD" (Josh.24:15).

"Then Jesus beholding him loved him, and said unto him, One thing thou lackest: go thy way, sell whatsoever thou hast, and give to the poor, and thou shalt have treasure in heaven: and come, take up the cross, and follow me" (Mk.10:21).

"Draw nigh to God, and he will draw nigh to you. Cleanse your hands, ye sinners; and purify your hearts, ye double minded" (Jas.4:8).

"See, I have set before thee this day life and good, and death and evil" (Dt.30:15).

"...How long halt ye between two opinions? if the LORD be God, follow him: but if Baal, then follow him. And the people answered him not a word" (1 Ki.18:21).

VI.   What Is the Decision Required by This Commandment?

1. Scripture is very forceful in telling us exactly what *not to do*:
   a. We must never steal, not even once.

   > "Thou shalt not steal" (Ex.20:15).

   b. We must never withhold tithes and offerings from God.

   > "Will a man rob God? Yet ye have robbed me. But ye say, Wherein have we robbed thee? In tithes and offerings. Ye are cursed with a curse: for ye have robbed me, even this whole nation. Bring ye all the tithes into the storehouse, that there may be meat in mine house, and prove me now herewith, saith the LORD of hosts, if I will not open you the windows of heaven, and pour you out a blessing, that there shall not be room enough to receive it" (Mal.3:8-10).

   c. We must never cheat our brother in anything.

   > "That no man go beyond and defraud his brother in any matter: because that the Lord is the avenger of all such, as we also have forewarned you and testified" (1 Th.4:6).

   d. We must never steal people (kidnap, enslave, or put them in bondage): the enslavement of people takes away a person's right to his own life.

   > "And he that stealeth a man, and selleth him, or if he be found in his hand, he shall surely be put to death" (Ex.21:16).

2. Scripture is also very forceful in telling us exactly *what to do*:

    a. We must practice the golden rule: be honest, fair, and just with all people; treat others as we would want to be treated.

> "Recompense to no man evil for evil. Provide things honest in the sight of all men" (Ro.12:17).
> "Therefore all things whatsoever ye would that men should do to you, do ye even so to them: for this is the law and the prophets" (Mt.7:12).

    b. We must love our neighbor as ourselves.

> "Master, which is the great commandment in the law? Jesus said unto him, Thou shalt love the Lord thy God with all thy heart, and with all thy soul, and with all thy mind. This is the first and great commandment. And the second [is] like unto it, Thou shalt love thy neighbour as thyself" (Mt.22:36-39).

    c. We must be temperate, controlled in all things.

> "And every man that striveth for the mastery is temperate in all things. Now they do it to obtain a corruptible crown; but we an incorruptible" (1 Cor.9:25).

    d. We must learn to be content with what we have; learn that we brought nothing into this world, and we can carry nothing out.

> "For we brought nothing into this world, and it is certain we can carry nothing out. And having food and raiment let us be therewith content" (1 Tim.6:7-8).
> "Let your conversation [behavior, conduct, life] be without covetousness; and be content with such things as ye have: for he hath said, I will never leave thee, nor forsake thee" (Heb.13:5).

    e. We must channel our desires toward eternal, heavenly treasures, not toward the temporary things of the earth.

> "Set your affection on things above, not on things on the earth" (Col.3:2).

    f. We must quit stealing and go to work: we must even work long and hard in order to earn more so that we can earn enough to help others.

> "Let him that stole steal no more: but rather let him labour, working with his hands the thing which is good, that he may have to give to him that needeth" (Eph.4:28).

g. We must realize this astounding truth: what we measure to others will be measured to us.

"Give, and it shall be given unto you; good measure, pressed down, and shaken together, and running over, shall men give into your bosom. For with the same measure that ye mete withal it shall be measured to you again" (Lk.6:38).

h. We must learn the phenomenal, unbelievable promise of God: that we are not to get things by stealing, but by prayer and hard work.

"Let him that stole steal no more: but rather let him labour, working with his hands the thing which is good, that he may have to give to him that needeth" (Eph.4:28).
"Ye have not, because ye ask not" (Jas.4:2).

i. We must learn to work hard and trust God for the necessities of life. Stealing shows that we fail to trust God and His care for us.

"But seek ye first the kingdom of God, and his righteousness; and all these things [clothing, food, shelter] shall be added unto you" (Mt.6:33).
"But my God shall supply all your need according to his riches in glory by Christ Jesus" (Ph.4:19).
"For we hear that there are some which walk among you disorderly, working not at all, but are busybodies. Now them that are such we command and exhort by our Lord Jesus Christ, that with quietness they work, and eat their own bread" (2 Th.3:11-12).

j. We must realize that stealing is a terrible sin: the thief shall face the terrifying judgment and condemnation of God.

"Not every one that saith unto me, Lord, Lord, shall enter into the kingdom of heaven; but he that doeth the will of my Father which is in heaven. Many will say to me in that day, Lord, Lord, have we not prophesied in thy name? and in thy name have cast out devils? and in thy name done many wonderful works? And then will I profess unto them, I never knew you: depart from me, ye that work iniquity" (Mt.7:21-23).
"And as it is appointed unto men once to die, but after this the judgment" (Heb.9:27).
"For what shall it profit a man, if he shall gain the whole world, and lose his own soul? Or what shall a man give in exchange for his soul?" (Mk.8:36-37).
"And I will say to my soul, Soul, thou hast much goods laid up for many years; take thine ease, eat, drink, [and] be merry. But God said unto him, [Thou] fool, this night thy soul shall be required of thee:

then whose shall those things be, which thou hast provided? So [is] he that layeth up treasure for himself, and is not rich toward God" (Lk.12:19-21).

"That no man go beyond and defraud his brother in any matter: because that the Lord is the avenger of all such, as we also have forewarned you and testified" (1 Th.4:6).

"Woe unto them that decree unrighteous decrees, and that write grievousness which they have prescribed; To turn aside the needy from judgment, and to take away the right from the poor of my people, that widows may be their prey, and that they may rob the fatherless! And what will ye do in the day of visitation, and in the desolation which shall come from far? to whom will ye flee for help? and where will ye leave your glory?" (Is.10:1-3).

k. We must realize that stealing is a terrible sin. Stealing causes loss for the victim...
   - perhaps something frivolous such as jewelry, a television, a stereo
   - perhaps something essential such as money, food, a job, or even life

The thief acted on a desire of the heart and took what did not belong to him. The commandment against stealing is one of the Ten basic Commandments of God:

"Thou shalt not steal" (Ex.20:15).

Commandment Nine
Concerns Man's Word and
Character—Never Lie
Exodus 20:16

Contents

Commandment Nine Concerns Man's Word and Character— Never Lie, Ex.20:16

COMMANDMENT 9: Concerns *man's word & character:* **Forbids lying or speaking falsely against anyone**	16 Thou shalt not bear false witness against thy neighbour.

Lying—bearing false testimony against people—is common to all of us. We have all lied. Sometime in the past we have all...

- told a little white lie
- told a half-truth
- gossiped, not really knowing the truth
- cast a suggestive hint or insinuated an untruth about someone
- raised an eyebrow, shrugged a shoulder, or made some motion to indicate something untrue or to keep from disclosing the truth
- twisted the truth
- discredited or slandered someone
- sought to escape blame by skirting around the truth
- boasted or exaggerated the truth in order to boost ourselves
- tried to place blame elsewhere by failing to come forth with the truth

Scripture emphatically declares: "All men are liars" (Ps.116:11). Lying is so common that it is condoned, accepted, and even expected by many people. But lying is not ever justified. Silence sometimes is, but not lying, not answering dishonestly. Leaders, both business and political, can say or promise anything and people either accept or overlook their twisting of the truth. For many...

- a person's character, his word and integrity, seem to matter little
- making false claims and promises has become a way of life
- there is a feeling that a person just cannot survive nor get ahead unless he twists the truth to boost himself
- telling the truth and being honest have fallen by the wayside

Lying—bearing false witness—threatens the very foundation of society. Nothing can survive when it is filled with lies, not for long: not families, friendships, businesses, clubs, schools, churches, communities, governments. Any organization or group will collapse in the wake of mistrust and broken, severed relationships.

This is the great concern of the ninth commandment, the concern for truth, that we build our lives upon truth: build our families, friendships, businesses, clubs, schools, churches, communities, and governments upon truth. *Commandment Nine Concerns Man's Word and Character: Never Lie* (v.16).

I. Who is to obey this commandment? How long was this commandment to be in force (v.16)?

II. What is forbidden by this commandment (v.16)?

III. What are the Biblical consequences of breaking this commandment?

IV. What are the Biblical benefits of keeping this commandment?

V. What is the teaching of Jesus Christ concerning this commandment?

VI. What is the decision required by this commandment (v.16)?

I. Who Is to Obey This Commandment? How Long Was This Commandment to Be in Force?

Some commentators say that this commandment was initially given to govern testimony in legal courts, to make absolutely sure that no one ever lied or gave a false testimony in court. There is no question, this commandment does govern a person who gives evidence in court: his testimony must always be true. But the commandment is much broader than this; it covers far more than just legal testimony. God is declaring that no person is ever to lie against a neighbor, not on any occasion. We must never bear a false witness *against* a neighbor, and we must never bear false witness *to* a neighbor. We must always tell the truth, the whole truth, and nothing but the truth.

> "Wherefore putting away lying, speak every man truth with his neighbour: for we are members one of another" (Eph.4:25).
> "Lie not one to another" (Col.3:9).
> "Thou shalt not bear false witness against thy neighbour" (Ex.20:16).
> "Thou shalt not raise a false report: put not thine hand with the wicked to be an unrighteous witness" (Ex.23:1).

Was this commandment given to govern only the ancient Israelites, only those who lived before Christ came? Was lying a problem only for the ancient world? Or, is lying still a serious problem? The answer is obvious. This commandment is needed today as much as it was needed by the ancient world. God's concern for righteousness upon the earth is as strong today as it has ever been. "You shall not bear false witness: you shall never lie"—this commandment was given to *you*. *You* are not to lie, not ever.

> "These six things doth the LORD hate: yea, seven are an abomination unto him: A proud look, a lying tongue, and hands that shed

innocent blood, An heart that deviseth wicked imaginations, feet that be swift in running to mischief, A false witness that speaketh lies, and he that soweth discord among brethren" (Pr.6:16-19).

"But I say unto you, That every idle word that men shall speak, they shall give account thereof in the day of judgment. For by thy words thou shalt be justified, and by thy words thou shalt be condemned" (Mt.12:36-37).

II. What Is Forbidden by This Commandment?

1. This commandment is broken by telling any untruth of any kind. Man's concept of lying is this: "If I lie, it is justifiable; but if you lie to me, it is unforgivable." But to God, lying is lying. The word "lying" (sheqer) means that which is false, untrue. It is untruthfulness, deception, misrepresentation, exaggeration.

Note how Scripture itself defines a false witness:
⇒ A false witness is a person who breathes out lies.

"A faithful witness will not lie: but a false witness will utter [breathe out] lies" (Pr.14:5).
"A false witness shall not be unpunished, and he that speaketh lies shall not escape" (Pr.19:5).

⇒ A false witness is a person who shares a false report.

"Thou shalt not raise a false report: put not thine hand with the wicked to be an unrighteous witness" (Ex.23:1).

⇒ A false witness is a person who deceives.

"He that speaketh truth showeth forth righteousness: but a false witness deceit" (Pr.12:17).

As pointed out earlier, when some people look at the ninth commandment, they think of a courtroom scene and think that lying against someone in court is what is being forbidden. But as the Scriptures above show, *bearing false witness* means far more than just not lying against someone in court. Bearing false witness means any kind of lying. Hosea 4:2 clearly shows this. When Hosea charged the people with breaking several of the commandments, he did not charge them with bearing false witness in court. He charged them with lying in their day-to-day affairs:

"Hear the word of the LORD, ye children of Israel: for the LORD hath a controversy with the inhabitants of the land, because there is no truth, nor mercy, nor knowledge of God in the land. By swearing, and lying, and killing, and stealing, and committing adultery, they break out, and blood toucheth blood" (Hos.4:1-2).

2. There are several forms or kinds of lies, and they must be diligently guarded against.

a. There is slander: thinking something bad about a person and sharing it; misrepresenting something about someone; tearing down the reputation and life of a person by spreading bad news about him.

> "Whoso privily [secretly] slandereth his neighbour, him will I cut off: him that hath an high look and a proud heart will not I suffer" (Ps.101:5).
> "He that hideth hatred with lying lips, and he that uttereth a slander, is a fool" (Pr.10:18).

b. There is rumor or gossip or tale-bearing: spreading little or big tales, idle or active tales, whether imagined or real; spreading the evil news that one has imagined in his mind or has heard.

> "And withal they learn to be idle, wandering about from house to house; and not only idle, but tattlers also and busybodies, speaking things which they ought not" (1 Tim.5:13).
> "But let none of you suffer as a murderer, or as a thief, or as an evildoer, or as a busybody in other men's matters" (1 Pt.4:15).
> "Thou shalt not go up and down as a talebearer among thy people" (Lev.19:16).
> "A talebearer revealeth secrets: but he that is of a faithful spirit concealeth the matter" (Pr.11:13).
> "A froward man soweth strife: and a whisperer separateth chief friends" (Pr.16:28).
> "Where no wood is, there the fire goeth out: so where there is no talebearer, the strife ceaseth" (Pr.26:20).

c. There are suggestive hints or insinuations: arousing a bad impression about someone; stirring the idea that something might possibly be true; planting in the mind the possibility of something improper or indecent.

> "Thou shalt not raise a false report: put not thine hand with the wicked to be an unrighteous witness" (Ex.23:1).
> "Take ye heed every one of his neighbor, and trust ye not in any brother: for every brother will utterly supplant, and every neighbor will walk with slanders" (Jer.9:4).

d. There is deception: thinking or wanting something to be true, accepting it as true and sharing it; tricking oneself and others into thinking something is true; deceiving oneself and others by accepting bad news as true when the truth is really not known; causing oneself and others to believe bad news.

> "He that speaketh truth showeth forth righteousness: but a false witness deceit" (Pr.12:17).
> "Be not a witness against thy neighbor without cause; and deceive not with thy lips" (Pr.24:28).

e. There are false charges and criticism: accusations made against a person to a third party; sharing the faults and failures of a person with someone other than the person himself; talking about the weaknesses and failures of a person with someone else; condemning, blaming, and censoring a person with others.

> "Blessed are ye, when men shall revile you, and persecute you, and shall say all manner of evil against you falsely, for my sake. Rejoice, and be exceeding glad: for great is your reward in heaven: for so persecuted they the prophets which were before you" (Mt.5:11-12).
> "Having a good conscience; that, whereas they speak evil of you, as of evildoers, they may be ashamed that falsely accuse your good conversation in Christ" (1 Pt.3:16).
> "For I have heard the slander of many: fear was on every side: while they took counsel together against me, they devised to take away my life" (Ps.31:13).

f. There is exaggeration and blown up flattery: stretching the truth about a person; excessively praising someone; falsely representing someone; painting a false picture of a person.

> "Let me not, I pray you, accept any man's person; neither let me give flattering titles unto man" (Job 32:21).
> "He that goeth about as a talebearer revealeth secrets: therefore meddle not with him that flattereth with his lips" (Pr.20:19).
> "A lying tongue hateth those that are afflicted by it; and a flattering mouth worketh ruin" (Pr.26:28).
> "He that rebuketh a man, afterward shall find more favor than he that flattereth with the tongue" (Pr.28:23).
> "A man that flattereth his neighbor spreadeth a net for his feet" (Pr.29:5).
> "The LORD shall cut off all flattering lips, and the tongue that speaketh proud things" (Ps.12:3).
> "But as we were allowed of God to be put in trust with the gospel, even so we speak; not as pleasing men, but God, which trieth our hearts. For neither at any time used we flattering words, as ye know, nor a cloke of covetousness; God is witness" (1 Th.2:4-5).
> "He that saith unto the wicked, Thou art righteous; him shall the people curse, nations shall abhor him" (Pr.24:24).

g. There are innumerable ways in which we lie, such as...

- perjury
- boasting
- telling half-truths
- breaking vows
- shifting blame
- brainwashing
- seeking to discredit someone

- sharing a convenient lie
- making up an excuse
- twisting the truth to protect oneself
- seeking to escape responsibility or punishment

- raising an eyebrow, shrugging the shoulder, or snickering—doing anything that indicates something is untrue or that disavows knowledge of the truth

3. A lie has at least three terrible effects upon people.
   a. Lying misrepresents the truth. It camouflages and hides the truth. The person lied to does not know the truth; therefore, he has to act or live upon a lie. If the lie is serious, it can be very damaging:
      ⇒ A lie about a business deal can cost money and cause terrible loss.
      ⇒ A lie about loving someone can stir emotions that lead to destruction.
      ⇒ A lie about the salvation of the gospel can cost a person the hope of eternal life.

   b. Lying deceives a person. It leads a person astray. A person deceives...
      - to get what he wants
      - to seduce someone
      - to cover up or hide something
      - to cause harm or hurt

   The point to see is that lying is a deception, and deception eventually causes misunderstanding, disappointment, bewilderment, helplessness, emotional upheaval, loss, and sometimes immorality and destruction.
   c. Lying builds a wrong relationship, a relationship built upon sinking sand. Two people cannot possibly be friends or live together if the relationship is based upon lies. Lying destroys...
      - confidence
      - assurance
      - security
      - love
      - trust
      - hope

4. Four facts need to be noted about lying or bearing false witness.
   a. False witness is usually shared with loved ones and good friends, with people we feel can be trusted. Therefore, we always feel that our loved ones and friends can be trusted with the *bad news*. However, what is overlooked is that our loved ones and friends have good friends whom they feel can be trusted. And so the bad news is spread further and further afield; more damage and hurt is done to people and to the cause of Christ. God knows this is the way people are. This is the reason God forbids His people from sharing failure, whether true or untrue, except in dealing with the person involved with the issue.

b. Bearing tales about a person, whether true or untrue, always hurts the person. The person being talked about has feelings just like we do: feelings that are subject to being cut and hurt and suffering pain. Therefore, when tales are shared, we are eventually going to cause pain and hurt, sometimes a great deal of pain, to the person and his loved ones. (Imagine how God feels about this.)

> "All that hate me whisper together against me: against me do they devise my hurt" (Ps.41:7).
> "The words of a talebearer are as wounds, and they go down into the innermost parts of the belly" (Pr.18:8).
> "A man that beareth false witness against his neighbour is a maul [hammer], and a sword, and a sharp arrow" (Pr.25:18).

c. The person who bears tales, giving false witness, shall be judged by God, no matter who he is.

> "Being filled with all unrighteousness...deceit...whisperers, backbiters....Who knowing the judgment of God, that they which commit such things are worthy of death, not only do the same, but have pleasure in them that do them" (Ro.1:29-30, 32).
> "Whoso privily [secretly] slandereth his neighbour, him will I cut off: him that hath an high look and a proud heart will not I suffer" (Ps.101:5).
> "A false witness shall not be unpunished; and he that speaketh lies shall perish" (Pr.19:9).

d. If a person truly loves, he will not bear false witness about anyone. If there is a problem or some questionable report, he will deal with the person himself, seeking to restore him to the faith. Note: love does not deal with a person in harshness, downgrading him, but in love and tenderness and in *strength*, being guided by the Holy Spirit of God.

> "Brethren, if a man be overtaken in a fault, ye which are spiritual, restore such an one in the spirit of meekness; considering thyself, lest thou also be tempted. Bear ye one another's burdens, and so fulfil the law of Christ" (Gal.6:1-2).
> "I have seen his ways, and will heal him: I will lead him also, and restore comforts unto him and to his mourners" (Is.57:18).
> "Set a watch, O Lord, before my mouth; keep the door of my lips" (Ps.141:3).

5. The source of lies and lying is Satan. He was the first ever to lie; therefore, he is called the father of lies. The person who lies follows in the footsteps of Satan and is called by Scripture a "child of the devil."

> "Ye are of [your] father the devil, and the lusts of your father ye will do. He was a murderer from the beginning, and abode not in the truth, because there is no truth in him. When he speaketh a lie, he speaketh of his own: for he is a liar, and the father of it" (Jn.8:44).

6. The source of truth is God. Note Scripture declares time and again that God is the God of truth.

> "God is not a man, that he should lie; neither the son of man, that he should repent: hath he said, and shall he not do it? or hath he spoken, and shall he not make it good?" (Num.23:19).
>
> "He is the Rock, his work is perfect: for all his ways are judgment: a God of truth and without iniquity, just and right is he" (Dt.32:4).
>
> "And now, O Lord GOD, thou art that God, and thy words be true, and thou hast promised this goodness unto thy servant" (2 Sam.7:28).
>
> "Happy is he that hath the God of Jacob for his help, whose hope is in the LORD his God: Which made heaven, and earth, the sea, and all that therein is: which keepeth truth for ever" (Ps.146:5-6).
>
> "That he who blesseth himself in the earth shall bless himself in the God of truth; and he that sweareth in the earth shall swear by the God of truth; because the former troubles are forgotten, and because they are hid from mine eyes" (Is.65:16).
>
> "God forbid: yea, let God be true, but every man a liar; as it is written, That thou mightest be justified in thy sayings, and mightest overcome when thou art judged" (Ro.3:4).
>
> "In hope of eternal life, which God, that cannot lie, promised before the world began" (Tit.1:2).
>
> "Wherein God, willing more abundantly to show unto the heirs of promise the immutability of his counsel, confirmed it by an oath: That by two immutable things, in which it was impossible for God to lie, we might have a strong consolation, who have fled for refuge to lay hold upon the hope set before us" (Heb.6:17-18).

7. The very foundation or basis of society is truth. Families, businesses, organizations, clubs, neighbors, or communities in any society will disintegrate and collapse unless the members are truthful with one another. If we lie and deceive one another, the consequences are hurtful, damaging, and often devastating. Wrong decisions are made and wrong actions are taken. Lies and deception—bearing false witness—are often what cause...

- divorce
- job loss
- unemployment
- severed relationships
- pain and hurt
- failure
- bankruptcy
- collapse
- vengeance
- retaliation
- abuse
- accident
- suffering
- imprisonment
- death

8. A critical question needs to be asked when dealing with lying or telling the truth. Should we ever tell the truth bluntly or harshly? In a court of law, the truth must always be spoken straight to the point: directly and straightforward. But when dealing in personal, face-to-face relationships, we should not intentionally cause pain, hurt, embarrassment, or shame. We should never deliberately wound a person with a blunt, harsh statement of the truth. Truth is to be spoken in love and kindness not in harshness and ugliness.

> **"But speaking the truth in love, may grow up into him in all things, which is the head, even Christ" (Eph.4:15).**
> **"Let all bitterness, and wrath, and anger, and clamour, and evil speaking, be put away from you, with all malice: And be ye kind one to another, tenderhearted, forgiving one another, even as God for Christ's sake hath forgiven you" (Eph.4:31-32).**

Thought.
William Barclay has an excellent statement on this point:

> "When we speak about telling the truth, one special point arises. Must we always tell the truth baldly and bluntly? For instance, if a person has played a game or sung a song or given some kind of performance, and not done very well, must we say that he was no good, or is there any harm in the polite compliment which will encourage him, even if it is not strictly true? Must we tell the truth, even when it is unpleasant and when it might hurt?
>
> "Someone has given us a valuable rule about this. There are three questions we should always ask about anything we say about anyone else, or to anyone else. The first question is: *Is it true?* And, of course, if it is not true, then it must not be said at all. The second question is: *Is it necessary?* If it is necessary, it will have to be said, but there are not many times when politeness and courtesy need to be disregarded. The third question is: *Is it kind?* It is hardly ever a duty to be unkind. There are ways and ways of telling the truth. You can tell it in a way that is deliberately designed to wound and hurt; there are people who take a delight in seeing other people wince when something is said. On the other hand, it was said of Florence Allshorn, a great teacher, that, when she had some criticism to make, she always made it, as it were, with her arm round your shoulder. She spoke the truth; she said what was necessary; but she took care to say it kindly and in a way that would help and not hurt. And that is the best rule of all."[1]

---

[1] William Barclay. *The Old Law & The New Law*, p.43-44.

III. What Are the Consequences of Bearing False Witness, of Lying?

When this commandment is broken, the false words dig deep into the heart. Damaging words often do more harm than a physical blow. The person who breaks this commandment becomes a willing partner of the "father of all lies" and "the accuser" of believers, of those who truly follow God.

> "Ye are of your father the devil, and the lusts of your father ye will do. He was a murderer from the beginning, and abode not in the truth, because there is no truth in him. When he speaketh a lie, he speaketh of his own: for he is a liar, and the father of it" (Jn.8:44).

> "And I heard a loud voice saying in heaven, Now is come salvation, and strength, and the kingdom of our God, and the power of his Christ: for the accuser of our brethren is cast down, which accused them before our God day and night" (Rev.12:10).

1. The person who lies—consistently lies—will not inherit the kingdom of God: he will be sentenced to hell.

> "But the fearful, and unbelieving, and the abominable, and murderers, and whoremongers, and sorcerers, and idolaters, and all liars, shall have their part in the lake which burneth with fire and brimstone: which is the second death" (Rev.21:8).

> "And there shall in no wise enter into it any thing that defileth, neither whatsoever worketh abomination, or maketh a lie: but they which are written in the Lamb's book of life" (Rev.21:27).

> "Blessed are they that do his commandments, that they may have right to the tree of life, and may enter in through the gates into the city. For without [the heavenly city] are dogs, and sorcerers, and whoremongers, and murderers, and idolaters, and whosoever loveth and maketh a lie [practices falsehood]" (Rev.22:14-15).

2. The person who lies and does not repent will not escape: he shall face the judgment of God and perish.

> "Thou shalt destroy them that speak leasing [tell lies]: the LORD will abhor the bloody and deceitful man" (Ps.5:6).

> "The LORD shall cut off all flattering lips, and the tongue that speaketh proud things" (Ps.12:3).

> "A false witness shall not be unpunished, and he that speaketh lies shall not escape" (Pr.19:5).

> "A false witness shall not be unpunished, and he that speaketh lies shall perish" (Pr.19:9).

> "And I will come near to you to judgment; and I will be a swift witness against the sorcerers, and against the adulterers, and against false swearers, and against those that oppress the hireling in his

wages, the widow, and the fatherless, and that turn aside the stranger from his right, and fear not me, saith the LORD of hosts" (Mal.3:5).

3. The person who lies will be separated from God.

"Whoso privily slandereth his neighbour, him will I cut off: him that hath an high look and a proud heart will not I suffer" (Ps.101:5).
"He that worketh deceit shall not dwell within my house: he that telleth lies shall not tarry in my sight" (Ps.101:7).

4. The person who lies sins against God.

"If a soul sin, and commit a trespass against the LORD, and lie unto his neighbour in that which was delivered him to keep, or in fellowship, or in a thing taken away by violence, or hath deceived his neighbour; Or have found that which was lost, and lieth concerning it, and sweareth falsely; in any of all these that a man doeth, sinning therein" (Lev.6:2-3).

5. The person who lies rebels against God and ignores His law.

"That this is a rebellious people, lying children, children that will not hear the law of the LORD" (Is.30:9).
"But thou shalt say unto them, This is a nation that obeyeth not the voice of the LORD their God, nor receiveth correction: truth is perished, and is cut off from their mouth" (Jer.7:28).

6. The person who lies forgets God.

"This is thy lot, the portion of thy measures from me, saith the LORD; because thou hast forgotten me, and trusted in falsehood" (Jer.13:25).

7. The person who lies perverts the Word of God.

"And the burden of the LORD shall ye mention no more: for every man's word shall be his burden; for ye have perverted the words of the living God, of the LORD of hosts our God" (Jer.23:36).

8. The person who lies about following God is a hypocrite: he flatters God, but his own heart betrays his true feelings.

"And they remembered that God was their rock, and the high God their redeemer. Nevertheless they did flatter him with their mouth, and they lied unto him with their tongues. For their heart was not right with him, neither were they stedfast in his covenant" (Ps.78:35-37).

9. The person who lies follows after the father of lies, Satan.

> "Ye are of [your] father the devil, and the lusts of your father ye will do. He was a murderer from the beginning, and abode not in the truth, because there is no truth in him. When he speaketh a lie, he speaketh of his own: for he is a liar, and the father of it" (Jn.8:44).
>
> "But Peter said, Ananias, why hath Satan filled thine heart to lie to the Holy Ghost, and to keep back part of the price of the land? Whiles it remained, was it not thine own? and after it was sold, was it not in thine own power? why hast thou conceived this thing in thine heart? thou hast not lied unto men, but unto God" (Acts 5:3-4).

10. The person who lies is a fool.

> "He that hideth hatred with lying lips, and he that uttereth a slander, is a fool" (Pr.10:18).

11. The person who lies will be turned into a fool by God.

> "[God] frustrateth the tokens of the liars, and maketh diviners mad; that turneth wise men backward, and maketh their knowledge foolish" (Is.44:25).
>
> "Causing the omens of boasters to fail, Making fools out of diviners, Causing wise men to draw back, And turning their knowledge into foolishness" (Is.44:25, NASB).
>
> "I am the one who shows what liars all false prophets are, by causing something else to happen than the things they say. I make wise men give opposite advice to what they should and make them into fools" (Is.44:25, LIVING PARAPHRASE).

12. The person who lies will have a life marked by deceit.

> "He that speaketh truth showeth forth righteousness: but a false witness deceit" (Pr.12:17).
>
> "Be not a witness against thy neighbour without cause; and deceive not with thy lips" (Pr.24:28).
>
> "Being filled with all unrighteousness, fornication, wickedness, covetousness, maliciousness; full of envy, murder, debate, deceit, malignity; whisperers, Backbiters, haters of God, despiteful, proud, boasters, inventors of evil things, disobedient to parents, Without understanding, covenantbreakers, without natural affection, implacable, unmerciful" (Ro.1:29-31).
>
> "What then? are we better than they? No, in no wise: for we have before proved both Jews and Gentiles, that they are all under sin; As it is written, There is none righteous, no, not one: There is none that understandeth, there is none that seeketh after God. They are all

gone out of the way, they are together become unprofitable; there is none that doeth good, no, not one. Their throat is an open sepulchre; with their tongues they have used deceit; the poison of asps is under their lips: Whose mouth is full of cursing and bitterness: Their feet are swift to shed blood: Destruction and misery are in their ways: And the way of peace have they not known: There is no fear of God before their eyes. Now we know that what things soever the law saith, it saith to them who are under the law: that every mouth may be stopped, and all the world may become guilty before God. Therefore by the deeds of the law there shall no flesh be justified in his sight: for by the law is the knowledge of sin" (Ro.3:9-20).

"Thou givest thy mouth to evil, and thy tongue frameth deceit" (Ps.50:19).

"Thou lovest evil more than good; and lying rather than to speak righteousness....Thou lovest all devouring words, O thou deceitful tongue" (Ps.52:3-4).

13. The person who lies only deceives himself; he has an empty religion.

"If any man among you seem to be religious, and bridleth not his tongue, but deceiveth his own heart, this man's religion is vain" (Jas.1:26).

14. The person who lies causes discord among people.

"A false witness that speaketh lies, and he that soweth discord among brethren" (Pr.6:19).

15. The person who lies destroys the reputations and lives of people.

"An hypocrite with his mouth destroyeth his neighbour: but through knowledge shall the just be delivered" (Pr.11:9).

16. The person who lies will have a reputation of being a gossip, of being mean and malicious, and sometimes evil.

"A man that beareth false witness against his neighbour is a maul [hammer], and a sword, and a sharp arrow" (Pr.25:18).

17. The person who lies will have a life marked by a critical spirit that is quick to judge the actions of others.

"Speak not evil one of another, brethren. He that speaketh evil of his brother, and judgeth his brother, speaketh evil of the law, and judgeth the law: but if thou judge the law, thou art not a doer of the law, but a judge" (Jas.4:11).

18. The person who lies causes hatred and ruin in the lives of many.

> "A lying tongue hateth those that are afflicted by it; and a flattering mouth worketh ruin" (Pr.26:28).
>
> "A lying tongue hates those it crushes, and a flattering mouth works ruin" (Pr.26:28, NASB).

19. The person who lies causes the corrubtion of society.

> "In transgressing and lying against the LORD, and departing away from our God, speaking oppression and revolt, conceiving and uttering from the heart words of falsehood. And judgment is turned away backward, and justice standeth afar off: for truth is fallen in the street, and equity cannot enter. Yea, truth faileth; and he that departeth from evil maketh himself a prey: and the LORD saw it, and it displeased him that there was no judgment" (Is.59:13-15).
>
> "Take ye heed every one of his neighbour, and trust ye not in any brother: for every brother will utterly supplant, and every neighbour will walk with slanders. And they will deceive every one his neighbour, and will not speak the truth: they have taught their tongue to speak lies, and weary themselves to commit iniquity" (Jer.9:4-5).

20. The person who lies causes God's people to make wrong decisions.

> "Behold, I am against them that prophesy false dreams, saith the Lord, and do tell them, and cause my people to err by their lies, and by their lightness; yet I sent them not, nor commanded them: therefore they shall not profit this people at all, saith the Lord" (Jer.23:32).

21. The person who lies causes wickedness to spread to others.

> "If a ruler hearken to lies, all his servants are wicked" (Pr.29:12).
>
> "If a ruler pays attention to falsehood, All his ministers become wicked" (Pr.29:12, NASB).

22. The person who lies will become enslaved to many sins.

> "And even as they did not like to retain God in their knowledge, God gave them over to a reprobate mind, to do those things which are not convenient; Being filled with all unrighteousness, fornication, wickedness, covetousness, maliciousness; full of envy, murder, debate, deceit, malignity; whisperers, Backbiters, haters of God, despiteful, proud, boasters, inventors of evil things, disobedient to parents" (Ro.1:28-30).

23. The person who lies will have a life marked by destruction and defilement.

"And the tongue is a fire, a world of iniquity: so is the tongue among our members, that it defileth the whole body, and setteth on fire the course of nature; and it is set on fire of hell" (Jas.3:6).

IV. What Are the Benefits of Keeping This Commandment?

Our word is our bond. If a man's word is trusted, Scripture declares he will be greatly blessed.

1. A person who tells the truth and shares in the glorious salvation of God will receive blessings and righteousness from the Lord.

"He that hath clean hands, and a pure heart; who hath not lifted up his soul unto vanity, nor sworn deceitfully. He shall receive the blessing from the LORD, and righteousness from the God of his salvation" (Ps.24:4-5).

2. A person who tells the truth and belongs to the LORD will derive joy from God's Word.

"I hate and abhor lying: but thy law do I love" (Ps.119:163).

3. A person who tells the truth and follows God will be delivered.

"The words of the wicked are to lie in wait for blood: but the mouth of the upright shall deliver them" (Pr.12:6).

4. A person who tells the truth and belongs to the LORD will be assured of his eternity.

"The lip of truth shall be established for ever: but a lying tongue is but for a moment" (Pr.12:19).

5. A person who tells the truth and follows God will not be brought to shame.

"A righteous man hateth lying: but a wicked man is loathsome, and cometh to shame" (Pr.13:5).

6. A person who tells the truth and obeys God can be counted on to be a faithful witness.

"A faithful witness will not lie: but a false witness will utter lies" (Pr.14:5).

> "A true witness delivereth souls: but a deceitful witness speaketh lies" (Pr.14:25).

7. A person who tells the truth and is a true believer in Jesus Christ will be trusted to put his words into action.

> "My little children, let us not love in word, neither in tongue; but in deed and in truth" (1 Jn.3:18).

8. A person who tells the truth and trusts in Christ as his Savior proves to others that the Spirit of truth lives in his heart.

> "And I will pray the Father, and he shall give you another Comforter, that he may abide with you for ever; Even the Spirit of truth; whom the world cannot receive, because it seeth him not, neither knoweth him: but ye know him; for he dwelleth with you, and shall be in you" (Jn.14:16-17).

9. A person who tells the truth and has saving faith in Christ will be able to speak the truth in love, right from his heart.

> "But speaking the truth in love, may grow up into him in all things, which is the head, even Christ" (Eph.4:15).
> "And the woman said to Elijah, Now by this I know that thou art a man of God, and that the word of the Lord in thy mouth is truth" (1 Ki.17:24).
> "LORD, who shall abide in thy tabernacle? who shall dwell in thy holy hill? He that walketh uprightly, and worketh righteousness, and speaketh the truth in his heart. He that backbiteth not with his tongue, nor doeth evil to his neighbour, nor taketh up a reproach against his neighbour" (Ps.15:1-3).

10. A person who tells the truth and has been gloriously saved by Jesus Christ will appear righteous, not deceitful, before the world.

> "He that speaketh truth showeth forth righteousness: but a false witness deceit" (Pr.12:17).

11. A person who tells the truth and follows God walks without shame before God.

> "But he that doeth truth cometh to the light, that his deeds may be made manifest, that they are wrought in God" (Jn.3:21).

12. A person who tells the truth and trusts in Christ as his Savior will strive to have a disciplined mind focused on the truth.

"Finally, brethren, whatsoever things are true, whatsoever things are honest, whatsoever things are just, whatsoever things are pure, whatsoever things are lovely, whatsoever things are of good report; if there be any virtue, and if there be any praise, think on these things" (Ph.4:8).

13. A person who tells the truth and follows God will not need to twist God's Word to justify his behavior or lifestyle.

"Study to show thyself approved unto God, a workman that needeth not to be ashamed, rightly dividing the word of truth" (2 Tim.2:15).

14. A person who tells the truth and lives a righteous life will live in God's presence both now and forever.

"LORD, who shall abide in thy tabernacle? who shall dwell in thy holy hill? He that walketh uprightly, and worketh righteousness, and speaketh the truth in his heart" (Ps.15:1-2; cp. v.3-5).

V. What Is the Teaching of Jesus Christ Concerning This Commandment?

1. Jesus Christ declared that God commanded man not to lie.

"He saith unto him, Which? Jesus said, Thou shalt do no murder, Thou shalt not commit adultery, Thou shalt not steal, Thou shalt not bear false witness," (Mt.19:18; cp. Mk.10:19; Lk.18:20).

Thought.
Scripture is clear: lying is wrong.

"Thou shalt not bear false witness against thy neighbour" (Ex.20:16).
"Thou shalt not raise a false report: put not thine hand with the wicked to be an unrighteous witness" (Ex.23:1).
"These six things doth the LORD hate: yea, seven are an abomination unto him: A proud look, a lying tongue, and hands that shed innocent blood, An heart that deviseth wicked imaginations, feet that be swift in running to mischief, A false witness that speaketh lies, and he that soweth discord among brethren" (Pr.6:16-19).
"Wherefore putting away lying, speak every man truth with his neighbour: for we are members one of another" (Eph.4:25).

2. Jesus Christ declared that men are responsible for every word they speak and will give an account in the day of judgment.

> "But I say unto you, That every idle word that men shall speak, they shall give account thereof in the day of judgment" (Mt.12:36).

Thought.

a) A man's words expose his true nature: what he is like beneath the surface.

b) A man's words expose what he is down deep within his heart: his motives, desires, and ambitions.

c) A man's words expose his true character: good or bad, kind or cruel.

d) A man's words expose his mind, what he thinks: pure or impure thoughts, clean or dirty thoughts.

e) A man's words expose his spirit, what he believes and pursues: the legitimate or illegitimate, the intelligent or ignorant, the true or false, the beneficial or wasteful.

> "Whoso privily slandereth his neighbour, him will I cut off: him that hath an high look and a proud heart will not I suffer" (Ps.101:5).
>
> "Being filled with all unrighteousness...deceit...whisperers, backbiters" (Ro.1:29-30).
>
> "But the fearful, and unbelieving, and the abominable, and murderers, and whoremongers, and sorcerers, and idolaters, and all liars, shall have their part in the lake which burneth with fire and brimstone: which is the second death" (Rev.21:8).

3. Jesus Christ declared that Satan is the father of lies, and that the liar has a life that marks him as a child of the devil.

> "Ye are of your father the devil, and the lusts of your father ye will do. He was a murderer from the beginning, and abode not in the truth, because there is no truth in him. When he speaketh a lie, he speaketh of his own: for he is a liar, and the father of it" (Jn.8:44).

Thought.

Anything that is not true is false—whether a lie, thoughts, ideas, words, or acts. Lying is of the devil and exposes a person to be a child of the devil. A person is certainly not of God if he is lying. His father is not the Father of Jesus Christ.

> "But Peter said, Ananias, why hath Satan filled thine heart to lie to the Holy Ghost, and to keep back part of the price of the land? Whiles it remained, was it not thine own? and after it was sold, was it not in thine own power? why hast thou conceived this thing in thine heart? thou hast not lied unto men, but unto God" (Acts 5:3-4).
>
> "I have not written unto you because ye know not the truth, but because ye know it, and that no lie is of the truth. Who is a liar but he that denieth that Jesus is the Christ? He is antichrist, that denieth

the Father and the Son. Whosoever denieth the Son, the same hath
not the Father: (but) he that acknowledgeth the Son hath the Father
also" (1 Jn.2:21-23).

"A false witness shall not be unpunished, and he that speaketh
lies shall not escape" (Pr.19:5).

"But the fearful, and unbelieving, and the abominable, and murderers, and whoremongers, and sorcerers, and idolaters, and all liars,
shall have their part in the lake which burneth with fire and brimstone: which is the second death" (Rev.21:8).

4. Jesus Christ declared that our words will either justify or condemn us.

"For by thy words thou shalt be justified, and by thy words thou
shalt be condemned" (Mt.12:37).

Thought.

The same law stated by Christ is common to man. A man is judged to be
guilty or not guilty based upon the testimony of his words.

- Words that are kind, gracious, loving, edifying, and profitable will testify for us and justify us in the day of judgment.
- Words that are ugly, dirty, filthy, angry, spiteful, gossiping, grumbling,
  or murmuring will testify against us and condemn us in the day of
  judgment.

"He that hideth hatred with lying lips, and he that uttereth a
slander, is a fool" (Pr.10:18).

"Death and life are in the power of the tongue: and they that love
it shall eat the fruit thereof" (Pr.18:21).

"A false witness shall not be unpunished, and he that speaketh
lies shall perish" (Pr.19:9).

"And the tongue is a fire, a world of iniquity: so is the tongue
among our members, that it defileth the whole body, and setteth on
fire the course of nature; and it is set on fire of hell" (Jas.3:6).

"Speak not evil one of another, brethren. He that speaketh evil of
his brother, and judgeth his brother, speaketh evil of the law, and
judgeth the law: but if thou judge the law, thou art not a doer of the
law, but a judge" (Jas.4:11).

5. Jesus Christ declared that men will slander and speak evil of His people.

"Blessed are ye, when men shall revile you, and persecute you,
and shall say all manner of evil against you falsely, for my sake. Rejoice, and be exceeding glad: for great is your reward in heaven: for
so persecuted they the prophets which were before you" (Mt.5:11-12).

Thought.

What is to be the believer's attitude toward persecution?

⇒ It is *not* to be retaliation, pride, spiritual superiority.

⇒ It *is* to be joy and gladness.

The persecuted are promised great rewards:

a) The Kingdom of Heaven—*now*. The persecuted believer experiences...
- a special honor (Acts 5:41)
- a special consolation (2 Cor.1:5)
- a special closeness, a glow of the Lord's presence (1 Pt.4:14)
- a greater witness for Christ (2 Cor.1:4-6)

b) The Kingdom of Heaven—*eternally* (Heb.11:35f; 1 Pt.4:12-13; Mt.19:23-24).

> "For I have heard the slander of many: fear was on every side: while they took counsel together against me, they devised to take away my life" (Ps.31:13).
> "Having a good conscience; that, whereas they speak evil of you, as of evildoers, they may be ashamed that falsely accuse your good conversation in Christ" (1 Pt.3:16).
> "Yea, and all that will live godly in Christ Jesus shall suffer persecution" (2 Tim.3:12).
> "Beloved, think it not strange concerning the fiery trial which is to try you, as though some strange thing happened unto you: But rejoice, inasmuch as ye are partakers of Christ's sufferings; that, when his glory shall be revealed, ye may be glad also with exceeding joy. If ye be reproached for the name of Christ, happy are ye; for the spirit of glory and of God resteth upon you: on their part he is evil spoken of, but on your part he is glorified" (1 Pt.4:12-14).
> "Marvel not, my brethren, if the world hate you" (1 Jn.3:13).

VI. What is the Decision Required by This Commandment?

Telling the truth is not an option. We must learn to conquer lying; to guard, prevent, and keep ourselves from lying. Scripture tells us:

1. We must obey God; keep His commandment: never bear false witness nor deceive a neighbor.

> "Thou shalt not bear false witness against thy neighbour" (Ex.20:16).
> "Keep thy tongue from evil, and thy lips from speaking guile" (Ps.34:13).
> "Be not a witness against thy neighbour without cause; and deceive not with thy lips" (Pr.24:28).

2. We must never spread a false report nor help a wicked person by lying for him.

> "Thou shalt not raise a false report: put not thine hand with the wicked to be an unrighteous witness" (Ex.23:1).

3. We must never bear false witness, but rather we are to love one another.

> "Owe no man any thing, but to love one another: for he that loveth another hath fulfilled the law. For this, Thou shalt not commit adultery, Thou shalt not kill, Thou shalt not steal, Thou shalt not bear false witness, Thou shalt not covet; and if there be any other commandment, it is briefly comprehended in this saying, namely, Thou shalt love thy neighbour as thyself. Love worketh no ill to his neighbour: therefore love is the fulfilling of the law" (Ro.13:8-10).

4. We must always speak the truth, and we must always speak the truth in love.

> "But speaking the truth in love, [that we] may grow up into him in all things, which is the head, even Christ" (Eph.4:15).
>
> "These are the things that ye shall do; Speak ye every man the truth to his neighbour; execute the judgment of truth and peace in your gates" (Zech.8:16).

5. We must teach every living person—especially our children and the youth of the world—the Word of God, the Ten Commandments.

> "And these words, which I command thee this day, shall be in thine heart: And thou shalt teach them diligently unto thy children, and shalt talk of them when thou sittest in thine house, and when thou walkest by the way, and when thou liest down, and when thou risest up" (Dt.6:6-7).
>
> "All scripture is given by inspiration of God, and is profitable for doctrine, for reproof, for correction, for instruction in righteousness" (2 Tim.3:16).
>
> "Wherefore laying aside all malice, and all guile [deception], and hypocrisies, and envies, and all evil speakings [slander, lying], As newborn babes, desire the sincere milk of the word, that ye may grow thereby" (1 Pt.2:1-2).

6. We must put away lying—put away all falsehood—and speak only the truth.

> "Sanctify them through thy truth: thy word is truth" (Jn.17:17).

> "Wherefore putting away lying [falsehood], speak every man truth with his neighbour: for we are members one of another" (Eph.4:25).

7. We must put off the old man of lying and put on the new man of righteousness.

> "Lie not one to another, seeing that ye have put off the old man with his deeds; And have put on the new man [of righteousness], which is renewed in knowledge after the image of him that created him" (Col.3:9-10).

8. We must stop all corrupt, unwholesome talk and slander (a type of lying); we must be kind and forgiving toward one another.

> "Let no corrupt communication [unwholesome talk] proceed out of your mouth, but that which is good to the use of edifying, that it may minister grace unto the hearers....Let all bitterness, and wrath, and anger, and clamour, and evil speaking [slander], be put away from you, with all malice: And be ye kind one to another, tenderhearted, forgiving one another, even as God for Christ's sake hath forgiven you" (Eph.4:29, 31-32).
>
> "Wherefore laying aside all malice, and all guile, and hypocrisies, and envies, and all evil speakings" (1 Pt.2:1).

9. We must be diligent—stand guard—keep our tongues from deception and lying.

> "Keep thy tongue from evil, and thy lips from speaking guile" (Ps.34:13).
>
> "Whoso keepeth his mouth and his tongue keepeth his soul from troubles" (Pr.21:23).
>
> "Take ye heed every one of his neighbour, and trust ye not in any brother: for every brother will utterly supplant, and every neighbour will walk with slanders" (Jer.9:4).

10. We must pray, ask God to guard our tongues from lying.

> "Set a watch, O LORD, before my mouth; keep the door of my lips" (Ps.141:3).

"Commandment Ten...

Commandment Ten Concerns Man's Desires and Security—Never Covet Exodus 20:17

Contents

Commandment Ten Concerns Man's Desires and Security— Never Covet, Ex.20:17

COMMANDMENT 10: Concerns *man's desires & security*: **Forbids coveting anything that belongs to a neighbor—his house, wife, servant, workers, animals, or anything else**	17 Thou shalt not covet thy neighbour's house, thou shalt not covet thy neighbour's wife, nor his manservant, nor his maidservant, nor his ox, nor his ass, nor any thing that is thy neighbour's.

Covetousness is a sin given little attention. Few sermons are ever preached and few lessons ever taught on covetousness. And there are even fewer books written on the subject. This is surprising, for covetousness is one of the most prevailing evils of society. Simply stated, covetousness is a predominant desire or thought, a desire or thought that craves, lusts, and yearns, that just eats away at the human heart. It is covetousness...

- that craves the things of the world
- that craves the things of others

Covetousness can and often does enslave the human soul: it often destroys a person or causes the destruction of other people. Covetousness is what causes and leads to so many of the other sins:

⇒ A person covets a woman and commits adultery.

⇒ A person covets money or property and steals or kills.

⇒ A person covets recognition and acceptance, or he seeks to escape suspicion; therefore, he lies.

⇒ A person feels unattractive, unhealthy, inadequate, or poor; and he covets what someone else has to the point of wishing that something bad would happen to the person.

Covetousness is terribly destructive. It is a desire or thought that will gnaw away at the mind until it consumes a person. A covetous thought or desire left unchecked can be so consuming that it almost forces a person to act. In such covetous moments, only the power of God can enable us to withstand the temptation. Only God can keep us from reaching out and taking what is not ours. Covetousness is a sin of the human heart that causes so many of the problems within society.

This is the critical importance of this commandment: *Commandment Ten Concerns Man's Desires and Security—Never Covet*, 20:17.

I.   Who is to obey this commandment? How long was this commandment to be in force (v.17)?

II. What is forbidden by this commandment (v.17)?

III. What are the Biblical consequences of breaking this commandment?

IV. What are the Biblical benefits of keeping this commandment?

V.   What is the teaching of Jesus Christ concerning this commandment?

VI. What is the decision required by this commandment (v.17)?

I.   Who Is to Obey This Commandment? How Long Was This Commandment to Be in Force?

Beyond question, covetousness is the most serious infection that corrupts man's heart. Covetousness always has been and always will be the prevailing sin of man's heart. Before man ever carries out any sin, covetousness—the desire, the lust, the thought—is aroused within his heart. Man covets, desires, lusts to sin; and then he carries out the act of sin.

The point is clear and forceful: as long as man exists and God rules over the earth, there will be a need for this tenth commandment, a need for man to heed the demand of God: "You shall not covet" (v.17).

Now, who is to obey this commandment? Note the verse: "You." Everyone of us. Every generation of man is to obey this commandment.

> **"Thou shalt not covet thy neighbour's house, thou shalt not covet thy neighbour's wife, nor his manservant, nor his maidservant, nor his ox, nor his ass, nor any thing that is thy neighbour's" (v.17).**

II.   What Is Forbidden by This Commandment?

Commandment ten concerns man's desires and security. How is this commandment broken, violated? This commandment forbids coveting anything that belongs to our neighbor: his house, wife, servant, workers, animals, or anything else. A man should be able to live in peace and feel secure. He should not have to worry about someone's coveting and stealing what he has. God wants man to feel secure and protected. God wants man to know that his wife and family, his property and possessions, his joy and anything else he has is secure and protected against the covetousness and theft of people.

1. The Hebrew word for "covet" (hamad) means to desire, crave, want, long for, thirst for, yearn for, lust after. *Coveting* is a neutral word; that is, coveting can be good as well as bad, legitimate as well as illegitimate.

    a. The Bible clearly says that there is a *legitimate covetousness*, that God has planted within man certain inalienable desires, desires that we are entitled to, desires that are good. We all have legitimate desires for love, joy, and peace; legitimate desires to be secure, successful, fulfilled, and satisfied.

      ⇒ The Bible says that every good and perfect gift comes from God Himself. This being so, we should actually *seek after* and *covet* good and perfect gifts.

> "Every good gift and every perfect gift is from above, and cometh down from the Father of lights, with whom is no variableness, neither shadow of turning" (Jas.1:17).

      ⇒ The Bible says that the excellent qualities of life and the best gifts of God are to be coveted.

> "Blessed [are] they which do hunger and thirst after righteousness: for they shall be filled" (Mt.5:6).
> "But covet earnestly the best gifts: and yet show I unto you a more excellent way" (1 Cor.12:31).
> "The fear of the LORD is clean, enduring for ever: the judgments of the LORD are true and righteous altogether. More to be desired are they than gold, yea, than much fine gold: sweeter also than honey and the honeycomb" (Ps.19:9-10).

      ⇒ The Bible even says that God gives us the ability to get wealth and that we should work so diligently that we can actually earn enough to meet the needs of others.

> "Let him that stole steal no more: but rather let him labour, working with his hands the thing which is good, that he may have to give to him that needeth" (Eph.4:28).

    b. The Bible clearly says there is an *illegitimate covetousness*, that man commits evil when he desires another person's wife or property, or any other possession belonging to the person.

> "Thou shalt not covet thy neighbour's house, thou shalt not covet thy neighbour's wife, nor his manservant, nor his maidservant, nor his ox, nor his ass, nor any thing that is thy neighbour's" (Ex.20:17).

> "But fornication, and all uncleanness, or covetousness, let it not be once named among you, as becometh saints" (Eph.5:3).
>
> "Mortify [put to death] therefore your members which are upon the earth; fornication, uncleanness, inordinate affection, evil concupiscence, and covetousness, which is idolatry" (Col.3:5).

2. Covetousness is an inward sin, a sin of the heart and mind: it is a *desire*, a *thought* within the heart and mind. This commandment differs from the other commandments in this very fact, differs rather significantly: covetousness is not the outward sin; it is the inward *desire* and *thought* that leads to the outward sin.

Remember, the first nine commandments dealt primarily with outward acts, with such acts as lying, stealing, and killing. But this tenth commandment deals with the human heart, with inward feelings, desires, thoughts, and attitudes. But note: the first nine commandments *also involved* the desires and thoughts of a person. Before a person ever lies, steals, or kills, the desire or thought to take such action arises in his heart and mind. The desire to do something always precedes the actual act. A man commits immorality because he desires a person. A woman steals because she either desires the thing stolen or the excitement of stealing. In dealing with the first nine commandments, we discussed this fact, the fact that the evil forbidden was aroused first of all in the heart and mind of a person, that the evil was basically a heart problem.

This is the very reason God has covered coveting last, listed it as the tenth commandment. Coveting (desiring, lusting,) is the first thing that happens before a person commits the outward sin. The sin is *aroused* within the heart before it is committed; the evil act is *thought about* before it is done. This commandment underlies all the commandments: coveting—the desire or thought—takes place within the human heart and mind before any of the nine commandments are publicly or secretly committed. Before a person ever commits the sinful act, he desires and thinks about what someone else has, his...

- home
- spouse
- servant
- livestock
- horse
- vehicle
- property
- money
- clothing
- appearance
- personality
- looks
- position
- power
- recognition
- job
- opportunity
- influence

The list could go on ad infinitum. We commit the sin of covetousness when our *hearts and minds* are set on some possession, so set that we...

- crave, long, and lust after it
- are consumed with getting it
- give ourselves over to pursuing it
- give top priority and first attention to it
- focus our hearts, minds, energy, and time to securing it

Covetousness is being so consumed with getting something that we become gripped and enslaved by it. Our hearts become focused upon *a person, a possession, a thing, something other than God.* This is the reason Scripture declares that covetousness is idolatry:

> **"For this ye know, that no whoremonger, nor unclean person, nor covetous man, who is an idolater, hath any inheritance in the kingdom of Christ and of God" (Eph.5:5).**

Thought 1.

Maxie Dunnam has an excellent application on this commandment:

> "Most of us are guilty of looking at others, comparing ourselves to them, and seeing ourselves come out on the short end. We torture ourselves in this fashion, drive ourselves to depression by self-pity, thinking we deserve more. When we find ourselves jealous of what life is for someone else, dreaming of how happy we would be if we were in someone else's situation, it's a dead giveaway that we are falling into the subtle, seductive hands of covetousness.
>
> "How often do we convince ourselves that other people always get the breaks and not us? How recently have we thought that we were deprived of opportunity? We look at our peers, friends our own age, and see where they are in life, and we're plagued with the notion that they had far more opportunity than we did.
>
> "You probably have not associated that with coveting, but whatever name you give it, it is exactly that, and it is destructive....
>
> "We convince ourselves that we have a sort of cosmic right to an equal share of the good things of life. That's a fallacious idea, and it plays folly in our lives. There's no equality to being in the right place at the right time.
>
> "There is no cosmic right that is ours to have an equal share of what everybody else has. If you're prone to leaning in that direction, consider how you would feel if you were averaged out with the world's two billion starving people. You see, we always want to be averaged up and not down."[1]

Thought 2.

Matthew Henry has a very graphic application:

> "'O that such a man's house were mine! Such a man's wife mine! Such a man's estate mine!' This is certainly the language of discontent at our own lot, and envy at our neighbour's; and these are the sins principally forbidden here."[2]

---

[1] Maxie Dunnam. *Mastering the Old Testament, Volume 2: Exodus,* p.267-268.
[2] Matthew Henry. *Matthew Henry's Commentary,* Vol. 1, p.362-363.

Thought 3.

The covetous life has been described as follows by an unnamed author:

"The passion to possess is an ugly sin no matter how we look at it. But when the object of our passion belongs to some one else, as the Tenth Commandment says "thy neighbor", this sin takes on an even uglier hue. When we covet something "out there", something that is available and waiting to be claimed, we limit most of the destruction to ourselves. But, when we covet that which belongs to others, we bring those people into the situation, and jeopardize our attitudes toward them and our relationships with them.

"Someone may covet a starting position on a sports team or another individual's job. This person, consumed with envy, may scheme and wish for his nemesis to be hurt, or miss a deadline, or lose an account, in order to claim his position. Or, what about coveting someone else's spouse? This person berates their own mate, feeds discontent with insensitive comparisons, and undermines another's marriage with subtle (or, not-so-subtle) advances. Some selfish siblings count the days to their parents' death as they covet the inheritance money.

"Coveting what belongs to another person is a serious offense on two counts. First, it indicates our lack of love for our neighbor, our relative, our friend, or whoever owns what we desire. The first and great commandment has to do with love; but, covetousness stands in direct opposition to love. When we place our affections on an inheritance, we remove our love from the person who's bequeathing it to us. When we see our neighbor's wife as the object of our desire, we begin to view our neighbor as the object of our disdain. When we scheme to get someone else's job, we reveal our calloused, insensitive heart. When we wish another person illness, injury, or bad fortune, we make it clear that the ONLY person we care about is 'NUMBER ONE', ourselves. When we covet what belongs to someone else, we displace the owner. In our minds, we kick him out of the game, or out of the job, or out of the marriage."[3]

III.   What are the Biblical Consequences of Breaking This Commandment?

The person who breaks this commandment totally disregards trust in God's provision. Instead of being content with what God has provided, this person...

• wants more	• envies more	• lusts for more	• longs for more
• needs more	• sees more	• hungers for more	• thirsts for more
• craves more	• desires more	• wishes for more	• requires more

---

[3]   From the Sunday School material: *Ten Overlooked Principles in Building Successful Families,* derived from Adrian Rogers' *Ten Secrets For A Successful Family.*

The person who habitually breaks this commandment will never be satisfied. His flesh and sinful nature will always long for more. God clearly warns: there are bitter consequences for breaking this commandment.

1. There are the consequences upon God.
   a. The covetous person rejects God: His care, His kingdom, and His righteousness.

   > "But seek ye first the kingdom of God, and his righteousness; and all these things shall be added unto you" (Mt.6:33).
   > "Let your conversation be without covetousness; and be content with such things as ye have: for he hath said, I will never leave thee, nor forsake thee" (Heb.13:5).

   b. The covetous person becomes an enemy of God.

   > "(For many walk, of whom I have told you often, and now tell you even weeping, that they are the enemies of the cross of Christ: Whose end is destruction, whose God is their belly, and whose glory is in their shame, who mind earthly things)" (Ph.3:18-19).
   > "Ye adulterers and adulteresses, know ye not that the friendship of the world is enmity with God? whosoever therefore will be a friend of the world is the enemy of God" (Jas.4:4).

2. There are the consequences upon one's family and others.
   a. The covetous person sometimes ruins lives and families, causing terrible pain, suffering, and division.

   > "And he said, Thy brother came with subtilty, and hath taken away thy blessing. And he said, Is not he rightly named Jacob? for he hath supplanted me these two times: he took away my birthright; and, behold, now he hath taken away my blessing. And he said, Hast thou not reserved a blessing for me? And Isaac answered and said unto Esau, Behold, I have made him thy lord, and all his brethren have I given to him for servants; and with corn and wine have I sustained him: and what shall I do now unto thee, my son? And Esau said unto his father, Hast thou but one blessing, my father? bless me, even me also, O my father. And Esau lifted up his voice, and wept. And Esau hated Jacob because of the blessing wherewith his father blessed him: and Esau said in his heart, The days of mourning for my father are at hand; then will I slay my brother Jacob" (Gen.27:35-38, 41).
   > "And it came to pass in an eveningtide, that David arose from off his bed, and walked upon the roof of the king's house: and from the roof he saw a woman washing herself; and the woman was very beautiful to look upon. And David sent and inquired after the woman. And one said, Is not this Bath-sheba, the daughter of Eliam, the wife of Uriah the Hittite? And David sent messengers, and took

her; and she came in unto him, and he lay with her; for she was purified from her uncleanness: and she returned unto her house. And the
woman conceived, and sent and told David, and said, I am with
child....And it came to pass in the morning, that David wrote a letter
to Joab, and sent it by the hand of Uriah. And he wrote in the letter,
saying, Set ye Uriah in the forefront of the hottest battle, and retire
ye from him, that he may be smitten, and die. And it came to pass,
when Joab observed the city, that he assigned Uriah unto a place
where he knew that valiant men were. And the men of the city went
out, and fought with Joab: and there fell some of the people of the
servants of David; and Uriah the Hittite died also....And when the
wife of Uriah heard that Uriah her husband was dead, she mourned
for her husband. And when the mourning was past, David sent and
fetched her to his house, and she became his wife, and bare him a son.
But the thing that David had done displeased the LORD" (2 Sam.11:2-
5, 14-17, 26-27).

b. The covetous person sometimes oppresses people and steals from them.

"And they covet fields, and take them by violence; and houses,
and take them away: so they oppress a man and his house, even a
man and his heritage" (Mic.2:2).

"And Jacob was wroth, and chode with [admonished, re-
proached] Laban: and Jacob answered and said to Laban, What is
my trespass? what is my sin, that thou hast so hotly pursued after
me? Whereas thou hast searched all my stuff, what hast thou found
of all thy household stuff? set it here before my brethren and thy
brethren, that they may judge betwixt us both. This twenty years
have I been with thee; thy ewes and thy she goats have not cast their
young, and the rams of thy flock have I not eaten. That which was
torn of beasts I brought not unto thee; I bare the loss of it; of my
hand didst thou require it, whether stolen by day, or stolen by night.
Thus I was; in the day the drought consumed me, and the frost by
night; and my sleep departed from mine eyes. Thus have I been
twenty years in thy house; I served thee fourteen years for thy two
daughters, and six years for thy cattle: and thou hast changed my
wages ten times. Except the God of my father, the God of Abraham,
and the fear of Isaac, had been with me, surely thou hadst sent me
away now empty. God hath seen mine affliction and the labour of my
hands, and rebuked thee yesternight" (Gen.31:36-42).

c. The covetous person causes grief for his entire family because of his pur-
suit of dishonest money.

"He that is greedy of gain troubleth his own house; but he that
hateth gifts [bribes] shall live" (Pr.15:27).

d. The covetous person sometimes enslaves other people for money.

> "And the patriarchs, moved with envy, sold Joseph into Egypt: but God was with him" (Acts 7:9).

e. The covetous person sometimes seeks to make a profit in sinful and evil ways.

> "And it came to pass, as we went to prayer, a certain damsel possessed with a spirit of divination met us, which brought her masters much gain by soothsaying: The same followed Paul and us, and cried, saying, These men are the servants of the most high God, which show unto us the way of salvation. And this did she many days. But Paul, being grieved, turned and said to the spirit, I command thee in the name of Jesus Christ to come out of her. And he came out the same hour. And when her masters saw that the hope of their gains was gone, they caught Paul and Silas, and drew them into the marketplace unto the rulers" (Acts 16:16-19).

> "For a certain man named Demetrius, a silversmith, which made silver shrines for Diana, brought no small gain unto the craftsmen; Whom he called together with the workmen of like occupation, and said, Sirs, ye know that by this craft we have our wealth. Moreover ye see and hear, that not alone at Ephesus, but almost throughout all Asia, this Paul hath persuaded and turned away much people, saying that they be no gods, which are made with hands" (Acts 19:24-26).

3. There are the consequences upon oneself, one's day-to-day life.

a. The covetous person sometimes becomes an adulterer.

> "But I say unto you, That whosoever looketh on [covets] a woman to lust after her hath committed adultery with her already in his heart. And if thy right eye offend thee, pluck it out, and cast it from thee: for it is profitable for thee that one of thy members should perish, and not that thy whole body should be cast into hell" (Mt.5:28-29).

> "And it came to pass in an eveningtide, that David arose from off his bed, and walked upon the roof of the king's house: and from the roof he saw a woman washing herself; and the woman was very beautiful to look upon. And David sent and inquired after the woman. And one said, Is not this Bath-sheba, the daughter of Eliam, the wife of Uriah the Hittite? And David sent messengers, and took her; and she came in unto him, and he lay with her; for she was purified from her uncleanness: and she returned unto her house" (2 Sam.11:2-4).

b. The covetous person becomes an idolater, one who refuses to acknowledge God as LORD and Master.

"Mortify therefore your members which are upon the earth; fornication, uncleanness, inordinate affection, evil concupiscence, and covetousness, which is idolatry" (Col.3:5).

c. The covetous person is greedy and will suffer many sorrows and much grief.

"So are the ways of every one that is greedy of gain; which taketh away the life of the owners thereof" (Pr.1:19).

"For the love of money is the root of all evil: which while some coveted after, they have erred from the faith, and pierced themselves through with many sorrows" (1 Tim.6:10).

d. The covetous person is unsatisfied, unfulfilled, and unhappy.

"Yea, they are greedy dogs which can never have enough, and they are shepherds that cannot understand: they all look to their own way, every one for his gain, from his quarter" (Is.56:11).

"Then I returned, and I saw vanity under the sun. There is one alone, and there is not a second; yea, he hath neither child nor brother: yet is there no end of all his labour; neither is his eye satisfied with riches; neither saith he, For whom do I labour, and bereave my soul of good? This is also vanity, yea, it is a sore travail" (Eccl.4:7-8).

"He that loveth silver shall not be satisfied with silver; nor he that loveth abundance with increase: this is also vanity" (Eccl.5:10).

"All the labour of man is for his mouth, and yet the appetite is not filled" (Eccl.6:7).

e. The covetous person has a warped perspective on the value of material things.

"And he said unto them, Take heed, and beware of covetousness: for a man's life consisteth not in the abundance of the things which he possesseth" (Lk.12:15).

f. The covetous person is misguided, placing his trust in accumulated riches and wealth.

"They that trust in their wealth, and boast themselves in the multitude of their riches; None of them can by any means redeem his brother, nor give to God a ransom for him" (Ps.49:6-7).

"Be not thou afraid when one is made rich, when the glory of his house is increased; For when he dieth he shall carry nothing away: his glory shall not descend after him" (Ps.49:16-17).

"Lo, this is the man that made not God his strength; but trusted in the abundance of his riches, and strengthened himself in his wickedness" (Ps.52:7).

"Riches profit not in the day of wrath: but righteousness delivereth from death" (Pr.11:4).

"He that trusteth in his riches shall fall: but the righteous shall flourish as a branch" (Pr.11:28).

g. The covetous person does not receive the answers to his prayers.

"From whence come wars and fightings among you? come they not hence, even of your lusts that war in your members? Ye lust, and have not: ye kill, and desire to have, and cannot obtain: ye fight and war, yet ye have not, because ye ask not. Ye ask, and receive not, because ye ask amiss, that ye may consume it upon your lusts" (Jas.4:1-3).

h. The covetous person is envious of the prosperity of the wicked.

"But as for me, my feet were almost gone; my steps had well nigh slipped. For I was envious at the foolish, when I saw the prosperity of the wicked" (Ps.73:2-3).

i. The covetous person will become sick from what he covets.

"Hast thou found honey? eat so much as is sufficient for thee, lest thou be filled therewith, and vomit it" (Pr.25:16).

j. The covetous person is a hypocrite.

"And they come unto thee as the people cometh, and they sit before thee as my people, and they hear thy words, but they will not do them: for with their mouth they show much love, but their heart goeth after their covetousness" (Ezk.33:31).

k. The covetous person is doomed to a life of unfruitfulness.

"And these are they which are sown among thorns; such as hear the word, And the cares of this world, and the deceitfulness of riches, and the lusts of other things entering in, choke the word, and it becometh unfruitful" (Mk.4:18-19).

l. The covetous person is worldly and carnal, a prisoner to the flesh, enslaved and given over to his lust and filled with coveteousness.

"And even as they did not like to retain God in their knowledge, God gave them over to a reprobate mind, to do those things which are not convenient; Being filled with all unrighteousness, fornication, wickedness, covetousness, maliciousness; full of envy, murder, debate, deceit, malignity; whisperers" (Ro.1:28-29).

"But they that will be rich fall into temptation and a snare, and into many foolish and hurtful lusts, which drown men in destruction and perdition" (1 Tim.6:9).

"Lust not after her beauty in thine heart; neither let her take thee with her eyelids" (Pr.6:25).

4. There are the consequences of judgment.
   a. The covetous person is deceived and will not inherit the kingdom of God.

   "Nay, ye do wrong, and defraud, and that your brethren. Know ye not that the unrighteous shall not inherit the kingdom of God? Be not deceived: neither fornicators, nor idolaters, nor adulterers, nor effeminate, nor abusers of themselves with mankind, Nor thieves, nor covetous, nor drunkards, nor revilers, nor extortioners, shall inherit the kingdom of God" (1 Cor. 6:8-10).

   "For this ye know, that no whoremonger, nor unclean person, nor covetous man, who is an idolater, hath any inheritance in the kingdom of Christ and of God" (Eph.5:5).

   b. The covetous person will face the severe judgment of God.

   "(For many walk, of whom I have told you often, and now tell you even weeping, that they are the enemies of the cross of Christ: Whose end is destruction, whose God is their belly, and whose glory is in their shame, who mind earthly things)" (Ph.3:18-19).

   "And shall receive the reward of unrighteousness, as they that count it pleasure to riot in the daytime. Spots they are and blemishes, sporting themselves with their own deceivings while they feast with you; Having eyes full of adultery, and that cannot cease from sin; beguiling unstable souls: an heart they have exercised with covetous practices; cursed children....For if after they have escaped the pollutions of the world through the knowledge of the Lord and Saviour Jesus Christ, they are again entangled therein, and overcome, the latter end is worse with them than the beginning. For it had been better for them not to have known the way of righteousness, than, after they have known it, to turn from the holy commandment delivered unto them" (2 Pt.2:13-14, 20-21).

   c. The covetous person is a castaway who will lose his soul.

   "For what is a man profited, if he shall gain the whole world, and lose his own soul? or what shall a man give in exchange for his soul?" (Mt.16:26; cp. Mk.8:36-37).

   "For what is a man advantaged, if he gain the whole world, and lose himself, or be cast away?" (Lk.9:25).

"And he said unto them, Take heed, and beware of covetousness: for a man's life consisteth not in the abundance of the things which he possesseth. And he spake a parable unto them, saying, The ground of a certain rich man brought forth plentifully: And he thought within himself, saying, What shall I do, because I have no room where to bestow my fruits? And he said, This will I do: I will pull down my barns, and build greater; and there will I bestow all my fruits and my goods. And I will say to my soul, Soul, thou hast much goods laid up for many years; take thine ease, eat, drink, [and] be merry. But God said unto him, [Thou] fool, this night thy soul shall be required of thee: then whose shall those things be, which thou hast provided? So [is] he that layeth up treasure for himself, and is not rich toward God" (Lk.12:15-21).

d. The covetous person is to be disciplined by the church, cut off from Christian fellowship.

"But now I have written unto you not to keep company, if any man that is called a brother be a fornicator, or covetous, or an idolater, or a railer, or a drunkard, or an extortioner; with such an one no not to eat" (1 Cor.5:11).

e. The covetous person is lost, passing away without God.

"For all that is in the world, the lust of the flesh, and the lust of the eyes, and the pride of life, is not of the Father, but is of the world. And the world passeth away, and the lust thereof: but he that doeth the will of God abideth for ever" (1 Jn.2:16-17).

IV. What Are the Biblical Benefits of Keeping This Commandment?

There are many great promises that can be claimed by the person who is content in the LORD and does not covet.

1. A person who is content in the LORD and truly seeks the LORD will have everything he needs.

"But seek ye first the kingdom of God, and his righteousness; and all these things shall be added unto you" (Mt.6:33).
"But my God shall supply all your need according to his riches in glory by Christ Jesus" (Ph.4:19).

2. A person who is content in the LORD and faithful will have plenty of God's provisions.

`   "I will abundantly bless her provision: I will satisfy her poor with bread" (Ps.132:15).

"Honour the LORD with thy substance, and with the firstfruits of all thine increase: So shall thy barns be filled with plenty, and thy presses shall burst out with new wine" (Pr.3:9-10).

"For the seed shall be prosperous; the vine shall give her fruit, and the ground shall give her increase, and the heavens shall give their dew; and I will cause the remnant of this people to possess all these things" (Zech.8:12).

3. A person who is content in the LORD and lives a righteous life will be blessed, even when the hard times come.

"Behold, the eye of the Lord is upon them that fear him, upon them that hope in his mercy; To deliver their soul from death, and to keep them alive in famine" (Ps.33:18-19).

"The Lord knoweth the days of the upright: and their inheritance shall be for ever. They shall not be ashamed in the evil time: and in the days of famine they shall be satisfied" (Ps.37:18-19).

4. A person who is content in the LORD will find pleasures and be satisfied forevermore.

"Thou wilt show me the path of life: in thy presence is fulness of joy; at thy right hand there are pleasures for evermore" (Ps.16:11).

"And ye shall eat in plenty, and be satisfied, and praise the name of the LORD your God, that hath dealt wondrously with you: and my people shall never be ashamed" (Joel 2:26).

5. A person who is content in the LORD and *continually seeks* the LORD will prosper in all he does.

"Keep therefore the words of this covenant, and do them, that ye may prosper in all that ye do" (Dt.29:9).

"Then shalt thou prosper, if thou takest heed to fulfil the statutes and judgments which the LORD charged Moses with concerning Israel: be strong, and of good courage; dread not, nor be dismayed" (1 Chron.22:13).

"And they rose early in the morning, and went forth into the wilderness of Tekoa: and as they went forth, Jehoshaphat stood and said, Hear me, O Judah, and ye inhabitants of Jerusalem; Believe in the LORD your God, so shall ye be established; believe his prophets, so shall ye prosper" (2 Chron.20:20).

"And he sought God in the days of Zechariah, who had understanding in the visions of God: and as long as he sought the LORD, God made him to prosper" (2 Chron.26:5).

"And in every work that he began in the service of the house of God, and in the law, and in the commandments, to seek his God, he did it with all his heart, and prospered" (2 Chron.31:21).

"And he shall be like a tree planted by the rivers of water, that bringeth forth his fruit in his season; his leaf also shall not wither; and whatsoever he doeth shall prosper" (Ps.1:3).

6. A person who is content and obedient in the LORD will be greatly blessed and have much success.

"And all these blessings shall come on thee, and overtake thee, if thou shalt hearken unto the voice of the LORD thy God" (Dt.28:2).

"This book of the law shall not depart out of thy mouth; but thou shalt meditate therein day and night, that thou mayest observe to do according to all that is written therein: for then thou shalt make thy way prosperous, and then thou shalt have good success" (Josh.1:8).

"Many, O LORD my God, are thy wonderful works which thou hast done, and thy thoughts which are to us-ward: they cannot be reckoned up in order unto thee: if I would declare and speak of them, they are more than can be numbered" (Ps.40:5).

"Many, O LORD my God, are the wonders which Thou hast done, And Thy thoughts toward us; There is none to compare with Thee; If I would declare and speak of them, They would be too numerous to count" (Ps.40:5, NASB).

"A faithful man shall abound with blessings: but he that maketh haste to be rich shall not be innocent" (Pr.28:20).

"Bring ye all the tithes into the storehouse, that there may be meat in mine house, and prove me now herewith, saith the LORD of hosts, if I will not open you the windows of heaven, and pour you out a blessing, that there shall not be room enough to receive it" (Mal.3:10).

7. A person who is content in the LORD will find that his job promotion and positions come from the LORD.

"So now it was not you that sent me hither, but God: and he hath made me a father to Pharaoh, and lord of all his house, and a ruler throughout all the land of Egypt" (Gen.45:8).

"The LORD maketh poor, and maketh rich: he bringeth low, and lifteth up" (1 Sam.2:7).

"Now therefore so shalt thou say unto my servant David, Thus saith the LORD of hosts, I took thee from the sheepcote, from following the sheep, to be ruler over my people, over Israel" (2 Sam.7:8).

"Go, tell Jeroboam, Thus saith the LORD God of Israel, Forasmuch as I exalted thee from among the people, and made thee prince over my people Israel" (1 Ki.14:7).

> "For promotion cometh neither from the east, nor from the west, nor from the south. But God is the judge: he putteth down one, and setteth up another" (Ps.75:6-7).
>
> "And he changeth the times and the seasons: he removeth kings, and setteth up kings: he giveth wisdom unto the wise, and knowledge to them that know understanding" (Dan.2:21).

8. A person who is content in the LORD will be rewarded for his faithfulness and for having the right priorities.

> "And he said unto him, Well, thou good servant: because thou hast been faithful in a very little, have thou authority over ten cities" (Lk.19:17).
>
> "For ye have need of patience, that, after ye have done the will of God, ye might receive the promise" (Heb.10:36).
>
> "By faith Moses, when he was come to years, refused to be called the son of Pharaoh's daughter; Choosing rather to suffer affliction with the people of God, than to enjoy the pleasures of sin for a season; Esteeming the reproach of Christ greater riches than the treasures in Egypt: for he had respect unto the recompence of the reward" (Heb.11:24-26).
>
> "And God said to Solomon, Because this was in thine heart, and thou hast not asked riches, wealth, or honour, nor the life of thine enemies, neither yet hast asked long life; but hast asked wisdom and knowledge for thyself, that thou mayest judge my people, over whom I have made thee king: Wisdom and knowledge is granted unto thee; and I will give thee riches, and wealth, and honour, such as none of the kings have had that have been before thee, neither shall there any after thee have the like" (2 Chron.1:11-12).

9. A person who is content in the LORD will, if needed, experience God's miraculous care and provision.

> "Yea, forty years didst thou sustain them in the wilderness, so that they lacked nothing; their clothes waxed not old, and their feet swelled not" (Neh.9:21).

10. A person who is content in the LORD is a recipient of God's grace: he receives what he does not deserve.

> "And I have given you a land for which ye did not labour, and cities which ye built not, and ye dwell in them; of the vineyards and oliveyards which ye planted not do ye eat" (Josh.24:13).

11. A person who is content in the LORD personally knows the Source of his supply.

"Not that I speak in respect of want: for I have learned, in whatsoever state I am, therewith to be content....But my God shall supply all your need according to his riches in glory by Christ Jesus" (Ph.4:11, 19).

12. A person who is content in the LORD knows that everything belongs to God.

"The earth is the Lord's, and the fulness thereof; the world, and they that dwell therein" (Ps.24:1).

13. A person who is content in the LORD has a firm faith in God's ability to provide for his needs.

"O fear the Lord, ye his saints: for there is no want to them that fear him" (Ps.34:9).

"I have been young, and now am old; yet have I not seen the righteous forsaken, nor his seed begging bread" (Ps.37:25).

"God hath spoken once; twice have I heard this; that power belongeth unto God. Also unto thee, O Lord, belongeth mercy: for thou renderest to every man according to his work" (Ps.62:11-12).

14. A person who is content in the LORD understands that life and material possessions are temporal.

"And said, Naked came I out of my mother's womb, and naked shall I return thither: the Lord gave, and the Lord hath taken away; blessed be the name of the Lord" (Job 1:21).

15. A person who is content in the LORD *learns* to be content no matter the circumstances and problems.

"Not that I speak in respect of want: for I have learned, in whatsoever state I am, therewith to be content. I know both how to be abased, and I know how to abound: every where and in all things I am instructed both to be full and to be hungry, both to abound and to suffer need" (Ph.4:11-12).

"But godliness with contentment is great gain. For we brought nothing into this world, and it is certain we can carry nothing out. And having food and raiment let us be therewith content" (1 Tim.6:6-8).

16. A person who obeys the LORD is content in the LORD and has his prayers answered.

"And whatsoever we ask, we receive of him [contentment], because we keep his commandments, and do those things that are pleasing in his sight" (1 Jn.3:22).

V. What Is the Teaching of Jesus Christ Concerning This Commandment?

1. Jesus Christ declared that man should never defraud (cheat) his neighbor, i.e., never covet anything belonging to his neighbor.

> "Thou knowest the commandments, Do not commit adultery, Do not kill, Do not steal, Do not bear false witness, Defraud not, Honour thy father and mother" (Mk.10:19).

Thought.

Scripture is clear: covetousness is wrong. We must never covet: we must never cheat our neighbor out of anything.

> "Thou shalt not covet thy neighbour's house, thou shalt not covet thy neighbour's wife, nor his manservant, nor his maidservant, nor his ox, nor his ass, nor any thing that is thy neighbour's" (Ex.20:17).
> "Take heed, and beware of covetousness" (Lk.12:15).
> "But fornication, and all uncleanness, or covetousness, let it not be once named among you" (Eph.5:3).
> "Let your conversation [behavior, conduct] be without covetousness" (Heb.13:5).

2. Jesus Christ declared that man should beware of coveteousness because man's life is more than accumulating material things.

> "And he said unto them, Take heed, and beware of covetousness: for a man's life consisteth not in the abundance of the things which he possesseth" (Lk.12:15).

Thought.

We must be content with what God has provided for us. Within the heart of every man is the desire to have more and more. God has promised to provide everything that His people *need*. The greedy or coveteous person is unwilling to wait for God to provide; consequently, his passion for more is never quenched.

> "Not that I speak in respect of want: for I have learned, in whatsoever state I am, therewith to be content. I know both how to be abased, and I know how to abound: every where and in all things I am instructed both to be full and to be hungry, both to abound and to suffer need. I can do all things through Christ which strengtheneth me" (Ph.4:11-13).
> "Let your conversation [behavior, conduct] be without covetousness; and be content with such things as ye have: for he hath said, I will never leave thee, nor forsake thee. So that we may boldly say,

The Lord is my helper, and I will not fear what man shall do unto me" (Heb.13:5-6).

"Ye lust, and have not: ye kill, and desire to have, and cannot obtain: ye fight and war, yet ye have not, because ye ask not. Ye ask, and receive not, because ye ask amiss, that ye may consume it upon your lusts" (Jas.4:2-3).

"(For many walk, of whom I have told you often, and now tell you even weeping, that they are the enemies of the cross of Christ: Whose end is destruction, whose God is their belly, and whose glory is in their shame, who mind earthly things)" (Ph.3:18-19).

"Love not the world, neither the things that are in the world. If any man love the world, the love of the Father is not in him. For all that is in the world, the lust of the flesh, and the lust of the eyes, and the pride of life, is not of the Father, but is of the world" (1 Jn.2:15-16).

3. Jesus Christ declared that a man who covets (lusts, craves) after beauty in his heart has committed adultery and sexual immorality.

"But I say unto you, That whosoever looketh on a woman to lust after her hath committed adultery with her already in his heart" (Mt.5:28).

Thought.

Coveting and lusting after a woman can never be justified. Sex is never right when a person covets another person to whom he or she is not married. The Bible does not teach that sex is wrong. But the Bible does teach that sex outside of marriage is wrong, and the wrong use of sex is sin. Sex has been given by God for at least three reasons.

a) Sex causes a person to be attracted to another person. Therefore, sexual attraction is one of the major tools that brings about marriage (Gen.2:18, 21-25).

b) Sex is a tool with which to love. Sex, properly rooted and expressed in God, is one of the deepest and richest involvements and expressions of love (Eph.5:28-32).

c) Sex creates life. God has given man the privilege of being sub-creators of life—under Him (Gen.1:29).

Adultery is often said to be sexual unfaithfulness by a married person. This is true, but it is much more. Man's idea of adultery is shattered by Christ. Christ says adultery is not only the actual act, but adultery is committed by any one of five acts:

a) A deliberate look.

b) Passion within the heart: desiring and lusting.

c) The actual act of sex with someone other than one's own spouse.

d) Divorce relationships (Mt.5:32; 19:9-11; Mk.10:11-12; Lk.16:18).

e) Spiritual unfaithfulness toward God or apostasy from God (Mt.12:39; 16:4; Mk.8:38; Jas.4:4; cp. Ezk.16:15f; 23:43f).

"Lust not after her beauty in thine heart; neither let her take thee with her eyelids" (Pr.6:25).

"Ye adulterers and adulteresses, know ye not that the friendship of the world is enmity with God? whosoever therefore will be a friend of the world is the enemy of God" (Jas.4:4).

"Know ye not that the unrighteous shall not inherit the kingdom of God? Be not deceived: neither fornicators, nor idolaters, nor adulterers, nor effeminate, nor abusers of themselves with mankind, Nor thieves, nor covetous, nor drunkards, nor revilers, nor extortioners, shall inherit the kingdom of God" (1 Cor.6:9-10).

"And it came to pass in an eveningtide, that David arose from off his bed, and walked upon the roof of the king's house: and from the roof he saw a woman washing herself; and the woman was very beautiful to look upon. And David sent and enquired after the woman. And one said, Is not this Bath-sheba, the daughter of Eliam, the wife of Uriah the Hittite? And David sent messengers, and took her; and she came in unto him, and he lay with her; for she was purified from her uncleanness: and she returned unto her house" (2 Sam.11:2-4).

4. Jesus Christ declared that we must not seek the things of this earth, but rather seek first the kingdom of God and His righteousness.

"But seek ye first the kingdom of God, and his righteousness; and all these things shall be added unto you" (Mt.6:33).

Thought.

Only God can meet the need of the heart that cries out for more and more. Things will never satisfy us. When we die and pass on into the spiritual world, we can take nothing with us because we have no strength, no energy, no power, no way for our spirits to carry away material possessions.

"For what shall it profit a man, if he shall gain the whole world, and lose his own soul? Or what shall a man give in exchange for his soul?" (Mk.8:36-37).

"For we brought nothing into this world, and it is certain we can carry nothing out" (1 Tim.6:7).

"A faithful man shall abound with blessings: but he that maketh haste to be rich shall not be innocent" (Pr.28:20).

"Yea, they are greedy dogs which can never have enough, and they are shepherds that cannot understand: they all look to their own way, every one for his gain, from his quarter" (Is.56:11).

"Then I returned, and I saw vanity under the sun. There is one alone, and there is not a second; yea, he hath neither child nor brother: yet is there no end of all his labour; neither is his eye satisfied with riches; neither saith he, For whom do I labour, and bereave my soul of good? This is also vanity, yea, it is a sore travail" (Eccl.4:7-8).

"He that loveth silver shall not be satisfied with silver; nor he that loveth abundance with increase: this is also vanity" (Eccl.5:10).

5. Jesus Christ declared that we must not lay up treasure upon earth, but rather lay up treasure in heaven.

"Lay not up for yourselves treasures upon earth, where moth and rust doth corrupt, and where thieves break through and steal: But lay up for yourselves treasures in heaven, where neither moth nor rust doth corrupt, and where thieves do not break through nor steal" (Mt.6:19-20).

Thought.

It is easier to covet earthly things than heavenly things for four reasons:
⇒ They are seen and can oftentimes be handled.
⇒ They are sought by most people, and other people influence us. A person is either worldly minded or heavenly minded (Ro.8:5-7).
⇒ They are to varying degrees necessary for life.
⇒ They are present, ever before us, and many can be possessed right now.

The things on earth are insecure for three reasons:
⇒ They can be stolen, eaten up, or destroyed.
⇒ They do not last; they waste away.
⇒ A person cannot take a single thing with him when he passes from this world into the next.

"Hast thou found honey? eat so much as is sufficient for thee, lest thou be filled therewith, and vomit it" (Pr.25:16).

"And the cares of this world, and the deceitfulness of riches, and the lusts of other things entering in, choke the word, and it becometh unfruitful" (Mk.4:19).

"For all that is in the world, the lust of the flesh, and the lust of the eyes, and the pride of life, is not of the Father, but is of the world. And the world passeth away, and the lust thereof: but he that doeth the will of God abideth for ever" (1 Jn.2:16-17).

"Thou wilt show me the path of life: in thy presence is fulness of joy; at thy right hand there are pleasures for evermore" (Ps.16:11).

VI.   What Is the Decision Required by This Commandment?

Note that covetousness is not a material or physical thing. We cannot see nor touch covetousness—only the results of it. Covetousness is an arousal, a passion that arises within our hearts and minds: it involves thoughts, desires, cravings, attitudes, longings, lusts. And these inward feelings and thoughts are far more difficult to control than outward acts. Nevertheless, this is exactly what God demands. He expects a strong decision, a clear cut decision: that we *never covet*. This is the tenth and final great commandment of God: "You shall not covet" (20:17).

1. We must stamp out the very first thought or urge to covet (desire or lust). The excellent commentator Arthur Pink says this:

"[Covetousness] is the first film or shadow of an evil thought, the imperfect embryo of a sin before it is shaped in us or has any lineaments or features. This is what the Scripture refers to as 'every imagination of the thoughts' of the human heart. Such imaginations are expressly declared to be 'evil' (Gen.6:5). Such are the first risings of our corrupt nature toward those sins which are pleasing to our sensual inclinations. They are to be steadfastly watched, hated, and resisted. They are to be stamped upon as the sparks of a dangerous fire, for as soon as they begin to stir within us they pollute our souls. Just as the breathing upon a mirror sullies it, leaving a dimness there, so the very first breathings of an evil desire or thought within one's breast defile the soul."[4]

2. We must not covet (desire, lust) the things of this world.

"Thou shalt not covet thy neighbour's house, thou shalt not covet thy neighbour's wife, nor his manservant, nor his maidservant, nor his ox, nor his ass, nor any thing that is thy neighbour's" (Ex.20:17).

"Neither shalt thou desire thy neighbour's wife, neither shalt thou covet thy neighbour's house, his field, or his manservant, or his maidservant, his ox, or his ass, or any thing that is thy neighbour's" (Dt.5:21).

"Now these things were our examples, to the intent we should not lust after evil things, as they also lusted" (1 Cor.10:6).

"Love not the world, neither the things that are in the world. If any man love the world, the love of the Father is not in him. For all that is in the world, the lust of the flesh, and the lust of the eyes, and the pride of life, is not of the Father, but is of the world" (1 Jn.2:15-16).

3. We must beware and guard against the very first urging and thought of covetousness.

"And he said unto them, Take heed, and beware of covetousness: for a man's life consisteth not in the abundance of the things which he possesseth" (Lk.12:15).

---

[4]   Arthur Pink. *The Ten Commandments*, p.64.

"Casting down imaginations, and every high thing that exalteth itself against the knowledge of God, and bringing into captivity every thought to the obedience of Christ" (2 Cor.10:5).

4. We must put to death the arousal and growth of covetousness (desires, lusts) in our hearts.

"Mortify therefore your members which are upon the earth; fornication, uncleanness, inordinate affection, evil concupiscence, and covetousness, which is idolatry" (Col.3:5).

5. We must not covet (lust, crave) after women.

"Lust not after her beauty in thine heart; neither let her take thee with her eyelids" (Pr.6:25).

"But I say unto you, That whosoever looketh on a woman to lust after her hath committed adultery with her already in his heart" (Mt.5:28).

6. We must not fellowship with a covetous person.

"But now I have written unto you not to keep company, if any man that is called a brother be a fornicator, or covetous, or an idolater, or a railer, or a drunkard, or an extortioner; with such an one no not to eat" (1 Cor.5:11).

7. We must not envy sinners, no matter who they are or what they have.

"Let not thine heart envy sinners: but be thou in the fear of the LORD all the day long" (Pr.23:17).

"Be not thou envious against evil men, neither desire to be with them" (Pr.24:1).

8. We must covet (desire, long for) only the good things of life.

"But covet earnestly the best gifts: and yet show I unto you a more excellent way" (1 Cor.12:31).

"Wherefore, brethren, covet to prophesy, and forbid not to speak with tongues" (1 Cor.14:39).

9. We must not seek first the things of this earth, but rather seek first the kingdom of God and His righteousness.

"But seek ye first the kingdom of God, and his righteousness; and all these things shall be added unto you" (Mt.6:33).

10. We must not lay up treasure upon earth, but rather lay up treasure in heaven.

> **"Lay not up for yourselves treasures upon earth, where moth and rust doth corrupt, and where thieves break through and steal: But lay up for yourselves treasures in heaven, where neither moth nor rust doth corrupt, and where thieves do not break through nor steal" (Mt.6:19-20).**

11. We must walk in the Spirit of God not in the lusts of the flesh.

> **"This I say then, Walk in the Spirit, and ye shall not fulfill the lust [covetousness, desires] of the flesh" (Gal.5:16).**

12. We must pray and seek God for the things we need and want, not covet them.

> **"Ye lust [covet, desire], and have not: ye kill, and desire to have, and cannot obtain: ye fight and war, yet ye have not, because ye ask not" (Jas.4:2).**

13. We must not attempt to serve (covet, long after) both God and money.

> **"No servant can serve two masters: for either he will hate the one, and love the other; or else he will hold to the one, and despise the other. Ye cannot serve God and mammon. And the Pharisees also, who were covetous, heard all these things: and they derided him" (Lk.16:13-14).**

14. We must be content with what we have.

> **"Let your conversation be without covetousness; and be content with such things as ye have: for he hath said, I will never leave thee, nor forsake thee. So that we may boldly say, The Lord is my helper, and I will not fear what man shall do unto me" (Heb.13:5-6).**

Now, note the verse just quoted, Heb.13:5-6. The Preacher's Outline & Sermon Bible® says this in its commentary on this great passage, Hebrews 13:5-6:

"1. 'Covetousness' (aphilarguros) means loving money or possessions. A person can love money, property, estates, houses, cars—anything on earth. Thomas Hewitt points out that the Greek word for 'conversation' (tropos) means *manner of life*, or *the way of thought and life*.[5] The believer's very thoughts are to be free from covetousness. His thoughts are to be focused upon Christ and the glorious hope of eternity, not upon this passing world and its possessions. The believer is to have no secret lust for the things of this world.

"2. A believer is to be content with what he has. This does not mean that a believer is not to improve himself, nor that he is not to work and make money and be wise in investments. Scripture teaches the very opposite: we are to work and invest and make money. We are to make enough so that we can meet the needs of the world. What this passage means is that we are to be...

- satisfied with our lot in life: our ability, capacity, job, position, opportunities, and on and on
- satisfied with the home, possessions, clothing, goods and everything else we have, whether it is little or nothing
- satisfied with our present condition

"Again, this does not mean that we do not plan and focus upon improving everything around us—ranging from our personal possessions over to the world's economy and environment. Believers are to work and labor more diligently than anyone else in the world. But while we labor, we know...

- God never leaves us nor forsakes us (Job 1:5)
- God is our helper, and we are secure no matter what men may do to us (Ps.118:6)

"Even if the world's economy and peace collapsed, believers—true believers—would be secure in God. God provides for His dear followers until He is ready to take them home to heaven (Mt.6:33). Matthew Henry sums it up well:

"'This promise contains the sum and substance of all the promises. I will never, no, never leave thee, nor ever forsake thee. Here are no fewer than five negatives heaped together, to confirm the promise; the true believer shall have the gracious presence of God with him in life, at death, and for ever.'[6]"[7]

---

5   Thomas Hewitt. *The Epistle to the Hebrews.* "Tyndale New Testament Commentaries." (Grand Rapids, MI: Eerdmans Publishing Co., Began in 1958), p.206.

6   Matthew Henry. *Matthew Henry's Commentary*, Vol.6, p.962.

7   *The Preacher's Outline & Sermon Bible*, Vol. 11, p.196-197.

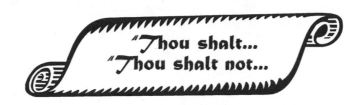

"Thou shalt...
"Thou shalt not...

The Purposes For the Law: Why God Gave the Ten Commandments to the World Exodus 20:18-26

Contents

The Purposes For the Law: Why God Gave the Ten Commandments to the World
Exodus 20:18-26

THE PURPOSES FOR THE LAW		
1. To reveal the glorious majesty & holiness of God: Showing that a great barrier—a great gulf—exists between man and God **2. To reveal man's need for a mediator, for a person who can approach God on behalf of man** **3. To test man** a. To see if man will walk in the fear & reverence of God b. To see if man will truly obey God & not sin c. To see if man will trust the mediator appointed by God **4. To teach that God alone is the LORD:** He alone has truly revealed Himself, has spoken to man	18 And all the people saw the thunderings, and the lightnings, and the noise of the trumpet, and the mountain smoking: and when the people saw it, they removed, and stood afar off. 19 And they said unto Moses, Speak thou with us, and we will hear: but let not God speak with us, lest we die. 20 And Moses said unto the people, Fear not: for God is come to prove you, and that his fear may be before your faces, that ye sin not. 21 And the people stood afar off, and Moses drew near unto the thick darkness where God was. 22 And the LORD said unto Moses, Thus thou shalt say unto the children of Israel, Ye	have seen that I have talked with you from heaven. 23 Ye shall not make with me gods of silver, neither shall ye make unto you gods of gold. 24 An altar of earth thou shalt make unto me, and shalt sacrifice thereon thy burnt offerings, and thy peace offerings, thy sheep, and thine oxen: in all places where I record my name I will come unto thee, and I will bless thee. 25 And if thou wilt make me an altar of stone, thou shalt not build it of hewn stone: for if thou lift up thy tool upon it, thou hast polluted it. 26 Neither shalt thou go up by steps unto mine altar, that thy nakedness be not discovered thereon.
		from heaven **5. To teach how God alone is to be approached & worshipped** a. No idolatry: No gods whatsoever are to be made or worshipped b. No pageantry 1) The altar of worship was to be of earth: A non-showy, non-costly material provided (created) by God alone 2) The altar of worship was to be made of natural, undressed stones: A material provided by God, not defiled & polluted by man c. No immodest behavior: The altar was not to have steps that would expose a person's nakedness (symbolized self-righteousness, man ascending up to God)

Scripture is clear: God gave the Ten Commandments as the basic law to govern all people. But why? Why exactly did God give the Ten Commandments to the world? What were His purposes? What did God have in mind? What were His reasons for instituting the Ten Commandments to be the basic law for all men to obey?

We must understand God's reasons, His purposes for giving the Ten Commandments, in order to gain the greatest benefit from them. A careful study of the present passage tells us why God gave the law. Five very specific purposes can be gleaned from the experience of Israel right after receiving the Ten Commandments. This is the all-important subject of this Scripture: *The Purposes For the Law: Why God Gave the Ten Commandments to the World*, Ex.20:18-26.

I. The Ten Commandments were given to reveal the glorious majesty and holiness of God: Showing that a great barrier—a great gulf—exists between man and God (v.18).

II. The Ten Commandments were given to reveal man's need for a mediator, for a person who can approach God on behalf of man (v.19).

III. The Ten Commandments were given to test man (v.20-21).

IV. The Ten Commandments were given to teach that God alone is the LORD: He alone has truly revealed Himself, has spoken to man from heaven (v.22).

V. The Ten Commandments were given to teach how God alone is to be approached and worshipped (v.23-26).

I. The Ten Commandments Were Given to Reveal the Glorious Majesty and Holiness of God: Showing That a Great Barrier—a Great Gulf—Exists between Man and God.

"And all the people saw the thunderings, and the lightnings, and the noise of the trumpet, and the mountain smoking: and when the people saw it, they removed, and stood afar off" (v.18).

Glance to chapter 19 of Exodus and note what had happened to Israel at the foot of Mount Sinai: God's holy presence had descended to the top of the mountain in what was probably the most spectacular, terrifying storm and cloud ever witnessed upon earth. Note the glorious description: there was...

- thunder and lightning (19:16)
- the constant blast of a loud trumpet (19:16)
- a flaming fire that engulfed the mountain (19:18)
- a cloud of bellowing smoke that arose as though from a huge volcanic eruption (19:18)
- the violent quaking of the mountain, a quaking that never stopped trembling (19:18)

The people reacted just as any of us would have: they withdrew from the foot of the mountain; they shrunk back from God's holy presence. They feared for their lives; feared lest the holy presence of God strike out at them (v.19). Obviously, they were sensing a great gulf between the holy presence of God and their own sinful, human nature. They sensed a deep, terrifying distance between the majesty and holiness of God's person and their own human condition—a condition of weakness, failure, shortcoming, and sinfulness. They knew that the majesty of God being displayed upon the mountain, the majesty they were witnessing, could strike them dead at any moment (v.19). Thus they shrunk back and withdrew from God's holy presence.

This was the very point that God wished to convey to the people: He is the very embodiment of *majestic glory and holiness*. There is a great gulf—a chasm, an abyss, a terrifying separation—between Himself and man, between what He Himself is and what man is. Again, God is the very embodiment of *majestic glory and holiness*; therefore, the very law of God—the Ten Commandments, the very *words* which God spoke—were holy and glorious (Ro.7:12, 14, 16). The law of God and the Ten Commandments were the very expression of God's being. Therefore, people were to obey God's law or else face the consuming brilliance and terrifying judgment of God's glory and holiness.

Thought.

This was the first reason God gave the law: to reveal His majestic glory and holiness, that there is a *great gulf*, a terrifying separation between God and man.

> "But your iniquities have separated between you and your God, and your sins have hid his face from you, that he will not hear" (Is.59:2).
>
> "But we are all as an unclean thing, and all our righteousnesses are as filthy rags; and we all do fade as a leaf; and our iniquities, like the wind, have taken us away" (Is.64:6).
>
> "And there is none that calleth upon thy name, that stirreth up himself to take hold of thee: for thou hast hid thy face from us, and hast consumed us, because of our iniquities" (Is.64:7).
>
> "And beside all this, between us [in heaven] and you [in hell] there is a great gulf fixed: so that they which would pass from hence to you cannot; neither can they pass to us, that [would come] from thence" (Lk.16:26).
>
> "For all have sinned, and come short of the glory of God" (Ro.3:23).
>
> "If we say that we have no sin, we deceive ourselves, and the truth is not in us" (1 Jn.1:8).
>
> "And GOD saw that the wickedness of man was great in the earth, and that every imagination of the thoughts of his heart was only evil continually" (Gen.6:5).
>
> "Who can say, I have made my heart clean, I am pure from my sin?" (Pr.20:9).

II.   The Ten Commandments Were Given to Reveal Man's Need for a Mediator, for a Person Who Can Approach God for Man, a Person Who Can Represent Man before God.

>"**And they said unto Moses, Speak thou with us, and we will hear: but let not God speak with us, lest we die**" (v.19).

Apparently, the people had heard the booming voice of God speaking out from the cloud covering the mountain. Scripture suggests that God's booming voice actually spoke and gave the Ten Commandments directly to the people:

>"**The LORD talked with you face to face in the mount out of the midst of the fire**" (Dt.5:4).
>
>"**These words the LORD spake unto all your assembly in the mount out of the midst of the fire, of the cloud, and of the thick darkness, with a great voice: and he added no more. And he wrote them in two tables of stone, and delivered them unto me. And it came to pass, when ye heard the voice out of the midst of the darkness, (for the mountain did burn with fire,) that ye came near unto me, even all the heads of your tribes, and your elders; And ye said, Behold, the LORD our God hath showed us his glory and his greatness, and we have heard his voice out of the midst of the fire: we have seen this day that God doth talk with man, and he liveth. Now therefore why should we die? for this great fire will consume us: if we hear the voice of the LORD our God any more, then we shall die. For who is there of all flesh, that hath heard the voice of the living God speaking out of the midst of the fire, as we have, and lived? Go thou near, and hear all that the LORD our God shall say: and speak thou unto us all that the LORD our God shall speak unto thee; and we will hear it, and do it**" (Dt.5:22-27).

Two terrifying events were happening: the people were witnessing the awesome sight of God's glory and majesty, and they were actually hearing the booming voice of God Himself declare the Ten Commandments. Both struck a deep sense of unworthiness in the people. They became keenly aware of the vast difference—the enormous gulf—between God and man, the vast difference...

*   between God's holy nature and man's sinful nature
*   between God's awesome power and man's helplessness before that power
*   between what God is like and what man is like

The sight of God's majestic glory and the hearing of God's booming voice revealed a startling fact to the people: there was a *great gulf* between man and God, and the people sensed the *gulf* deeply. They were so aware of God's holiness and their sinfulness—so aware of the vast difference between God's awesome person and their humanity—that they did not want God to speak directly to them, not anymore. They obviously feared some pronouncement of judgment upon them (v.19).

The point is this: they sensed the need for a mediator, for a person to approach God for them, a person who could represent them before God. They wanted God's messenger to be their mediator: they wanted Moses to approach God, to receive God's message, and then to bring God's message back to them. Note what the people promised: they would hear and obey the word of God (v.19).

This great sense and need for a mediator led to one of the great promises in Scripture, the promise of God's Perfect Mediator, the Lord Jesus Christ. As God's Perfect Mediator, Jesus Christ was to stand before God for all people of all ages. Note what Moses himself was later to proclaim to the people:

> "The LORD thy God will raise up unto thee a Prophet from the midst of thee, of thy brethren, like unto me; unto him ye shall hearken; According to all that thou desiredst of the LORD thy God in Horeb [Mt. Sinai] in the day of the assembly, saying, Let me not hear again the voice of the LORD my God, neither let me see this great fire any more, that I die not. And the LORD said unto me, They have well spoken that which they have spoken. I will raise them up a Prophet from among their brethren, like unto thee, and will put my words in his mouth; and he shall speak unto them all that I shall command him. And it shall come to pass, that whosoever will not hearken unto my words which he shall speak in my name, I will require it of him" (Dt.18:15-19).

Thought.

The Ten Commandments—that is, our failure to keep the Ten Commandments—show how far short we come, how far away we are from God. The Ten Commandments show our great need for a mediator, for someone to approach God and to intercede for us. That Someone, that Person, is Jesus Christ. Jesus Christ is our Mediator, the Person who approaches God for us.

> "For there is one God, and one mediator between God and men, the man Christ Jesus; Who gave himself a ransom for all, to be testified in due time" (1 Tim.2:5-6).
> "Forasmuch then as the children are partakers of flesh and blood, he also himself likewise took part of the same; that through death he might destroy him that had the power of death, that is, the devil; And deliver them who through fear of death were all their lifetime subject to bondage. For verily he took not on him the nature of angels; but he took on him the seed of Abraham. Wherefore in all things it behoved him to be made like unto his brethren, that he

might be a merciful and faithful high priest [mediator] in things pertaining to God, to make reconciliation for the sins of the people" (Heb.2:14-17).

"Wherefore he is able also to save them to the uttermost that come unto God by him, seeing he ever liveth [as the mediator] to make intercession for them" (Heb.7:25).

"But now hath he obtained a more excellent ministry, by how much also he is the mediator of a better covenant, which was established upon better promises" (Heb.8:6).

"And for this cause he is the mediator of the new testament, that by means of death, for the redemption of the transgressions that were under the first testament, they which are called might receive the promise of eternal inheritance" (Heb.9:15).

III. The Ten Commandments Were Given to Test Man.

Note the word *fear*: two kinds of fear are mentioned in this verse:
⇒ A *tormenting fear* (yare): the fear that defeats a person, that keeps a person from acting and doing what he should.
⇒ A *respectful, honoring fear* (yirah): the fear of God that arouses a person to reverence and obey God.

"And Moses said unto the people, Fear not: for God is come to prove you, and that his fear may be before your faces, that ye sin not. And the people stood afar off, and Moses drew near unto the thick darkness where God was" (v.20-21).

Moses encouraged the people not to be gripped with a tormenting fear of God. God was not out to destroy them but to test them. God had actually given them the Ten Commandments to test them (v.20).

Remember, the people had earlier promised to do all that the LORD had said. They had made a strong profession and commitment to the LORD. Remember what had happened:

"And Moses came and called for the elders of the people, and laid before their faces all these words which the LORD commanded him. And all the people answered together, and said, All that the LORD hath spoken we will do. And Moses returned the words of the people unto the LORD" (Ex.19:7-8).

Now the LORD was going to use the Ten Commandments to test the people:
⇒ To see if the people would truly walk in the fear and reverence of God. He had given the people a glimpse of the majestic glory and holiness of God. Would they keep the sight before their minds and obey

the commandments, the commandments given by the Lord of glory and holiness?

⇒ To see if the people would truly obey God and not sin, not break the Ten Commandments.

⇒ To see if the people would trust the mediator appointed by God (v.21). Note that Moses approached the cloud and thick darkness where God was. He was God's appointed mediator to represent the people before God. Would the people trust and follow him as they journeyed to the promised land?

Thought.

Did Israel pass the test of God? Tragically, no. Israel did what so many have done down through the ages: promised to obey God but failed to follow through.

a) Many have rejected God: refused to walk in the fear and reverence of God.

b) Many have disobeyed the Ten Commandments and lived in sin.

c) Many have rejected God's appointed mediator, the Lord Jesus Christ.

"Now therefore, if ye will obey my voice indeed, and keep my covenant, then ye shall be a peculiar treasure unto me above all people: for all the earth is mine" (Ex.19:5).

"Beware of him, and obey his voice, provoke him not; for he will not pardon your transgressions: for my name is in him" (Ex.23:21).

"Behold, I set before you this day a blessing and a curse; A blessing, if ye obey the commandments of the LORD your God, which I command you this day: And a curse, if ye will not obey the commandments of the LORD your God, but turn aside out of the way which I command you this day, to go after other gods, which ye have not known" (Dt.11:26-28).

"Ye shall walk after the LORD your God, and fear him, and keep his commandments, and obey his voice, and ye shall serve him, and cleave unto him" (Dt.13:4).

"And the people said unto Joshua, The LORD our God will we serve, and his voice will we obey" (Josh.24:24).

"And Samuel said, Hath the LORD as great delight in burnt offerings and sacrifices, as in obeying the voice of the LORD? Behold, to obey is better than sacrifice, and to hearken than the fat of rams" (1 Sam.15:22).

"For the time is come that judgment must begin at the house of God: and if it first begin at us, what shall the end be of them that obey not the gospel of God?" (1 Pt.4:17).

IV. The Ten Commandments Were Given to Teach That God Alone Is the LORD: He Alone Has Truly Revealed Himself, Has Truly Spoken to Man from Heaven.

> **"And the Lord said unto Moses, Thus thou shalt say unto the children of Israel, Ye have seen that I have talked with you from heaven" (v.22).**

Remember, God's name—the LORD—means the LORD of salvation, deliverance, redemption, and revelation.

Think for a moment about all the so-called gods declared and worshipped by people. No matter who the so-called gods are, there is only one LORD, only one true and living God who can save, deliver, and redeem people, who can reveal Himself. Who is He? Note this verse:

> **"And the LORD said unto Moses, Thus thou shalt say unto the children of Israel, Ye have seen that I have talked with you from heaven" (v.22).**

The LORD truly revealed Himself; He "has talked with you [man] from heaven" (v.22). The LORD is the only living and true God who has spoken to man and given man the Ten Commandments. (See Commandment Two, p. 67, for more discussion concerning how God has revealed Himself through His Son, Jesus Christ.)

Thought.

The point is clear: God revealed Himself; He came down upon Mt. Sinai and gave the Ten Commandments to prove that He alone is the LORD who can save and redeem man. Man must, therefore, obey the LORD; man must do what the LORD says to be saved and redeemed.

> **"Not every one that saith unto me, Lord, Lord, shall enter into the kingdom of heaven; but he that doeth the will of my Father which is in heaven" (Mt.7:21).**
>
> **"And to you who are troubled rest with us, when the Lord Jesus shall be revealed from heaven with his mighty angels, In flaming fire taking vengeance on them that know not God, and that obey not the gospel of our Lord Jesus Christ" (2 Th.1:7-8).**
>
> **"Blessed are they that do his commandments, that they may have right to the tree of life, and may enter in through the gates into the city" (Rev.22:14).**
>
> **"Now therefore, if ye will obey my voice indeed, and keep my covenant, then ye shall be a peculiar treasure unto me above all people: for all the earth is mine" (Ex.19:5).**

"This day the LORD thy God hath commanded thee to do these statutes and judgments: thou shalt therefore keep and do them with all thine heart, and with all thy soul" (Dt.26:16).

"But if ye will not obey the voice of the LORD, but rebel against the commandment of the LORD, then shall the hand of the LORD be against you, as it was against your fathers" (1 Sam.12:15).

"For if the word spoken by angels was stedfast, and every transgression and disobedience received a just recompense of reward; How shall we escape, if we neglect so great salvation; which at the first began to be spoken by the Lord, and was confirmed unto us by them that heard him...?" (Heb.2:2-3).

V. The Ten Commandments Were Given to Teach How God Alone Is to Be Approached and Worshipped.

"Ye shall not make with me gods of silver, neither shall ye make unto you gods of gold. An altar of earth thou shalt make unto me, and shalt sacrifice thereon thy burnt offerings, and thy peace offerings, thy sheep, and thine oxen: in all places where I record my name I will come unto thee, and I will bless thee. And if thou wilt make me an altar of stone, thou shalt not build it of hewn stone: for if thou lift up thy tool upon it, thou hast polluted it. Neither shalt thou go up by steps unto mine altar, that thy nakedness be not discovered thereon" (v.23-26).

Note three instructions spelled out by God.

1. There is to be no idolatry in worship: no so-called *imaginary* gods are to be made or worshipped (v.23). This, of course, would include the gods of man's imagination, the gods that men dream up. There is only one true and living God, the Father of the Lord Jesus Christ. He alone is to be worshipped. No other so-called gods are to be worshipped.

2. Worship is not to be full of pageantry, not to be ostentatious, flashy, or showy. Any altar built by the Israelites was to be made of earth, the plainest and simplest material of all (v.24). The altar of earth was, of course, to be a temporary center of worship until the tabernacle was erected. Note: if an altar of stone were to be built, only undressed stones were to be used. The stone was not to be touched by any tool of man. Touching it with any tool or giving any shape to the stone was considered by God to be a defilement (v.25). The point being made was that worship was to be totally free of any ostentation or flashiness. Worship was not to be showy, not even the focus of worship, which was the altar. Nothing was to distract from the people's worship.

3. Worship is to involve no unrefined or disrespectful behavior, none whatsoever. Note that the altar of the Israelites was to have no steps (v.26). In ancient times, it was the common practice to build high altars with steps leading up to the top of the altars. As the priest climbed the steps of the altar, his nakedness was often exposed to the people standing at the bottom of the altar. God was declaring that there was to be no disrespectful behavior, no immoral behavior ever associated or conducted in the worship services of His people.

Note this fact as well: altars of that day were built high, symbolizing that man was ascending up to God, offering himself and his offering to the false god. But God forbids this, forbids it for four reasons:

⇒ Man cannot climb up in righteousness: he has no righteousness to offer up to God.

⇒ Man cannot ascend up to God. God has to descend down to man (reveal Himself to man).

⇒ Man cannot climb up and break through to heaven; he cannot enter the spiritual world; God has to enter the physical world.

⇒ Man cannot climb man-made steps to reach God; the mediator of God has to stand before God for man.

Thought.

Three lessons are clearly seen in this point.

a) We must never approach and worship any person nor any false god dreamed up by man. There is only one true and living God, the Father of the Lord Jesus Christ. He and He alone is the one true and living God; consequently, He and He alone is to be approached and worshipped.

> "Take heed to yourselves, that your heart be not deceived, and ye turn aside, and serve other gods, and worship them" (Dt.11:16).
>
> "But unto the place which the LORD your God shall choose out of all your tribes to put his name there, even unto his habitation shall ye seek, and thither thou shalt come" (Dt.12:5).
>
> "Let all the earth fear the LORD: let all the inhabitants of the world stand in awe of him" (Ps.33:8).
>
> "I am the LORD: that is my name: and my glory will I not give to another, neither my praise to graven images" (Is.42:8).
>
> "Little children, keep yourselves from idols. Amen" (1 Jn.5:21).

b) We must never worship God for show—with a spirit of ostentation, flashiness, or pride.

> "Therefore when thou doest [thine] alms, do not sound a trumpet before thee, as the hypocrites do in the synagogues and in the streets, that they may have glory of men. Verily I say unto you, They have their reward" (Mt.6:2).

"And when thou prayest, thou shalt not be as the hypocrites [are]: for they love to pray standing in the synagogues and in the corners of the streets, that they may be seen of men. Verily I say unto you, They have their reward" (Mt.6:5).

"Moreover when ye fast, be not, as the hypocrites, of a sad countenance: for they disfigure their faces, that they may appear unto men to fast. Verily I say unto you, They have their reward" (Mt.6:16).

"But all their works they do for to be seen of men: they make broad their phylacteries, and enlarge the borders of their garments" (Mt.23:5).

c) We must never be disrespectful nor irreverent in our worship; we must never pollute nor defile our worship.

"And he said, Draw not nigh hither: put off thy shoes from off thy feet, for the place whereon thou standest is holy ground" (Ex.3:5).

"Ye shall keep my sabbaths, and reverence my sanctuary: I am the LORD" (Lev.19:30).

"And the captain of the LORD'S host said unto Joshua, Loose thy shoe from off thy foot; for the place whereon thou standest is holy. And Joshua did so" (Josh.5:15).

"God is greatly to be feared in the assembly of the saints, and to be had in reverence of all them that are about him" (Ps.89:7).

"Keep thy foot when thou goest to the house of God, and be more ready to hear, than to give the sacrifice of fools: for they consider not that they do evil" (Eccl.5:1).

"And the Jews' passover was at hand, and Jesus went up to Jerusalem, And found in the temple those that sold oxen and sheep and doves, and the changers of money sitting: And when he had made a scourge of small cords, he drove them all out of the temple, and the sheep, and the oxen; and poured out the changers' money, and overthrew the tables; And said unto them that sold doves, Take these things hence; make not my Father's house an house of merchandise" (Jn.2:13-16).

"But if I tarry long, that thou mayest know how thou oughtest to behave thyself in the house of God, which is the church of the living God, the pillar and ground of the truth" (1 Tim.3:15).

"But the LORD is in his holy temple: let all the earth keep silence before him" (Hab.2:20).

SUBJECT INDEX

DISCOVER THE GREAT VALUE of the Subject Index. The Subject Index gives you...
- A practical list of subjects that can be easily developed for preaching, teaching, or for personal Bible study
- Support Scriptures or cross references for the Subject
- A wealth of topics that will meet your own personal need

DISCOVER THE GREAT VALUE of the Index for yourself. Quickly glance below to the very first subject of the Index of <u>What the Bible Says About the Ten Commandments</u>. It is:

ABORTION (See **MURDER**)
Discussed. The needs of the mother who has aborted her child. p.197-198

Turn to the page and note the discussion. You will immediately see the GREAT VALUE of the INDEX.

OUTLINE & SUBJECT INDEX

Capital punishment. p.190
Justified war. p.190
Self-defense. p.190
Meaning. p.189-190

**LANGUAGE - LAN-
GUAGES**
Kinds of. Foul. p.109

LAW, The
Obeyed by Jesus Christ. p.16
Purpose of the l.
    To arouse people to seek
    both life & the prom-
    ised land. p.11-12
    To be a guide who
    would lead people to
    Christ. p.11
    To mark believers as the
    priests of God. p.8
    To mark believers as the
    true followers of God. p.8
    To show man how to
    live a peaceful & pro-
    ductive life upon earth.
    p.12
    To show man that he
    can never be justified
    by the l. p.9
    To show man that he is
    sinful. p.9
    To show man that he
    needed a Mediator to
    approach God. p.10-11
    To show man that he
    needs a Savior who
    can deliver him from
    the curse & penalty of
    the l. p.9-10
Type - Symbol of. A
schoolmaster or guardian
who brings us to Christ.
p.11
What the l. cannnot & does
not do.
    It cannot give life to
    man. p.13
    It cannot justify a person
    from sin. p.12-13
    It cannot make a person
    perfect. p.12
    It cannot make a person
    righteous. p.13
    It cannot save a person
    because no person can
    keep the law. p.12

LAWLESSNESS
Discussed.
    People have become de-
    sensitized & hardened
    to l. p.187
    The media focuses upon
    l. p.187

LAZY - LAZINESS
Warning. p.139

LIE - LIAR - LYING (See
DECEPTION)
Benefits of *not* lying.
    p.273-275
Christ & His teaching con-
    cerning man's word &
    lying. p.275-278
Discussed. Three terrible
    effects upon people.
    p.264
Duty. To protect or guard
    oneself from l. p.278-280
Fact.
    Causes pain & suffering
    for other people.
    p.264-265
    Is common to everyone.
    p.259
    Is usually shared with
    loved ones & good
    friends. p.264-265
Judgment of. Is judged by
    God. p.265
Kinds of - How one lies.
    Charges & criticism.
    p.263
    Deception. p.262
    Exaggeration & flattery.
    p.263
    Rumor, gossip, or tale-
    bearing. p.262
    Slander. p.262
    Suggestive hints or in-
    sinuations. p.262
    Unlimited ways. List.
    p.264
Meaning.
    Includes all forms of
    false speech. 261
    That which is false, un-
    true. p.261
Results. Consequences of l.
    p.268-273
Source. Satan is the father
    of lies. p.265

LIFE (See **SALVATION**)

LIFE, SANCTITY OF
Duty.
    To respect the sanctity
    of life. p.189
    To teach the sanctity of
    life & the brotherhood
    of man. p.209
Results. Ten benefits to the
person who respects the
sanctity of life. p.201-204

LORD, THE
Meaning. p.31-32

LUST
Fourteen demands that
    forbid lusting or covet-
    ing. p.303-307

MAJESTY
Of God. (See **GLORY OF
GOD**)
    Discussed. p.313

MAN (See **JUDGMENT;
LUST; SIN**; Related Sub-
jects)
    Separation from God. great
    gulf between God & m.
    p.313-315
    Value - Worth of m.
    Created in the image &
    likeness of God. p.189
    Is God's master crea-
    tion. p.189
    Is God's precious pos-
    session. p.189
    Is God's priceless prop-
    erty. p.189
    Is God's royal master-
    piece. p.189

MARRIAGE - MARRIED
Duty - Essentials.
    To keep m. pure. Not to
    commit adultery.
    p.215, 218
    To leave parents &
    cleave to spouse. p.181

MEDIA
Discussed. The m. focus
    upon lawlessness, vio-
    lence, killing, & immor-
    ality. p.187

MEDIATOR (See **JESUS
CHRIST**, Mediator)
Fact.
    Jesus Christ is God's
    Perfect Mediator.
    p.315-316
Work of Christ as Media-
tor.
    Approaches God for us.
    p.315-316

MINISTER (See **MINIS-
TRY - MINISTERING**)

**MINISTRY - MINISTER-
ING** (See **BELIEVERS;
MINISTERS** for more dis-
cussion)
Duty in relation to others.
    To m. to suicidal people
    & their families. p.199

ACKNOWLEDGMENTS AND BIBLIOGRAPHY

Every child of God is precious to the Lord and deeply loved. And every child as a servant of the Lord touches the lives of those who come in contact with him or his ministry. The writing ministry of the following servants have touched this work, and we are grateful that God brought their writings our way. We hereby acknowledge their ministry to us, being fully aware that there are so many others down through the years whose writings have touched our lives and who deserve mention, but the weaknesses of our minds have caused them to fade from memory. May our wonderful Lord continue to bless the ministry of these dear servants, and the ministry of us all as we diligently labor to reach the world for Christ and to meet the desperate needs of those who suffer so much.

THE REFERENCE WORKS

Archer, Gleason L. Jr. *A Survey of Old Testament Introduction*. Chicago, IL: Moody Bible Institute of Chicago, 1974.

Baker's Dictionary of Theology. Everett F. Harrison, Editor-in-Chief. Grand Rapids, MI: Baker Book House, 1960.

Brown, Francis. *The New Brown-Driver-Briggs-Gesenius Hebrew-English Lexicon*. Peabody, MA: Hendrickson Publishers, 1979.

Cruden's Complete Concordance of the Old & New Testament. Philadelphia, PA: The John C. Winston Co., 1930.

Dake's Annotated Reference Bible, The Holy Bible. Finis Jennings Dake. Lawrenceville, GA: Dake Bible Sales, Inc., 1963.

Elwell, Walter A., Editor. *The Evangelical Dictionary of Theology*. Grand Rapids, MI: Baker Book House, 1984.

Funk & Wagnalls Standard Desk Dictionary. Lippincott & Crowell, Publishers, 1980, Vol.2.

Geisler, Norman. *A Popular Survey of the Old Testament*. Grand Rapids, MI: Baker Book House, 1977.

Good News Bible. Old Testament: © American Bible Society, 1976. New Testament: © American Bible Society, 1966, 1971, 1976. Collins World.

Harrison, Roland Kenneth. *Introduction to the Old Testament*. Grand Rapids, MI: Eerdmans Publishing Company, 1969.

Kelley, Page H. *Exodus: Called for Redemptive Mission*. January Bible Study. Nashville, TN: Convention Press, 1977.

Kohlenberger, John R. III. *The Interlinear NIV Hebrew-English Old Testament*. Grand Rapids, MI: Zondervan Publishing House, 1987.

Life Application® Bible. Wheaton, IL: Tyndale House Publishers, Inc., 1991.

Lindsell, Harold and Woodbridge, Charles J. *A Handbook of Christian Truth*. Westwood, NJ: Fleming H. Revell Company, A Division of Baker Book House, 1953.

Lockyer, Herbert. *All the Books and Chapters of the Bible*. Grand Rapids, MI: Zondervan Publishing House, 1966.

Lockyer, Herbert. *All the Men of the Bible*. Grand Rapids, MI: Zondervan Publishing House, 1958.

Lockyer, Herbert. *The Women of the Bible*. Grand Rapids, MI: Zondervan Publishing House, 1967.

Martin, Alfred. *Survey of the Scriptures*, Part I, II, III. Chicago, IL: Moody Bible Institute of Chicago, 1961.

McDowell, Josh. *Evidence That Demands A Verdict*, Vol.1. San Bernardino, CA: Here's Life Publishers, Inc., 1979.

Miller, Madeleine S. & J. Lane. *Harper's Bible Dictionary*. New York, NY: Harper & Row Publishers, 1961.

Nave's Topical Bible. Orville J. Nave. Nashville, TN: The Southwestern Company. Copyright © by J.B. Henderson, 1921.

Nelson's Expository Dictionary of the Old Testament. Merrill F. Unger & William White, Jr. Nashville, TN: Thomas Nelson Publishers, 1980.

New American Standard Bible, Reference Edition. La Habra, CA: The Lockman Foundation, 1975.

New International Version Study Bible. Grand Rapids, MI: Zondervan Bible Publishers, 1985.

New Living Translation, Holy Bible. Wheaton, IL: Tyndale House Publishers, Inc., 1996.

NIV Exhaustive Concordance. (Grand Rapids, MI: Zondervan Corporation, 1990).

Orr, William. *How We May Know That God Is*. Wheaton, IL: Van Kampen Press, No date given.

Owens, John Joseph. *Analytical Key to the Old Testament,* Vols.1, 2, 3. Grand Rapids, MI: Baker Book House, 1989.

Pilgrim Edition, Holy Bible. New York, NY: Oxford University Press, 1952.

Roget's 21st Century Thesaurus, Edited by Barbara Ann Kipfer. New York, NY: Dell Publishing, 1992.

Rosen, Ceil and Moishe. *Christ In The Passover*. Chicago, IL: Moody Press, 1978.

Slemming, C.W. *Made According To Pattern*. Fort Washington, PA: Christian Literature Crusade, 1983.

Stone, Nathan J. *Names of God.* Chicago, IL: Moody Press, 1944.

Strong's Exhaustive Concordance of the Bible. James Strong. Nashville, TN: Thomas Nelson, Inc., 1990.

The Amplified Bible. Scripture taken from THE AMPLIFIED BIBLE, Old Testament copyright © 1965, 1987 by the Zondervan Corporation. The Amplified New Testament copyright © 1958, 1987 by The Lockman Foundation. Used by permission.

The Hebrew-Greek Key Study Bible, New International Version. Spiros Zodhiates, Th.D., Executive Editor. Chattanooga, TN: AMG Publishers, 1996.

The Holy Bible in Four Translations. Minneapolis, MN: Worldwide Publications. Copyright © The Iversen-Norman Associates: New York, NY, 1972.

The Interlinear Bible, Vol.1, 2, & 3, Translated by Jay P. Green, Sr. Grand Rapids, MI: Baker Book House Company, 1976.

The International Standard Bible Encyclopaedia, Edited by James Orr. Grand Rapids, MI: Eerdmans Publishing Company, 1939.

The NASB Greek/Hebrew Dictionary and Concordance. (La Habra, CA: The Lockman Foundation, 1988).

The New Compact Bible Dictionary, Edited by T. Alton Bryant. Grand Rapids, MI: Zondervan Publishing House, 1967. Used by permission of Zondervan Publishing House.

The New Scofield Reference Bible, Edited by C.I. Scofield. New York, NY: Oxford University Press, 1967.

The New Thompson Chain Reference Bible. Indianapolis, IN: B.B. Kirkbride Bible Co., Inc., 1964.

The Open Bible. Nashville, TN: Thomas Nelson Publishers, 1975.

The Zondervan Pictorial Encyclopedia of the Bible, Vol.1. Merrill C. Tenney, Editor. Grand Rapids, MI: Zondervan Publishing House, 1982.

Theological Wordbook of the Old Testament, Edited by R. Laird Harris. Chicago, IL: Moody Bible Institute of Chicago, 1980.

Vine's Complete Expository Dictionary of Old and New Testament Words. W.E. Vine, Merrill F. Unger, William White, Jr. Nashville, TN: Thomas Nelson Publishers, 1985.

Webster's Seventh New Collegiate Dictionary. Springfield, MA: G. & C. Merriam Company, Publishers, 1971.

Wilson, William. *Wilson's Old Testament Word Studies.* McLean, VA: MacDonald Publishing Company, No date given.

Wood, Leon. *A Survey of Israel's History.* Grand Rapids, MI: Zondervan Publishing House, 1982.

Young's Analytical Concordance to the Bible. Robert Young. Grand Rapids, MI: Eerdmans Publishing Company, No date given.

Young, Edward J. *An Introduction to the Old Testament.* Grand Rapids, MI: Eerdmans Publishing Company, 1964.

THE COMMENTARIES

Barclay, William. *The Letters to the Philippians, Colossians, and Thessalonians.* "Daily Study Bible Series." Philadelphia, PA: Westminster Press, Began in 1953.

Barclay, William. *The Old Law & The New Law.* Philadelphia, PA: The Westminster Press, 1972.

Barnes' Notes, Exodus to Esther. F.C. Cook, Editor. Grand Rapids, MI: Baker Book House, No date given.

Bush, George. *Commentary on Exodus.* Grand Rapids, MI: Kregel Publications, 1993.

Bush, George. *Exodus.* Minneapolis, MN: Klock & Klock Christian Publishers, Inc., 1981.

Childs, Brevard S. *The Book of Exodus.* Philadelphia, PA: The Westminster Press, 1974.

Cole, R. Alan. *Exodus.* "The Tyndale Old Testament Commentaries." Downers Grove, IL: Inter-Varsity Press, 1973.

Dunnam, Maxie. *Mastering the Old Testament,* Vol.2. Dallas, TX: Word Publishing, 1987.

Durham, John I. *Understanding the Basic Themes of Exodus.* Dallas, TX: Word, Inc., 1990.

Durham, John I. *Word Biblical Commentary, Exodus.* Waco, TX: Word, Inc., 1987.

Ellison, H.L. *Exodus.* Philadelphia, PA: The Westminster Press, 1982.

Fretheim, Terence E. *Exodus, Interpretation.* Louisville, KY: John Knox Press, 1991.

Gaebelein, Frank E. *The Expositor's Bible Commentary,* Vol.2. Grand Rapids, MI: Zondervan Publishing House, 1990.

Gill, John. *Gill's Commentary,* Vol.1. Grand Rapids, MI: Baker Book House, 1980.

Hayford, Jack W., Executive Editor. *Milestones to Maturity.* Nashville, TN: Thomas Nelson Publishers, 1994

Henry, Matthew. *Matthew Henry's Commentary,* 6 Volumes. Old Tappan, NJ: Fleming H. Revell Co., No date given.

Heslop, W.G. *Extras from Exodus.* Grand Rapids, MI: Kregel Publications, 1931.

Hewitt, Thomas. *The Epistle to the Hebrews*. "Tyndale New Testament Commentaries." Grand Rapids, MI: Eerdmans Publishing Co., Began in 1958.

Hucy, F.B. Jr. *A Study Guide Commentary, Exodus*. Grand Rapids, MI: Zondervan Publishing House, 1977.

Hyatt, J.P. *The New Century Bible Commentary, Exodus*. Grand Rapids, MI: Eerdmans Publishing Company, 1971.

Keil-Delitzsch. *Commentary on the Old Testament*, Vol.1. Grand Rapids, MI: Eerdmans Publishing Company, No date given.

Life Change Series, Exodus. Colorado Springs, CO: NavPress, 1989.

Maclaren, Alexander. *Expositions of Holy Scripture*, 11 Vols. Grand Rapids, MI: Eerdmans Publishing Company, 1952-59.

McGee, J. Vernon. *Thru The Bible*, Vol.1. Nashville, TN: Thomas Nelson Publishers, 1981.

Meyer, F.B. *Devotional Commentary on Exodus*. Grand Rapids, MI: Kregel Publications, 1978.

Napier, B. Davie. *Exodus*. "The Layman's Bible Commentary," Vol.3. Atlanta, GA: John Knox Press, 1963.

Pink, Arthur. *Gleanings in Exodus*. Chicago, IL: Moody Bible Institute of Chicago, Moody Press, No date given.

Pink, Arthur W. *The Ten Commandments*. Grand Rapids, MI: Baker Books, 1994.

Reapsome, James. *Exodus*. Downers Grove, IL: InterVarsity Press, 1989.

Salmond, S.D.F.. *The Epistle to the Ephesians*. "The Expositor's Greek Testament," Vol.3. Grand Rapids, MI: Eerdmans Publishing Co., 1970.

Sarna, Nahum M. *Exploring Exodus*. New York, NY: Schocken Books Inc., 1986.

Strauss, Lehman. *Devotional Studies in Galatians & Ephesians*. Neptune, NJ: Loizeaux Brothers, 1957.

The Biblical Illustrator, Exodus. Edited by Joseph S. Exell. Grand Rapids, MI: Baker Book House, 1964.

The Epistle of Paul to the Ephesians. "Tyndale New Testament Commentaries." Grand Rapids, MI: Eerdmans, No date listed.

The Interpreter's Bible, 12 Vols. New York, NY: Abingdon Press, 1956.

The Preacher's Outline & Sermon Bible®. Chattanooga, TN: Leadership Ministries Worldwide, 1993.

The Pulpit Commentary. 23 Volumes. Edited by H.D.M. Spence & Joseph S. Exell. Grand Rapids, MI: Eerdmans Publishing Company, 1950.

Thomas, W.H. Griffith. *Through the Pentateuch Chapter by Chapter*. Grand Rapids, MI: Eerdmans Publishing Company, 1957.

Wuest, Kenneth S.. *Ephesians and Colossians*. "Word Studies in the Greek New Testament," Vol.1. Grand Rapids, MI: Eerdmans Publishing Co., 1966.

Youngblood, Ronald F. *Exodus*. Chicago, IL: Moody Press, 1983.

OTHER SOURCES

Anderson, Norman. *Issues of Life and Death*. Downers Grove, IL: InterVarsity Press, 1977.

Briscoe, Stuart. *The Ten Commandments*. Wheaton, IL: Harold Shaw Publishers, 1986.

Geisler, Norman. *Ethics: Alternatives and Issues*. Grand Rapids, MI: Zondervan, 1971.

McGee, J. Vernon. *Love Liberation and the Law*. Nashville, TN: Thomas Nelson Publishers, 1995.

Rogers, Adrian. *Ten Secrets For A Successful Family*. Wheaton, IL: Crossway Books, 1996.

PURPOSE STATEMENT

LEADERSHIP MINISTRIES WORLDWIDE

exists to equip ministers, teachers, and laymen in their
understanding, preaching, and teaching of God's Word
by publishing and distributing worldwide
The Preacher's Outline & Sermon Bible®
and related *Outline* Bible materials,
to reach & disciple men, women, boys, and girls for Jesus Christ.

•MISSION STATEMENT•

1. To make the Bible so understandable - its truth so clear and plain - that men
   and women everywhere, whether teacher or student, preacher or hearer,
   can grasp its Message and receive Jesus Christ as Savior; and...
2. To place the Bible in the hands of all who will preach and teach God's Holy
   Word, verse by verse, precept by precept, regardless of the individual's
   ability to purchase it.

The *Outline* Bible materials have been given to LMW for printing and especially
distribution worldwide at/below cost, by those who remain anonymous. One fact,
however, is as true today as it was in the time of Christ:

• The Gospel is free, but the cost of taking it is not •

LMW depends on the generous gifts of Believers with a heart for Him and a love and
burden for the lost. They help pay for the printing, translating, and placing *Outline*
Bible materials in the hands and hearts of those worldwide who will present God's
message with clarity, authority and understanding beyond their own.

LMW was incorporated in the state of Tennessee in July 1992 and received IRS 501(c) 3 nonprofit status in March 1994. LMW is an international, nondenominational mission organization.
All proceeds from USA sales, along with donations from donor partners, go 100% into under-
writing our translation and distribution projects of *Outline* Bible materials to preachers,
church & lay leaders, and Bible students around the world.

8/97 © 1997. Leadership Ministries Worldwide

PO Box 21310 - Chattanooga, TN 37424 • (423) 855-2181 • FAX (423) 855-8616
• E-Mail - outlinebible@compuserve.com — Web site: www.outlinebible.org •

LEADERSHIP
MINISTRIES
WORLDWIDE

The
Preacher's
Outline
&
Sermon
Bible

Sharing

The

OUTLINED

BIBLE

With the World!